GYÖRGY LIGETI

Of Foreign Lands and Strange Sounds

GYÖRGY LIGETI

Of Foreign Lands and Strange Sounds

Edited by
Louise Duchesneau
and Wolfgang Marx

THE BOYDELL PRESS

First published 2011
The Boydell Press, Woodbridge

ISBN 978 1 84383 550 9

The Boydell Press is an imprint of Boydell & Brewer Ltd
PO Box 9, Woodbridge, Suffolk IP12 3DF, UK
and of Boydell & Brewer Inc.
668 Mount Hope Ave, Rochester, NY 14620, USA
website: www.boydellandbrewer.com

A catalogue record for this book is available
from the British Library

The publisher has no responsibility for the continued
existence or accuracy of URLs for external or third-party
internet websites referred to in this book, and does not
guarantee that any content on such websites is, or will
remain, accurate or appropriate.

Papers used by Boydell & Brewer Ltd are natural,
recyclable products made from wood grown in
sustainable forests

Designed and typeset in FF Scala and Scala Sans by
David Roberts, Pershore, Worcestershire

Printed and bound by CPI Group (UK) Ltd,
Croydon, CRO 4YY

Contents

Illustrations

Photographs

Photographs 1–13 © Ines Gellrich; 14 © Erika Krauß

Figures

Colour plates

The plates appear between pp. 170 and 171.

All sketches (Figures 7–12 and Colour plates 1–16) courtesy of the György Ligeti Collection, Paul Sacher Foundation Basel

Foreword

I first met Ligeti in 1989 at a Royal Festival Hall series of concerts entitled *Ligeti by Ligeti*. I had always loved his work and was very keen that the Philharmonia Orchestra play more of his music. Over the years I got to know him better and in 1994, at a Ligeti festival in Gütersloh, I really discovered the depth of his music and we struck up a friendship. After that, we used to meet in Paris where we would often have breakfast together in his favourite hotel at Place de la Sorbonne.

One morning, I spoke of my frustration at not finding enough of his recordings in music shops. Ligeti explained that his recordings were spread across too many different recording labels and that they were of uneven quality. On the spur of the moment I suggested: 'Why don't we record all your music again, past and future, under your artistic supervision?' There was a long silence and Ligeti replied, 'let me think about it'. I did not have to wait long for a positive response!

Over a period of ten years we succeeded in recording his complete works for Sony and Warner. The project was ambitious, conflictual and sustained throughout by Ligeti's persistent search for perfection.

I loved Ligeti's dry sense of humour and engaging personality. He knew how much I enjoyed his company (often shared over a plate of delicious French cheese) and he seemed at ease with me. This was not always the case; many people in the music 'industry' made him tense and nervous. He could be quite sarcastic and less than diplomatic with those he did not care for. Ligeti was aware of his own great talent, but was not over-confident. Although he knew he was regarded as one of the great composers of his time, he often questioned his contribution and was plagued with doubt in the last years of his life.

This later pessimism obviously reflected the darkness Ligeti had lived through. He witnessed the worst of mankind's cruel madness, losing most of his family in Nazi death camps. Even over the brightest pages of his music there always looms a dark shadow and so I have always felt that listening to Ligeti's music means discovering a little bit more about humanity and therefore a little bit more about myself.

During the last couple years of his life, illness caused Ligeti to become angry and resentful. He was imprisoned in his own body, unable to move freely or to compose and this made him profoundly unhappy. It was so painful to see him shutting himself off from the outside world, refusing to see or talk to anyone.

I saw Ligeti for the last time in Vienna, a few weeks before he died. When, before parting, I told him that next time I would bring a couple of good cheeses from Paris, his eyes did not light up like they usually did. I knew he no longer wanted to live and remembered Vassily Grossman's words: 'What music resurrects in the soul of a man about to die is neither hope nor thought, but simply the blind, heart-breaking miracle of life itself'.

My sad memories of his last years are now fading. I still miss Ligeti but for me his music and his mischievous smile remain more alive than ever. His works have already joined the small canon of masterpieces of post-war music, and I am glad that friends, colleagues, former students and musicologists have come together to produce this volume. It contains not only reflections on Ligeti as student, teacher and friend but also new insights into how he wrote his music, its structure and its meaning, and the way he received inspiration from a wide range of musical and extra-musical concepts. These texts help us better understanding the composer and his music and make it clear why he will have something to say to us for a long time to come.

Vincent Meyer
London, November 2010

Contributors

SIMHA AROM is Emeritus director of research at the French National Centre for Scientific Research (Centre National de la Recherche Scientifique – CNRS). A musician who later became an ethnomusicologist, his field of research is Central African polyphony as well as the scales, the temporal organisation, the modelling of patterns and the cognitive aspects of musical oral tradition (orality). He developed methods of interactive experimentation for which he received the Médaille d'Argent of the CNRS. His book *African Polyphony and Polyrhythm* (Cambridge, 1991) was rewarded with the prestigious ASCAP Deems Taylor Award for Excellence in Music Literature. In 2008 he was laureate of the Prix International Fyssen (Paris) as well as the Koizumi Fumio Prize for Ethnomusicology (Tokyo). Simha Arom is a frequent guest lecturer at distinguished universities such as Princeton, Yale, UCLA, MIT, Cambridge, and he has worked closely with IRCAM in Paris. Composers like György Ligeti, Luciano Berio and Steve Reich have made use of the musical procedures he discovered.

JONATHAN W. BERNARD is Professor of Music Theory at the School of Music, University of Washington. His articles and chapters on the music of Varèse, Bartók, Carter, Messiaen, Ligeti, Zappa, Feldman, minimalism, popular music, the history of theory, and the history of 20th-century compositional practice have appeared in numerous scholarly journals and anthologies. His books include *The Music of Edgard Varèse* (New Haven, 1987), *Elliott Carter: Collected Essays and Lectures, 1937–1995* (Rochester, NY, 1997), and, most recently, *Joël-François Durand in the Mirror Land* (Seattle, 2005).

CIARÁN CRILLY lectures on Modernism and Music Performance at University College Dublin. His PhD (2008), entitled *The (Syn)Aesthetics of Modernism*, was an examination of the relationship between music and visual art in the early 20th century. He has given papers and published on Arnold Schoenberg as painter, Erik Satie's late collaborations, György Ligeti, and music in the films of Alfred Hitchcock. Ciarán also works as a conductor and violinist.

LOUISE DUCHESNEAU studied piano and musicology in Ottawa and Montreal, Canada, and has received a doctorate in musicology at Hamburg University, Germany. She then lectured at that institution for ten years (systematic musicology). From 1983 to 2005 she was György Ligeti's assistant. In that capacity she wrote and translated programme and CD booklet notes, helped organise concerts, conferences, recordings and festivals of Ligeti's music, was responsible for all his correspondence, for the negotiation of commission fees, for the scheduling of appointments (interviews, photo shoots, various meetings) as well as for managing the general contact between composer and the outside world. In 2006–7 she was part of musical director Kent Nagano's team at the Orchestre symphonique de Montréal in Montreal, Canada. Since her return to Germany in 2008, she has been a free-lance author and translator.

BENJAMIN DWYER is a graduate of Trinity College, Dublin, the Royal Academy of Music, London, and Queen's University, Belfast where he received his PhD. Equally known as a classical guitarist, composer, curator and musicologist, he teaches at the Royal Irish Academy of Music. He is an elected member of Aosdána (the Irish government-sponsored academy of creative artists), and recently was named an Associate of the Royal Academy of Music (London) for his 'outstanding contribution to the music profession.' Dwyer's work in new music has been notable. He founded the *Mostly Modern* series (now MUSIC21) in 1991, which has been a central platform for contemporary music in Ireland for the past two decades. He is also a founder-member of the new music ensemble *Vox21*. In 2007 he curated the *Remembering Ligeti* festival – the first major retrospective of the composer's work following his death. His essays appeared in *The Journal of Music* and *The Musical Times*.

TIBORC FAZEKAS was born in Szekszárd, Hungary, in 1951. He studied Hungarian as well as English language and literature at Eötvös-Lóránd University in Budapest. He received a teacher's certificate in 1975 and was awarded a doctorate in 1977 with a dissertation entitled *Historical and Linguistic Assessments of the Origin of the Bukovina Szekler*. From 1975 to 1978 he was research assistant for the history of the Hungarian language and dialectology at Eötvös-Lóránd University. From 1978 to 1982 he was lecturer at the Finno-Ugrian Department of the Georg-August University in Göttingen. From 1982 to 1984 he was head-consultant at the Education and Culture Ministry in Budapest and, since 1984, he is lecturer for Hungarian language and culture at the Finno-Ugrian Institute of Hamburg University. His main fields of research are Hungarian dialectology, sociology of languages, methodology of language teaching, regional and cultural study of Hungary, translation studies, history of Finno-Ugrian linguistics and literary criticism.

The photographer INES GELLRICH first encountered the music of György Ligeti in April 1978 when she heard (and saw) the German première of the opera *Le Grand Macabre* in Hamburg. Her father, Heinz Gellrich, was then the head of scenic design at the Hamburg State Opera and his teenage daughter would often sit in at the rehearsals of the numerous ballet and opera productions. She studied photography in Bielefeld (Germany) and, in 1989, chose to portray György Ligeti for her final-year project. The famous composer was always on his guard against anyone who might steal even a little of his precious time, so when asked if he would allow Ines Gellrich to photograph him, he answered: 'Let her come to London, to the South Bank Festival, and tell her I will not pose.' She met the challenge and the photos she took of Ligeti in London marked the beginning of a professional friendship which ended only with Ligeti's death. A compilation of many of her Ligeti photos – *Un/Endlichkeiten. Begegnungen mit György Ligeti, 1989–2003* (Freiburg, 2008), became her unexpected legacy. In June 2010 Ines Gellrich died at the age of 47.

PAUL GRIFFITHS was born in Wales in 1947 and worked for thirty years as a music critic in London and New York. He is known particularly as a writer on new and recent music, his *Modern Music and After* (Oxford, 1995), now in its third edition, being the standard work on music since 1945. But he has also covered a much broader span in *The Penguin Companion to Classical Music* (London, 2006) and *A Concise History of Western Music* (Cambridge, 2006), both of which have been widely translated. He had the unforgettable experience of meeting Ligeti on several occasions, in London, Århus and Hamburg, and wrote a short book on him and his music. For more information see www.disgwylfa.com.

ILDIKÓ MÁNDI-FAZEKAS, born in Budapest in 1954, is Lecturer for Hungarian literature at the Institute for Finno-Ugrian Studies at Hamburg University. She studied Hungarian language and literature as well as library science at Eötvös-Loránd University in Budapest. She was awarded a teacher's certificate in 1977 and a PhD in 1978; her dissertation focused on forms of Hungarian short prose at the beginning of the 20th century. From 1977 to 1992 she was a research assistant for Hungarian Literature at Eötvös-Loránd University. Between 1990 and 1994 she was a freelance author and translator for the Hungarian issue of *Sandra*, a journal published by Gruner + Jahr, and from 2000 to 2002 she was a freelance teacher at the Hamburg School of Foreign Languages and Commerce. Since 2001 she is a member of the Rehabilitation and Prevention research institute at Hamburg University, since 2007 she is a member of 'Europol and Data Protection in Europe', a research project of Mannheim University. The focus of her work and research are the history of Hungarian literature, stylistics, cultural history (especially film and music history), intercultural communication and the social structure of Budapest culture.

WOLFGANG MARX, born in 1967 in Bremen, is Senior Lecturer at the School of Music, University College Dublin. He studied musicology and philosophy in Hamburg and worked for several years as author and product manager for classical labels and festivals. Apart from György Ligeti his research interests include the representation of death in music (with a particular focus on requiem compositions) and the theory of musical genres. Among his publications are *Klassifikation und Gattungsbegriff in der Musikwissenschaft* (Hildesheim, 2004) and *Lontano – 'Aus weiter Ferne': Zur Musiksprache und Assoziationsvielfalt György Ligetis* (Hamburg, 1997). He is co-editor of the *Frankfurter Zeitschrift für Musikwissenschaft* and executive editor of the *Journal of the Society for Musicology in Ireland*.

HEINZ-OTTO PEITGEN, born in 1945 in Nümbrecht-Bruch, is one of the most prominent researchers in the field of fractal geometry. After teaching for a number of years in Bonn he became Professor of Mathematics at Bremen University in 1977. He was Professor of Mathematics at the University of California at Santa Cruz, 1985–91; since 1991 he has been Professor of Mathematics and Biomedical Sciences at the Florida Atlantic University in Boca Raton, Florida. In 1995 he founded the Center for Medical Image Computing, MeVis Research GmbH, now the Frauenhofer MEVIS – Institute for Medical Image Computing. His research emphasizes dynamical systems, numerical analysis, image and data analysis, as well as the use of computers in image-based medical diagnostics. In 1992 he was elected a member of the European Academy of Sciences and Arts, and in 2008 to the Göttingen Academy of Sciences.

FRIEDEMANN SALLIS is Professor at the University of Calgary. He obtained his PhD in musicology under the direction of the late Carl Dahlhaus at the Technische Universität Berlin. His writings include a book on the early works of György Ligeti, the co-edition of *A Handbook to Twentieth-Century Musical Sketches* (Cambridge, 2004), and numerous articles on 20th-century music. As well as sketch studies, Dr. Sallis's areas of expertise include the interaction of historical and theoretical perspectives in 20th-century music, aesthetics, and issues concerning music and identity. He has received Fellowship Grants from the Paul Sacher Foundation (Basle) and since 1997 he has been awarded five successive research grants by the Social Sciences and Humanities Research Council of Canada.

WOLFGANG-ANDREAS SCHULTZ, born in 1949 in Hamburg, studied musicology, philosophy and composition in Hamburg with Ernst Gernot Klussmann und György Ligeti. He was awarded a PhD in musicology in 1974 and a diploma in music theory in 1975. He taught at Hamburg University and the Musikhochschule Hamburg, and from 1977 was György Ligeti's teaching assistant. Since 1988 he has been Professor of Composition and Music Theory at the Musikhochschule Hamburg. His compositions include the operas *Sturmnacht* and *Achill unter den Mädchen*, his first symphony *Die Stimmen von Chartres*, *Shiva* (a dance poem for flute and orchestra), the chamber symphony *Die Sonne von Tabriz*, three string quartets, a violin and a cello sonata, piano music and songs. He has written several essays on the philosophy of music, including *Avantgarde und Trauma* (Berlin, 2005) and *Das Ineinander der Zeiten: Kompositionstechnische Grundlagen eines evolutionären Musikdenkens* (Berlin, 2001).

MANFRED STAHNKE was born in 1951 in Kiel. In 1966 he started to study piano, composition and musicology in Lübeck, Freiburg and Hamburg and in the United States (Urbana, IL, and Stanford, CA). In 1973 he passed his exams in music theory and composition in Freiburg. In 1979 he earned his doctorate in Hamburg with Constantin Floros; the subject of his thesis was Pierre Boulez' Third Piano Sonata. Manfred Stahnke studied composition in Freiburg in 1970–3 with Wolfgang Fortner, and from 1973–4 with Klaus Huber. From 1974 his principal professor was György Ligeti. Stahnke's works have received prizes and awards. He has dealt with aspects of contemporary music at international symposiums and has written numerous essays. He has been a lecturer in, among other places, Wellington (New Zealand), Tongyeong (South Korea), Buenos Aires (Argentina) and Montreal (Canada). In 1992 he founded the ensemble Chaosma. Since 1999 he has been a member of the Music Advisory Board of the Goethe Institut. In the same year he was elected a member of the Free Academy of the Arts in Hamburg.

RICHARD STEINITZ is Emeritus Professor at the University of Huddersfield. He studied at King's College Cambridge and composition with Goffredo Petrassi in Rome on an Italian government scholarship. In 1978 he was a prize winner in the BBC Young Composers Competition and in 1981 was joint winner of the Clements Memorial Prize for Chamber Music. In 1978 he also founded and was for 23 years artistic director of Huddersfield Contemporary Music Festival, one of the most important new music festivals in the world, for which he was awarded an OBE in 1995. Richard has long been active as a musicologist and writer. His book *György Ligeti: Music of the Imagination* (London, 2003) is the most extensive study of the composer in English and won an award 'for excellence' from the American Society of Composers, Authors and Publishers in 2004. He is currently completing a comprehensive history of the first 33 years of the Huddersfield Festival, to be published by the University of Huddersfield Press and Jeremy Mills Publishing at the end of 2011.

Acknowledgements

György Ligeti was always eager to have recordings made of those performances of his works he deemed exemplary and authoritative because, in his mind, these recordings would eventually replace him as keepers of an 'authentic' Ligeti tradition. Towards the end of his life he had the great dream of having all his works recorded with musicians of his choice. To that end he approached several record companies only to be told that the project was impossible to realise without a patron. Upon hearing about Ligeti's dilemma Vincent Meyer spontaneously offered to fulfill this dream and, true to his word, generously funded this unique musical legacy. Informed of our, albeit much less prestigious project, he agreed to share with us some of his memories of Ligeti as well as provide our publication with abundant financial support. For this we sincerely thank him.

We also would like to thank the Seed Funding Programme of University College Dublin for its financial support, without which we never would have been able to embark on such a substantial undertaking.

Near to every one of our authors has had to make his way to Basle to the reading room of the Paul Sacher Foundation. There, along with many other collections available for study, are housed Ligeti's manuscripts, sketches, recordings, correspondence and other documents. We would like to thank everyone at the Paul Sacher Foundation who has made our life and work easier by providing liberal access to these treasures, as well as for the unfailing assistance and pertinent advice we received, especially Dr. Felix Meyer and Dr. Ulrich Mosch for their keen interest in the book, music librarian Evelyne Diendorf for her always sympathetic reaction to any request and, most of all, Dr. Heidy Zimmermann, the 'guardian angel' of the Ligeti collection for her patience, her support and her expertise.

Ines Gellrich had photographed Ligeti since 1989 till his last public appearance in Vienna 2003. Some of her photos of Ligeti have appeared repeatedly in concert programmes, CD booklets, newspapers and other publications. To illustrate this book we chose with Ines some of her less-known photos, for instance the one of Ligeti with his tea cup or the one of Simha Arom with an African musician. It is very sad indeed that she did not live to see the publication of a book she anticipated with so much pleasure. We thank her for these beautiful and unique images.

Since the very beginning Boydell & Brewer have accompanied and guided us steadily in this project. We particularly thank Michael Middeke for his encouragement and his willingness to live with the delays and problems we confronted him with. It was a pleasure working with him.

Preface

When György Ligeti died on 12 June 2006 in Vienna everyone connected with the world of contemporary music agreed that one of the foremost composers of the second half of the 20th century had passed away.[1] Ligeti was far more than 'the greatest of Transylvanian composers' as Alex Ross once wrote, tongue-in-cheek;[2] he had not only once, but several times over the course of his life, introduced new ways of composing and thinking about music. As early as the late 1950s he developed a technique of dense polyphony, his 'micropolyphony', which showed that there were other paths a composer could take to stay clear of both the Scylla of total serialism and the Charybdis of indeterminacy. With his 'meccanico style' which he used not only in his harpsichord piece *Continuum* but also in his Piano Études of the 1980s, he helped stretch the limits of what was thought to be technically possible for a human being to play. This piece was also, along with the *Poème symphonique for 100 Metronomes* (1962), a kind of starting point for his many fruitful experiments with complex polyrhythmic textures. Moreover, his fascination with new and unorthodox tuning systems led to the unique sound world of his instrumental works of the 1980s and 90s. But perhaps that for which we should be the most grateful is hinted at in a recent publication by Richard Taruskin:

> We have lots of new music, God knows, that reduces listeners to their cerebral cortex and, in opposition to that, lots ... that reduces them to their autonomic nervous system. ... György Ligeti ..., and only a few others, [have] seen the need to treat ... listeners as fully conscious, fully sentient human beings.[3]

Ligeti taught us how to listen, to his music as well as to the music of others. In the 20th century all composers of art music have had to navigate their own way between 'avant-garde' music which many see as a purely intellectual exercise and those musical styles blamed of sustaining the modern-day version of Hanslick's 'pathological listening'. Indeed, this is certainly one of the 20th century's crucial challenges to any composer of art music as combining both extremes in order to generate a new musical

---

[1] See, for example, the obituaries by Stephen Plaistow, 'Gyorgy Ligeti', *The Guardian*, 14 June 2006, http://www.guardian.co.uk/news/2006/jun/14/guardianobituaries.artsobituaries, accessed 15 August 2010; [no author], 'György Ligeti', *The Times*, 13 June 2006, http://www.timesonline.co.uk/tol/comment/obituaries/article674092.ece, accessed 15 August 2010; Richard Dyer, 'Gyorgy Ligeti; influential composer of wry, startling pieces', *Boston Globe*, 13 June 2006, http://www.boston.com/news/globe/obituaries/articles/2006/06/13/gyorgy_ligeti_influential_composer_of_wry_startling_pieces/?rss_id=Boston+Globe+ − +Obituaries, accessed 15 August 2010.

[2] Alex Ross, 'Ligeti Split', *The New Yorker*, 28 May 2001, http://www.therestisnoise.com/2004/05/ligeti_2001.html, accessed 15 August 2010.

[3] Richard Taruskin, 'A Sturdy Musical Bridge to the Twenty-first Century', in *The Danger of Music and Other Utopian Essays* (Berkeley, Los Angeles, London, 2009), pp. 98–103, at pp. 100–1. Taruskin's article is about Steve Reich, and he actually lists Ligeti and Conlon Nancarrow as the 'few others' alongside the American minimalist.

language has eluded most of them. Nevertheless, Ligeti's works are not only complex, multi-layered constructions, they are also simply fascinating to listen to. Just ask any one of the millions of viewers of *2001: A Space Odyssey* or *Eyes Wide Shut*.

Ligeti was not only a prolific composer but also an equally captivating lecturer and interview partner. He was widely read, interested in the latest ideas not just in the arts but in all areas of human endeavour and would openly express his strong moral and political views. Ligeti's own writings and interviews have become indispensable to any scholar of his music.

This volume is the first edited volume on Ligeti and his music in any language since the composer's death.[4] The concept goes back to a festival entitled 'Remembering Ligeti' which was organized by Benjamin Dwyer, Gavin O'Sullivan and Wolfgang Marx in Dublin in November 2007. Its mixture of concerts, movie screenings and lectures constituted the first sizable festival of Ligeti's music since the composer's death in June 2006. The idea for the present collection of essays was therefore born out of the desire not only to preserve the spirit of the Dublin gathering but also to share some of its findings with a broad public of interested music-lovers. The book project, however, quickly outgrew the range of the festival. New authors agreed to take part, while most of the contributors present in Dublin (Richard Steinitz, Paul Griffiths, Benjamin Dwyer, Ciarán Crilly, Wolfgang Marx) either changed their topics or developed them in greater detail. Also, colleagues, friends and students were invited to share their memories of Ligeti, thus helping to provide a more complete picture not only of Ligeti the composer but also Ligeti the student, the teacher, the colleague and the friend.

The volume opens with a look at György Ligeti the student and the influence Sándor Veress's teaching had on the young composer in Budapest in the late 1940s ('"We play with the music and the music plays with us": Sándor Veress and his Student György Ligeti'). In this chapter Friedemann Sallis focuses on the impact Veress had on his most famous student, not only in terms of how their personal relationship developed in Hungary and later in the West, but also regarding the stylistic influences Veress's work had on some of Ligeti's compositions of the early 1950s (notably *Musica ricercata*).

Benjamin Dwyer's article also focuses on one of Ligeti's early Hungarian works, the Cello Sonata. In an attempt to identify stylistic features which did not change over the course of the composer's career, he links this work to the Viola Sonata, one of Ligeti's later works ('Transformational Ostinati in György Ligeti's Sonatas for Solo Cello and Solo Viola'). Dwyer defines 'transformational ostinati' as a compositional device common to both works and traces the ideas underlying this technique to Machaut's isorhythmic motets.

Ligeti was influenced not only by Hungarian music and by his teachers, but also by other aspects of Hungarian culture. Ildikó Mándi-Fazekas and Tiborc Fazekas, who teach Hungarian philology and literary criticism

---

[4] A very useful compilation of Ligeti's own writings, the *Gesammelte Schriften* (*Complete Writings*), should have been published in 2003 for his 80th birthday, but only came out in 2007.

at Hamburg University, acquaint us with the colourful poetry of Sándor Weöres and its effect on and use in Ligeti's music ('Magicians of Sound – Seeking Ligeti's Inspiration in the Poetry of Sándor Weöres'). As native speakers they are able to offer a unique glimpse in both artists' common background as well as to their lifelong attachment to Hungarian language and culture. Weöres was as interested in the quality of the sound of words and syllables he used as material in his poems as Ligeti was in his treatment of that which he set to music. Works such as *Aventures* or the *Nonsense Madrigals*, for instance, show the composer's proximity to the poet's ideas and methods.

An influence which formed Ligeti's outlook on life and determined his artistic choices like no other was his experience as a victim of violence, oppression and tyranny. In his youth he was a member of the Hungarian minority in Romania and during the 1950s he endured the Stalinist communist regime. But it was the murder of his father, brother and several other members of his family in the concentration camps, which shaped his feelings about life and death. Wolfgang Marx investigates Ligeti's attitude towards death as it is reflected in works such as the *Requiem* and *Le Grand Macabre* ('"Make Room for the Grand Macabre!" The Concept of Death in György Ligeti's Œuvre'). He shows that ambiguity and irony are both key concepts in the composer's attempts to deal with the catastrophe which was forced on him at a very young age.

Always curious, Ligeti never ceased to learn and was always affected by developments not only in music but also in literature, culture or science. Two of the most important influences during his later years were chaos theory, more specifically fractal geometry, and the music of Sub-Saharan Africa. In both fields he was fortunate to have encountered leading experts. Both men became his friends and describe here how they met Ligeti, how they interacted with him and what, in their opinion, made their knowledge and expertise so relevant to this contemporary composer. Heinz-Otto Peitgen is one of the world's leading specialists on fractal geometry. In his chapter ('Continuum, Chaos and Metronomes – A Fractal Friendship') he explains how and why chaos theory and fractal geometry became important for Ligeti's composition. Many of his later works, such as the Piano Concerto or the Piano Études, are based on apparent chaos, on those small changes in the repetition of patterns which, in the end, inevitably cause major digressions in the process. Yet it also becomes clear that while fractal geometry provided Ligeti with a scientific inspiration for his compositional techniques, a work like *Poème symphonique* – written long before he discovered fractal geometry – shows that the underlying ideas were there long before and were thus genuinely Ligeti's.

Simha Arom, also a survivor of the Holocaust, introduced Ligeti to African polyrhythmic music, a discovery which was to be crucial to his work in the 1980s ('A Kinship Foreseen: Ligeti and African Music – Simha Arom in Conversation'). Many of the polyrhythmic textures in the late concertos and in the Piano Études can be traced back to models found in African music. After a short introduction on African polyrhythm, Arom discusses the importance of African music for Ligeti's music.

Recorded music had a special place in Ligeti's life and in his work. It was as much a pleasant pastime as an unquestionable source of new ideas and inspiration, and it allowed him to become acquainted with the music of many different cultures and historical periods. As Louise Duchesneau points out in her chapter ('"Play it like Bill Evans": György Ligeti and Recorded Music'), Ligeti amassed a vast collection of records over the years, of which many are now housed in the Paul Sacher Foundation. Based on the author's personal experience as the composer's long-time assistant, her text (which contains a list of the LPs now held in Basel) gives an insight into this source of Ligeti's inspiration.

Now also gathered in Basel at the Paul Sacher Foundation, Ligeti's sketches have been recently made available to musicologists. Their study promises new insights not only into Ligeti's compositional practices and into the genesis of many of his works, they also reveal many of his musical and extra-musical sources. Two chapters are based on in-depth studies of these sketches. Jonathan W. Bernard ('Rules and Regulation: Lessons from Ligeti's Compositional Sketches') proposes a five-fold classification of the different types of sketches (jottings, drawings, charts, tables, musical notation) and shows how Ligeti utilized these at different stages of the composition of the Kyrie from the *Requiem*. In his essay Richard Steinitz focuses on Ligeti's sketches from the early 1980s ('À qui un hommage? The Genesis of the Piano Concerto and the Horn Trio'). He too shows how Ligeti would sometimes require several attempts to marshal his thoughts and visualize his general ideas until he finally reached the stage at which he could actually begin the composition in musical notation. He was often dissatisfied with his own ideas, but would eventually find a way forward – a process which could take months or years before it bore fruit. Steinitz's analysis also reveals how much Ligeti could be influenced by the music of other composers or musical cultures; there are well-known references (such as the one to Beethoven's sonata 'Les Adieux' in the Horn Trio) but also unexpected links to composers such as Monteverdi and Janáček.

Both Bernard's and Steinitz's essays clearly show that future analytical studies of Ligeti's work will not be able to ignore the source material now available in Basel, and that a command of Hungarian will be more than helpful.

The relationship between teacher and student is often two-sided; Ligeti's students in Hamburg not only received instruction, they also influenced the development of his compositional style. Initially a student of Ligeti's, Wolfgang-Andreas Schultz later became his assistant, teaching his students counterpoint as well as other music theory subjects. An accomplished composer himself, his chapter ('Craft and Aesthetics – The Teacher György Ligeti') focuses on the relationship between technical proficiency and aesthetic quality. This discussion of what was a recurring topic in the conversations between the teacher and his students gives us an insight into how composers can critique each other's works in a productive way. Manfred Stahnke – like Schultz also a composer and professor at the Hamburg Musikhochschule – focuses in his article ('The Hamburg Composition Class') on the often heated discussions between teacher and students and on the role those students from different cultural backgrounds played in this context. He also reflects on Ligeti's teaching 'methods' and his relationship to other contemporary composers. In this chapter there is as much to learn about Ligeti the man as about Ligeti the composer.

It is well known that Stanley Kubrick made use of some of Ligeti's micropolyphonic works in *2001: A Space Odyssey* (1968) and in so doing introduced the composer to a broader public. Kubrick later used Ligeti's music in two other films, most famously in his last, *Eyes Wide Shut*. In his chapter ('The Bigger Picture: Ligeti's Music and the Films of Stanley Kubrick') Ciarán Crilly analyses the different roles the music plays in these motion pictures and discusses the specific way in which Kubrick dealt with his (usually pre-existing) film music.

Finally, Paul Griffiths looks at the development of Ligeti's orchestral settings ('Invented Homelands: Ligeti's Orchestras'). The composer's preferences for certain instruments or sound colours are assessed as well as the sometimes thinner, sometimes thicker textures of his concerti and the possible aesthetic reasons for these choices.

While all articles deal with Ligeti, his music and creative process, only a few authors presented what can be understood as a more or less analytical approach to his music (Benjamin Dwyer, Wolfgang Marx, Jonathan W. Bernard, Richard Steinitz and Paul Griffiths). Two articles were written by music-loving non-musicians (Heinz-Otto Peitgen and Ildikó Mándi-Fazekas and Tiborc Fazekas) and three pertain to the relationship between teacher and student (Friedemann Sallis, Manfred Stahnke and Wolfgang-Andreas Schultz). There is only one article which is presented as an interview, to our mind an elegant and straightforward format for these reminiscences of a long friendship (Simha Arom). Finally there are two articles about Ligeti and the media (Ciarán Crilly and Louise Duchesneau).

It is our wish to present the music-loving public as well as the professional musicians and musicologists with a selection of informative as well as, in the highest sense, entertaining essays about a composer whose works have never stopped delighting and charming his many admirers. The chosen sequence of the articles, vaguely chronological although seemingly without a specific order, maybe reflects our unconscious desire to imitate Ligeti's own unorthodox eloquence. Those of us who had the good fortune to hear him speak will never forget how he would meander through his talks, jumping to a new topic before he finished the first and ending at times, to the bewilderment of his listeners, on a completely different plane of thought. Those who could catch up with him were truly privileged but all of us benefited from his brilliance and extraordinary spirit.

Louise Duchesneau, Wolfgang Marx
Hamburg/Dublin, November 2010

Ligeti drinking tea at home
(Hamburg, 9 November 1989)

1 'We play with the music and the music plays with us':[1] Sándor Veress and his Student György Ligeti

FRIEDEMANN SALLIS

> The philosophy of music has thrived on claims about the language
> of music as bound or not bound to a nation, as free, expressive, and
> creative. But exiled musicians challenged two basic views: that music
> is a language and, relatedly, that creativity is causally or otherwise
> connected to the condition either of exile or of home.
>
> Lydia Goehr[2]

Late in his career, György Ligeti acknowledged his debt to Sándor Veress, with whom he studied composition at the Franz Liszt Academy from 1945 to 1948. In 1993 (the year after Veress's death) Ligeti dedicated the third movement, entitled 'Facsar', of his six-movement Sonata for Solo Viola to the memory of 'my dear composition teacher Sándor Veress who died in Bern and who was an unjustly neglected composer'.[3] As we find in so many of Ligeti's late compositions, the movement alludes in obvious ways to his Hungarian past and a sense of identity, which he once described as that indestructible culture of his childhood.[4] Marked 'Andante cantabile ed espressivo, with swing', the movement has a poignancy that is partially explained by its title. 'Facsar' means to wrestle or to distort, and the music does take the attentive listener through a series of distorted, twisted modulations. Ligeti also notes that in Hungarian the word 'facsar' can be associated 'with the bitter sensation felt in the nose when one is about to cry'.[5] The over-riding sadness of this slow-moving dance is captured by this aspect of the title. The Sonata and especially the third movement's belated acknowledgement open a window on to a fascinating aspect of Ligeti's past that has yet to be completely elucidated.

[1] György Ligeti, 'Kótaismertetések' [Score Review], trans. Zuzana Finger and Friedemann Sallis, in Friedemann Sallis, *An Introduction to the Early Works of György Ligeti* (Cologne, 1996), p. 227. The reference for the original Hungarian text is György Ligeti, 'Kótaismertetések', *Zene-pedagógia* [Music Pedagogy] 2/3 (March 1948), p. 43.

[2] Lydia Goehr, *The Quest for Voice: Music, Politics, and the Limits of Philosophy* (Oxford, 1998), p. 181.

[3] György Ligeti, 'Preface', trans. Lindsay Gerbracht, in *Sonata for Solo Viola* (Mainz, 2001). In my opinion, Ligeti's statement contains a trace of culpability. As I was preparing my PhD thesis on Ligeti's early works in the late 1980s/early 1990s, I met the composer on numerous occasions in Hamburg and Berlin. On one occasion I distinctly remember him asking me if I had Veress's address and telephone number, because at that time I was residing in Switzerland. The question surprised me because I had mistakenly assumed that he would have been in contact with his former professor. Thinking back on this request after having read Ligeti's words explaining his dedication led me to suspect that Ligeti may have felt that he too had neglected his former professor.

[4] Ligeti, cited in Richard Steinitz, *György Ligeti: Music of the Imagination* (London, 2003), p. 251. The original statement was published in Tünde Szitha, 'A Conversation with György Ligeti', *Hungarian Musical Quarterly* 3/1 (1992), p. 14.

[5] Ligeti, 'Preface', in *Sonata for Solo Viola*, n.p.

Sándor Veress (1907–92) belongs to that generation of Hungarian-born composers who found themselves squeezed between illustrious teachers and famous students: Béla Bartók (1881–1945) and Zoltán Kodály (1882–1967) on the one side, and Ligeti (1923–2006); György Kurtág (1926–) on the other. As a result, Veress's work has not received the critical attention it deserves and his impact as a teacher remains poorly understood, at least with regard to those who studied with him in Budapest. Veress learned composition with Kodály during the late 1920s. His international career as a composer began with the successful première of his String Quartet no. 2 by the Végh Quartet at the 1935 ISCM festival in Prague. At the time, he was working as Bartók's research assistant at the Hungarian Academy of Sciences, a position he held from 1934 to 1938.[6] In 1943 Veress replaced Kodály as professor of composition at the Liszt Academy and held this post until January 1949, when he left Hungary because of the worsening political situation, even though he was an active member of the Hungarian Communist Party. Veress had joined the Party in 1945 because he thought that it could be an efficient vehicle for reform.[7] At that time many Hungarian artists and intellectuals, including Ligeti and Kurtág, agreed, though it must be added that not all became members of the Party. Rachel Beckles Willson observes that in the new, post-war environment, his membership in the Party may well have compensated for earlier political ties and affiliations.[8] Veress's relationships to the war-time and post-war political regimes appear ambiguous. During the war he is reported to have actively intervened to help Bence Szabolcsi (who was interned in a labour camp because he was Jewish) emigrate to Palestine.[9] Such an attempt could only have been made because, as Bartók's former assistant and as professor of composition at the Liszt Academy (as of 1943), Veress was in good standing within the Budapest musical establishment. At the same time Veress used this status to pursue his goals as a composer and clearly benefited from it during the war.[10] Be that as it may, during 1948 Veress began to have second thoughts about his future in Hungary, and his misgivings became very personal in nature. Veress was a good friend of Gyula Rajk, the eldest brother of László Rajk, Foreign Minister

[6] Ferenc Bónis, 'Musical Life: Three Days with Sándor Veress the Composer, Part II', *New Hungarian Quarterly* 29/109 (Spring 1988), pp. 217–25, at p. 221.

[7] Veress makes this claim in a letter to Paul Sacher, dated 8–18 May 1950, conserved in the Sándor Veress Collection of the Paul Sacher Foundation.

[8] Rachel Beckles Willson, 'Veress and the Steam Locomotive in 1948', in *Sándor Veress: Komponist – Lehrer – Forscher*, ed. Doris Lanz and Anselm Gerhard (Kassel, 2008), pp. 20–5, at p. 24.

[9] György Kroó, cited in Beckles Willson, 'Veress and the Steam Locomotive in 1948', p. 24. This claim was originally published in György Kroó, *Szabolcsi Bence*, vol. 2 (Budapest, 1994), pp. 505–6.

[10] Lest the outside observer jump to hasty conclusions concerning Veress's actions and decisions, it should also be noted that to the end of his life, Ligeti continued to regard Veress as an example of moral rectitude. 'Veress war ein hundertprozentig geradliniger Mensch mit einem unglaublichen Ethos.' Ligeti cited in Simone Hohmaier, '"Veress war ein Vorbild, aber kein guter Lehrer": Zur Frage einer kompositorischen Veress-Rezeption bei Kurtág und Ligeti', in *Sándor Veress*, ed. Lanz and Gerhard, pp. 142–58, at p. 143. Ligeti's statement was initially published in *'Träumen Sie in Farbe?', György Ligeti im Gespräch mit Eckhard Roelcke* (Vienna, 2003), pp. 64f.

and high-ranking member of the Communist Party. Rajk was arrested, and charged with treason on 15 June 1949. In September he was sentenced to death and executed on 15 October, marking the culmination of a political trial orchestrated by the Moscow wing of the Party led by Mátyás Rákosi. Rajk's execution is now seen as one of the public events that marked the beginning of the Stalinist regime in Hungary.[11] Veress's close contact with members of the Rajk family was no doubt one of the reasons contributing to his decision not to return to Hungary in 1949.[12] During the summer of 1949 Veress moved to Berne, Switzerland, to take a temporary teaching position at the university. He would reside in the Swiss capital for the rest of his life. All told, Veress taught composition for a mere five and a half years at the Liszt Academy and, as Richard Steinitz has accurately observed, during that time he made the most of possessing a passport, undertaking long trips for the promotion of his music.[13] Yet he did have a tangible impact on Hungarian music culture, both as a composer and as a teacher.

Veress was undoubtedly an inspiring professor and left an indelible mark on many in Hungary and later in Switzerland.[14] That a professor should have left a lasting impression on his students is hardly surprising. Tracing the precise nature of these relationships is a complex task. The legacies of the artist and the teacher are not the same. The former is constituted primarily by a body of work that can be measured. The latter is usually evaluated through the actions of students, among whom subgroups and tendencies form and disintegrate, further ramifying the teacher's legacy.[15] Furthermore, it is impossible to completely separate a composer's work from his legacy as a teacher of composition and this overlap can render reports of a composer's teaching ambiguous. Towards the end of his life, Ligeti noted that he admired Veress as a teacher less for his attention to technical detail and more as an example of aesthetic and moral leadership, adding that Ferenc Farkas, the political opportunist (with whom Ligeti studied after Veress emigrated), was a much better teacher of compositional technique. He specifically criticized Veress's apparently poor knowledge of the classical counterpoint as transmitted by Knud Jeppesen.[16] The assessment seems overstated and problematic. Apart from Ligeti's critique, we cannot know how well Veress communicated what he

[11] The other was the arrest on 26 December 1947 of Cardinal-primate József Mindszenty on charges of anti-state activities. Ignác Romsics, *Hungary in the Twentieth Century*, trans. Tim Wilkinson (Budapest, 1999), pp. 258 and 272–3 respectively.

[12] Bónis, 'Musical Life: Three days with Sándor Veress the composer, Part III', *New Hungarian Quarterly* 29/111 (Autumn 1988), pp. 208–14, at p. 209.

[13] Steinitz, *György Ligeti: Music of the Imagination*, p. 23.

[14] In the year of Veress's death (1992), a large number of compositions dedicated to his memory were written by many of his former students: Heinz Holliger, Vladislav Jaros, György Kurtág, György Ligeti, Heinz Marti, and Roland Moser, to mention only a few.

[15] Like the pedagogical legacies of Arnold Schoenberg, Nadia Boulanger and Olivier Messiaen, Veress's is complex because of the international, multicultural nature of his career.

[16] Ligeti, cited in Hohmaier, 'Veress war ein Vorbild, aber kein guter Lehrer', p. 143.

knew about counterpoint to his students in Budapest in the years following the war.[17] We do know that his compositions, notably the *Billegetőmuzsika* [*Fingerlarks*] written during the war (see below), attest beyond any shadow of a doubt that he had a thorough knowledge of classical counterpoint. Finally, Veress was committed to transmitting his interpretation of Bartók's legacy, and as Simone Hohmaier repeatedly points out, when evaluating Veress's impact as a teacher it is sometimes impossible to separate his influence from that of Bartók.[18] An exhaustive examination of such complex networks of relationships is of course not possible in the scope of this essay. Consequently, we will focus our attention on one specific case: the impact Veress had on Ligeti's early career and how this teacher-student relationship evolved after their emigration.

Veress and Ligeti: the professor and his student

Ligeti was accepted into Veress's class following a successful entrance examination taken in September 1945.[19] Documents, both public and private, suggest that within a relatively short period of time he became one of Veress's favourite students and that they developed and maintained a mutual admiration and respect for one another that outlasted Ligeti's period of study. Between 1948 and 1956 Ligeti published 18 reviews and articles in Hungarian and German, and in these he referred to Veress on numerous occasions.[20] The most obvious example is a short article entitled 'Von Bartók bis Veress', the second in a series entitled 'Neues aus Budapest' published in *Melos*.[21] In it Ligeti reports on noteworthy musical events of 1948: a series of concerts presenting Bartók's major works (Ligeti found the Sonata for Solo Violin particularly impressive) and a visit to Budapest by Olivier Messiaen involving lectures and concerts (which impressed Ligeti far less). The fact that the article's title puts Veress on the same level as Bartók speaks volumes on Ligeti's opinion of the significance of his professor's contribution as a composer. The article was published in February 1949 just after Veress had left Hungary. In the increasingly Stalinist context, one can hardly underestimate the political implications entailed in underscoring the importance of a composer whose prolonged stays in Western Europe were irritating the authorities.[22] Of course, when

---

[17] To know this a broader study would have to be undertaken of a representative number of Veress's Budapest students. This has not been done and it may well be too late to do this now.

[18] Simone Hohmaier, ''Veress war ein Vorbild, aber kein guter Lehrer'. Zur Frage einer kompositorischen Veress-Rezeption bei Kurtág und Ligeti', pp. 142–58.

[19] György Ligeti, 'Begegnung mit Kurtág im Nachkriegs-Budapest', in *György Kurtág*, Musik der Zeit 5 (Bonn, 1989), pp. 14–16.

[20] For English translations of the Hungarian writings, see Sallis, *An Introduction*, pp. 226–61.

[21] György Ligeti, 'Neues aus Budapest: von Bartók bis Veress', *Melos* 16/2 (February 1949), pp. 60–1. Until recently this document has gone unnoticed in Ligeti scholarship. This author first became aware of it in 1995 while examining Veress's voluminous correspondence with his Hungarian publisher Cserépfalvi written in 1949–50 and conserved at the Paul Sacher Foundation.

[22] The Veress Collection contains a letter written by József Révai, member of the Party's Central Committee and Minister of Public Education in the Rákosi government with responsibility for cultural affairs, addressed to 'Kedves

the article was published Ligeti could not have known that Veress would never return. However, given their close relationship, he must have been aware of Veress's misgivings of the political situation.

Evidence of the admiration and trust that Veress and Ligeti had for one another can also be found in their personal correspondence. In an undated letter addressed to his housekeeper, Margit (her surname remains unknown), Veress wrote that the most valuable object in his Budapest apartment was the piano.[23] He then explicitly mentioned Ligeti, whom he described as a very careful person, and stated that if someone like him were to ask about it, there would be no problem in letting him have the instrument.[24] Ligeti did not correspond with Veress until after he left Hungary in late 1956. A short but intensive correspondence began shortly after Ligeti's arrival in December as a refugee in Vienna. These letters between the former teacher and student tell us great a deal about their relationship, as well as providing a wealth of information on their respective perspectives concerning the political situation and contemporary music in Hungary and Europe. The first letter written by Ligeti appears to be lost. A copy of Veress's reply, dated 19 December 1956, is conserved in the Sándor Veress Collection of the Sacher Foundation. Ligeti's main purpose in writing was to ask Veress to help him and his wife obtain asylum in Switzerland. In his reply Veress responded that the list of Hungarians to be granted refugee status in Switzerland was unfortunately full. However, he went out of his way to help his former student, encouraging him not to give up hope and adding a great deal of practical advice, tips, names and addresses. For example, he suggested alternatives to Switzerland as a place of immigration, including the United Kingdom, North America and the German Federal Republic, though he was not sure whether Ligeti would consider the last possibility given his experiences during the War.[25] He also advised Ligeti to solicit the help of Alfred Schlee and provided the latter's office address at Universal Edition. The same day Veress sent a letter to Schlee asking him to help his former student.[26] Ligeti responded quickly on Christmas Day 1956, heartily thanking Veress for his help. He was

Veress Elvtárs!' [Dear Comrade Veress!]. In it he orders Veress to return to Hungary immediately. Among other things, Révai noted that, according to his sources, Veress had complained about the absence of the necessary tranquility for creative work in Hungary. Observing that the Party's recently adopted cultural policy aimed at guaranteeing the material basis for all creative activity, he bluntly stated that Veress's reasons for staying abroad were simply no longer valid. The tenor of the letter is such that it must have reinforced Veress's resolve not to return and one can only wonder if this was not the writer's intent. Révai to Veress, 12 October 1949, Sándor Veress Collection, Paul Sacher Foundation.

[23] Margit (surname unknown) was the Veress family's housekeeper in Budapest. Claudio Veress, email message to the author, 8 October 2007.

[24] Veress to Margit, n.d., Sándor Veress Collection, Paul Sacher Foundation. The letter is undated, through the content and other contextual information, it seems probable that the letter was written within a few years, if not months of Veress's departure from Hungary.

[25] Veress to Ligeti, 19 December 1956, Sándor Veress Collection of the Paul Sacher Foundation.

[26] Veress to Schlee, 19 December 1956, Sándor Veress Collection of the Paul Sacher Foundation.

particularly grateful for the fact that when he visited the offices of Universal Edition, the letter from Veress had already arrived. Ligeti continued to hope that he and his wife would be able to settle in Switzerland. However, he also acknowledged that he was considering the German Federal Republic and the United States, though he added ruefully that moving from Budapest to anywhere in North America would be tantamount to moving from one provincial situation to another. This letter also includes fascinating hints of what was to come. Explaining that during the past eight years he had had little time to work, he stated that from now on he would rather live in poverty than not have enough to time to compose. He also noted that he had only been able to bring a few manuscripts with him, but added that he was nonetheless brimming with plans and ideas. In particular, he mentioned manuscript copies of a string quartet (*Métamorphoses nocturnes*, 1953–4), two choruses (*Éjszaka – Reggel* [Night – Morning], 1955) and sketches for a work in progress (no doubt the first movement of *Apparitions*, which was then entitled *Víziók* [Visions], 1956).[27] Veress responded on 10 January 1957 with another long letter containing more advice and encouragement.[28]

The first thing one notices in this exchange is the fact that whereas Ligeti begins his letters with the formal 'Kedves Tanár Úr' (Dear Mr. Professor), Veress responds with 'Kedves Barátom' (My dear friend). Though he does systematically use the polite rather than the familiar pronominal form, the tone of Veress's advice and encouragement is full of empathy, suggesting a strong friendship based on mutual respect and admiration. This sentiment is also found in letters to third parties. One such correspondent was Endre Gaál, a Hungarian musician who had immigrated to Canada some time between the end of World War II and the Hungarian Revolution. Gaál wrote to Veress on 1 June 1958 from Georgeville, Quebec, asking for information about Veress's former student because he (Gaál) had been asked to write an article on Ligeti.[29] Veress responded on 17 June 1958 noting that Ligeti was a talented musician, a good composer and an honest, trustworthy person. He was also quite proud of what his former student had achieved since he (Veress) had left Hungary in 1949. He stated that he had met Ligeti on numerous occasions in the past six months and had had the opportunity to hear a performance of Ligeti's first string quartet, *Métamorphoses nocturnes*.[30] Veress felt that the quartet was a high-quality work on a European level, in striking contrast to the horrible provincialism

---

[27] Ligeti to Veress, 25 December 1956, Sándor Veress Collection of the Paul Sacher Foundation.

[28] Veress to Ligeti, 10 January 1957, Sándor Veress Collection, Paul Sacher Foundation.

[29] Gaál to Veress, 1 June 1958, Sándor Veress Collection, Paul Sacher Foundation. From the correspondence it is clear that Gaál was not only a colleague, but also close friend of Veress. Gaál begins his letter with the familiar 'Kedves Sanyi' [Dear Alex] and Veress responded likewise. Not much is known about Gaál beyond the fact that he was a pianist and appears to have been active as a teacher. His letters demonstrate that he was a very well informed about the current situation with regard to musicians and composers in Budapest, suggesting that his immigration to Canada must have occurred in the post-war period.

[30] Veress may well be referring to the work's first performance given by the Ramor String Quartet in Vienna on 8 May 1958.

into which Hungarian music had sunk since his own departure.[31] Perhaps Veress had detected something of his teaching in this music?

Veress's *Billegetőmuzsika/Fingerlarks* (1940–6) and Ligeti's *Musica ricercata* (1951–3)

A close examination of the compositions Ligeti wrote just before he began work on the string quartet reveals possible connections to Veress's music, notably to a collection of 70 short pieces for piano students (77 if alternate versions of the same pieces are counted) entitled *Billegetőmuzsika* written during World War II.[32] The work appears to have been an important project for the composer and is closely related to music written in the 1930s during his so-called 'Sonatina Period', particularly with regard to the pervasive use of imitative counterpoint. Veress also felt that this collection filled a pedagogical niche that had been left open by his predecessors.

> I had long planned something like it, but it became particularly topical at that time when we did much for the renewal of Hungarian musical education, and there emerged the need in instrumental music for a cycle like this for children, one with an artistic object ... . I felt the need of some music similar to that which Kodály and Bartók had written for choirs, that is to say a series of short piano pieces based on folksongs, something perhaps similar than Bartók's cycle *For Children* – in short music for beginners.[33]

The collection was published in 1947 by Cserépfalvi, one of the main private music publishing firms in Hungary between 1945 and 1948. A literal translation of *Billegetőmuzsika* would be 'Waggling Music.' For the bilingual (Hungarian/English) publication, Veress chose *Fingerlarks* as his English title, which will be used hereafter. Both the Hungarian and the English titles suggest an outgoing, carefree attitude, as befits the pedagogical function of the collection. The light tone of voice suggested by both titles is however belied by the work's dedication. Veress composed this work in memory of Jenő Deutsch, an excellent musician and good friend, 'who in the hard times had disappeared during his forced labour service'.[34]

The pieces of the collection are organized in sections, each devoted to an aspect of piano technique: scales, phrasing, tied notes, dotted rhythms, syncopations, broken chords, etc.; and, underscoring the pedagogical nature of the work, they become progressively more difficult as the student moves through each section. From a stylistic point of view, the whole collection owes much to Bartók. On the one hand, every one of the pieces in *Fingerlarks* is based on a specific folk music source, each carefully identified in an index at the end of the volume, as is the case in *For Children*. On the other hand, the contrapuntal treatment is so intensive that in many cases the folksong identity of the source tends to subside into the background reminding us of Bartók's collection of 27 pieces for children's or women's

---

[31] Veress to Gaál, 17 June 1958, Sándor Veress Collection, Paul Sacher Foundation.

[32] In a later edition, the number of pieces was expanded to 88. Bónis, 'Musical Life, Part II', p. 224.

[33] Ibid.

[34] Ibid.

choir, entitled *Bartók Béla kórusművei* [Béla Bartók's Choral Music].[35] In his 'Introductory Words' Veress explicitly cites the first four volumes of *Mikrokosmos* and the *44 Duos* for two violins as models.[36]

The seventh movement of Ligeti's *Musica ricercata* contains traces of his former teacher's influence that can be linked to *Fingerlarks*. This movement exists in three distinct versions, linking three important compositions of the early 1950s: *Szonatina* for piano four hands, the third movement, 1950; *Musica ricercata*, 11 pieces for piano solo, seventh movement, 1951–3; *6 Bagatell fúvósötösre* [Six Bagatelles for Wind Quintet], third movement, 1953. The compositions are part of a group of five works related stylistically.[37] In writing these compositions, Ligeti consciously attempted to take stock of his situation in terms of style and compositional technique so as to work his way out of what he saw as a technical and aesthetic impasse. Following their completion, Ligeti's next major achievement was *Métamorphoses nocturnes*. The string quartet announces his assimilation of the musical legacy he had received as a student and at the same time looks toward new horizons. Stylistically, it belongs with the group of five instrumental compositions that precede it.[38]

How do Veress's *Fingerlarks* relate to *Musica ricercata*? First, the intense use of imitative counterpoint that permeates *Fingerlarks* is generally characteristic of Ligeti's early output, including the *Musica ricercata*. From *Invenció* (1948) to *Omaggio a Girolamo Frescobaldi* (1953) counterpoint and linear structure were hallmarks of the compositional technique that Ligeti learned as a student. Second, on a more detailed level one can also link the seventh movement of the *Musica ricercata* to a specific piece in Veress's *Fingerlarks*. We know that Ligeti had a high opinion of the collection from a short review he wrote in early 1948: 'If we play through these small pieces created with modest means, we are conscious that we are confronted with the greatest works perfected in the smallest form.'[39] In the review, Ligeti singled out for special praise 'Dudanóta' [Bagpipe Tune] (piece no. 50; see Example 1): '... at last – for the first time – something new since "The Cricket Marries".'[40] This title ('The Cricket Marries') refers to the folk song on which 'Kanásznóta' [Swineherd's Song] (piece 37 in volume II of Bartók's *For Children*) is based. Of interest here is not the relationship Ligeti drew between the pieces by Bartók and Veress, but rather between Veress's 'Dudanóta' and the seventh movement of his *Musica ricercata*.

The music of the second half of Veress's 'Dudanóta' and that of the seventh movement of Ligeti's *Musica ricercata* use an *ostinato* to accompany a relatively simple folk melody and in both cases the melody and the *ostinato* are metrically unsynchronized (see Example 2). In Veress's case we have a six-note pattern that is also harmonically ambiguous (based on the

---

[35] Bartók completed these choral pieces in 1935–6; at this time Veress was working as his assistant.

[36] Sándor Veress, 'Introductory Words', in *Billegetőmuzsika* (Budapest, 1947).

[37] The other two works are *Rongyszőnyeg* [Rag Carpet], three pieces for piano solo (1950–1) and *Omaggio a G. Frescobaldi*, ricercar for organ solo (1953).

[38] For more on this important phase of Ligeti's career see Sallis, *An Introduction*, pp. 100–21, and Steinitz, *György Ligeti: Music of the Imagination*, pp. 53–61.

[39] Ligeti, 'Kótaismertetések', p. 227.

[40] Ibid., p. 228.

trichord C, F♯, G) against a 4/4 metre and in Ligeti's piece, a seven-note pattern based on a pentatonic scale (C, E♭, F, G, B♭) is set against a melody in 3/4 metre.

Beyond this rather anecdotal similarity of construction, one also notes that the progression of Ligeti's piece seems to replicate some of the basic features of Veress's piano method. The piece begins with a 27-bar melody that is repeated three times. Each time Ligeti embellishes it with an ever more complex contrapuntal treatment. At the first repetition (Example 3a), he doubles the melody a third below. At the second repetition (Example 3b) the melody is in Steinitz's words, 'shadowed canonically by a version

Example 1 Sándor Veress, *Fingerlarks*, 'Dudanóta', bars 9–22

Example 2 Ligeti, *Musica ricercata*, VII, bars 1–12

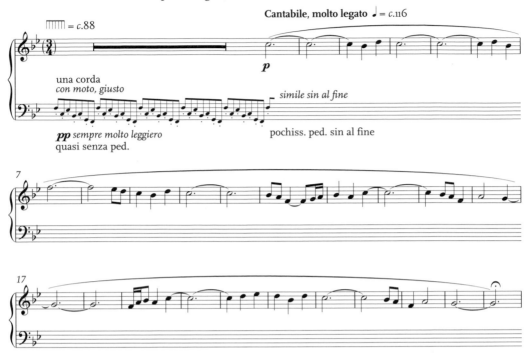

of itself in E flat'.[41] The high point of the piece is achieved in the third repetition (Example 3c) with a full-fledged three-voice contrapuntal version of the melody played by the right hand above the continuously repeating pentatonic ostinato.

The right-hand melodic material of this piece does not refer to 'Dudanóta' directly, rather it 'plays' with the melody in the same way that Veress wanted his young piano students to 'play games' with the melodies in *Fingerlarks*. In his review Ligeti, emphasized precisely this aspect of the Veress's method.

> We play with the music and the music plays with us. Here is a piece in which music can also be turned on its head: your right hand plays the left and your left the right. No plain mechanics: you must listen ... Here you can strike thirds to the melody ... . There you can also strike things which are not at all in the score ... . Your fingers, tempted to play, catch you up and you don't know what carries you away: your hands? ... your imagination? ... You have strayed far off in the 'prohibited' regions, you play topsy-turvy – your teacher, the parents must not listen![42]

In the seventh movement from the *Musica ricercata* Ligeti employs many of the techniques used throughout *Fingerlarks*: doubling a melody by thirds, imitative counterpoint, canon, etc. For Veress, these embellishments and contrapuntal devices were intended to give the student more freedom

---

[41] Steinitz, *György Ligeti: Music of the Imagination*, p. 57.

[42] Ligeti, 'Kótaismertetések', pp. 227–8.

Example 3 Ligeti, *Musica ricercata*, VII: (a) bars 28–35 (right hand only);
(b) bars 56–62 (right hand only); (c) bars 82–95 (right hand only)

within which his or her musical fantasy could better develop and this intention has wider social implications.[43] In a paper entitled 'Folk Music in Musical and General Education', presented at the first Conference organized by the International Folk Music Council held in Basel, Switzerland (13–18 September 1948), Veress drew a direct link between the encouraging of artistic freedom through improvisation and the enabling of political and social freedom in civil society.

> The fact that the achievements of modern science and technique have become widespread enables the man of today to delve into the past in a much wider sense than ever before. Our preoccupation with the past is of deeper significance in our lives than it was in that of our ancestors. This can also be traced in our music-making. There have never before been so many printed editions of *Ur*-texts

43 Veress, 'Introductory Words'.

as during the past thirty years, because music historians have never devoted themselves to such detailed research into the past as they do nowadays. In addition to its obvious advantages, this preoccupation with the past also has its disadvantages. For one thing, it influences the practical part of our music-making in a one-sided way by making it somewhat exaggeratedly adhere to the printed text, resulting, of course, in the neglect of the ability to improvise. This leads finally to a mechanical kind of music-making which we so frequently see in the virtuoso type of our times. Viewing this generally, I consider as one of the greatest dangers of our age the mechanical type of individual who slowly loses his ability to act freely. I also think that teaching in general today should fight this menace with every means in its power. And realising the importance of music in education, a great part of this work lies in the hands of the music teachers, who should utilise the psychological effect of music to enable men to preserve the spark of individuality.[44]

At the end of his paper, Veress specifically used excerpts from *Fingerlarks* to illustrate his ideas musically.[45]

When he wrote his review in early 1948, Ligeti could hardly have imagined that he would be going back to *Fingerlarks* five years later to find a way out of a technical and aesthetic impasse he then found himself in. And yet, in his review he presciently noted that these modest musical games were 'also deadly serious and more important than much conceited solemnity'.[46] For Ligeti, their importance lay in their ability to open new horizons and free the student from convention, a lesson which in a few years would prove to be very valuable indeed. Thus when Ligeti felt the need to go back to basics in the early 1950s he looked to ideas, concepts and compositional techniques that he had received from Veress.[47] It goes without saying that these ideas, concepts and techniques were part and parcel of a larger Hungarian legacy derived mainly from the work of Bartók and Kodály. But it now seems clear that Veress had also made tangible and indeed critically important contributions to that legacy at the same time as he served as a major conduit of information between the generation of his mentor and teacher on the one hand, and that of his students on the other. There is, of course, no explicit reference to Veress anywhere in the *Musica ricercata*; in the early 1950s writing a work in homage to one's former teacher who had recently fled to the West would have been reckless in the extreme.

---

[44] Sándor Veress, 'Folk Music in Musical and General Education', *Journal of the International Folk Music Council* 1 (1949), pp. 42–3.

[45] Ibid., p. 43.

[46] Ligeti, 'Kótaismertetések', p. 228.

[47] The same can also be said of György Kurtág, though at a later stage in his career. See Friedemann Sallis, 'Teaching as a Subversive Art: Sándor Veress's "Billegetőmuzsika (Fingerlarks)" and György Kurtág's "Játékok (Games)"', in *Sándor Veress*, ed. Lanz and Gerhard, pp. 159–71.

Epilogue: The composer as immigrant and the exile

Ironically, the crisis through which Ligeti passed during the early 1950s set him on a path that would ultimately lead him away from his former teacher. The music composed during this period permitted him to gain a measure of independence from the so-called New Hungarian School then being promoted in Hungary by former Kodály students who had gained positions of influence within the musical establishment. In his letters to Veress, Ligeti was scathing in his criticism of what he called the 'Wall of China' atmosphere and the provincialism that reigned at the Liszt Academy.[48] Veress could not have agreed more, though he also felt compelled to warn his former student that not all that glowed in the West was gold.[49] Nevertheless, within 18 months of this exchange, Veress began to have serious doubts about the aesthetic direction his former student's music was taking. After having presented a very positive portrait of Ligeti as a person and of his compositions written before 1956 in his letter written to Gaál in June 1958, Veress added a decidedly negative assessment of his former student's most recent work. Veress noted with obvious disappointment that Ligeti had become a member of what he (Veress) called the 'Secret Sect' of electronic music at Cologne Radio. Though this took nothing away from Ligeti's innate musical abilities, he (Veress) no longer understood what Ligeti was trying to write. Recalling the critique he had made ten years earlier of rationalist tendencies in Western society and the concomitant loss of individuality, he expressed his concern that Ligeti's current production, together with a great deal of contemporary art, constituted a dangerous sign that Western culture was losing its way as it moved inexorably towards extreme rationalization and spiritual sterility. He added sadly that on the occasion of a recent visit, Ligeti had even attempted to persuade him that his new compositions were part an organic evolution of the European tradition.[50] Veress remained unconvinced, stating that in his opinion Ligeti's new compositions 'written on millimetre paper' could no longer be considered music at all. He concluded pessimistically that the music of his former student had become an incomprehensible monstrosity.[51] Three months later Veress received another letter from Ligeti in which he again solicited Veress's help and advice with regard to finding

[48] Ligeti to Veress, 25 December 1956, Sándor Veress Collection of the Paul Sacher Foundation. As an example of the impact socialist realism had at that time, Ignác Romsics cites Pál Kadosa's cantata *Terjed a fény* [The Light Spreads] 'in which 93 of the 221 words of text are nothing more than sung or shouted declamations of Stalin's name'. Romsics, *Hungary in the Twentieth Century*, p. 289.

[49] Veress to Ligeti, 19 December 1956, Sándor Veress Collection of the Paul Sacher Foundation.

[50] This is precisely one of the points Ligeti raises in his article 'Wandlungen der musikalischen Form'. The article was first published in *Die Reihe* 7 ('Form – Raum') in 1960. Ligeti actually wrote the essay in November–December 1958, and was clearly thinking about the article's contents when he visited Veress earlier that year. For more on the genesis of this important text, see Sallis, *An Introduction*, p. 212.

[51] Veress to Gaál, 17 June 1958, Sándor Veress Collection, Paul Sacher Foundation.

a job in Switzerland, where he still hoped to settle.[52] Veress responded in a letter shorter than those written the previous year, saying that the job situation was difficult and regretted that he could do no better than provide Ligeti with an honest but negative assessment of his chances of finding employment in Switzerland.[53] No further correspondence between Veress and Ligeti is conserved at the Sacher Foundation, suggesting that from this point onwards, the respective careers of the former teacher and student took each in very different directions.

It is interesting to briefly compare how Veress and Ligeti approached and handled the challenges of emigration. Bruno Nettl suggests that we should apply the terms and categories of sociology and ethnomusicology when attempting to understand what happens when composers, musicians and music scholars migrate, and builds his argument around a strong, albeit conventional distinction between the concept of exile and emigration. First he notes that all migrants are refugees in one way or another: 'no one just does it on a lark'. Referring to the German musicians and intellectuals who moved to North America in the 1930s (among whom were his parents), he observes that most, whether they arrived voluntarily or because of forces out of their control, saw themselves for a time as refugees and then became exiles or immigrants, depending on whether they expected to return or not.[54] This is of course a relatively standard way of differentiating composers such as Bartók and Arnold Schoenberg on the one hand, and Igor Stravinsky, Edgard Varèse and Kurt Weill on the other. As widespread as it may be, this sharp distinction can appear artificial and rather abstract when applied to specific cases. For example, in a recent conference paper Sabine Feisst has pointed out that even though his serious work remained firmly attached to his Austro-German heritage, as a new citizen Schoenberg made considerable efforts to adapt to the trappings and habits of the American middle class.[55]

Coming back to Nettl's categories, Veress and Ligeti were both clearly political refugees. Veress, who recognized the warning signs early, had the opportunity and the means to leave Hungary legally in 1949. Ligeti decided to flee only after the catastrophe of the failed revolution in late 1956 and left on foot under cover of darkness. The situation with regards to human rights was of course a prime concern to both, but they also left for

---

[52] Liget to Veress, 10 September 1958, Sándor Veress Collection, Paul Sacher Foundation.

[53] Veress to Ligeti, 3 October 1958, Sándor Veress Collection, Paul Sacher Foundation.

[54] Bruno Nettl, 'Displaced Musics and Immigrant Musicologists: Ethnographical and Biographical Perspectives', in *Driven into Paradise: The Musical Migration from Nazi Germany to the United States*, ed. Reinhold Brinkmann and Christoph Wolff (Berkeley, 1999), pp. 54–65, at p. 55.

[55] Sabine M. Feisst, 'Arnold Schoenberg–American', conference paper presented on 4 November 2007 at the annual meeting of the American Musicological Society in Quebec City, Canada. See also the complex relationships of place and identity that always remained part of Darius Milhaud's work in Marie-Noëlle Lavoie, 'Identité, emprunts et régionalisme: judaïcité dans les œuvres de Milhaud Durant l'entre-deux-guerres', in *Musique, arts et religion dans l'entre-deux-guerres*, ed. Sylvain Caron and Michel Duchesneau (Lyons, 2009), pp. 57–70.

musical reasons. As we noted above in their private correspondence, both agreed that under the current regime legitimate creative activity was no longer possible. However, having taken the decision to emigrate for similar reasons, Veress and Ligeti reacted differently to the environments into which they moved.

On the one hand, Veress successfully immigrated to Switzerland. Though he did not officially become a Swiss citizen until months before his death, he nevertheless was, as professor of music and ethnomusicology at the University of Berne, one of the pillars of Switzerland's musical establishment. In his correspondence he openly admitted that though his move to Switzerland had not been part of his travel plans, he was thankful that things had worked out the way they did.[56] Ligeti, on the other hand, failed in his attempt to immigrate to Switzerland. He eventually did become an Austrian citizen, but he never really settled in Vienna in the same way that Veress made Berne his home. On the contrary, Ligeti used the Austrian capital as a convenient resting point as he moved around Western Europe and North America following increasingly alluring career opportunities.

If we examine the two not merely as social individuals requiring visas, passports and some form of legal residency status, but as composers, a different picture emerges. As a composer in Western Europe, Veress very quickly found himself marginalized in relation to what would become the post-war avant-garde. Over time he did obtain a secure teaching position in Berne that enabled him to maintain his standard of living and provided him with a form of professional security.[57] But at the same time, his post-war compositions written mainly in Switzerland never achieved the success that his pre-war work seemed to portend. The Hungarian-born critique John Weissmann writing from London in 1955 summed up Veress's predicament in the following terms.

> From his Swiss vantage point he has surveyed the European scene with the objective detachment of a visitor from another planet, untainted by the recently formed traditions and unburdened by the dangerous conventions of the day. Like most open-minded creative musicians, he explored the dodecaphonic method of composition, regarding it merely as an enrichment of his technical armoury, feeling no obligation to apply it consistently and without his music becoming intellectualized. In fact, his spontaneous, undoctrinaire approach made it possible for him to achieve the highly original fusion of serial technique with a folk-music inspired utterance of decidedly tonal inclinations.[58]

Whereas, from an aesthetic point of view, Veress remained something of a musical exile in Western Europe, Ligeti clearly succeeded with remarkable

---

[56] Veress to Ligeti, 10 January 1957, Sándor Veress Collection, Paul Sacher Foundation.

[57] One could argue that his situation resembled that of the North American university composer, which after World War II became exceedingly widespread throughout that continent.

[58] John Weissmann, 'Guide to Contemporary Hungarian Composers. (1) The Early Decades of the Twentieth Century', *Tempo* 35 (1955), pp. 24–30, at p. 30.

ease in establishing a place for himself in the West European new music scene. In fact he was so successful that his music became a defining element and marker of that scene. Thus depending on whether we view Veress and Ligeti as citizens or as composers, both appear to have been both immigrants and exiles at the same time, but for different reasons.[59] The divergent destinies of teacher and student illustrate the difficulties that can arise when sociological categories are applied to composers and creative artists too crudely. Though they may work well in describing individuals and groups in civil society that move from one place to another, they are awkward and ill suited when dealing with creative artists if we do not take into account the aesthetic side of their activities.

Despite the fact that they appear to have lost contact with one another in the early 1960s, Ligeti never forgot the lessons he learned from Veress during the few years he studied with him in post-war Budapest. The playful attitude or pose that Ligeti would so often adopt in relation to the stylistic and technical conventions inherited from the past (which we find clearly exhibited in *Invenció* written in 1948 while Ligeti was still studying with Veress) is a possible outward sign of how Veress may have indirectly influenced Ligeti's development as a composer.[60] But the most important lesson Ligeti took to heart must surely be Veress's enduring commitment to individual freedom as a necessary condition of basic human dignity and creative activity. Ligeti recognized from the outset that this idea was a motivating factor in the composition of *Fingerlarks* and it remained part of Ligeti's artistic credo throughout his career.[61]

[59] This double perspective reminds us of Lydia Goehr's contention that in the 20th century, the discourse of music and musicians in exile is necessarily double-sided. Composers are usually both resisters and adapters. Goehr, *The Quest for Voice*, pp. 174ff., esp. pp. 182–94.

[60] For more on *Invenció* and its relationships with models from the past, see Friedemann Sallis, 'La transformation d'un héritage: *Bagatelle* op. 6 n° 2 de Béla Bartók et *Invenció* (1948) pour piano de György Ligeti', *Revue de musicologie* 83/2 (1997), pp. 281–93.

[61] I would like to heartily thank Zuzana Finger for her work in translating this text as well as other Hungarian texts cited in this article. I would also like to thank the Faculté des études supérieures et de la recherche de l'Université de Moncton for providing funds to pay for the translation of letters conserved in the Sándor Veress Collection of the Paul Sacher Foundation.

Ligeti during a rehearsal of his Cello Sonata at home
(Hamburg, 9 November 1989)

2 Transformational Ostinati in György Ligeti's Sonatas for Solo Cello and Solo Viola

BENJAMIN DWYER

Leaving aside the works for piano and harpsichord, the Sonata for Solo Cello (1947–53) and the Sonata for Solo Viola (1991–4) are among the most important works by György Ligeti for solo instrument. It is curious therefore that, despite the 40-odd years that separate them, they occupy somewhat similar ground: a regard for Hungarian and Romanian folk elements, a more than passing tribute to Béla Bartók, and a lyricism that marks both Ligeti's early and late periods. The relationship of these two sonatas to the indigenous music of his homeland and its spiritual father might indicate that Ligeti felt that a bowed stringed instrument represented the most natural medium for music of such affiliations: itinerant gypsy violin music and Bartók's Sonata for Solo Violin hover over both works. It should be kept in mind, however, that the Sonata for Solo Cello represented (for its time) a serious rebellion from the demands imposed upon Ligeti during the late 1940s and early 1950s by an oppressive Stalinist regime, which considered any art displaying modernist tendencies to be decadent and anathema to its totalitarian ideology. In contrast, the Sonata for Solo Viola is something of a home-coming: it is significant among those works that characterize the composer's re-embracing of folk elements and a new-found lyricism into his musical palette following a long middle period of avant-garde exploration. Despite their perceived traditionalism, both works occupy an evolutionary space: one broke free from ideological strictures and opened out into an enticing freedom promised by the European avant-garde of the 1950s, the other acted as 'a rebellion against the established conventions of the avant-garde'[1] and veered back towards an affiliation with earlier stimuli.

The Sonata for Solo Viola inherits many rhythmic and structural features from both the Violin Concerto and the Études for Piano. Indeed, each movement is a kind of 'study' relating to specific aspects of the instrument. The Sonata is also concerned with fundamental notions of the variation and transformation of a melody – remarkably similar (considering the distance in time of composition) to those utilized in the earlier *Dialogo* from the Sonata for Solo Cello. Given the historic pedigree and clear delineations of the 'theme and variation' genre, the processes Ligeti employs in both sonatas are best understood as a series of ostinati of varying types. Derived from the Italian meaning 'stubborn', the word *ostinato* refers to a motif or phrase that persistently repeats. Ligeti's use of a repeating 'ground' (*Chaconne chromatique, Lamento*), the repetition of melodic phrases (*Hora lungă, Facsar*, and, in the cello piece, *Dialogo*), the reiteration of rhythmic structures (*Loop*), or even entire segments (*Prestissimi con sordino*), indeed renders the term 'ostinato' an apt choice. As variation and alteration are generated through these reiterations, the most apposite term to describe these mutational processes would be transformational ostinato. This essay will provide a brief background to the composition of both sonatas, and

---

[1] György Ligeti, *Chamber Music*, György Ligeti Edition 7, Sony Classical 62309 (1998), programme note, trans. Annieles McVoy and David Feurzeig, n.p.

it will highlight some of their more distinctive attributes. However, the investigation will concentrate on the specifics of Ligeti's employment of what I am terming transformational ostinati as a means to develop and vary his material.

Transformational ostinati as gender types

The Sonata for Solo Cello was not planned as one might expect. Like the Sonata for Solo Viola, the cello work had an unusual genesis and development that were dictated by outside forces rather than by planned and controlled intent. The Sonata was composed over a five-year period that saw extraordinary changes in Hungarian society – a fact that impacted its development strongly. The score bears two dates – 1948 and 1953, as the two-movement work was not planned originally as such. Despite its obvious qualities, the first movement, *Dialogo*, is essentially a student work composed when Ligeti was only 25 years of age for a fellow pupil at the Kolozsvár Conservatory in Budapest: a female cellist, Annus Virány, with whom he was secretly in love. It was conceived originally as a short self-contained piece. Apparently, Ligeti's shy and cryptic advances did not meet with much success and *Dialogo* remained unperformed. Meanwhile, political change was imminent and by 1949 the People's Republic of Hungary was installed under Stalinist dominance. From this period onwards, severe restrictions were placed on cultural activity: practically all modernist art was condemned as decadent and duly banned. New music came under the same restrictions – 'all "modern" music was banned in Hungary that is, not only Schoenberg, Berg, Webern and Stravinsky, but even Britten and Milhaud.'[2]

Ligeti was forced to work amidst this claustrophobic atmosphere. The new regime's harsh policies, which led to the imprisonment or disappearance of many, destroyed any of his lingering affiliations with this caricature of Socialism. The new political reality also influenced Ligeti's growing desire to write a more radical type of music. Once commenting that fascism did not like dissonance, his movement away from the conservative folk idioms favoured by the party apparatchiks was at least one way of preserving his own internal, personal freedom. However, those compositions that displayed 'progressive' characteristics remained censored or hidden.

In 1953, at the request for a sonata by the cellist Vera Dénes, Ligeti composed a second work, which he added to *Dialogo*. *Capriccio* provides a structural contrast to the former: the introduction, exposition, development, recapitulation and coda aspects of standard sonata form are generally adhered to. Together they would comprise the Sonata for Solo Cello (dedicated to Ligeti's friend, the Swedish musicologist, Ove Nordwall). The new Sonata was presented to the Composers' Union, which controlled artistic activities in Hungary at the time. Considering the work too 'formalist', the Union denied Ligeti the rights to both publication and public performance. Although it did permit Dénes to make a recording for Hungarian Radio, it was broadcast only once and Ligeti had to wait 26

---

[2] György Ligeti, *Aventures, Nouvelle Aventures, etc.*, György Ligeti – The Ligeti Project V, Teldec Classics 8573-88262-2 (2004), programme note to CD, trans. Louise Duchesneau.

years for its première, which took place at the English Bach Festival in 1976, given by Rohan de Saram.

Ligeti describes the first movement, *Dialogo* (marked *Adagio, rubato, cantabile*), as a representation of a hypothetical dialogue between two people. In a characteristic concern for idiomatic writing, the four strings of the cello are employed separately to help delineate individual voices, and to suggest aspects of 'masculinity' and 'femininity'. Relying, therefore, on 'standardized' definitions, the 'gender' of given phrases may be appreciated and categorized depending upon the range of the melodies – the higher, more plaintive lines can be read as 'feminine' and the lower, more resonant phrases could be interpreted as 'masculine'. Leaving aside contemporary philosophical and socio-political notions of gender, it is easier to understand this simplified binary as an aspirational dialogue between a shy, naïve, male composer and an unsuspecting female cellist. The work comprises two parts of six sections each. Part One contains two 'themes' of two types (A-type and B-type, see Example 4)[3] and four transformational ostinati. Part Two further develops the two 'theme' types through an additional six transformational ostinati.

Example 4 Sonata for Solo Cello, first movement, *Dialogo*, bars 2 and 6

A-Type 'theme'

B-Type 'theme'

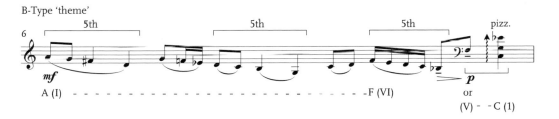

'Masculine' and 'feminine' characteristics emanate from both 'theme' types depending on the range. Despite their affinity with traditional models, these 'themes' do not derive from original folk sources. That both 'theme' types (A and B) end on the dominant (V) and sub-mediant (VI) respectively, adds to the excursionist nature of each: they suggest an inquisitive inclination that heightens the dialectic between the two protagonists. Along with these, and the following ten transformational ostinati, Ligeti also incorporates a number of pizzicato chords executed with glissandi at the opening and closing of the work; they further arbitrate between the first three phrases. Following the appearance of the first pizzicato chord, the A-type 'theme' is presented on the C string, the lowest on the instrument. Resonant and broad in character, the melody embodies what might be considered a 'masculine' character (see

---

[3] Example 4 and all following examples from the Cello Sonata are taken from György Ligeti, *Sonata for Solo Cello*, score (Mainz, 1990).

Table 1 Sonata for Solo Cello, first movement, *Dialogo*: formal structure

Section	Phrase type	Gender
Pizzicato introduction		
(1) A-type 'theme'		masculine
Pizzicato interlude		
(2) t.o. 1	A-Type	feminine
(3) B-type 'theme'		feminine
Pizzicato interlude		
(4) t.o. 2	A-type	masculine
(5) t.o. 3	B-type	feminine with accompaniment
(6) t.o. 4	A-type	masculine with accompaniment
(7) t.o. 5	A-type	feminine with dialogue
(8) t.o. 6	B-type	feminine with accompaniment
(9) t.o. 7	A-type	masculine with dialogue
(10) t.o. 8	B-type	feminine & masculine
(11) t.o. 9	B-type	feminine with accompaniment
(12) t.o. 10	A-type	masculine with dialogue
Pizzicato coda		

Table 1: A-type 'theme' [masculine], and Example 5, top stave). Following a pizzicato interlude, the first transformational ostinato appears. Presented a twelfth higher and executed entirely on the D string, this music displays what might be allowed as a 'feminine' quality. Some double stops are employed in transformational ostinati (henceforth abbreviated to t.o.) 3 and 4 that act as subtle accompaniments. Table 1 shows the structural plan for the entire movement outlining gender suggestions and 'theme'-type affiliations.

Example 5 isolates the A-type 'theme' and the six transformational ostinati relating to it (nos. 1, 2 and 4 from Part One, and nos. 5, 7, and 10 from Part Two). This provides an opportunity to observe for the first time the way in which transformational ostinati function and the results they glean. As noted, the term *ostinato* signifies a motif or phrase that persistently repeats. In this case, it is a phrase, which is represented by the A-type 'theme' in its 'masculine' range (top stave). The subsequent transformational ostinati progressively transform the original.

T.o. 1, for example, maintains the exact contour and note values, but (as noted) places the phrase up a compound fifth, offering a 'feminine' version. T.o. 2 replicates the original almost exactly, except for the penultimate note, which slightly but effectively alters the shape of the cadence. T.o. 4 (the next one that relates to the A-type 'theme') stays in the 'masculine' range but transforms the original through phrase prolongation and the introduction of accompaniment touches. The following relevant transformational ostinati (nos. 5, 7 and 10), which appear in Part Two, further develop the 'theme' through the following: a tempo change, phrase prolongation, the introduction of new voices to create a dialogue between the parts, the

Example 5 Sonata for Solo Cello, first movement, *Dialogo*: A-type 'theme', and its related transformational ostinati (nos. 1, 2, 4, 5, 7 and 10)

incorporation of dynamic markings, and further explorations of 'feminine' and 'masculine' ranges. Example 6 shows similar processes in the transformation of the B-type 'theme', although prolongation is abandoned.

The interval of the perfect fifth emerges as one of the most influential factors in the work. It dominates in two distinctive ways: as mentioned, the 'themes' move from a tonic point (I) to a dominant point (V), while the sub-phrases within the B-type 'theme' are dominated by the fifth interval (see Example 4 and Table 2).[4] Furthermore, the relationship between the 'themes' and some of their transformational ostinati is governed by the fifth. This fact means that the very construction of the phrase development is often built upon a fifth hierarchy: a design that naturally emanates from the tuning system of the cello: C–G–D–A [IV–III–II–I].

---

[4] Note: The B-Type 'theme' ends not on a (V) but rather a (VI) or F. However, this harmonic point is related by a fifth to the following pizzicato interlude in C (F to C or I–V). The C is then connected by a fifth relationship to the following t.o. 2 starting on G. Taken together, these three sections form a cycle of 5ths relationship: F–C–G. Further note that the F♯, the higher pitch of the final dyad of t.o. 4 acts as a leading note to the opening G of t.o. 5 in Part Two.

Example 6 Sonata for Solo Cello, first movement, *Dialogo*: B-type 'theme',
and its related transformational ostinati (nos. 3, 6, 8 and 9)

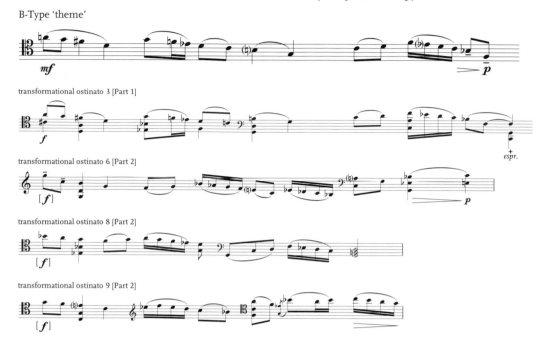

Part One of *Dialogo* sets out the two 'themes', the following four transformational ostinati, their genders, and their types. Apart from some additional accompaniment notes, the phrases are delineated clearly and stated simply. Part Two makes greater strides in development, transforming the thematic material in more elaborate ways. Therefore, successive transformational ostinati create considerable dynamism and dialectic tension, the repetition of each becoming more interrogative and speculative. Additionally, whereas the A-type 'theme' dominates in Part One, the B-type 'theme', which might be considered the more strident of the two, dominates in Part Two giving the latter a more dramatic impact. That stridency is enhanced by the increased rate at which the transformational ostinati recur, prolongation (as noted) not being a feature of Part Two. In fact, t.o. 9 and 10 sound as if they have been cut short, which enhances dramatic tension in the work. Despite the dominance of B-type music, the final and tenth transformational ostinato returns us (in a somewhat fragmented manner) to the opening A-type material and to the opening 'theme' (though here up an octave), which provides a frame for the entire movement and a suitable close to the piece. Although the Sonata for Solo Cello is an early work, it remains a very important addition to the solo cello repertoire. Significantly, it provides in its *Dialogo* movement an early example of Ligeti's use of the transformational ostinato technique, which was to become such a central feature in the Sonata for Solo Viola. That technique allowed him to ingeniously transform relatively simple 'themes' into hybridized phrases of hidden complexity.

Table 2 Sonata for Solo Cello, first movement, *Dialogo*:
harmonic construction of Part One

Section	Harmonic progression
Pizzicato introduction	
(1) A-type 'theme'	G (I) – D (V) – (Pizzicato interlude)
(2) t.o. 1	D (I) – A (V) – (Pizzicato interlude)
(3) B-type 'theme'	A (I) – F (VI)
(4) Pizzicato interlude in C	
(5) t.o. 2	G (I) – D (V) [D is dominant of A]
(6) t.o. 3	A (I) – (F)
(7) t.o. 4	G (I) – D (V)

Transformational ostinati and the harmonic series

Like the cello sonata, the Sonata for Solo Viola also had an unusual compositional development. Written in stages between 1991 and 1994, the composition and first performances of its six movements do not correlate to the order of the finished score. The violist Garth Knox premièred *Loop* (the first movement to be written but now the Sonata's second) at a commemoration concert in Vienna in 1991 given by the Arditti Quartet for Alfred Schlee, Ligeti's first publisher in the West. Although just a short piece, *Loop* was written with the clear intention of being included into a more substantial sonata. Consequently, *Facsar* appeared next in 1993. Written as a tribute to Sándor Veress, Ligeti's old composition professor who had died in March the previous year in Berne, *Facsar* would become the Sonata's third movement. When Klaus Klein offered a platform for a full sonata at the Gütersloh Festival, it provided Ligeti with the focus and inspiration to compose four more movements and complete the Sonata for Solo Viola as we know it today.[5] The German violist, Tabea Zimmermann, whose 'particularly vigorous and pithy ... yet always tender' sound was an inspiration for Ligeti, gave the première at the German festival in 1994.[6]

Ligeti's desire to re-embrace his traditional folk heritage and distance himself from the European avant-garde is realized most pertinently in the first movement of the Sonata for Solo Viola. It is not known if he was aware of an important precedent – *Hora Staccato*, written in 1906 by the Romanian composer and violinist Grigoraş Dinicu (1889–1949), but Ligeti's appropriation of the *hora lungă* ingenuously reconnected him to

[5] Klaus Klein has been an important cultural attaché to the city of Gütersloh. He was very active in the promotion of all its cultural events. In addition to his significant connection with Ligeti, one of the most noteworthy contributions he made before retiring was the development and opening of the new concert hall in the city.

[6] György Ligeti, *Sonata for Solo Viola*, score, preface, trans. Lindsay Gerbracht (Mainz, 1991). Tabea Zimmermann's performance at the WDR Cologne concert in 1990 actually ignited Ligeti's interest in composing a sonata for viola. The first and last movements are dedicated to her.

both his immediate homeland and to the spiritual father of Romanian and Hungarian music, Béla Bartók. Sometime around 1912 Bartók first came across the *hora lungă* in the territories of Maramureş and Satu-Mare – geographical, historical and ethno-cultural regions in northern Transylvania. Such was its significance that Bartók later admitted that his encounter with the *hora lungă* was the most important development of his musicological career.[7] Subsequent research has revealed similar music found as far west as Albania and Algeria, and as far east as Tibet, western China, and Cambodia. Ligeti himself highlighted the 'striking similarity' of the *hora lungă* 'to the *Cante jondo* in Andalucía and ... folk music in Rajastan', so its use in the Sonata for Solo Viola invokes expansive folk traditions of varying shades and influences.[8]

The structure of Ligeti's *Hora lungă* offers a fine example of the transformational ostinato process (see Table 3). Its opening 'theme' consists of nine notes that Ligeti develops through a series of six extended transformational ostinati. The first three transformational ostinati start on the note C and end on the note G (see Example 7 for t.o. 1).[9] The underpinning of the melodic material with these two pitches somewhat corrodes what might otherwise have been a work considered to be centred on an F tonality. Nonetheless, the rivalry between the prominent tonal centres of F, C and G, coupled by the ever-increasing dialectic of the transformational ostinati, creates an accumulating tension in the movement.

Table 3 Sonata for Solo Viola, first movement, *Hora lungă*:
formal structure

Bars	Section	Harmonic progressions
1–2	'theme'	
2–5	t.o. 1	C–G
5–8	t.o. 2	C–G
9–14	t.o. 3	C–G
14–16	[Interlude]	
16–19	t.o. 4	
19–32	t.o. 5	
32–7	t.o. 6	

Following t.o. 3 (bar 14), a small interlude is introduced: a sweeping arpeggiated gesture executed on a single string. Opening on the note C, it rises in natural harmonics culminating on C_2, pre-empting the extended use of the same harmonic series in the final transformational ostinato starting at bar 32. The semiquaver rest following the final C of the interlude (the only rest in the entire movement) offers a visual marker

---

[7] Jay Rahn, 'Text-Tune Relationships in the *Hora Lunga* Versions Collected by Bartók', *Yearbook of the International Folk Music Council* 8 (1976), pp. 89–96, at p. 89.

[8] György Ligeti, *Sonata for Solo Viola* (Mainz, 2001), preface.

[9] Example 7 and all following examples from the Viola Sonata are taken from: György Ligeti, *Sonata for Solo Viola* (Mainz, 1991).

Example 7 Sonata for Solo Viola, first movement, *Hora lungă*, bars 1–6

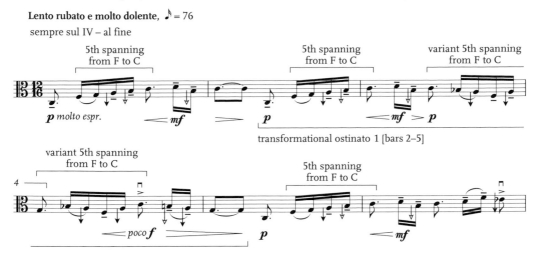

dividing the work into two sections. The second half of the work comprises t.o. 4, 5 and 6. Although number 4 covers only four bars, the following one, over a 14-bar development, brings the work to an intense climax. It notably amplifies the range of the instrument to a C_I at the *ffff* dynamic in bar 29. As mentioned, the final transformational ostinato (t.o. 6) is executed throughout in natural harmonics.

Table 4 clearly shows the expanding range of pitches: material unfolds exponentially in each half of the work (the second half markedly so) that figuratively suggests an ever-increasing sense of diffusion and ethereality. The earthy, defined nature of the folk 'theme' is extended and augmented consistently by each successive transformational ostinato towards evermore hypothetical permutations.

Microtonality has always been an important feature of Ligeti's work. Rather than employing it in an arbitrary manner in *Hora lungă*, he utilizes the natural microtonal discrepancies offered by the harmonic series, and in so doing parallels certain developments in the spectral music of Tristan Murail, Horatiu Radulescu and Gérard Grisey. Certain notes from a given harmonic series resonate marginally below or above what would be an exact pitch in their well-tempered equivalents. For example, where a semitone equals 100 cents, the fifth harmonic of the series is –14 cents (in the case of the C fundamental in Example 8, this is a slightly flattened E), while the seventh harmonic is –31 cents (a B♭ further flattened almost a third of a semitone), and so on.

The notation of the Sonata for Solo Viola utilizes three different downward arrows to signify these distinct natural downward deviations. Bars 16/17 offer examples of their use. The first is a quarter tone lower

Example 8 Harmonic series on the note C

Table 4 Sonata for Solo Viola, first movement, *Hora lungă*: expansion of range with successive transformational ostinati

t.o. 1	t.o. 2	t.o. 3	Interlude	t.o. 4	t.o. 5	t.o. 6
						C
						b
						b
						a
						g
						F♯
						e
						d
						c
						b♭
						g
						e
					C	c
					b	
		A♭			a♭	
		g♭			g♭	g
	F	f		F	f	
	e♭	e♭		e♭	e♭	
D	d	d		d	d	
c	c	c		c	c	c
b	b	b		b	b	
a	a	a		a	a	
g	g	g		g	g	
f	f	f		f	f	
C	C	C	Interlude	C	C	C

(−49 cents), being the 11th harmonic of the scale. The second is about a sixth of a tone lower (−31 cents), being the seventh harmonic, and the third is a rather slight deviation (−14 cents), being the fifth harmonic of a series.

Hora lungă is performed entirely on the C string of the viola. Previously, Ligeti had employed the single string idea in the second movement of the Violin Concerto (*Aria, Hoquetus, Choral*), in which phrases are played entirely on the G string for 74 bars of the *Aria*. Furthermore, *Facsar* (the third movement of the Sonata, but written before *Hora lungă*) also employs the C string for a considerable period. Referring to the use of the C string, Garth Knox commented on an interesting point he observed while working with Ligeti on *Facsar*. At this time Ligeti was already beginning to compose *Hora lungă*, and it seems that the employment of the C string for the opening 'theme' of *Facsar* led to its use for the entirety of the former. Ligeti told Knox that, 'he had a better idea' for the C string, evidently referring to his subsequent and exclusive use of it in *Hora lungă*. Once the decision was made, Ligeti's imagination was kindled. He then enquired, 'How high can you go?' The use of the C string for an entire work was something of a stroke of genius – 'It is the one string by which the viola can be really identified,' Knox comments.[10] Ligeti's unique approach to writing for the C string guarantees an original sound in that it is 'necessary to produce the harmonics of F while playing normally on the C string, and by controlling the accuracy of the intonation by ear; one operates to some extent starting from imaginary strings.'[11] Thus, the three downward arrow signs utilized in the score (see Example 9) are used with the notes A (–14 cents); E♭ (–31 cents) and B (–49 cents) – respectively the fifth, seventh and 11th degrees of the harmonic series on F (see Table 5).

Example 9   Notation arrows used in *Hora lungă*

(1)↓   (2)↓   (3)↓

While utilizing the altered third and fourth degrees of the imaginary F series, Ligeti also occasionally resorts to their well-tempered pitch versions, as can be observed in bar 7 (see the standard note B in the last four semiquaver group) and in bars 28/9 (where the standard note B occurs three times and the standard note A appears twice). The inclusion of these notes results in two slightly different pitch-classes that play against each other. This use of alternative scale patterns further parallels another common trait of the *hora lungă* genus: the third and fourth degrees of its scale fluctuate between their exact, slightly flat and slightly sharp pitch versions.

Table 5   Harmonic series on F fundamental

Harmonic	1	2	3	4	5	6	7	8	9	10	11	12	13	14	15	16
Pitches	F	F	C	F	A	C	E♭	F	G	A	B	C	D♭	E♭	E	F
Pitch deviation (cents)	0	0	+2	0	–14	+2	–31	0	+4	–14	–49	+2	+41	–31	–12	0

Ligeti's use of the imaginary F harmonic series has further implications in the final section of the movement. As noted, the work is divided into six transformational ostinati based on a 'theme'. The final transformational ostinato commences in bar 32 and is performed (for the first time in the work) solely on harmonics. As the entire movement (and, therefore, also the final transformational ostinato) is executed on the C string, all these harmonics naturally emanate from the harmonic series of the fundamental C, thus offering a second and distinct pitch series to the

---

[10] Garth Knox, telephone interview with the author, 25 June 2009.

[11] Pierre Gervasoni, 'Interview with György Ligeti', *World*, 27 September 1997, reprinted online at http://members.lycos.fr./yrol/MUSIC/LIGETI/ligeti2.htm (trans. Josh Ronsen, October, 2003), accessed on 3 August 2011.

imaginary F harmonic series upon which the previous five ostinati have been constructed. Consequently, the tonal character and pitch class of the last transformational ostinato is different. If it is accepted that the work is centred upon an F tonality (even if, as we have noted, the prominence of the C and G pitches competes with this suggestion), a dominant shade has been cast over the cadential material of this last transformational ostinato (the same, of course, could be said of the Interlude, which, being also based on the harmonic series of the C string, may be seen as a cadential moment for the first half of the movement).

The shift in tonal character also explains what might have been viewed initially as rogue notes in bars 29 and 30: the Bb, F♯ and E (third note-group of bar 29 and first note-group of bar 30), which have the downward arrow signs attached. These notes do not correlate to those in the imaginary F harmonic series. They do, however, correspond exactly to the seventh, eleventh and fifth degrees of the harmonic series on C (see Example 8), though performed here not as natural harmonics but as normally executed notes (and, thus, appearing out of context in the fifth transformational ostinato). Therefore, in bars 29/30, right at the climax of the entire movement, Ligeti pre-empts the later use of the C harmonic series with these notes; as they appear in a transformational ostinato based on the F series, these hybrids can be seen as a modulatory force in the work. This dominant attribute of the final transformational ostinato brings the music into ungrounded territory and further adds to the ethereal and imagined quality of the fading melodies disappearing through the dissolving filmy harmonics.

Nancarrow and the isorhythmic motet as models for transformational ostinati

Transformational ostinati in *Loop* concentrate on the manipulation of rhythm and pulse. Numerous processes Ligeti employs in his music from the 1970s onwards emerge out of his familiarity with 14th-century polyphony (the first movement of *Three Pieces for Two Pianos* (1976), *Monument*, and *Loop* are foremost among them). From 1980 the mechanical 'studies' of Conlon Nancarrow (1912–97) also exercise a significant influence.

In 1966, Ligeti turned to Guillaume de Machaut (1300–77) in preparation for *Lux aeterna*. The French master also provided a significant model for the *Hoquetus* (middle) section of the second movement of the Violin Concerto, which is directly influenced by his *Hoquetus David* motet (1360), where the *Alleluia nativitas* melody in the tenor is stated four times and treated isorhythmically. An isorhythmic motet is constructed around two central principles: the *talea*, that is, the order of durations or rhythms, and the *color*, or pitch series of the melody. An isorhythmic construction is often varied by strict or free rhythmic diminution in the repetition of the *color*. Occasionally, composers utilize a long and more elaborate *talea* to create larger scale works. In this case, each *color* and *talea* constitutes a substantial structural section of the composition. Often, a long *color* is repeated several times according to different mensuration rules, making its execution faster by a fixed proportion each time: a technique that fashioned the diminution motet.

Ligeti opens *Loop* with a melodic gesture comprising four dyads played over three bars. Having flagged this motif, the music continues with a further series of 45 dyads (from bar 4 to 20) that represent the *talea* and *color* from which the entire movement will be constructed (Example 10). As these double-stops differ in note length, sometimes comprising two or three note values connected by ties, it is useful to consider them as 'syllables', of which there are 45. The time signature for the entire movement alternates between 8/16 (most often divided into 5+3, though not exclusively) and 10/16 (most often in 4+6 groupings).

Example 10 Sonata for Solo Viola, second movement, *Loop* (extending over bars 4–20)

As they constitute the subject material for the entire work, the *talea* and *color* of 45 dyads represent the 'theme', which is developed through the employment of eight transformational ostinati. The *color* never alters, but Ligeti subjects the *talea* to ever-diminishing rhythmic values in a mechanistic *reductio ad absurdum*. The initial *talea* 'theme' requires 148 semiquavers to be completed, the eighth and final transformational ostinato requires only 48, down to 32% – or a reduction of 68% (see Table 6).

Table 6 Sonata for Solo Viola, second movement, *Loop*: formal structure

Bars	Section	Duration (semiquavers)
4–20	*Talea* ('theme')	148
20–33	t.o. 1	122
33–45	t.o. 2	108
46–56	t.o. 3	94
56–65	t.o. 4	84
65–73	t.o. 5	71
73–80	t.o. 6	64
80–6	t.o. 7	52
86–91	t.o. 8	48

Thus, displaying rhythmic/structural characteristics very similar to that of a Diminution Motet, *Loop* acutely contrasts the augmentational processes of the preceding *Hora lungă*. The full extent of the rhythmic contraction can be observed when the music in bar 92, which is effectively an abortive attempt at a ninth transformational ostinato, is compared with the opening motivic gesture covering bars 1 and 2 (Example 11).

If Machaut helped provide a compositional model for *Loop*, Conlon Nancarrow showed how that model could be realized in a contemporary idiom. His pianola 'studies' are replete with canons in augmentation or diminution, and he often constructs *prolation canons* (where each voice executes the same melody but at different speeds), all of which provided important precedents for Ligeti.[12] The sudden, explosive finish to *Loop* – the score indicates 'as if torn off' – is indicative of many of the piano Études (themselves deeply influenced by Nancarrow) that extirpate in a spiral of self-destruction. Furthermore, the increasing complexity makes *Loop* an advanced technical study for viola: one note of every dyad in the work is played with an open string, and as the movement proceeds, the performer is gang-planked into evermore dangerous left-hand leaps and bow manipulations. The score instructs the performer to play *'with swing'*,[13] and Nancarrow's studies and his Sonatina for piano from 1941 (particularly its second movement – *Moderato – Più allegro*) may have suggested the unusual mix of focused complexity and quirky jazz evident in *Loop*. Although the seriousness of the former seems to contradict the humour of the latter, the attendant double-aesthetic is a central facet of Ligeti's music.

Example 11 Sonata for Solo Viola, second movement, *Loop*, bars 1/2 and bars 91/2

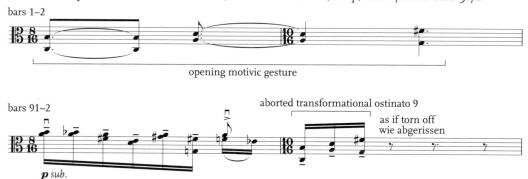

bars 1–2

opening motivic gesture

bars 91–2

aborted transformational ostinato 9

as if torn off
wie abgerissen

p sub.

[12] An interesting parallel exists between Ligeti's models for the *Sonata for Solo Viola* and Stravinsky's chamber music from the early 1950s, much of which explores similar processes. It was a period when Stravinsky was beginning to be influenced both by aspects of serialism and the counterpoint of 14th-, 15th- and 16th-century composers. For example, observe the use of augmentation, diminution and prolation canons in the first movement of the Septet 1952/3, while the Cantata of 1951/2 shows the influence of Heinrich Isaac (1450–1517) and Guillaume Dufay (1397–1474).

[13] In this respect, Ligeti was influenced by the performance style of Stéphane Grappelli.

Transformational ostinati as melodic, harmonic & textural generators

In contrast to *Loop*, *Facsar*, the third movement of the Sonata for Solo Viola, shifts attention away from rhythmic concerns towards an exploration of melody, harmony and texture. Ligeti presents his 'theme' over the first ten bars. The ensuing transformational ostinati also last ten bars. Therefore, the developmental process ignores prolongation or diminution. Despite a short *Più mosso* covering five bars (bars 60–4), the reassuring length-consistency of the transformational ostinati with that of the 'theme' certainly provides a contrast to the feckless acceleration of *Loop*. What at first seems like a ninth transformational ostinato at bar 91 (the first three bars follow the 'thematic' contour) veers off into a coda of six bars (bars 91–6).

Facsar certainly embodies its meaning of 'to screw' or 'to wring'. The idea here is to extract as much melodic, harmonic and textural variety from the 'theme' as possible. Concerning melodic development alone, Example 12 indicates the slow metamorphosis the 'theme' undergoes. T.o. 1–3 display minimal melodic alteration (note: new notes within a given transformational ostinato are marked with an asterisk, notes altered enharmonically are not identified). Although double and triple stops have been introduced, t.o. 1, 2 and 3 alter respectively only two, two and six notes of the original 'theme'. However, from t.o. 4 onwards, new pitch classes are introduced, though in most cases the melodic contour of the 'theme' is adhered to.

The strict length regularity of the 'theme' and transformational ostinati offer a perfect formal design. This might be the very reason why Ligeti attempts to erode the attendant overt structural subdivisions. In bars 40/1, for example, Ligeti phrases over the barline; *tenuto* markings are restricted to the first three quavers of bar 40 and the second and third quavers of 41, thereby avoiding an emphasis on the first beat of 41, that is, the beginning of the new transformational ostinato (see Example 13a). Meanwhile, in bars 60/1 Ligeti employs the heading *Più mosso* and the dynamic marking *ff*, not at bar 61 where one might expect them (the beginning of a new transformational ostinato) but at bar 60, marginally before it (see Example 13b). He further obscures the division between t.o. 6 and 7 by running a crescendo line from bar 70 to bar 72 (see Example 13c), and executes the same in reverse for the next division by insisting upon a diminuendo line from bar 78 to 86, well inside the boundaries of t.o. 8 (see score and Example 13d). Ligeti effectively overlays the divisions of each transformational ostinato with musical, dynamic and gestural instructions that contrive to conceal them. All function cumulatively to avoid the prescriptive influence of the measured structural design.

In reference to these points, it is worth noting Garth Knox's observations while working with Ligeti on *Facsar*. By this time the movement had already been composed and therefore no alterations were made to any notes during the session. However, they worked closely together on numerous aspects of articulation and dynamics. During the session, Ligeti requested Knox to perform *Facsar* many times, placing the climax at different points and experimenting with rates and lengths of

Example 12 Sonata for Solo Viola, third movement, *Facsar*: 'theme', eight
transformational ostinati and coda

Example 13 Sonata for Solo Viola, third movement, *Facsar*

(a) bars 40–1

end of t.o. 3   beginning of t.o. 4

(b) bars 60–1

end of t.o. 5

Più mosso   beginning of t.o. 6

(c) bars 70–2

end of t.o. 6   beginning of t.o. 7

(d) bars 80–1

end of t.o. 7   beginning of t.o. 8

dim. poco a poco _ [etc.]

crescendos.[14] These practical revisions indicate that Ligeti arrived at his final decisions regarding tempo changes and dynamics through experimentation and intuitive processes rather than by structurally based decisions.

The phrase transformations within *Facsar* relate to alterations of the 'thematic' line and its contours. Harmonic variation is achieved through note addition, which also substantially enriches the texture of the music resulting in numerous dyads and triads; the gradual thickening of the texture transforms the wire-sculptured terseness of the 'theme'. Furthermore, this additive process generates an evolving polyvalent harmonic language. Ligeti's alertness to tradition is deeply ingrained, but the resultant triads do not form an harmonic unity. The rate at which autonomous harmonies interpolate prevents any appreciation of a central harmonic focus point. This ambiguity is further enlivened by the substantial use of the open strings of the instrument: a central constituent of the harmonic language throughout the Sonata. In *Facsar* Ligeti employs

[14] Garth Knox, telephone interview with the author, 25 June 2009.

a conventional harmony for the music written before the climax. He refers to music following the climax (from t.o. 6 onwards) as emanating from an 'imaginary harmony', meaning that its harmonic language has little allegiance to structured, organized pitch class systems but rather emanates from intuitive and suggestive impulses.[15] The result is an harmonic complex of insurgent tonal entities.

Transformational ostinati as continuum

In *Prestissimo con sordino* (dedicated to Klaus Klein), Ligeti divides the interest between line and rhythm. The instruction – *so schnell wie möglich* (as fast as possible) – presents the violist with one of the most virtuoso works in the entire repertoire. In this regard, the fourth movement of Paul Hindemith's Viola Sonata, op. 25, no. 1, seems likely to have been an important precedent. With its subtitle *Wild* and its constant flowing figurations from which accented notes are emphasized, it is remarkably similar to the later work. Sharing his opinions about Hindemith's music in general and the op. 25, no. 1 in particular, Ligeti confided to Garth Knox that, 'I didn't like the music very much, except for one piece, I wish I'd written it.'[16] However, the very opening of Ligeti's own Violin Concerto offers the most immediate template for *Prestissimo con sordino*, with its juxtaposition of rhythmically punctuated notes emerging from the quieter web of arpeggios and melismatic phrases. This accentuation of line was almost certainly a conscious decision: Ligeti commented to Knox that he wanted to 'use some bits left over from the Violin Concerto' and even admitted later that, 'it does work better on the viola!'[17] Written throughout in connected meandering quavers (even attached across barlines), visually, the notation of *Prestissimo con sordino* implies one long, single gesture. Given the emphasis on continuity, it would seem that formal design is neglected, but Ligeti has simply camouflaged its structure within the music leaving very few visual clues for the detection of architectural signposts.

The movement comprises 34 bars in 12/4 time subdivided into two parts of 14 and 10 quaver lengths respectively: this subdivision is identified in the score by a broken barline. Despite the deliberate obfuscation, the formal design of this movement is straightforward:

> – introductory material
> – 'theme'
> – transformational ostinato

The placement, however, of these sections within the work is by no means obvious. The 'theme' starts in the second part of bar 2, that is, on the 15th quaver beat of that bar (immediately following the broken barline), and continues until bar 18 (up to the tenth quaver beat). The transformational ostinato (which repeats the melodic material outlined in the 'theme' with certain modifications) starts on the 11th quaver beat of bar 18 and continues until the 15th quaver beat of bar 34, whereupon the movement is brought to a sudden close with a C♯ minor triad (see Example 14). The material

[15] Ibid.
[16] Ibid.
[17] Ibid.

Example 14 Sonata for Solo Viola, fourth movement, *Prestissimo con sordino*, bars 2, 18, and 34

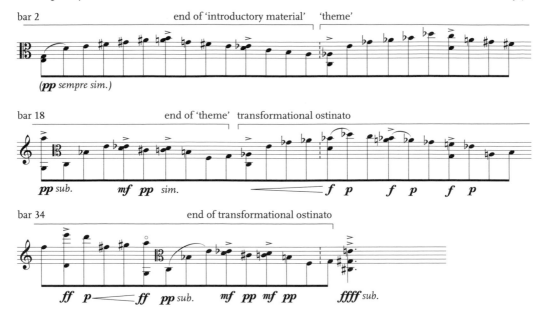

that opens the work and lasts until the point where the 'theme' begins (38 quavers covering bar 1 and the first part of bar 2), may, for convenience, be called introductory material, but the total absence of any individuating characteristics in this material refuses much nomenclature.

The so-called 'introductory material', the 'theme', and the transformational ostinato, devoid of distinguishing structural features and forming part of the single gesture of the entire movement, lead one to conclude that Ligeti rejected prescriptive structural blueprints. In other words, despite the repetition in the transformational ostinato of approximately 18 bars of music (or 398 notes!) from the 'theme', Ligeti wanted this work to be experienced as one single *Gestalt* – an uninterrupted continuum.

Despite the substantial reiteration, Ligeti's ingenious use of articulation, dynamics, and the controlled addition/subtraction of certain notes obfuscates any sense of repetition. As mentioned, *Prestissimo con sordino* comprises a long series of smooth, quaver notes played at high speed with a typical dynamic marking of *pp*. This line is interpolated at distances of two, four or six quaver positions with accented double-stops accompanied by louder dynamic markings: *mf, f, ff* or even *fff*. This juxtaposition sets up two melodic strata: one comprising quiet, seemingly continuous quavers, and the other a series of short, explosive outbursts (see Example 15).

Example 16 shows how Ligeti's fluid use of dynamics, the position shift of accent markings, and the addition and/or subtraction of notes radically alters our perception of two sections of music that are essentially the same. (Note: In Example 16, numbers have been added to assist in making comparisons: each number represents a given note in the 'theme', and its subsequent repetition in the transformational ostinato. Further observe that enharmonic notation has not been identified.)

Example 15 Sonata for Solo Viola, fourth movement, *Prestissimo con sordino*, bar 1–4

Typical of the general differences between the 'theme' and the transformational ostinato, the following points may be observed: –

There are additions and subtractions of notes. Note 6 (G) in the 'theme' appears in the transformational ostinato with an additional note (A). As this addition now forms a double-stop, it consequently gains an accent and a change of dynamic marking (from *p* to *mf*). Alternatively, double-stop 7 in the 'theme' (G♯/A) has been reduced to the single note G♯ in the transformational ostinato: no longer a double-stop, it loses its accent, and its dynamic marking is changed from *f* to *pp*. These alterations occur often throughout the transformational ostinato.

The dynamic markings, the lengths of dynamic hairpins, and their arrival points are all manipulated in the transformational ostinato in such a way as to significantly alter the original gestural shape and propulsion of the music. A major climax in the 'theme' requires a steady crescendo running from 15 right through to 37, culminating in a dynamic instruction of *fff*. The correlating passage in the transformational ostinato, however, displays significant differences: from 15 the passage undergoes a series

Example 16 Sonata for Solo Viola, fourth movement, *Prestissimo con sordino*, bars 15/16, and bars 31/2

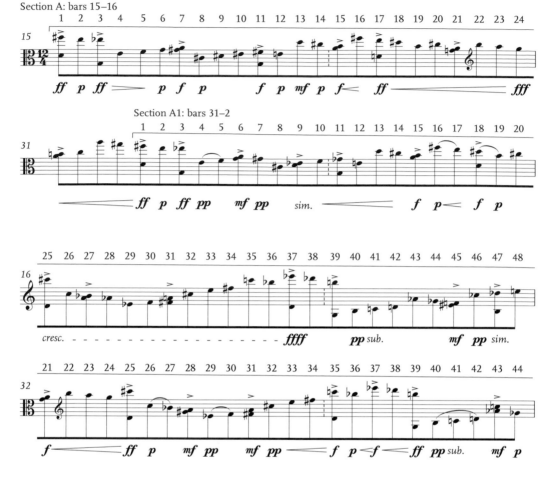

of contradictory dynamic instructions, giving the music a more jagged, inchoate character. When eventually it makes a climax, it does so on note 39 with an accompanying *ff* dynamic and not, as when originally presented, on note 37 with *fff*. Again, the transformational ostinato is replete with similar types of alteration.

Slurs are introduced only in the transformational ostinato. This slight change gives the music a significantly different articulation and renders the accented notes even more explosive.

These few examples might seem at first to be quite insignificant, but cumulatively they exercise a considerable modification in the transformational ostinato, so much so that they effectively render it new music. These alterations further highlight Ligeti's ear for detail and expose his uncanny ability to alter our aural perceptions by a subtle legerdemain.

Transformational ostinati and the *lamento* motif

In the fifth movement of the Sonata for Solo Viola (dedicated to his assistant of many years, Louise Duchesneau), Ligeti returned to one of his most characteristic signatures: the *lamento* motif. Written in 1985, the sixth Étude in Ligeti's monumental series for piano, *Automne à Varsovie* (Autumn in Warsaw), presented the *lamento* motif in its fullest grandeur and announced it as a central, recognizable feature that was to permeate much of his music from that moment onwards. It appears in numerous compositions including, among others, the Horn Trio, the Piano Concerto, the Violin Concerto, the *Hamburg Concerto*, and *Síppal, dobbal, nádihegedüvel*. Richard Steinitz has suggested that the *lamento* motif in early forms can be traced back to such works as the *Requiem* and the Double Concerto.[18] Other commentators have put forward the suggestion that aspects of it can be recognized in Ligeti's music dating as far back as the 1960s: in some of the thread fragments of *Lontano* (1967), for example. Ligeti himself suggests an indigenous source:

> In my music it's rather the melodic type of Romanian laments, the *bocet*, which appears; these are structured in a different way than the *Hora lungă*, although they are often similar in style and expression. By the way, there seems to be a similarity between the *bocet* and the Baroque lamento-bass.

He goes on to be more precise:

> This lament-ostinato appears in my music for the first time in the piano cycle *Musica ricercata*, which I composed between 1951 and 1953 while still in Budapest ... There I used a theme from a Frescobaldi ricercare which I changed a bit and added onto: a chromatic theme, which functions as the melodic fundament of the whole piece. I did the same thing later in the last movement of my Horn Trio, but also my first string quartet *Métamorphoses nocturnes* is actually based on the chromatic scale.[19]

Ligeti's clarifications on the genesis of the *lamento* and its subsequent use makes clear its centrality as a major *idée fixe* in his work.

The *lamento* motif consists of three phrases, the second and third longer than the one preceding them. The phrases descend in stepwise motion most often in whole tone or semitone movement, but occasionally with ascending leaps. Although different *lamento* examples display distinctive rhythmic formulae, the adopted *talea* is usually maintained throughout the work. Example 17 extracts the *lamento* from the opening seven bars of the movement (see upper staves).

---

[18] Richard Steinitz, *György Ligeti: Music of the Imagination* (London, 2003), p. 148.

[19] Denys Bouliane, 'Stilisierte Emotion: György Ligeti im Gespräch mit Denys Bouliane', *MusikTexte – Zeitschrift für neue Musik* 28–9 (March 1989), pp. 52–62, at p. 59 (trans. Louise Duchesneau). I am indebted to Louise Duchesneau for bringing this article to my attention.

Example 17 Sonata for Solo Viola, fifth movement, *Lamento*, bars 1–7

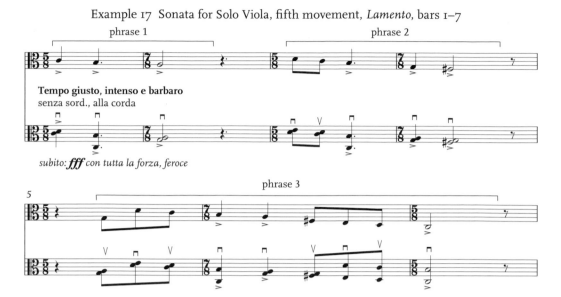

Formally, the work is divided into a *lamento* 'theme' and four ensuing transformational ostinati interspersed with contrasting interludes and ending with a short coda (see Table 7). Example 18 shows how each transformational ostinato develops upon and transforms the *lamento* 'theme'. (Note: the transformational ostinati cited are merely suggestions as alternative readings exist.) The original *lamento* ('theme') and the first two transformational ostinati begin on the notes C, F♯, and A respectively, presenting different registers for each. Although the three-phrase structure is always recognizable, the specific contour, length and note values are transformed and generally extended on repetition. The remaining two transformational ostinati are executed on harmonics giving the music an ethereal, if distant and cold quality.

Table 7 Sonata for Solo Viola, fifth movement, *Lamento*: formal structure

Bars	Section
1–7	lamento
9–11	interlude
12–18	t.o. 1
20–3	interlude
25–33	t.o. 2
34–40	interlude
41–9	t.o. 3
50–2	interlude
53–62	t.o. 4
63–4	coda

Example 18 Sonata for Solo Viola, fifth movement, *Lamento*, bars 1–7, 11/12–18, 25–34, 41–9, and 54–62

The interludes display aspects of accumulation and diminution. The first three are characterized by a *pp* dynamic marking and by the fact that each successive one develops incrementally. Example 19 shows how fragment B from interlude 1 is used in interlude 2, while fragments B and C from interlude 2 are used to extend interlude 3. Only the forceful interlude 4 introduces completely new harmonic material. The entire interlude system is rounded off with a short coda that returns to the opening fragment A (with an added C bass note), thus neatly framing the whole. Example 19 also gives a clear idea of the expansion and contraction of the interlude material, suggesting that this music is subject to its own autonomous logic.

The centrality of contrast has been noted, but Ligeti's manipulation of the relationships between pitch class and dynamics is ingeniously employed to delineate contrast at its most effective. In other works of Ligeti's which employ it, the general tenor of the *lamento* motif has nearly always been characterized by a certain nostalgia, a sad, song-like quality. In the opening of this work, however, the motif takes on a rather more angular and aggressive countenance: the score insists upon a *fff* dynamic with the performer instructed to play '*with full force*'. In addition, the double-stops of the *lamento* theme and t.o. 2 and 3 are comprised of major and minor seconds and sevenths only, giving them a harsh, grating sonority (see

Example 19 Sonata for Solo Viola, fifth movement, *Lamento*, interludes 1, 2, 3, 4, and coda

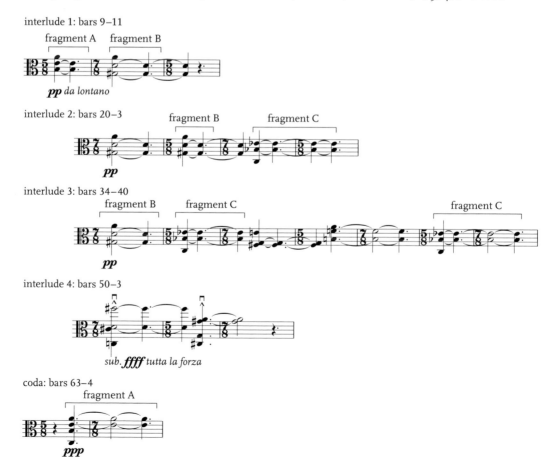

Example 17, lower staves). These pitch classes, therefore, correlate to the *fff* dynamics (see Table 8). In contrast, the two interludes that separate the first three *lamento* versions are constructed upon perfect fourths and fifths (with the occasional diminished 5th) resulting in clear, spatial harmonies (see Example 9 above). Consequently, these pitch classes are related to the *pp* dynamic markings employed for these sections. Thus, by bar 32 distinct correlations between pitch classes and dynamics have been firmly established for both *lamento*/transformational ostinati and interludes.

T.o. 3 and interlude 3, however, display traits of disintegration in relation to the established pitch/dynamic correlations. The final triad of t.o. 3 (the C, B and E of bars 32/3) juxtaposes a major seventh (as would be expected here) with a foreign perfect fourth (already identified as an interlude

Table 8 Sonata for Solo Viola, fifth movement, *Lamento*: shifting correlations between pitch class and dynamics

Established pitch & dynamic correlations	Bars	Section	Pitch classes	Correlating dynamics
	1–7	*lamento* 1	major/minor 2nds/7ths	*fff*
	9–11	interlude 1	perfect 4ths/5ths/dim. 5ths	*pp*
	12–18	*lamento* (t.o. 1)	major/minor 2nds/7ths	*fff*
	20–23	interlude 2	perfect 4ths/5ths/dim. 5ths	*pp*
	25–33	*lamento* (t.o. 2)	major/minor 2nds/7ths	*fff*
Mutating & modulating correlations				
	33	(t.o. 2) last bar only	major 7th/perfect 4th	*fff*
	34–40	interlude 3	perfect 4ths/5ths/dim. 5ths mixed with minor 2nds, minor 7ths/compound minor7ths	*pp*
Lamento adopts correlations from Interludes 1 & 2				
	41–49	*lamento* (t.o. 4)	perfect 4ths/5ths/dim. 5ths	*pp*
Interlude adopts correlations from *Lamentos* 1, 2 & 3				
	50–52	interlude 4	compound minor 2nds/ dim. 5ths compound major 3rds	*ffff*
Mixed correlations				
	53–62	*lamento* (t.o. 5)	major/minor 2nds /7ths	*ppp*
	63–64	coda	minor 7th/perfect 4ths	*ppp*

interval), introducing a pitch class mutation. Meanwhile, interlude 3, which should only comprise the established intervals of fourth, fifth and diminished fifth, has now also subsumed minor sevenths (bar 35), minor seconds (bar 36) and compound minor seconds (bar 39) into its pitch class. Ligeti has used the final triad of t.o. 3 and interlude 3 as a modulating force, as they have broken down the previously established correlations, initiating and enacting the transformation of forthcoming correlations that display distinctly new pitch/dynamic relationships.

By the time t.o. 4 appears at bar 41, its pitch/dynamic correlation has been completely transformed, adopting that of the earlier interludes 1 and 2 (see Example 19). Accordingly, interlude 4 has undergone the same process, appropriating what was the pitch/dynamic correlation for the *lamento* theme and t.o. 2–3 (see Example 18). The final and fifth transformational ostinato (starting bar 53) creates a mutation: it assumes the major seconds of the *lamento* theme and t.o. 2–3 but employs the *pp* dynamics that were previously connected to interludes 1 and 2. The short coda also mutates its intervals (minor seventh and perfect fourth). By this stage, a total transformation of the initial pitch/dynamic correlation has been achieved. As in so much of Ligeti's work, the manipulation of the minutest details has a hugely transformative effect. The modulation of the relationship between dynamics and pitch class is the central motor for variation in this movement.

Transformational ostinati and the chaconne

Chaconne chromatique follows *Lamento* naturally: the ground of the *Chaconne* bears a strong melodic and functional resemblance to the *lamento* motif. Both the rhythmic and chromatic nature of Ligeti's ground links it to an entire species of chaconnes and passacaglias established throughout the Renaissance and Baroque. Henry Purcell's 'Dido's Lament' (from the opera *Dido and Aeneas*, 1689) is a possible precedent for both Ligeti's *Lamento* and *Chaconne*. The chaconne as a structural device is remarkably similar to that of transformational ostinati. Indeed, the terms 'ground' and transformational ostinato are, effectively, interchangeable, in so long as they retain their contours and organizing function. However, as Ligeti in this work occasionally dismantles the ground and superimposes multiple ground fragments, the transformational ostinato, within which these alterations take place, becomes the organizing principle.

The transformational ostinati, as employed in this movement, bring into close quarters a number of simultaneously contradictory forces. On the one hand, the familiar chromatic integrity of the ground is increasingly eroded, while on the other, a growing sense of momentum is created with the ever-broadening textures of double, triple and quadruple-stops. Although forces of accumulation seek to obscure the rhythmic character (the *talea*) of the ground by the incorporation of quaver, semiquaver and triplet-quaver beats, a fundamental characteristic of that *talea* – the crochet/minim rhythmic unit – is increasingly enhanced in successive transformational ostinati with the use of quadruple-stops and intensifying dynamics (see bars 44, 53, 58 and 62). The three-phrase structure of the *lamento* motif is echoed and duplicated in the *Chaconne* ground, which covers eight bars in 3/4 time (see Example 20).

Example 20 Sonata for Solo Viola, sixth movement, *Chaconne chromatique*, bars 1–8

The full chromatic identity of the ground is maintained in the first transformational ostinato – bars 9–16 (see Example 21). Following this, however, forces of disintegration undermine that integrity and fractures begin to appear. The second transformational ostinato at bar 17 starts on an F♯. By the third crochet beat of bar 19, the chromatic line prematurely terminates and a new superimposed ground is introduced two crochet beats before the old line ends. A similar process takes place at bar 23 (see Example 21, third stave).

Starting on F♯, t.o. 3 (bar 25) manages a full ground, but thereafter the ground structure disintegrates (see Example 21, fifth stave). From the beginning of t.o. 4 (bar 34) we are presented with a series of ground fragments increasingly intensified by note accumulation and dynamic enhancement. Just as in *Facsar*, the texture thickens considerably, but the ground fragments are always attempting to break through (see Example 22, where the two lower staves extrapolate the hidden ground fragments for easier observation).

Despite the intense metamorphosis the music is forced to undergo, and the fracturing of the chromatic lines contained within its thick textures, the rhythmic character of the initial ground (and the ensuing transformational ostinati) do manage to maintain their general shape. The *talea* of the ground and its internal phrase structure (as observed in Example 21, first stave) cover eight bars and are maintained throughout with only some slight alterations.

Example 21 Sonata for Solo Viola, sixth movement, *Chaconne chromatique*

Ground ('theme'): bars 1–9

transformational ostinato 1: bars 9–16

transformational ostinato 2: bars 17–24

transformational ostinato 3: bars 25–34

transformational ostinato 4: bars 34–9

Example 22 Sonata for Solo Viola, sixth movement, *Chaconne chromatique*, bars 51–6

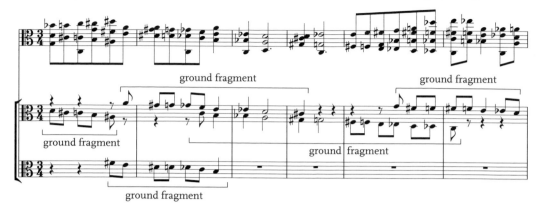

As Table 9 demonstrates, there are only three minor alterations to the *talea*. First, t.o. 7 should start at bar 57, but, directly following bar 56, Ligeti has inserted an extra bar (57) of triple-stop quavers accompanied by a crescendo marking directing momentum towards the bar 58, where the new transformational ostinato now enters. This amendment creates a greater climax approaching t.o. 8, but the *talea* of t.o. 7 has been altered in the process. Second, bar 73 (completing t.o. 8) is extended to a 4/4 bar (the only one in the work), and clearly Ligeti is providing a rhythmic surprise to usher in t.o. 9 at bar 74 in triplet quavers. Third, t.o. 9 itself is left short (see Example 23) – instead of comprising eight bars, there are only six (the chromatic line is preserved for two of the bars before its disintegration occurs; the remaining four bars act as a link to the new transformational ostinato at bar 80).

Table 9 Sonata for Solo Viola, sixth movement, *Chaconne chromatique*: phrase structures of ground and t.o. 1–11

Bars	Section	Phrase structure
1–8	Ground	112112
9–16	t.o. 1	112112
17–24	t.o. 2	112112
25–32	t.o. 3	112112
33–40	t.o. 4	112112
41–8	t.o. 5	112112
49–57	t.o. 6	112113
58–65	t.o. 7	112112
66–73	t.o. 8	11211.3
74–7 (–79)	t.o. 9	11(4)
80–7	t.o.10	112112
88–95	t.o.11	112112

Example 23 Sonata for Solo Viola, sixth movement, *Chaconne chromatique*, bars 74–9 (t.o. 9)

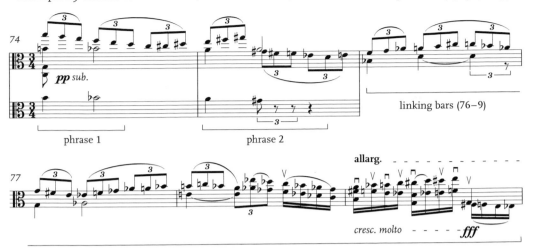

The music just discussed lasts a total of six bars (bars 74–9) and intensifies in a flurry of semiquaver double-stops. The attendant climax leads to a totally contrasting section at bar 80: headed *Meno mosso, molto cantabile*, and comprising the last two transformational ostinati, t.o. 10 and 11, this music dissipates the energy accumulated during the work before reaching a short coda of five bars' duration at bar 96. The *talea* of these last two transformational ostinati is almost completely preserved (except for the latter, where quavers are employed at just three points). The overall effect, however, is one of a return to the simplicity of the initial ground. Furthermore, its chromatic character is largely ignored in favour of an alternative comprising chords: melodic lines emerging from these chords bare no relation to the established *color*. Instead, Ligeti opts generally for chords comprising perfect fourths and fifths to which are added some minor thirds and major seconds. The overall harmonic sense is one of openness and acceptance, bringing Sonata for Solo Viola to a serene close.

Conclusion

> But don't consider that I take a model whatever it is, biological or otherwise ... theory interests me but not for a direct application.[20]

> Somewhere underneath, very deeply, there's a common place in our spirit where the beauty of mathematics and the beauty of music meet. But they don't meet on the level of algorithm or making music by calculation. It's much lower, much deeper – or much higher, you could say.[21]

The Sonata for Solo Cello and the Sonata for Solo Viola were composed at two pivotal points in Ligeti's career: the first when he was poised to

[20] Gervasoni, 'Interview with György Ligeti'.
[21] György Ligeti in a public conversation with Richard Steinitz (Huddersfield, 1993) published in Richard Steinitz, 'Music, Maths & Chaos', *Musical Times* 137/1837 (March 1996), pp. 14–20, at p. 14.

embrace the avant-garde, and the second, when he began to make a profound reconciliation with his Bartókian inheritance. When Ligeti argued as far back as 1949 (the period of the Cello Sonata) that 'Bartók's rigorous, tonal language is not classical ... not a "return to tonality" but rather a "progress to tonality"', he could have been talking about his own Viola Sonata of 1991–4.[22] This unusual symmetry, the balancing of relations between indigenous music and art music, parallels Ligeti's relationship between his dependence on compositional mechanisms and ready-made systems on the one hand, and his intuitive application of them in his music on the other. This essay has argued that the Cello and Viola Sonatas are connected through their employment of transformational ostinati as a method of expansion and development of musical material. Ligeti's varying employment of transformational ostinati has, I hope, been made clear. However, of cardinal interest are the various intuitive processes through which he erodes the very regulatory mechanisms upon which he depends. More specifically, Ligeti's attachment of 'gender' identities to phrases in *Dialogo*, his use of an imaginary F string in *Hora lungă*, his instruction to play *'with swing'* in the rigorously controlled *Loop*, his attenuation of architectural clarity in *Facsar* and *Prestissimo con sordino*, his highly improvisatory use of articulation and dynamic markings in *Facsar*, *Lamento* and *Chaconne chromatique*, and his erosion of the established dynamics/pitch-class relationships in *Lamento* and *Chaconne chromatique* all negate the potentially prescriptive effects of the transformational ostinati. Thus, his relationship to them is both dependent and anarchic. Ligeti's use (and abuse) of transformational ostinati in both sonatas demonstrates that contradiction is a central facet of his music and reveals what I have described elsewhere as his 'implausible fascination with both precision and imprecision'.[23]

[22] György Ligeti, 'Neue Musik in Ungarn', in *Gesammelte Schriften*, ed. Monika Lichtenfeld, vol. 1 (Mainz, 2007), pp. 51–5.

[23] Benjamin Dwyer, 'Laughing at the Chaos – György Ligeti (1923–2006)', *Journal of Music in Ireland* (Sept./Oct. 2007), p. 16.

Ligeti during a rehearsal of his Cello Sonata at home
(Hamburg, 9 November 1989)

3 Magicians of Sound –
Seeking Ligeti's Inspiration in the Poetry of Sándor Weöres

ILDIKÓ MÁNDI-FAZEKAS & TIBORC FAZEKAS

> A teljes lét: élet-nélküli.
> A teljes öröklét: idő-nélküli.
> A teljes működés: változás-nélküli.
> A teljes hatalom: erő-nélküli.
> A teljes tudás: adat-nélküli.
> A teljes bölcsesség: gondolat-nélküli.
> A teljes szeretet: érzés-nélküli.
> A teljes jóság: irány-nélküli.
> A teljes boldogság: öröm-nélküli.
> A teljes zengés: hang-nélküli.

> [The absolute existence is: existence without life.
> The absolute eternity is: eternity without time.
> The absolute action is: action without change.
> The absolute power is: power without strength.
> The absolute knowledge is: knowledge without information.
> The absolute wisdom is: wisdom without thoughts.
> The absolute love is: love without feelings.
> The absolute kindness is: kindness without direction.
> The absolute happiness is: happiness without joy.
> The absolute sound is: sound without tunes.][1]

This article will examine the diverse ways in which Sándor Weöres's poetry inspired György Ligeti's compositions, with particular regard to the personal, artistic and social circumstances under which these artists lived and worked. It will focus on the creative processes, as well as on the tendencies, similarities, experiments and resulting developments in poetry as well as in music. The extensive analyses of the individual works in the specialized literature will, of course, be taken into account; their cumulative discussion, however, is not the aim of the present study.

The poet

> Az igazság nem mondatokban rejlik, hanem a torzítatlan létezésben.
> Az öröklét nem az időben rejlik, hanem az összhang állapotában.

> [The truth lies not in sentences but in the undistorted existence.
> Eternity lies not in time but in the state of harmony.][2]

Sándor Weöres (1913–89) is one of the most exceptional poets of the 20th century, a period so full of exceptional artists in Hungary. His artistic

---

[1] The Hungarian version of this poem, 'Tíz erkély' [Ten Balconies], is published in Sándor Weöres, *Egybegyűjtött írások I–III* [Collected Works I–III] (Budapest, 1981), vol. 1, p. 681. The English translation is by Susanna Fahlström and is quoted from her monograph *Form and Philosophy in Sándor Weöres' Poetry*, Studia Uralica Upsaliensia 32 (Uppsala, 1999), p. 154.

[2] Sándor Weöres, 'Szembe-fordított tükrök' [Mirrors Inverted *vis-à-vis*], in *A teljesség felé* [In the Direction of Perfection, 1943–5], in Weöres, *Egybegyűjtött írások I–III*, vol. 1, p. 632.

inclinations became apparent at a very early age. Even though he grew up in sheltered albeit provincial circumstances he would react with the candour of a child to how art was then sometimes used in everyday life. Many of his contemporaries remember that, even as a child, he could not stand the singing in school or in church: he felt it was more like 'screeching' than music-making. Weöres would automatically reject a 'work of art' which appeared to be dishonest or forced, whether because of the 'artist's' inner attitude towards his work or because of an exterior 'reason' for the 'artistic activity', as this could only be seen as contempt for his own art. Very early on he made his own way. As he said himself, he had written his first poem at the age of three and he was first published at 14. At 15 he wrote a two-line poem, which in translation sounds something like this:

> I've already ended my career,
> You lads, follow now in my footsteps.[3]

Weöres was considered a child prodigy who always followed his own unique path. His early poems won their author the renowned Baumgarten Prize in 1935 and 1936. The prize money allowed him to travel, the following year, to Egypt, India, Ceylon, Malaya and the Philippines, and then all the way to Shanghai. What Weöres experienced during these travels left a deep impression on his thinking and his poetry. It especially enhanced his ability to mix literary traditions, art forms and subject matter from non-European cultures at the onset of civilization with the psychoanalysis-fed ideas and perceptions of a 'language artist'. Lóránt Czigány characterized Weöres's poetry in the following way:

> He employs all forms with equal ease, from complex metre and rhyme structures to free verse. He never refers directly to social or political causes, neither is he interested in relating personal experiences or describing nature. Instead, he roams freely in time and space, as a puckish spirit unfettered by earthly concerns. Furthermore, his imagination is a limitless source of poetic invention; he creates imaginary languages with startling sound and visual effects, or private myths, if he finds the wide range of mythological or anthropological references at his disposal inadequate for his poetic aims.[4]

(*Mutatis mutandis*, the elements and attributes of art mentioned here can also be applied to a great extent to Ligeti's music.) The critics unanimously hailed the publication of *Medúza* (Medusa) in 1944 as an epochal turning point in Weöres's art. Béla Hamvas judged him to be among the greatest European poets of the time:

> Mallarmé once said: 'La poésie était fourvoyée depuis la grande déviation homérique – Poetry followed a false path after the great Homeric digression'. When asked what came before Homer, he

---

[3] From the afterword by Barbara Frischmuth in Sándor Weöres, *Der von Ungern: Gedichte und fünf Zeichnungen*, trans. Barbara Frischmuth and Robert Stauffer (Frankfurt am Main, 1969), p. 101.

[4] Lóránt Czigány, *The Oxford History of Hungarian Literature* (Oxford, 1984), pp. 453–4.

answered: 'L'orphisme – orphism'. ... After the great Homeric digression which lasted over 2,500 years, and from which almost nobody escaped, it was Chénier, Hölderlin and Keats who began to return to the primitive state of poetry. At the end of the 19th century both Whitman and Mallarmé, today also Rilke in his last period, admit that the whole of European poetry was 'une grande déviation' – a great digression. Rilke's *Sonnets to Orpheus* and his *Elegies* both represent the final and irrevocable return to 'orphism', the primitive state of poetry.[5]

Contemporary critics recognized and pointed out the complexity of Weöres's often simple-form poems. In 1947 András Bajcsa, a friend of Weöres, described his poetry in the following way: 'Boldness; truthfulness of inspiration; originality; it has movement, therefore undergoes change; it is open to mythical powers; it is steeped in moral grandeur and transcendental joviality.'[6] Bajcsa is convinced of Weöres's modernity as 'Weöres's poetry is embedded in the art of his time, owing to identical existential problems, and is thus connected to modern (atonal) music and modern (abstract) visual arts.'[7]

Other than its power of association, it is the music, sound and rhythm of his texts which, since his childhood, characterized Weöres's poetry. On the one hand, both the vocal and instrumental forms of European musical tradition and music theory fascinated him. Weöres wrote 12 cycles of poems between 1938 and 1970, the *Symphonies I to XII*, whose titles clearly reveal a conscious application of compositional principles taken from music to the structuring of texts. Furthermore, he adopts such titles as *Rondo, Bolero, Pavane, Preludium, Fughetta, Cantilena*, but also *Rock and Roll*, etc., while, throughout his life, the structural principles of the fugue, the sonata or the concerto are reflected in many of his works. However, according to Imre Bori, another aspect must be mentioned to explain the decidedly sensual character of Weöres's language:

> In his poetry Weöres paves the way to a blueprint of a world language, and a new cosmogony is laid out ... (Here) the rules of poetic logic develop freely and generate endless variations, and the stream of ideas seems to be like a stream of images with which the poet gyrates over his unknown world. 'Life and death do not interest me, all I need is the harmony which is neither supported by matter, nor understood by reason ...'[8]

On the other hand, Weöres works intensively with the sound of words from existing or imaginary languages by focusing on their musical essence.

[5] Béla Hamvas, 'A Medúza' [The Medusa], in *Magyar Orpheus* [Hungarian Orpheus] (Budapest, 1999), pp. 213–17, at pp. 216–17.

[6] Tibor Tüskés, 'Weöres és a *Sorsunk*' [Weöres and the Journal *Sorsunk*], in *Magyar Orpheus*, pp. 177–91, at p. 191.

[7] Ibid.

[8] Imre Bori, 'A szintézisteremtő' [The Creator of Synthesis], in *Magyar Orpheus*, pp. 351–69, at p. 366.

The musical principle is not just a complementary or incidental phenomenon in Weöres's poetry, rather it is one of the most important elements of his expressive style. Music plays a primary role in many of his poems, especially in the picture poems, in the folk song variations – an offshoot of modern music history's folkloristic movement – and also generally in the poems' rhythmic proportions. All this lies beyond the mere sound (*Lautbild*) of the words. Weöres chose his raw material and composed his poetry according to principles similar to those of the modernist and avant-garde manner of the 20th century. We believe that a thorough analysis of the similarities between Bartók and Weöres would help us to discover an inner order in the poet's work which has been overlooked by numerous literary analyses until now.[9]

At this point, however, it must be pointed out that many of the principles found in the composition of Weöres's poems, particularly those which have to do with 'special effects', rest on certain characteristics of the Hungarian language (such as the fixed accentuation of words, the two kinds of vowel harmony, the clear quantity correlations between the sounds, etc.) and as such cannot really be translated into other languages: '... and so it is that the German translator is forced to capitulate again and again in the face of this mastery of forms. Hungarian is innately more malleable and its structure permits it to be rearranged with much more diversity than German.'[10] Even so, since 1970 three books of Weöres's poetry have been translated into English[11] and two into German,[12] while one book in French[13] and one in Swedish[14] contain translations of Weöres poems.

The 'Greeting' to the reader which opens his book of poems *Tüzkút* (Fountain of Fire, published 1964 in Paris as well as in Hungary) demonstrates Weöres's unwavering stance vis-à-vis his own role in relation to art and to his times, for it was published unmodified nearly 20 years later, in 1981, in his three-volume *Collected Writings*. This text seems to have been especially important to Weöres, and for this reason we quote it here:

> Forty years shy of the third millennium, I release my book into the year 2000, not knowing how long it will be kept safe there or indeed if it will even be liked, but confident that my work will prove the false prophecy of the 'Twilight of Humanity' (*Menschendämmerung*). Furthermore I hope that the new millennium finds neither pessimism nor nihilism within the pages of my book, but rather

---

[9] Ibid., p. 365.

[10] Barbara Frischmuth, *Sándor Weöres*, p. 102.

[11] *Selected Poems of Sándor Weöres and Ferenc Juhász*, trans. Edwin Morgan [for Sándor Weöres] and David Wevill [for Ferenc Juhász] (London, 1970); Sándor Weöres, *Eternal Moment: Selected Poems*, trans. William Jay Smith *et al.* (London, 1988); Sándor Weöres, *If All the World Were a Blackbird*, trans. Alexander Fenton (Aberdeen, 1985).

[12] Sándor Weöres, *Der von Ungern*; *Poesiealbum 135: Sándor Weöres*, trans. Annemarie Bostroem *et al.* (Berlin, 1978).

[13] Sándor Weöres, *Dix-neuf poèmes* (Paris, 1984).

[14] Sándor Weöres, *Hvisking I morket* (Oslo, 1977).

laughs at the intellectual bootlegging of spirits I attempted during this possible end of the spiritual prohibition. May it look back into my old eyes with the same cheerfulness with which I look forward into its smiling young eyes.

The nihilism found in these poems is, I think, nothing else than an insight into more or less foreign levels of style, idea and life: the unknown is always a kind of frightening emptiness, still it is a reality one must penetrate. And as to pessimism: at the bedside of that three-thousand-year-old resplendent wonder which is Europe, with its mercilessly greedy reign, our Asian blood sweats one hundred tears maybe, but not one more.

My intention is neither to bewitch nor to annoy those who cringe when they encounter anything unusual; it is of no interest to me whether I am understood or not. What I want is something else: to emit a living spark which sets alight instinct, emotion, reason, imagination, spirit as well as the whole being, for not only should one read the poem but also be read by it. I would like to see through you and to incite you to rearrange your closed, restricted and existential ego into an open, social, cosmic and infinite self. I call forth the communist individual who is conscious of the inconvenience of possessions, of status, of violence, and instead of asserting himself in the outside world, seeks to lift his physical-spiritual self to a higher, more worthy level.

Today we generally live in a state of terrified apprehension: 'What can I get? What am I missing?' We spend our whole lives shoving and pushing. It would be better to say: 'What can I give?' This carefree, calm, down-to-earth attitude bears fruit without fail, and the harvest in which also others can share is rich; you can give is very small, a greater gift will be repeatedly bestowed upon you and others. As long as I wish to be happy without others and against them, I am condemned to endless sacrifice and remorse. However, as soon as I share my joy with others, like a happy lover, there is no reason for any self-denial. This may seem incredible and unsettling to you, yet more and more of us go through this Copernican Revolution. This embryo which slumbers in the womb of Times Present should not miscarry: too many are dancing with the mother.

I yearn neither for success nor for glory in the present, and even less in the future. Poets think of the hereafter as an infallible divine tribunal; even though it is like a snotty kid who should be happy when I change its wet nappy, it should not hand me any laurels. It should wrestle with me like a child with his father and the fight should make it stronger. It should find me adequate and mold me to the usual conventions and regulations. Even in my grave I will accept those who do not appreciate my alleged or true madness, who courageously sidestep that Golden Idiot to reach such heights and challenges, of which even I cannot dream.[15]

This is how an exceptional artist expresses his self-determination, awake to the depth of instinct, couching his transcendental, magical content in

---

[15] Sándor Weöres, *Tűzkút* [Fountain of Fire] (Paris, 1964), pp. 6–7.

oftentimes simple, seemingly childish and fanciful terms; one who rejects all rules and expectations when it comes to the art of poetry, in which sound, emotion, rhythm, man's inner and outer world are brought together for a cosmic moment.[16] Entire generations of Hungarians have grown up listening to the immense number of musical settings of Weöres's poems. Some of these songs were already included in the basic teaching repertoire of nursery and primary schools in the early 1970s. The musical settings of Weöres's poems are 'sung poems', a genre which can be traced as far back as the 16th century in Hungary. In 1933 Zoltán Kodály was the first to compose a chorus on the poem *Öregek* (Elders); in 1940 he wrote a larger piece, *Norvég lányok* (Norwegian Girls). Even though these pieces were written for the concert hall, they give the impression of having been inspired by traditional folk music rather than by concert music. This ambiguity is also apparent in Ligeti's early adaptations of Weöres, *Éjszaka – Reggel* (Night – Morning, 1955), as well as *Magyar etüdök* (Hungarian Études, 1983), where the melodies sound like Hungarian folk music.

It is therefore not surprising that the texts of an artist who so resolutely worked according to his own rules would attract another artist who was similarly disposed, for not only did Weöres's poetry occupy an important place in György Ligeti's life and œuvre from the very beginning, but it influenced him decade after decade and attended his life's work. Weöres's enchanting verse would perhaps have been sufficient inspiration in itself, but the seemingly improvised strophes carried within them another impulse: that of the 'original' (minimalistic, primeval), magical, 'intrinsic' art which reveals itself in the various forms of folk art, poetry and music. Let us not forget that Ligeti also collected folk songs in the great tradition of Hungarian musicology. However, he used the collected material in a different way from what his great predecessors had done before him. During their lifetimes Weöres and Ligeti were at times singled out and recognized by political leaders, serving either as positive or negative examples. It was therefore nearly inevitable that such personalities who adamantly rejected conformism, manipulation and servitude would one day finally meet. Weöres constantly and openly kept 'to the periphery' of official culture while Ligeti actually left Hungary in 1956. Weöres's contemporary Miklós Vajda noted the following:

> Sándor Weöres ... totally lacked even a drop of vanity, jealousy, grievance or any other base passion, despite the fact that he, too, had been unable to publish for a substantial period. He was not terribly interested in where he happened to be, or with whom, at any given moment, which is not to say that he did not notice, and sometimes comment on, the things that were going on. He was uniformly pleasant and courteous with everyone at all times. Many was the occasion, each and every day, that I would be taken aback, on reaching for a cigarette, to see him smartly hasten over, and always get there, sometimes almost at a trot, even from the furthest corner of whatever place we were in, simply in order to offer me a match – he, the greatest genius whom I have been privileged to know up close

---

[16] On this subject see the detailed analysis in Fahlström, *Form and Philosophy in Sándor Weöres' Poetry.*

– before I, a nobody in comparison, had a chance to get out my lighter. Of course, I was not the only one to be accorded that and many similar gestures of solicitude, for he was the same with everyone else. Weöres was seemingly unconcerned about the success and fate of his work. It is apparent from his poems that he was fully aware of his poetic greatness, but he looked on his own person as merely the vehicle, the insignificant channel, of that greatness. It was his wife, Amy Károlyi, who kept him tethered to earth; without her, it is more than likely that Weöres would have just taken wing or forgotten to eat and died of starvation, though possibly not before drinking himself to death. It is perhaps the most considerable of Amy's merits, greater even than that of her delicate, intimately feminine lyric verse, that she was able to keep the impish sprite of a man in a fit state to be able to compose one of the most scintillating of all poetic œuvres of the twentieth century, so immense in its scope, depth and variety.[17]

The composer

Should I return to clearer diatonic structures or press ahead, towards completely blurred outlines of sound? – I wondered. (My answer to this was *Apparitions* and later *Atmosphères*.) [In these works,] so many rhythmic processes are superimposed that they cover one another, the result is a homogeneous [musical] 'mass'.[18]

György Ligeti set poems by Weöres to music at four different periods of his life, which coincided with four stages of his artistic development. By putting poems to music, either for choir or accompanied soloist, he was following a Hungarian musical tradition which regarded vocal and choral compositions as a particularly important point of reference in a composer's development. The early 19th century settings of poems by Sándor Petőfi (1823–49) reveal the traditionally close relationship between poetry and music. By the beginning of the 20th century these had become an integral part of the folksong repertoire and were even being collected as such by ethnographers. Under the banner of political emancipation, Petőfi's poetry integrated the elements and forms of Hungarian folk songs into high art while at the same time modernizing them. He created a 'new tone' that significantly differed from his successors' 'folkloristic' approach. That many popular songs of the second half of the 19th century appropriated his texts attests to how accurately he had touched the feelings of simple people. Béla Bartók (1881–1945) and Zoltán Kodály (1882–1967) were pursuing a similar goal when they integrated into their works folk songs they had themselves collected after the First World War. In this way they helped to establish new and modern directions in Hungarian music. With this background and in this context, Ligeti apparently encountered poems by Sándor Weöres early on. These sound as if they could be folk songs or even 'mere noises

---

[17] Miklós Vajda: '"If Any Harm Comes of This, I'll Kill You!": The True Story of Six Hungarian Poets' Grand Tour of Britain in 1980', *Hungarian Quarterly* 44/171 (Autumn 2003), pp. 85–96, at p. 87.

[18] *György Ligeti in Conversation with Péter Várnai, Josef Häusler, Claude Samuel and Himself* (London, 1983), p. 38.

of nature'; they simultaneously express absolute artistic freedom and touch on the greatest issues of mankind. Weöres was the first Hungarian poet after Petőfi and János Arany (1817–82) to use the framework of (not only Hungarian) folk songs in a programmatic way. He did not, however, follow the political goals that these 19th-century authors had adopted. Rather, what interested him in these seemingly simple forms were their complexity and structure as well as the ancient and universal experience of language as sound. For this reason, Weöres's poetry inevitably moved closer to issues which also preoccupied contemporary music. An example of this is the way his multiform texts are often joined together in cycles. 'As a contemporary form', the placing of individual pieces as if on a chain, a circle, a wreath, a bow or in loosely numbered series, 'aims for a kind of fragmented connectedness in a long series of poems or a combination of poetic lines and prose ...'.[19] Ligeti had set literary texts to music, mostly for choir, as early as the 1940s. Between 1942 and February 1946, while still in Kolozsvár (Cluj-Napoca, Romania), he composed many songs on texts by Goethe, Bálint Balassa (1554–94), Sándor Petőfi, János Arany, Endre Ady (1877–1919) and Attila József (1905–37) along with numerous settings of authentic Hungarian folk songs.[20] Then in 1946/7, just a year after moving to Budapest, the 23-year-old Ligeti turned his attention to poems by Weöres and composed a first piece which, in his list of works, is dated 10 November 1946.[21] In this same period Ligeti was also working on some of the poems from Weöres's cycle *Rongyszőnyeg* (Rag Carpet). Ligeti chose three poems from this cycle of 160 individual texts, which are subtitled 'Songs, Epigrams, Rhythm Samples, Sketches and Fragments': *Táncol a hold fehér ingben* (The moon is dancing in a white robe), *Gyümölcs-fürt* (A Cluster of Fruit) and *Kalmár jött nagy madarakkal* (A merchant has come with giant birds).[22] These poems, as well as the cycle *Magyar etüdök* which we will examine later, hold a special place within Weöres's body of work because they represent a play between the need to build a structure and the wish to remain flexible within the piece. Ligeti composed these songs when he was studying with Ferenc Farkas (1905–2000) at the Budapest Music Academy. Farkas, who had also been his teacher (and that of a whole generation) from 1941 at the Kolozsvár Conservatory, had taken up Bartók's compositional legacy and, along with Kodály, had pushed it in a different direction. In 1946 Farkas composed a cycle of 12 songs on poems by Weöres which had been published under the title *Fruit Basket*. Ligeti, a passionate advocate of

[19] Alison Hawthorne Deming, 'Science and Poetry: A View from the Divide', in *The Measured Word: On Poetry and Science*, ed. Kurt Brown (Athens, 2001), pp. 181–97, at p. 195; quoted in Ildikó Pethő, 'Weöres Sándor korai zenei kísérletei, a zenei sorozat' [Sándor Weöres's Early Musical Experiments, the Musical Series], in *Modern – magyar – irodalom – történet* [Modern – Hungarian – Literature – History], ed. Orsolya Kolozsi and Tímea Urbanik (Szeged, 2006), pp. 51–60, at p. 59.

[20] Friedemann Sallis, *An Introduction to the Early Works of György Ligeti* (Cologne, 1996), pp. 266–72.

[21] Ibid, p. 273.

[22] These settings as well as a further fragment ('Nagypapa leszállt a tóba' [Grandfather Descended into the Pond]) have been analysed in detail in Sallis, *An Introduction*, pp. 58–81.

the renewal of Hungarian music, praised this work in a review he wrote in 1948:

> The new Hungarian song literature is, unfortunately, sunk up to its neck in declamation. From all directions we hear decomposing, sick melodies. But now here is a cure; Farkas opens completely new avenues. He is following a new track: audacity. It is audacious to write simple songs which can be performed by singers and pianists at sight when hitherto the most horrible acrobatics were demanded by the music. It is audacious to write clear and beautiful music when the more dissonance the better was expected from the 'modernists'.[23]

In those days, even Bartók had fallen prey to the need for a 'new music' (in the sense of 'socialistic art') in Hungary. Given this, it is difficult to say how Ligeti would have written about new music without the imposed political guidelines, but his life's work shows that he had imagined the renewal of music in a totally different way.

One can see how Sándor Weöres attracted the attention of the ambitious Ligeti: on the one hand, he was then a highly admired and independent-minded artist, on the other hand, he was ignored by the official cultural policy makers who soon labelled him a 'bourgeois reactionary'. Thinking back on those times, Ligeti wrote:

> The *Three Weöres Songs* (*Három Weöres-dal*) from my first year of studies (1946) mark the beginning of a compositional development which was to be abruptly broken off two years later by the establishment of the Communist dictatorship. Before the fateful year 1948 I was a typical young leftist intellectual: anti-Nazi, opposed to the conservative Hungarian right, a believer in the Socialist Utopia.[24]

Apparently Ligeti met Sándor Weöres in 1947 and made the following comment about this meeting in an interview:

> A bit later and after having set to music three more poems of his, I think it was in 1947, I met him through common friends – you know, the intellectual Hungarian milieu was not that large and everybody more of less knew each other. I was thrilled to be able to show him what I had done and we always remained friends.[25]

Scholarly research on Ligeti, made considerably more complicated by his peregrinations (Romania, Hungary, Austria, Germany, Sweden, Japan, the United States), must still address the matter of his personal contact to Weöres as well as their exchange of letters.

---

[23] Quoted in Sallis, *An Introduction*, pp. 42–3.

[24] György Ligeti, Vocal Works, *György Ligeti Edition 4*, CD booklet, trans. Annelies McVoy and David Feurzeig, Sony Classical, SK 62311, pp. 9–10.

[25] Quoted in Sallis, *An Introduction*, pp. 120–1.

How Weöres's texts sustained Ligeti's artistic development

Sándor Weöres was one of Hungary's greatest poets, a modern poet, at the same time universal and experimental, who exploited like none other the rhythmic-metric and semantic possibilities and impossibilities of the Hungarian language. Profound and playful, elitist and vulgar, he was Hungary's Mozart.[26]

In the following years hardly anyone who had to do with Hungarian literature took notice of Weöres and he published only two children's books between 1947 and 1955. At the time, Weöres was writing his texts by hand in a notebook which had been personally given to him by the earlier Hungarian cultural minister Dezső Keresztury (1904–96). It was referred to by his friends as the 'Keresztury Codex', a sarcastic allusion to this medieval state of affairs. Meanwhile, Ligeti continued to focus his attention on earlier poems although he composed traditional folk song settings for the most part. However, poems by Weöres continued to appear in his work catalogue: *Hajnal* (Dawn, 1949), *Tél* (Winter, 1950), *Pletykázó asszonyok* (Gossiping Women, 1952). Ligeti even undertook an adaptation for piano of the *Rongyszőnyeg* cycle in 1951.[27] Then Ligeti, who seldom voiced an opinion on political matters but was all the more resolute when he composed in 1955, in the middle of another hopeless political turmoil, two pieces for choir on poems Weöres had written in 1945, *Éjszaka – Reggel*. Linked together in spite of their contrasting nature, these pieces were powerful symbols. The end of a dark era is heralded with unmistakable clarity at the end of the poem *Reggel* (though the Hungarian edition of Weöres's *Complete Writings* includes another, less expressive version of the concluding strophe):[28] 'Reggel van! Szép reggel!' (It's morning! A beautiful morning!) and in Ligeti's own English translation in the score: 'Ring well, bell! Ring, ring well!'[29] This piece marks a break with Bartók's tradition and musical heritage: 'These two short choruses play a key role in my stylistic development because they document the transition from Bartók-imitation to the building of my own mature style (complex polyphony and static sounds).'[30] Pure sound becomes increasingly important in his music, superseding melody and harmony. How important Weöres's texts were for his development as a composer is shown not only by Ligeti's constancy in using them again and again his whole life long, sometimes after intervals of many years, but also by how he treated them. For instance, he translated *Éjszaka – Reggel*[31] himself from the Hungarian to English and German and, if we compare the three versions – this aspect would be worth a study of its own – we notice that his translations are very free and place strong emphasis on the music and sound of the words.

---

[26] György Ligeti, *Gesammelte Schriften*, vol. 2, ed. Monika Lichtenfeld (Basel, 2007), p. 313.

[27] See Sallis, *An Introduction*, pp. 280–8.

[28] Weöres, *Egybegyűjtött írások I–III*, vol. 1, p. 377.

[29] György Ligeti, *Éjszaka/Night/Nacht – Reggel/Morning/Morgen*, Two Unaccompanied Choruses (1955), score (Mainz, 1973).

[30] Ligeti, *Gesammelte Schriften*, vol. 2, p. 165.

[31] Ligeti, *Éjszaka/Night/Nacht – Reggel/Morning/Morgen*.

For Ligeti, the decades after 1956 were momentous and full of contradictions. On the one hand, these were years of intense artistic development during which he became famous. On the other hand, after having fled his 'second' homeland Hungary, he was to live till the end of his life in a state of perpetual wandering. Ironically, these circumstances not only strengthened his development but seemingly did not diminish his attachment to Hungarian culture. After enjoying much success with large-scale innovative works, he turned once again to Weöres in 1983 and composed a 16-voice chorus on ten texts by Sándor Weöres, *Magyar etüdök*.

> These are snapshots of everyday occurrences so to speak – what is experimental here is first how I use rhythm and metre, and then the connotations arising from the Hungarian language. As I was putting some of these short poems to music I tried to reproduce Weöres's playful experimental manner in the musical structure.[32]

The creative link between Weöres and Ligeti becomes even clearer when we realize that Weöres's poems are compiled under the title *Polyrhythmia* in his collected works. 'These are extremely constructivist works.'[33] Significantly, Ligeti uses the same word to describe his own composition: 'The third piece, entitled 'Fair', is written for eight voices and consists of five different, independent tempo layers which come together to form a complex polyrhythmic structure.'[34] Also, acoustic subtlety seems to have inspired the two artists in other fields: Weöres and Ligeti were always attracted by boundaries and zones of transition, the 'neglected' areas of music and poetry fascinated them. They revolutionized their own art form precisely because they were able to discern new (and old), free (and nonetheless determinate) forms, means and inspiration, and to point towards lost, hidden and suppressed possibilities and itineraries. A comparison of their choice of titles could, for instance, uncover interesting parallels. The metronome as instrument inspired both artists; they both wrote/composed bagatelles, études, symphonies; the theatre/opera was for both challenging in a complex way; and 'unusual' titles such as Ligeti's *Artikulation, Ramifications, Apparitions, Continuum* or *Le Grand Macabre* and Weöres's *Áthallások* (Cross Talks), *Polyrhythmia, Átváltozások* (Metamorphoses), *Filigránok* (Filigree) or *Suite bourlesque* have become important 'brands' which immediately arouse the listener's attention.

Finally, at the end of his creative days, Ligeti came back to some of Weöres's 'children's poems' when he wrote the seven-part cycle *Síppal, dobbal, nádihegedűvel* (With Pipes, Drums, Reed Fiddles)[35] which is a kind of compendium of his artistic intent since all the characteristics of

[32] Ligeti, *Gesammelte Schriften*, pp. 286–7.
[33] Ligeti, *Gesammelte Schriften*, p. 287.
[34] Ligeti, *Gesammelte Schriften*, pp. 286–7.
[35] The authors prefer to appose the word 'reed' to 'fiddles' in the title of Ligeti's work as this correctly translates the Hungarian 'nádihegedűvel': *nádi* – reed and *hegedű* – fiddle. The 'official' English translation, however, is 'fiddle' without 'reed'. See list of works and score (Schott, ED 9602) as well as CD recording (*The Ligeti Project* III, 8573 – Teldec 87631-2). The translations into German: 'Schilfgeigen' and French: 'violons-roseaux', which are also contained in the CD booklet, both reflect the Hungarian original.

his music are quoted here in a brief, clear magician's hand, with irony and ease.

Weöres never wrote a cycle of poems under the title Ligeti chose for his composition. It was Ligeti himself who borrowed a line from a Hungarian nursery rhyme, *Gólya, gólya, gilice* (Stork, stork, turtledove), which enumerates the musical instruments ancient sorcerers used to heal wounds. The song cycle contains the following parts: 'Fabula' (Fable), 'Táncdal' (Dance Song), 'Kínai templom' (Chinese Temple), 'Kuli' (Coolie), 'Alma álma' (Dream), 'Keserédes' (Bitter-Sweet), 'Szajkó' (Parakeet), and bands together texts from very different periods: 'Fabula' (1957) stems from the album *Tűzkút* (1964), 'Táncdal' (1942) from *Elysium* (1946), 'Kínai templom' (1941) is included in *Medúza* (1944), 'Kuli' (1931/1967) appears in the collection *Merülő Saturnus* (Saturn Declining, 1968), 'Alma álma' is an excerpt from the poem 'Tizenkettedik szimfónia' (Twelfth Symphony, 1970) which is included in *Áthallások* (1976), 'Keserédes' is poem no. 67 from the cycle *Magyar etüdök*, written between 1947 and 1956, and 'Szajkó' comes from the volume *Ének a határtalanról* (Song from Infinity, 1980). Apparently Ligeti disregarded any chronological link between the texts. The seven miniatures which form *Síppal, dobbal, nádihegedűvel* cannot really be described as being settings of poems by Weöres; rather, they are witnesses of a congenial encounter between two artists. Both are able to recreate that which 'primitive' cultures, primal childlike naïveté and the human race once could do, but in the course of time have now forgotten. The elemental vigour of their creative spirit can only be matched by the greatness of Bartók: they were able, with words or sounds, to conjure up a primeval world, to descend into it and unearth man's position and role in building universal structures. For the world is more than mere human existence, the claim to perfection strives towards structures which are universal. In art, Weöres assumed that one should draw from the age-old rhythms which can free poetry of its unnecessary emotions (in the case of Hungarian poetry these are the German role models). His point of view is related to that of those great composers who seek to create a kind of harmony of the spheres as an antidote to the coarseness of the world – 'With pipes, drums and reed fiddles', like the shamans.

For Weöres, invoking this lost harmony is linked to all that is 'childlike' (he gazes at the world through the eyes of a wide-eyed child). The songs, sayings and game rhymes all have an internal and external musical envelope. The outer surface is the ancient melody of the poem, that basic music which inspired Weöres (rhythm, rhyme, groups of words interwoven in prosodic formula, 'nonsense' words). The inner musical layer is more abstract: here Weöres strives to sublimate the soul's unspoken sorrows into music. Instead of the words only evoking images, it is the heightened music of the words which takes effect here, the melody is often stronger than the content. 'These poems serve, as their models do, to free the human soul from its self-indulgent gallivanting, to call attention to its more profound and higher potential, to remind it of the universal and eternal scope of things ...'[36]

---

[36] Letter to Pál Lovász, in Tibor Tüskés, *A határtalan énekese, Fotográfiák, levelek, dokumentumok, Írások Weöres Sándorról* [Infinity's Songster, Photographs, Letters, Documents, Writings on Sándor Weöres] (Budapest, 2003), p. 132.

A short description of three of the poems illustrates the originality of the musical setting. Ligeti used the following poems to set nos. 2, 3 and 4 of the cycle:

No. 2
Táncdal

panyigai panyigai panyigai
ü panyigai ü
panyigai panyigai panyigai
ü panyigai ü

kudora panyigai panyigai
kudora ü
panyigai kudora kudora
panyigai ü

kotta kudora panyigai
kudora kotta ü
kotta panyigai kudora
panyigai kotta ü

ház panyigai kudora
ü kudora kotta ház
kudora ház panyigai
ü panyigai ház kotta

In this poem real Hungarian words and imaginary ones which 'sound' Hungarian are combined. The resulting text, composed with words chosen for their musical colour, can therefore not really be translated. In the booklet of the CD recording of this work, no English, German or French translation was included. The title of the song 'Dance Song' was followed by 'This text cannot be translated'.

No. 3

Kínai templom[37]				Chinesischer Tempel				Chinese Temple		
zent	Sankt	Holy	fönn	hoch	high	Négy	Vier	Four	maɟd	dann	then
ert	Park,	garden	lenn	tief	deep	fém	Stahl	metal	mély	tief	deep
ő	reich	wide	tág	weit	wide	cseng:	klingt:	ring:	csönd	Ruh	quiet
omb	Laub:	leaf:	éj	Nacht	night	Szép,	Schön,	Fair,	leng,	schwingt,	swings,
árt	groß	open	jő	kommt,	comes	Jó,	Gut,	Good,	mint	wie	like
öld	grün	green	kék	blau	blue	Hír,	Ruf,	Fame,	hült	kalt	cold
zárny,	Flug,	wing,	árny.	Fleck.	shape.	Rang,	Rang,	Rank,	hang.	Laut.	sound.

Here we simultaneously have a 'picture poem', a tone poem and an associative poem; as we see, the form, the vertical 'word beams' which flow from top to bottom, imitates the columns of a temple. The monosyllabic Hungarian words, which were chosen for their particular sound and were suggestively positioned in a row, combine everyday familiarity and exotic foreignness.

[37] Original Hungarian text from Weöres, *Egybegyűjtött írások I–III*, vol. 1, p. 335; German translation from Sándor Weöres, *Der von Ungern*, p. 11; the English version is a rough translation by Tiborc Fazekas.

No. 4

Kuli	Coolie
Kuli bot vág.	Coolie cane chop.
Kuli megy	Coolie go
Megy	go
csak guri-guri	only softly-softly
Riksa	Rickshaw
Autó	Car
Sárkányszekér	Dragon-carriage
Kuli húz riksa.	Coolie pull rickshaw.
Kuli húz autó.	Coolie pull car.
Kuli húz sárkányszekér.	Coolie pull dragon-carriage
Csak guri-guri	only softly-softly
Kuli gyalog megy.	Coolie go foot.
Kuli szakáll fehér.	Coolie beard white.
Kuli álmos.	Coolie sleepy.
Kuli éhes.	Coolie hungry.
Kuli öreg.	Coolie old.
Kuli babszem mákszem kis gyerek	Coolie bean poppyseed little child
ver kis kuli nagy rossz emberek.	Big wicked man beat little Coolie
Csak guri-guri	only softly-softly
Riksa	Rickshaw
Autó	Car
Sárkányszekér	Dragon-carriage
Ki húz riksa?	Who pull rickshaw?
Ki húz autó?	Who pull car?
Ki húz sárkányszekér?	Who pull dragon-carriage?
Ha kuli meghal.	Suppose Coolie dead?
Kuli meghal.	Coolie dead.
Kuli neeem tud meghal!	Coolie no-o-o-t now dead!
Kuli örök	Coolie immortal
Csak guri-guri	only softly-softly[38]

The text conveys timelessness and a momentary glimpse in a situation in which communication has broken down, where the tension created between opposites is nearly comical, although associations are allowed to run free. Exoticism and familiarity come together in an explosive mix. Weöres unlocks the world for us and our response is instinctively automatic, like an aeolian harp in the wind.

Weöres and his poetry seem to have had the rare ability to inspire Ligeti his whole life long. In his youth, after having survived an unimaginable catastrophe, he desperately needed freedom and the joy of experimentation. Later in Ligeti's life, as a permanent threat lay on the future of humanity, Weöres's poems, instead of freedom, provided the composer with an unconventional discipline he was free to choose and a state of equilibrium not bound by any rules. In the words of the poet:

> Ha pokolra jutsz, legmélyére térj:
> az már a menny: Mert minden körbe ér.

---

[38] Original Hungarian text from Weöres, *Egybegyűjtött írások I–III*, vol. 2, pp. 512–13; the English translation is quoted from Weöres, *Eternal Moment*, p. 115.

(If you go to hell, then go to the bottom of it:
that is heaven: For all things move around.)[39]

Concluding remarks

I don't think that poetry can inspire composers, rather it can become
the raw material they use. Music uses poetry as a mason uses the
skeleton of a building, its beams or girders, to flesh out a structure.
The composer gets his inspiration somewhere else, exactly like
the poet who is also not inspired by music but rather draws on his
personal experience; it is out of the virtually indeterminable matter
which swims through his soul that he forms his works. I don't believe
the inspiration that arts exert on one another is especially important.
But occasionally it can happen, of course.[40]

Both artists relied more on their own power of innovation – albeit in
different art forms – than on the traditions of their respective art. In his
poems Weöres rejected the conventional and established 'rules' of poetry
and, without a trace of an ideological artistic manifesto or personality cult,
embraced his own personal voice. Hence his poems sound like outbursts
from the 'primitive culture' of a bygone world where human language and
culture began, forgotten because it was stifled and shrouded by 'civilized
culture'. In its foreignness this art reveals 'uncultured' man's genuine
attributes, without any pretence of the virtue or morals which can so easily
be put aside. Ligeti deliberately opposed the established rules of convention
in music, and in doing so created a kind of 'anti-music', a music beyond
the existing boundaries. His encounter with the poetry of Weöres was
almost fated since both artists sought to portray, in their own way and in
their own art form, man's harrowing and awe-inspiring history without the
sheen of 'culture'. In this quasi-psychoanalytical display, every question
about human existence which is usually concealed, falls prey to ideology,
or is played down by culture, emerges amazingly plain and clear. Equally
plain and clear, however, is the awareness that a direct and simple answer
is impossible.

What could have become of the creative harmony between these two
artists had not the events of the 20th century separated them so brutally?
This must remain an open question. One can also pose this question
regarding other constellations, whether they appeared briefly, too late or not
at all. At a reading in the Hamburg Literaturhaus, we personally witnessed
György Ligeti's first meeting with Imre Kertész, the Hungarian writer
who later received the Nobel Prize for Literature. It was an exceptional
moment, to be able to see and experience how both artists immediately felt
an intense and deep mutual understanding. Ligeti and Kertész discussed
the responsibilities and possibilities of culture, they spoke of the fates of
individuals and artists alike in the 20th century and reflected what it all
meant. Meeting a Hungarian soul-mate in art (even if this occurred too

---

[39] Original Hungarian text from Weöres, *Egybegyűjtött írások I–III*, vol. 2, p. 9;
the English translation is quoted from Fahlström, *Form and Philosophy in
Sándor Weöres' Poetry*, p. 40.

[40] György Czigány, 'Vers, zene, Weöres Sándor' [Poetry, Music, Sándor Weöres],
in *Magyar Orpheus*, pp. 564–70, at p. 566.

late in his life) remained intensely important to Kertész and he endured, over and over and in a very personal way, the immeasurable loss caused by the time spent in isolation. Kertész describes this experience in a letter to Ferenc Fejtő (1909–2008):

> I try to remember what we talked about then. But it doesn't really matter in the end because we always talked about the same thing. I don't know if I was ever able to say how much I learned from you. Aside from very few exceptions, I learned about Hungary only through emigrants, either from the real emigrants or from those who had chosen inner emigration. And because of the weird state of affairs of the world which held me captive here, I failed to forge many a friendship which could have held great promise. If I had, for instance, been able to discuss the Kádár era with you through and through ... it's absurd but I sometimes toy with this idea. But I only met Ligeti very late, also Professor Klein or Tábori; and I never did meet Márai,[41] although after the war, when I was still a boy, I saw him on Zárda Street, taking a walk on the Serpentine at the foot of Rose Hill and another time swimming and sunning himself at the Lukács pool.[42]

Translated by Louise Duchesneau[43]

[41] George Klein, (Budapest 1925–), Professor emeritus, Research Group Leader, Microbiology and Tumorbiology Center (MTC), Karolinska Institute Stockholm; George Tábori (1913–2007), Hungarian writer and theatre director; Sándor Márai (1900–89), Hungarian writer.

[42] Imre Kertész, 'Hommage à Fejtő', in *Európa nyomasztó öröksége* [Europe's Gruelling/Oppressing Legacy] (Budapest, 2008), pp. 203–16, at p. 204.

[43] Translator's note: The text was translated from German into English. For her translation of the Hungarian quotations the translator made use of the original Hungarian texts (supplied by the authors) as well as of the German translation by the authors.

*Ligeti turning pages during a rehearsal
(London, October 1989)*

4 'Make Room for the Grand Macabre!' The Concept of Death in György Ligeti's Œuvre

WOLFGANG MARX

Two of György Ligeti's major works – the *Requiem* (1965) and the opera *Le Grand Macabre* (1978) – deal with the subject of death, apparently a topic which fascinated him during different periods of his life as a composer. The grim reaper was, it seems, nearly omnipresent in his artistic thoughts. This may not be too surprising in the case of a composer who was not only a survivor of the Holocaust but had also a keen interest in political and religious affairs, and not only abhorred all dictatorships, totalitarianism and any suppression of free thought, but all of the consequences which devolved from such systems. In this essay, these two works will be discussed with regard to what they reveal about Ligeti's view of death, as well as how a composer in his position chooses to engage with this topic in the late 20th century. It will focus on alienation effects, ambiguity, exaggeration and the grotesque as key concepts in all of these compositions. For, after all, Ligeti himself admitted that

> ... one dimension of my music bears the imprint of a long time spent in the shadow of death both as an individual and as a member of a group. Not that it lends a tragic quality to my music, quite the opposite. Anyone who has been through horrific experiences is not likely to create terrifying works of art in all seriousness. He is more likely to alienate.[1]

A Requiem for humanity

Ligeti attempted to write a requiem early on in his life. He was particularly fascinated by the 'Dies irae' sequence, which forms the longest and central part of the Latin Mass for the Dead. 'I always thought I should write a Requiem Mass just for the *Dies irae*', he admitted during an interview with Josef Häusler.[2] The poetic text attributed to Thomas of Celano appealed to his fondness for ambiguity and contrast: 'It is an extraordinarily colourful, almost comic-strip, representation of the Last Judgement. I find it particularly fascinating that the poet resorted to colourfulness to resolve fear.' It was not so much the religious content that interested the non-Christian Ligeti but rather the emotional contrasts, the exaggerated expressions of what he regarded as a 'mixture of fear and grotesque humour'.[3]

While still in Hungary he twice began to work on a requiem, at first still a student in the late 1940s and later in the early 1950s as a teacher at the Music Academy in Budapest (this latter one in a style he called 'pentatonic

[1] *György Ligeti in Conversation with Péter Várnai, Josef Häusler, Claude Samuel and Himself* (London, 1983), p. 21. 'alienate' and 'alienation effect' are here used in the sense of *Verfremdung* in Bertolt Brecht's epic theatre. See, for example, Bertolt Brecht, *Brecht on Theatre: The Development of an Aesthetic*, ed. and trans. John Willett (London, 1964).

[2] *György Ligeti in Conversation*, p. 47.

[3] Ibid, pp. 46–7.

serialism'), yet both attempts did not get very far. After fleeing to Austria in 1956 he once again contemplated writing a requiem, 'but now for the victims of the Hungarian Uprising'.[4] Again this project came to nothing. In 1961 Ligeti dedicated *Atmosphères* to Mátyás Seiber (1905–60), a fellow Hungarian composer also living in the West who had died in a car accident just a year earlier. As Harald Kaufmann points out, *Atmosphères* can be regarded as a requiem of sorts:

> While he was working on *Atmosphères* [Ligeti] had the idea to compose a Mass of the dead with this same material. He wants us to hear this work as a requiem which is emerging from some subterranean cave, very far away, beyond the range of conscious perception. ... In the middle of the composition there is a passage where the unwavering static sound suddenly breaks off. The piccolos' and violins' high notes become higher and more piercing until they suddenly tumble down to the depths of the double basses. ... Ligeti admits to have thought of a fall 'in Tartaro'. This is the moment at which a Dies irae might begin.[5]

When in 1961 he was commissioned to write a piece for the tenth anniversary of the Swedish new music series *Nutida Musik*, Ligeti decided that now the time had come to write a 'real' requiem. His fascination with the 'Dies irae' aside, there was another more personal reason why Ligeti wanted to write such a work. This he revealed in an interview, entitled *Close and Far Away at the Same Time: Being a Jew in Music*, which was broadcast on 3 November 1990 by Westdeutscher Rundfunk (West German Radio). In it, the composers György Ligeti and Mauricio Kagel – both Jewish, yet from different corners of the world (Hungary and Argentina) – were interviewed by the Argentinian composer Juan Allende-Blin.[6] Asked why he had chosen to compose a requiem, that is, Catholic church music, Ligeti explained:

> I stayed alive by coincidence. ... There is a deep-rooted – fear is perhaps not the right word for it. I would say: hate, yet a free-floating hate if this was possible. Yet my hate is not just directed against the National Socialists, but equally against the Soviet system ... Both were and still are terrible. ... And this hate, this fear, and in addition a kind of distance certainly influence my music. ... I am often asked how someone who is a Jew – even though not a practising one, I am not a member of any Jewish congregation yet I am not Christian either, I was not baptized – how could I write a requiem? I was even

---

[4] Richard Steinitz, *György Ligeti: Music of the Imagination* (London, 2003), p. 141.

[5] Harald Kaufmann, 'Strukturen im Strukturlosen: Über György Ligetis "Atmosphères"', in *Spurlinien: Analytische Aufsätze über Sprache und Musik* (Vienna, 1969), pp. 107–17, at pp. 114–15.

[6] *Nah und fern zugleich: Jude-Sein in der Musik: Ein Gespräch zwischen Juan Allende-Blin, Mauricio Kagel und György Ligeti*, Westdeutscher Rundfunk, 3 November 1990. The interview was part of a series entitled *Begegnung mit Israel* (Encountering Israel). It was conducted in German; all translations are by the author. I am grateful to Sophie Fetthauer for making me aware of this interview and providing me with both a recording and a transcript of it. The transcript was prepared by Marlin Pahl, to whom I am also indebted.

attacked by some, in the US, some friends – how could you do this? ...
I think this is the moment to clarify how I came to write a requiem. It
has political reasons.

Then, Ligeti recounts how, just after the communist takeover in 1948,
he was made president of the students' union at the Music Academy in
Budapest.

> In that winter 1948/9 ... the following happened, horrific from
> my point of view, who had no idea of how a secret police operated.
> I was called in along with representatives of other universities and
> institutes of technology ... and I was asked how many students there
> were at the Music Academy. I said about 900. 'Then please give
> us nine names next week' – it had to be 1 per cent; the communist
> system always operated on a quota system – nine names of openly
> catholic students. ... so catholicism is now the enemy (not so much
> Protestants, Jews etc.), and suddenly I am expected to denounce
> people. I am supposed to name nine church musicians. (There was a
> Catholic and a Calvinist section of church music.)[7]

The secret police even tried to 'seduce' him with a beautiful girl who was
to help convince him to hand over the names, yet Ligeti decided otherwise.

> ... then I went to an old friend, János Bartos, ... a devout Catholic,
> not a teacher of mine, yet someone I had a high opinion of, and I
> told him what had happened and asked him to warn everybody who
> is openly Catholic. I did not know all the people who were exposed
> as militant Catholics or anti-communists, yet I asked him to please
> warn them all. The next day I stepped down as president as I didn't
> want to be involved in something like this. ... I was not imprisoned,
> I had some problems, yet this was the reason I joined János Bartos's
> circle, those militant Catholics, and felt at home there. There was a
> kind of solidarity, not for religious reasons ... you have to stand by
> those who are discriminated against, who are declared enemies.
> So I became part of that group, without becoming a Catholic. This
> left a deep impression on me, and I thus started writing a requiem
> which was related to everybody, Jews and Catholics ..., all the tens
> of thousands of people who vanished in Hungary ... . I was part of a
> kind of private resistance movement, and this was where my urge to
> compose a requiem originated.[8]

As we see, Ligeti's admiration for the Hungarian Catholics' resistance to
the Soviet system played an important role in his motivation to write a Mass
for the Dead. The requiem he refers to at the end of the previous quotation
must have been the one Steinitz mentions as his first attempt to compose
such a piece. When Ligeti finally did write his *Requiem* in the early 1960s
he focused primarily on the 'Dies irae', which, as a consequence, became
the last movement of the piece – he composed only an Introitus, a Kyrie, a
'Dies irae' and a 'Lacrimosa' (which is part of the 'Dies irae' but in Ligeti's
Requiem forms a separate movement). Even so, it was the longest work he

[7] Ibid.
[8] Ibid.

had produced to date. A year later he wrote *Lux aeterna*, a setting of the requiem's closing liturgical text, yet in this case it is a separate, independent work.

Ligeti's first attempt at composing a requiem had been dedicated to the tens of thousands of people of all confessions who had vanished in Hungary, and with the second version he wished to honour the victims of the Hungarian uprising of 1956. Finished in 1965, his third attempt at composing a requiem is not dedicated to a single person or event but is rather a funeral mass for the whole of humanity.[9]

Ligeti is not the only 20th-century composer to have written a requiem with this kind of 'dedication'. Like him, many had not set out to write a piece of Catholic liturgy at all, but rather wanted to make use of the well-known traditional text for their personal statement about death.[10] This is not necessarily a reaction to an individual's death – although the compositional process is often triggered by a friend's or relative's demise –, but rather addresses the simultaneous death of large numbers of people as it occurs during wars and genocides.[11] This applies not only to what are arguably the other major requiem compositions of the 1960s, i.e. Benjamin Britten's *War Requiem* (1962) and Bernd Alois Zimmermann's *Requiem für einen jungen Dichter* (Requiem for a Young Poet, 1969), but also to the majority of requiem compositions written since the First World War and up to compositions such as Hans Werner Henze's *Requiem* (1993) or the *Requiem der Versöhnung* (Requiem of Reconciliation, 1995), a collaborative work by 15 composers to commemorate the 50th anniversary of the end of the Second World War.[12] A personal, non-liturgical approach gave all these composers the freedom to treat the original liturgical text individually, either by confronting it with other secular or religious texts (Britten, Zimmermann), by using only parts of it (Ligeti, Zimmermann) or by writing a purely instrumental composition (Henze). Death as addressed by these works is not the inevitable biological necessity we all have to face in the end but rather it is the result of political, ideological or religious strife that was not inevitable; these deaths were unnecessary at the time they occurred. In this sense death is not something to be passively endured; it can be fought and even prevented, so these requiems deal not with the afterlife but with the conditions we face here on earth. Thus these compositions not only commemorate or console but they have an

[9] Erkki Salmenhaara, *Das musikalische Material und seine Behandlung in den Werken 'Apparitions', 'Atmosphères', 'Aventures' und 'Requiem' von György Ligeti* (Regensburg, 1969), p. 166. Ligeti said this at a press conference and later tried to recant his statement which seemed to have been made in an unguarded moment, but of course the genie could not be squeezed back into the bottle.

[10] Compositions like Maurice Duruflé's *Requiem* (1947) are rather exceptions confirming this rule.

[11] For a more detailed discussion of this topic see Hans-Günther Bauer, *Requiem-Kompositionen in Neuer Musik: Vergleichende Untersuchungen zum Verhältnis von Sprache der Liturgie und der Musik* (Tübingen, 1984).

[12] This piece was initiated by Helmuth Rilling (who had also organized the first performance of another significant collaborative requiem composition, the Verdi-initiated *Messa per Rossini*, in 1988); the 15 composers represent different countries that fought each other during the war.

'educational' function as well and may even denounce political or military despots. By describing his requiem as a 'funeral mass for the whole of humanity' (Richard Steinitz calls the relevant section of his book 'The Requiem: A Cry for Humanity'),[13] Ligeti clearly attaches this educational function to his work as well. His reference to both the National Socialist and the Soviet systems in an earlier quotation above point to the same direction.

What distinguishes Ligeti from Britten, Zimmermann or Henze is that he had been a victim of genocide himself and composed not only as a survivor of the Holocaust, but also of the Soviet communist suppression in Hungary.[14] The fact that he had himself been close to death many times during the war gives his treatment of the requiem text a very special edge. He described his approach to the text as guided by 'the fear of death, the imagery of dreadful events and a way of cooling them, freezing them through alienation, which is the result of excessive expressiveness ...'.[15]

Ligeti's principal means of dealing with fear, dreadful events or horrific experiences seems to have been grotesque exaggeration, or 'excessive expressiveness'. The four movements combine most of the stylistic devices Ligeti had developed up to that time. As Marina Lobanova describes the work, it starts with a static beginning in the Introitus, proceeds to the less static Kyrie to reach the dramatic central piece, the 'Dies irae', before ending with the cathartic 'Lacrimosa'.[16] The Kyrie usually receives the most attention from scholars, as it is commonly recognized as being the most interesting (and also the most accessible) movement from an analytical point of view because of its highly complex and elaborate micropolyphonic texture.[17] The other three movements are often discussed in less detail.

Though less complex than the Kyrie, the Introitus is also a micropolyphonic piece. The micropolyphonic texture of this movement – the choir is divided in five groups of four parts each – makes understanding the text very difficult, with two exceptions. There are two passages in which the two lowest bass voices suddenly emerge alone in unison: the first time they sing 'Domine', later 'exaudi orationem meam'. 'Lord, hear my prayer' – this is the only comprehensible bit of text in this movement. The five vocal groups move upwards, from 'requiem' to 'lux', following the direction of the two main keywords of this movement. Yet 'Domine' is sung on D♯ and C♯ two octaves below middle C, while 'exaudi orationem meam' goes down a semitone to D and C♮ respectively. The fearful dying soul does not move upwards but appears to gradually sink further into despair.

The Kyrie has the briefest text of all the movements and, while it certainly is the most fascinating movement in terms of its compositional technique, it is perhaps least interesting regarding the emotional narrative of the work.

[13] Steinitz, *György Ligeti: Music of the Imagination*, p. 140.

[14] Not to mention his earlier experiences as a Jewish member of the Hungarian minority in Romania.

[15] *György Ligeti in Conversation*, p. 46.

[16] Marina Lobanova, *György Ligeti: Style, Ideal, Poetics* (Berlin, 2002), pp. 111–37.

[17] He spent nine months working on this movement alone. Jonathan W. Bernard in his analysis of the *Requiem* sketches also focuses on the Kyrie, for which Ligeti produced extensive sketch material; see pp. 149–67 in this volume.

Steinitz describes the 'Dies irae' as 'marked by violent contrasts between frenzied activity and frozen immobility, an explosion of the emotion locked inside the vast sweep of the "Kyrie"'[18] and as a 'wild, gesticulating sequence of kaleidoscopic images performed with exaggerated contrasts of manner by all participants'.[19] Here Ligeti adopts the experimental vocal style of his *Aventures* in which three vocalists try to convey their emotional state without words by singing in an imaginary nonsense language. They achieve this solely by switching between different (and often massively exaggerated) types of expression, helped by swift changes of dynamics, tempo and style. The 'Dies irae' has a text, of course, but it is often difficult to understand, so that the difference from *Aventures* may be less clear cut than perhaps initially thought. According to Marina Lobanova, the often very sudden, immediate changes of colours and contrasts as well as parallel contrasting semantic layers and textures help turn the *Requiem* away from being the expression of an individual's fear or grief towards a more general, 'objective' appeal:

> The extremes, the grotesque exaggerations, the heightened attention to detail and the colouristic brightness of the third movement of the Requiem are reminiscent of late Gothic. The emotions which are portrayed in the Dies irae have nothing to do with subjective experiences: taken to an extreme level of contrast and sharpness, they appear cold and detached.[20]

Finally the 'Lacrimosa' provides a 'hushed backward look at the previous events ... as if losing themselves in a numbed, glassy twilight.'[21] Lobanova's overall impression of the work reads as follows.

> The composer was aiming to convey a picture of the twentieth century apocalypse – of which he himself had been a witness – without descending into Romantic emotionality or naturalistic verisimilitude. During the genocide people ceased to be individual agents in what was taking place, but simply came to be identified with a particular social or ethnic group. Statements by individuals were an inadequate narrative on events which were a denial of everything human.[22]

The emotionally exaggerated, 'Gothic' and non-naturalistic settings of all movements allow for the alienating effect to take root: the audience hears the well-known texts as it has never heard them before and is left in an agitated rather than in a comforted state. Ligeti's *Requiem* (and particularly its central third movement) focuses on the death not of an individual but rather of a collective. It is something so horrific that it can only be approached in a surreal, sometimes even parodistic way: on the one hand, naturalism is in any case impossible to achieve, on the other, this is the only possible approach for a composer who is himself a victim to do justice to his experiences in his music. And so one can answer

---

[18] Steinitz, *György Ligeti: Music of the Imagination*, p. 145.

[19] Ibid., p. 148.

[20] Lobanova, *György Ligeti: Style, Ideal, Poetics*, p. 130.

[21] Steinitz, *György Ligeti: Music of the Imagination*, p. 145.

[22] Lobanova, *György Ligeti: Style, Ideal, Poetics*, p. 129.

Adorno's claim that one cannot write poetry – and, by extension, create art in general – after Auschwitz. It is still possible, but only in a very special way.

The *Requiem* moves from a static beginning, through the slightly more flowing Kyrie, on to the highly dramatic central 'Dies irae', only to return to the rather static (and more homophonic) 'Lacrimosa'. There is neither a pessimistic surrender to the powers of death nor the hopeful solace of a better afterlife; the musical survivors (the two soloists and a reduced orchestra in a much simplified homophonic texture) almost seem to depict a battlefield the day after a bloody encounter – the 'twentieth-century apocalypse' Lobanova referred to. This movement reminded Harald Kaufmann of the sound of a Beckettian void, a total inner emptiness.[23]

Ambiguity always plays a part in this work as it does in Ligeti's œuvre in general; the listener may sometimes wonder whether, despite its 'non-realism', a certain effect can be taken seriously or not. While individual gestures might be exaggerated and so appear surreal to us, the general picture they present when taken together still falls well short of truly rendering the horrors Ligeti and others experienced. Yet one element which is crucial to ambiguity and alienation is still (and must be) absent from the *Requiem*: humour, comedy and the element of farce. This was to be added in Ligeti's opera, *Le Grand Macabre*.

'The serious is always comic, and the comic frightening' – *Le Grand Macabre*

Since its première in Stockholm in 1978 *Le Grand Macabre* has become one of the most successful contemporary operas. Even before the first performance of its revised version in 1996 its popularity was rivalled only by some of John Adams's operas. Michel de Ghelderode's play, *La Balade du Grand Macabre*, is already a highly surreal, absurd piece of literature whose attributes were further heightened by Ligeti's music. However, the exaggerated expressiveness here could do what the requiem text did not permit: it takes the form of a farce. Ligeti believed that the comical elements were crucial in this case as they made the horror of death bearable: '*buffa* and *seria*, comedy and fear, are not simply mixed, but are rather two sides of ... the same coin: the serious is always comic, and the comic frightening.'[24] The story of Nekrotzar, who appears on earth to bring it to an end at midnight, yet miserably fails to do so when the time comes, is as surreal as it is comical:[25]

> ... although aware of the permanence of death, we cannot prevent ourselves from aspiring to eternal life; on the other hand, Ghelderode shows us, when the end of the world is about to occur, that Nekrotzar, exhausted by pleasure, weakened by over-indulgence in love-making

---

[23] Quoted after Salmenhaara, *Das musikalische Material und seine Behandlung ...*, p. 162.

[24] Lobanova, *György Ligeti: Style, Ideal, Poetics*, p. 222.

[25] This is one of the few operas during which the audience openly laughs for long stretches of the performance – and not at the expense of any intellectual concern with the matters in question.

and alcohol, no longer has the strength to accomplish the task of annihilation.[26]

In Ghelderode's *Balade* Nekrotzar is finally unmasked as a charlatan; he was never death in the first place. Ligeti changed this as he wanted to add an element of ambiguity to his opera.

> At last I had found a play about the end of the world, a bizarre, demoniacal, cruel, and also very comic piece, to which I wanted to give an additional dimension, that of ambiguity. ... one never knows whether he [Nekrotzar] really represents death or whether he is simply a charlatan. So *Le Grand Macabre* is an opera about death conceived as a farce.[27]

The opera is, however, far more effective if Nekrotzar really is death because this means that death can be outwitted. This way of dealing with the fear of death is always possible according to Ligeti: 'The threat of collective death is always present but we try to eliminate it from our consciousness and to enjoy to the maximum the days that are left to us.'[28] It is important to note that Ligeti here speaks of collective death – just like in the *Requiem*, this is not about individual biological death but about genocide and mass extermination.

Alienation effects are a crucial aspect of both the opera's libretto and music. It is a kind of absurd theatre, full of surprising, comical and surreal musical effects, also with elements of dadaism thrown in for good measure. Ligeti generally loves playing with avant-garde techniques of composition and in this opera it is a particularly good way of enhancing the surreal and alienating effects. A good example of this is Nekrotzar's triumphant arrival at Prince Go-Go's palace. One might expect fanfares at this point (perhaps akin to many 'Dies irae' settings), yet Ligeti does the unexpected. He begins with an ostinato subject, which is later successively joined by other parts (Example 24).[29] This subject is actually a quotation, referring to the passacaglia subject of the final movement of Beethoven's 'Eroica' Symphony (Example 25).[30]

Ligeti only quotes the precise rhythmic structure of Beethoven's subject but its melodic shape is left blurred. He can't quote Beethoven's melody exactly as the melodic material at this point is based on a 12-tone row which starts on F and finishes on G♭, consisting mainly of intervals of seconds, sevenths and tritones. Building this theme out of a 12-tone row, however, creates a problem: Beethoven's theme has 13 notes, while the row obviously has one fewer. This means that the last note of the rhythmic pattern is at the same time the first note of the second melodic row. As we can see in Example 24, the last note of the rhythmic theme is F – the note at the beginning of the example. At the end of the second iteration, the melodic

---

[26] *György Ligeti in Conversation*, p. 117.

[27] Ibid., p. 115.

[28] Ibid., p. 117.

[29] György Ligeti, *Le Grand Macabre*, revised version 1996, study score (Mainz, 2003), p. 201 (no. 451).

[30] Ludwig van Beethoven, Symphony No. 3 op. 55 in E flat Major *Eroica* (London, n.d.), pp. 128f.

row ends even earlier; now F and B, which are the first two notes of the next row, are the pattern's last notes. With each repetition of melodic row and rhythmic pattern these two parameters are more 'out of phase', as Steve Reich would put it. The melodic row begins earlier and earlier within the rhythmic pattern. In order to approximate the general contour of Beethoven's theme, Ligeti regularly moves the row's notes up or down an octave. As we can see in example 24, the first row begins with a leap up from F to B, while the same B is transposed downwards in the second presentation in order to allow for an upward movement B–B♭ at the theme's next beginning. After 12 presentations of the row, the rhythmic and melodic units coincide for the first time since the beginning, and would do so again should we hear the melody 24 times – however, the melody is played only 23 times.

Example 24 Ligeti, *Le Grand Macabre*, third scene, ostinato theme and its first repeat

Example 25 Beethoven, Symphony no. 3, 4th movement, bar 12

The 12-tone row used by Ligeti consists mainly of tritones, major and minor seconds and sevenths. The compositional technique reminds one of Steve Reich's 'phasing', also of the isorhythmic textures of music from the 14th and 15th centuries, in which melodic and rhythmic patterns can also be separated (*color* and *talea*). These are not always of equal length and can therefore also move 'out of phase'. Ligeti had a special interest in music of this period and utilized similar concepts later on in his Piano Études.

Allusions were Ligeti's favourite way of referring to a piece, a style or a composer. Yet although he was a master of allusion, one finds few direct quotations in his works. Rather he tried to imitate styles or works from within his own musical language, for example with the use of a particular instrumentation or a certain rhythmic pattern. The use of a recognizable Beethoven quotation here is therefore rather unusual. It is however not the only quote in this opera; in this *Le Grand Macabre* is special in Ligeti's œuvre as it contains quite a few more.[31]

---

[31] Apart from this Beethoven quotation, there is also a reference to Offenbach's 'Galop infernal' (also known as 'Can Can') from *Orphée aux enfers*, Schumann's 'Fröhlicher Landmann' from his *Album für die Jugend* and Liszt's *Grand Galop Chromatique*. Like the Beethoven reference, all of these are not literal

Ligeti was often inspired by paintings, literature or other arts and frequently spoke of these in interviews. Thus we know that among his inspirations for *Le Grand Macabre* were paintings by Pieter Breughel (hence 'Breughelland'), Hieronymus Bosch, Francisco de Goya and René Magritte, cartoons by Saul Steinberg and Roland Topor (many of these were also inspirations for his *Requiem*), the theatre of the absurd, literature by Edgar Allan Poe, Boris Vian, Charles Baudelaire and Alfred Jarry, as well as films by Charlie Chaplin and the Marx Brothers. These numerous sources make it difficult to link specific effects to individual inspirations but then ambiguity can be regarded as a central element of Ligeti's style.

As Nekrotzar enters the palace, the Beethoven theme is played along with allusions to several other styles (now clearly no quotations): a ragtime played by a solo violin, a Balkan dance rhythm in the bassoon, a flamenco theme in the Eb clarinet, a pseudo-medieval hymn *à la* Perotin in the oboe, a Hungaro-Scottish pentatonic march and finally a distorted samba in the bass trumpet. At the same time the percussion adds a cha-cha-cha in three different tempi. All this ends up being a large-scale collage (as already acknowledged by Ligeti in the score in Example 25). But let us return to our Beethoven theme. This is based on an unorthodox 12-tone row, which is not built according to the rules of modernist serialism, as there are no transpositions, inversions or retrogrades. Instead the row is subjected to compositional techniques more common in minimal music or in isorhythmic music of the late Middle-Ages. This leads to distortion on several levels: for instance, the rhythm of the 'Eroica' theme is quoted, but not the melody. The unconventional treatment of the 12-tone row is a sign of the composer's critical stance towards modernism and the avant-garde at the time the opera was composed. One might expect that Nekrotzar's entrance would be accompanied by triumphant music, so the reference to a symphony entitled 'Eroica' at first appears to make sense. But since Ligeti chose maybe the least heroic theme from this symphony the musical effect is almost as if Nekrotzar came tiptoeing into the room. A reference to the 'Eroica' Symphony raises expectations that the actual quotation will deliberately disappoint.

Towards the end of the opera (in the fourth and final scene) Ligeti alludes once again to serial compositional techniques when he writes a mirror canon based on a ten-note row.[32] This time he fulfils 'traditional' expectations and uses inversions and retrogrades – however with only an 'incomplete' ten-note row. In the case of the 'Eroica' reference the musical material was complete, but the compositional technique it was subjected to was 'incorrect', here the technique is 'correct' and it is the material which is incomplete. Distortion prevails once again.

---

quotations yet they are clearly recognizable. In other works, Ligeti rarely uses references as specific as these; the main exception would be the opening of the Horn Trio with its again 'distorted' yet still clear reference to the opening of Beethoven's piano sonata op. 81a, *Les Adieux*. For a more detailed discussion of this reference see Richard Steinitz's chapter in this volume (pp. 181ff.).

[32] Ligeti, *Le Grand Macabre*, study score, pp. 288f. This music accompanies the scene in which Nekrotzar – having realized that he failed to bring about the end of the world – starts to shrink and slowly fade away.

Another interesting example of Ligeti's musical depiction of death can be found at the end of the second scene. Here Nekrotzar reveals for the first time that the end of the world is imminent. Piet the Pot and the court astrologer Astradamors are horrified – but also a little bit ironic. Peter von Seherr-Toss correctly reads this scene as a parody of the Apocalypse: Nekrotzar's bombastic ranting is a grotesque exaggeration of the natural disasters which are unleashed before the opening of the seventh seal during the last judgement.[33] Nekrotzar, Piet and Astradamors sing three-line rhymed couplets. The poetic quality of the text is rather low and one cannot help feeling that achieving a proper rhyme was more important than the content of the song, which was of course intentional. Here are for example the initial stanzas in English and German. The text was originally written in German and it is clear that the translation in this case was more concerned with maintaining the poetic form than providing an accurate translation of the content.[34]

NEKROTZAR	NEKROTZAR
Fire and Death I bring,	Feuer und Feuersnot,
burning and shrivelling!	Flamme und Flammentod!
PIET, ASTRADAMORS	PIET, ASTRADAMORS
Awful our suffering!	Wir sind in größter Not.
NEKROTZAR	NEKROTZAR
Thunder and lightning flash!	Rache und Donnerklang,
Now comes the final crash!	Strafe und Untergang!
PIET, ASTRADAMORS	PIET, ASTRADAMORS
My mouth is dry as ash!	Bruder, es wird mir bang.
NEKROTZAR	NEKROTZAR
Torches of hell-fire glow!	Brennende Höllenglut,
Blood in the streets shall flow!	Strömendes Menschenblut!
PIET, ASTRADAMORS	PIET, ASTRADAMORS
Why do I tremble so?	Mensch, mir fehlt ganz der Mut!
NEKROTZAR	NEKROTZAR
My rage on all I vent,	All die im Zorn ich traf,
bringing them punishment!	Erfahren meine Straf'!
PIET, ASTRADAMORS	PIET, ASTRADAMORS
Death is so permanent!	Ei, das ist gar nicht brav.

This exchange between Nekrotzar's pompous drivel and Piet's and Astradamors' mostly shorter whinings carries on for quite a while.[35]

---

[33] Peter von Seherr-Toss, *György Ligetis Oper Le Grand Macabre: Erste Fassung, Entstehung und Deutung. Von der Imagination bis zur Realisation einer musik-dramatischen Idee* (Eisenach, 1998), 244ff.

[34] György Ligeti, *Le Grand Macabre*, György Ligeti Edition 8, Sony Classical, SK 62312, CD Booklet, pp. 102ff. The opera was written in German yet premièred in Swedish. Ligeti wanted each production of the opera to be given in the language of the country where it was being performed. So far there are versions in Swedish, German, English, French, Italian and Hungarian.

[35] Ibid.

Particularly in the German version, Piet's and Astradamors' replies seem not just frightened but sometimes also ironical. For example, the line 'Ei, das ist gar nicht brav' (which could be translated as 'Well, isn't he misbehaving?') clearly has an ironic or parodistic undertone.

Apart from the Revelation (or Apocalypse), this section appears to me to refer to another sacred text: the 'Dies irae', the sequence of the Mass for the Dead, a Latin poem made up of 19 three-lined stanzas. The first two stanzas are:

Dies irae, dies illa	Day of wrath and doom impending
Solvet saeclum in favilla,	David's word with Sibyl's blending!
Teste David cum Sybilla.	Heaven and earth in ashes ending!
Quantus tremor est futurus,	Oh, what fear man's bosom rendeth,
Quando iudex est venturus,	When from heaven the Judge descendeth,
Cuncta stricte discussurus?	On whose sentence all dependeth![36]

In the previous section we have already seen that Ligeti was fascinated by the text of the 'Dies irae' and that this in fact was one of the reasons he chose to compose his *Requiem*. In the opera the formal structure is in rhymed stanzas of three lines, most often beginning with two lines sung by Nekrotzar and one line of comment added by Piet and Astradamors. Poetry in general and three-lined stanzas in particular are quite rare in liturgical texts, while the dialogic structure of the episode also supports this reading. In the Latin sequence there is a quasi-neutral report written in the third person at the beginning, which later switches to a very emotional, highly moved poetic first person expressing fear in the face of the last judgement and begging for mercy. At the end of the sequence (in the 'Lacrimosa'), the third-person returns. This alternating principle becomes here a dialogue. Nekrotzar's lines are not quite emotionally neutral but certainly more descriptive, while the two respondents on the one hand express their fear, but also reinforce Nekrotzar's lines to the point where they become even more ridiculous – distortion again. Musically, Ligeti mostly ignores the natural emphases of the text and develops the dialogue as an extended crescendo, with more and more instruments gradually joining the singers. The vocal parts remain rhythmically as well as melodically rather similar, mainly set in triadic quavers with many note repetitions and phrases that tend to gradually move up over time in small intervals (seconds and thirds). The scene thus becomes more and more intense; the general impression is that of a gradually emerging hysteria.

A key to Ligeti's half-comical, half-tragic distorting approach to death can be found in the texts of another Hungarian Jewish Holocaust survivor: the author Imre Kertész, winner of the 2002 Nobel Prize for Literature. Kertész survived both Auschwitz and Buchenwald, and all his writings deal in some way or another with this experience. In an essay entitled 'Wem gehört Auschwitz?'[37] (Who does Auschwitz belong to?) from 1998

---

[36] English translation by William Josiah Irons (1848), http://everything2.com/title/Dies+Irae, accessed on 5 August 2010.

[37] Imre Kertész, 'Wem gehört Auschwitz?', in *Eine Gedankenlänge Stille, während das Erschießungskommande neu lädt* (Reinbek, 2002), pp. 145–54. All following translations of this text are by the author.

he compares two Holocaust movies, namely Steven Spielberg's *Schindler's List* and Roberto Benigni's *Life is Beautiful*. It may not be surprising that Kertész finds Spielberg's approach problematic. This is partly because the movie tried too hard to be naturalistic, which is ultimately impossible and bound to fail, but also because it offers its audience no guiding advice.

> I regard ... as kitsch any depiction that does not implicate the wide-ranging ethical implications of Auschwitz, and consequently any portrayal of MAN (written in capitals) – and with him the ideal of what is 'human' – which doesn't emerge from Auschwitz complete and undamaged.[38]

It may surprise one that Kertész actually likes *Life is Beautiful*. In this film, Benigni plays a Jewish prisoner who pretends to his son that their life in a concentration camp is only a game with clearly set rules and regulations at the end of which one can win a great prize – a real tank. The film is completely unrealistic and has moments of slapstick that, at first viewing, may appear rather inappropriate for this subject. Kertész, however, describes his impression as follows:

> While one can stand less and less the hero's slapstick-like moments, gradually the magician emerges behind the mask of the clown. He raises his wand, and suddenly each word, each centimetre of film is possessed of another spirit. ... The camp gate resembles the real gate of Birkenau as much as the man-of-war in Fellini's *Ship of Dreams* resembles the real flag ship of the Austro-Hungarian admiral. But this is about something completely different: the spirit, the soul of this film is authentic, it touches us with the power of old magic – the fairy tale.[39]

Later he adds:

> At first glance this fairy tale looks rather awkward on paper. ... But does not this [film's] invention have an essential equivalent in the real world? Even when you have smelled the stench of burned flesh you are not prepared to believe it could all be real. Rather you look for something which would make survival worthwhile, and a 'real tank' is exactly that kind of seductive promise for a child.[40]

So it is the fairy-tale character that is central to Kertész. To recreate the Holocaust in a naturalistic way is impossible – it will never be exactly right and could never replace the real experience (particularly not for those who are comfortably seated in a cinema with their popcorn), it will always trivialize. A fairy tale, however, focuses on one particular aspect or emotion, it can express hope, sadness or cruelty without having to be authentic. *Le Grand Macabre* is maybe such a fairy tale too – a tale in which death is outwitted in an alien and grotesque world. Everybody fears death, yet death turns out to be a toothless tiger that may roar very loudly but cannot bite when it matters.

[38] Ibid., p. 150.
[39] Ibid., p. 152.
[40] Ibid., pp. 152–3.

Artists who have gone through horrible experiences such as the Holocaust are unlikely to try to recreate those experiences in a naturalistic way in their art. They will rather choose the path of alienation effects. Kertész certainly advocates this position, and Ligeti – who befriended Kertész in the final years of his life – appears to have adopted a similar approach in this opera.

Ligeti and his co-librettist Michael Meschke have written a kind of secular last judgement for an apocalyptical world in which death does not win, for once and against all expectations. This utopia is created by the use of grotesque, parodistic, absurd and surreal effects and halfway dadaistic texts. Ligeti's music underlines this approach with its permanent ambiguity, its collage-like character, its allusions to styles and specific compositions and its mix of tragedy and farce. The composer does not just protest against death as something natural, but rather against death as he (and Kertész) experienced it during the Holocaust: death caused by dictators who decided completely arbitrarily who lives and who dies. The opera is itself a kind of fairy tale, set in an imaginary land and with a happy ending, and in its attitude towards death it displays a strong ethical component.

'Make Room for the Grand Macabre!'[41] Nekrotzar shouts early on in the opera. There can be no doubt that death occupied much 'room' in Ligeti's mind, and not only in the 1960s and 70s. 'A Long, Sad Tale', composed in 1993, is the last of his six *Nonsense Madrigals*. Again Ligeti chooses a rather surreal subject matter, texts which are partly grotesque and speak of death (in this case the texts were written by William Brighty Rands and Lewis Carroll) and provides them with even more ambiguous music. Based on his own experience as a victim of two totalitarian systems, the *Requiem* is his first major attempt to deal with the extermination of millions of people, the arbitrariness and injustice of dictatorships and the fear of death. Already in this work an ultimately impossible naturalism is replaced by surrealist mannerisms, a grotesque style and – at least in part – a certain over-expressiveness, all of which permeate his new approach to the age-old text. This tendency is even more obvious in the countless absurd features of the opera (many of which – like the car horn preludes, the choice of character names or the singing style, register and appearance of certain protagonists such as the chief of the Gepopo, for example – could not be explored here). Imre Kertész's reading of art engaging with the Holocaust appears to provide a useful approach to Ligeti's musical reactions to his own past; *Le Grand Macabre* can certainly be read as a fairy tale in which anything is possible, but the *Requiem* falls into this category too (certainly the 'Dies irae', but in a broader aesthetic context the other movements as well). Collective death brought on by politicians, ideologues and demagogues is unbearable, and laughing at (as well as about) death is a way of making it bearable, at least up to a point. We must all conquer our fear of death and this battle can be fought by everybody.

---

[41] György Ligeti, *Le Grand Macabre*, György Ligeti Edition 5, booklet, p. 72.

*Ligeti at a conference in Gütersloh
(May 1990)*

5 Continuum, Chaos and Metronomes – A Fractal Friendship

HEINZ-OTTO PEITGEN

In the beginning there was chaos

When I first met György Ligeti in 1985 I had no idea of the effect he would have on my life. My friend, the physicist Peter Richter, and I had just finished putting together a large exhibition of as yet unpublished images from mathematics for the Goethe-Institut (Frontiers of Chaos – Computer Graphics Face Complex Dynamics). The exhibition had been assembled in two identical copies and started its world tour nearly simultaneously at the Museum of Modern Art in Oxford and at the Exploratorium in San Francisco. The images showed computer experiments from the fields of chaos research and fractal geometry, some of which our mentor, the Nobel Prize winner Manfred Eigen, had shown Ligeti. He was electrified by these images and absolutely wanted to know more about them, as well as about the experiments through which they had been produced. As a result, two people met who knew nothing of each other, and doors in a completely new world opened for both of us. I had always loved music but had the usual misgivings when it came to new music. This explains why I had no idea then who Ligeti was. With hindsight I see that this was a good thing, as it was the only way of meeting him candidly and without prejudice.

Everything changed when, from pure acquaintances, we became close friends. Today I cannot imagine my life without new music and, above all, without Ligeti's music. Those who had the pleasure of meeting him might find my account uninteresting and dull because his brilliant manner, his piercing questions, as well as his caustic criticism – in appearance always deceptively mild[1] – can hardly be put in words. However dissimilar Ligeti's origin and life as a musician was from my scientific background, we both saw that what we did was, in some way, remarkably connected and interwoven. To lay open these connections was not only uniquely enriching for us but it also helped to advance knowledge. He introduced me to new music and to him I opened the doors to the study of fractals, fractal geometry and other fields of mathematics. I remember a long conversation we had in a hotel in Bremen after a concert of his works. The main piece in the programme, which was part of the Musikfest Bremen in 1997, was his Violin Concerto, played by Christian Tetzlaff and the Deutsche Kammerphilharmonie Bremen. The concert took place in the aerospace hangar of the DASA (Deutsche Aerospace Aktiengesellschaft, which later became EADS), an unusual venue normally used to assemble objects for space travel. Ligeti and I were to have introduced the individual works of the programme and the concert was sold out, surely because the master himself had been announced. I had prepared myself well because I knew that he would not limit himself only to the subjects we had agreed upon. His associative way of speaking often led him from one topic to other very

---

[1] Following his funeral, which took place on 26 June 2006, I attended the commemorative concert at the Mozart Hall in Vienna. It was there that I heard from his composition students that Ligeti could also criticize without any 'mitigating' packaging.

remote reflections. Therein lay precisely its charm, but on stage, in front of 1,000 spectators, the challenge to the moderator can only be mastered with thoughtful preparation. This certainly paid off in my case because as Ligeti arrived from Hamburg late in the afternoon, he immediately exclaimed upon entering the hall: 'Impossible! It's hopeless. You can't play my Concerto in here. The acoustics are awful.' This put Christian Tetzlaff in an awkward situation. He had prepared extremely well and, together with the conductor Christian Hommel, had adjusted his playing to the difficult acoustics. He could not, however, disagree with the composer. And without the main piece in the programme, a talk with Ligeti during the concert did not make much sense. We discussed back and forth at great length and after I had tried to use the weight of our friendship to save the situation, Ligeti finally accepted that we play the Concerto but without him being present. He went back to his hotel and I had 30 minutes to prepare for my solo role as moderator. The audience accepted Ligeti's indisposition, everything went well and the Violin Concerto was a great success. That's just the way he was: he would not tolerate even the slightest compromise on quality. When we met the next day, we discussed the role of infinity and its many forms in mathematics, also Gödel's incompleteness theorem. One can really get bogged down over this question and he certainly did. I remember very well his outburst of pure joy as I explained how Bernhard Riemann had placed infinity on one point – the North Pole of a sphere – and so made it easier to manipulate. Naturally, he always wanted to hear about the latest news from chaos research. He did not like the word 'chaos' at all, because he thought it was too populistic, and he overestimated the possibilities of convincing the mathematical community to choose a better word.

Public awareness of chaos research reached its peak in the mid-1980s. Looking back one could say it was only hype. Scientific hypes often have two sides: because the expectations are incredibly high, disappointment over the unfulfilled hopes soon sets in. In reality, however, the discovery of chaos broadened and changed our view of mathematics and natural science, and we see that in the meantime scientists have been quietly developing countless practical applications for it. But first we should ask ourselves: what is chaos and what is it about?

Chaos: a lesson from weather forecasting

In 1961 Ligeti composed an orchestral piece entitled *Atmosphères*. Its 'content' consisted of fluctuation, turbulence and flowing forms. At the same time Edward N. Lorenz was simulating weather patterns with the help of a computer. This research led eventually to the discovery of 'strange attractors' and the dynamic systems which would cause a scientific revolution in the following years. However, it was only in 1984, when he discovered the computer graphics Peter Richter and I had made of the Julia and Mandelbrot sets,[2] that Ligeti noticed how similar this new branch of mathematics was to his compositions.

---

[2] See György Ligeti, 'Rhapsodische Gedanken über Musik, besonders über meine eigenen Kompositionen (1991)', in *Gesammelte Schriften*, vol. 2, ed. Monika Lichtenfeld (Mainz, 2007), p. 131.

Edward N. Lorenz died on 16 April 2008 at the age of 90. Not only was he one of the fathers of chaos theory but, following quantum theory and the theory of relativity, he enriched 20th-century science with its third ground-breaking discovery. Man has always sought to predict the weather and, till the beginning of the last century, the strategy was simple: meteorologists had amassed a treasure trove of weather patterns they had recorded and based their forecasts on the way the current weather pattern would fit into an earlier sequence. That seemed to make sense: if, for instance, today's weather pattern is the same as one from a certain day two years ago, it stands to reason that it should also develop in the same way it did then. For some reason, however, this method was not very successful.

In 1922 the great British meteorologist Lewis Fry Richardson came up with a revolutionary new approach. He created a precise mathematical model – for which the formulae and equations fill a whole book – which describes the physical development of weather patterns, and he suggested calculating future weather by measuring the state of today's weather. His great individual achievement made it possible to integrate the hitherto archaic science of meteorological observation and interpretation into the modern natural sciences. But the dream of applying Richardson's work to any practical use only came true after the first computers were developed at the end of the 1940s. Since then, meteorologists have striven to fulfil Richardson's vision and meteorologists were convinced that, by using more and more powerful computers, this goal will be reached some day.

Edward N. Lorenz was working in this same spirit when, in 1960, he discovered something strange, which he later called the 'butterfly effect'.[3] Initially, he only investigated a mathematically simplified weather pattern, but found that even the smallest inaccuracies in the measurements of current weather could, in the end, lead to predictions of completely different weather patterns. It was only a few years later that the word 'chaos' would be applied to such situations. *Chaos is the practical loss of predictability in the presence of a strictly valid mathematical law.* Here 'practical' means that the forecast is based on a measurement, and, as we know, measurements are always a bit unreliable. Lorenz' discovery puts Richardson's dream into perspective because we know today that weather can only be forecast at best for two to three weeks. This is an example of how *one* single scientist can disconcert a whole scientific community. However, the importance of Lorenz also lies in the fact that he broke new ground and in so doing, created chaos theory's first components, which subsequently proved to be so productive that natural scientists in the 1970s and 80s found chaos nearly everywhere in nature. Therefore, one can speak with good reason of a new view of nature. Since Galileo and Newton, modern mathematics-based sciences had nurtured the dream that man would one day be able to see into the future. Chaos theory claims that, on the contrary, reliable forecasts of long-term developments in nature are the exception rather than the rule. Even where the future is predetermined by natural laws and appears to be accessible to us in principle, in many cases we cannot and will never be able to reliably predict it.In other words, for us as intelligent observers

---

[3] 'The flap of a butterfly's wings in Rio de Janeiro can set off a tornado in Texas' is how Lorenz explained his discovery to his fellow meteorologists.

the future is more open-ended than we thought before the discovery of chaos.

The history of chaos theory also teaches us that even the opinion of a majority of scientists cannot guarantee that something will be true. Mathematics clearly and irrevocably shows us our limits to identify or even manipulate the future.

To find chaos in a mathematical or scientific sense means, so to speak, to discover butterflies in something, that is, to realize how the smallest inaccuracies, mistakes or disturbances can have a powerful, unexpected impact on a process, a development, or an event. At present, my work deals with the improvement of medical diagnostics and therapy, and, about ten years ago, I discovered a trace of chaos in the risk evaluation in liver surgery.

Risk analysis in surgery

In order to understand the problems of surgical risk analysis during a resection – that is, the surgical removal – of a tumour from an organ, it is important to remember that there exists no sure method to diagnose where exactly a tumour starts and where it stops. The present standing of medical knowledge does not allow us to determine this with certainty. It is for this reason that the surgeon tries to operate in what he is absolutely sure is healthy tissue. He traces a safety margin around the tumour which he sees on the computer tomography scans, and he hopes that after the operation the pathologist will find the tumour enclosed in the removed lump of cells, or at least that no cancer cells are found in the resection surface, since leaving cancer cells in the organ would render the operation useless. The problem here is that an organ has several different kinds of vascular systems: it is interconnected within itself not only locally but also over a distance. Now, if a tumour with its safety margin is removed during the operation, parts of the vascular network will be inevitably injured, which, in turn, will cause an organ to malfunction in some of its parts in the long run. How do these risks depend on the location of the tumour? It took a series of complex experiments for me to discover that sometimes the smallest change in the positioning of a tumour could cause great differences of the effect on surgical risks – as we see, there are also butterflies in the distribution of risk in tumour surgery.

Chaos and crash tests

The auto industry organizes crash testing because cars have to be safe enough to protect passengers in the event of an accident. Whereas in the past a real car was demolished in every single test, today many of these tests are carried out on a computer. While engineers were developing mathematical procedures to help them create simulated tests that exactly reproduce reality, an unbelievable discovery was made: they found butterflies. That is, the crash results sometimes differed considerably from each other, for instance, when the angle of the direction in which the car crashed was minutely different. Once again, small differences can produce great effects. The mathematical methods helped finding exactly where the butterflies were located, or rather, which features of the car parts were responsible for the butterflies and how they could be avoided.

Chaos, Ligeti and super-signals

Two of Ligeti's works stand out for me because of their experimental and scientific character: the *Poème symphonique for 100 metronomes* (1962) and *Continuum* for harpsichord (1968). The idea of mechanical, ticking music haunted Ligeti since his childhood. It was associated with fantasies of a musical labyrinth and the infinity of gradually diminishing images, which can be seen when gazing into parallel mirrors. While composing the *Poème symphonique* Ligeti had in mind numerous superimposed grids, moiré patterns, which would result in changing rhythmic structures. He wanted to produce a rhythmic grid that is so thick at the beginning that it seemed practically continuous. Irregular grid structures, which emerge one after the other as the metronomes stop ticking, gradually replace this disordered but homogeneous blur. In this way, unpredictable patterns grow out of the uniformity of the opening. At the end we have a single metronome left ticking and the uniformity of the beginning is re-established.[4]

After composing the *Poème symphonique* Ligeti applied the same clockwork-like rhythmic process to various other pieces, the most characteristic of which is the harpsichord piece *Continuum*. The experimental nature of the *Poème symphonique* is obvious: even the set-up of the piece and the course it follows remind us of an experiment. On the other hand, when listening to *Continuum*, one does not get the impression that it is a refined and sophisticated experiment because the tension we hear is so wonderfully musical and captivating. It reminds us maybe of the solo cadence in the first movement of Bach's Fifth Brandenburg Concerto or of the C minor Prelude from Book 1 of the *Well-Tempered Clavier*. What we don't realize is that Ligeti is putting his listeners through a perceptual experiment. If we read the instructions in the score, it is immediately clear that he is interested in creating an effect, not just in stating ordinary tempo indications:

> Prestissimo = extremely fast, so that the individual tones can hardly be perceived, but rather merge into a continuum. Play very evenly, without articulation of any sort. The correct tempo has been reached when the piece lasts less than 4 minutes (not counting the long fermata at the end). The vertical broken lines are not bar lines – there is neither beat nor metre in this piece – but serve merely as a means of orientation.[5]

The piece has to be played just at the physiological limit of what is possible, or even beyond it, so that the notes can melt into a continuum. A film projector uses the same effect to insure that the individual frames are transformed into a continuous flow. In fact, the projector shows static images at 24 frames per second, but these go by so fast that we perceive them as part of a continuous succession and not as individual images. The flowing movement of the film does not exist, rather it is 'added on' by our

---

[4] See György Ligeti, *Poème symphonique for 100 Metronomes*, score, instructions for performance (Mainz, 1982); and György Ligeti, *Mechanical Music*, György Ligeti Edition 5, Sony Classical 62310 (1997), p. 12.

[5] György Ligeti, *Continuum*, score, instructions for performance (Mainz, 1970), p. 4.

perception of it. Musical notes can also behave in a similar way. If I tap, let's say, ten times a second absolutely regularly on a table, I can still hear the individual taps. If I could tap 440 times a second, which is of course physically impossible, the taps would melt into one note and I would hear something close to a concert A. What happens when two people tap at the same time? Let's say one taps 440 a second and the other 441 a second. What do we perceive? A 'mixture' of two notes maybe? No, what we perceive is a simple rhythmic pattern, which pulsates over the span of a second. Our visual perception can experience similar phenomena as is shown in the following simple experiment.

In Figure 1 at the top we have a series of vertical lines, all positioned within the same (small) distance from each other; they represent a basic rhythm. Under this, in the middle, we have another series of lines, with the distance between them widened by exactly 5% (a slower rhythm, so to speak). And finally, at the bottom, we see both series of lines superimposed and we notice that where both series are superposed, a new, much slower rhythm emerges (slowed down to approximately factor 20). One could say that new rhythms are formed when two nearly similar rhythms are placed one on top of another.

Today I find these facts completely trivial and, as a scientist, I would have learned about them already during my student years. The truth, however, is that I have Ligeti to thank for making me aware of these connections. Since then, I hear and see in a newer, richer way. During our conversations, the names of Steve Reich and Conlon Nancarrow were often mentioned. At first, I didn't give this much thought but Ligeti repeated them over and over again. This helped me to discover what he was talking about and for this I will be eternally grateful. He not only opened my eyes to the

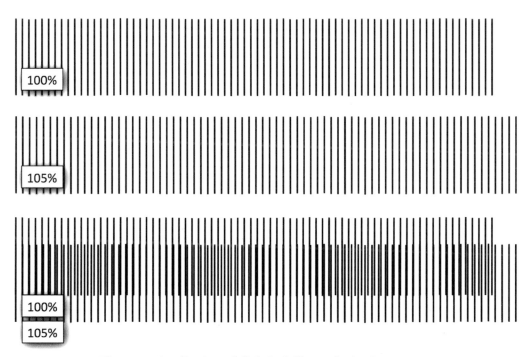

Figure 1 Visualization of slightly different rhythmic patterns

interconnectedness between his own work and that of Steve Reich, Iannis Xenakis and Jean-Claude Risset, but also introduced me to new music in a way that allows me to explore it on my own with much greater pleasure.

The perceptual elements we mentioned above are especially important to Steve Reich's earlier compositions, for instance *Piano Phase* (1967). I recently had the chance to discuss this with Steve Reich and was surprised to hear that he was not aware that his music had any connection to current brain research. In fact, this aspect did not really interest him. And this even though *Piano Phase* and *Come Out* (1966) could be interpreted as perceptual experiments. In the case of Ligeti, the relationship between composition and effect was virtually reversed. He followed the advancement of brain research with great interest and extraordinary insight, and there is no doubt that his enthusiasm for current scientific advances was the unifying inspiration behind his creative work. And yet one reads practically nothing about this. Therefore it is worth exposing these connections and looking once again at *Continuum* (Example 26).

In the right hand we hear a repeated two-note motive, B♭–G, and in the left hand the same motive but inverted, G–B♭. Both motives, or rhythmic units, seem to shimmer when played together. The two-note motives are organized in periods of eight, and each period is separated by a broken vertical line. After nine periods, Ligeti adds an F to the right hand, thus creating a three-note motive, B♭–G–F, while the two-note motive continues in the left hand. This tiny change leads to a rhythmic complexity which can be called 'virtual', that is, nothing has been changed rhythmically – we still have evenly played quavers although we hear uneven rhythms. A trace of chaos: small variations lead to big effects. One could say that Ligeti has built in a butterfly. The beginning of the piece is completely uniform. But as soon as you add a third note in one hand, here an F, it will stick out and sound as if it were held while the other two are just blurred. The rhythmic patterns which are produced by the interplay between the two hands are musical figures of a 'second order', that is, they are not directly produced by the player but are illusionary patterns which are produced by overlapping grids of different speeds.[6] One finds many examples of Ligeti using similar procedures, for instance in the first Étude for Piano, *Désordre* (1985).

After having found traces of chaos in Ligeti's music, let us look at another important point. Scientists like to speak now about 'deterministic chaos'. In the past, the word 'chance' was used when experimental observation failed to establish an order, that is, when it was impossible to predict the further course of the observed events. For example, imagine that you are looking at someone throwing a coin. It will always be either heads or tails. Even if you watch thousands of throws, you cannot predict whether the next throw will be heads or tails. You will have the same problem at the roulette table where there are also no patterns for the sequence of events, at least when the table is in good functioning order. Nevertheless, players are always trying to find a pattern. For instance, if the number 7 hasn't appeared in the past half-hour, they think it will come up next. Deterministic chaos means that we may have a strict mathematical law for some natural phenomenon, for

---

[6] See György Ligeti, 'Zwischenbilanz in Toronto (1973)' and 'Monument-Selbstportrait-Bewegung Drei Stücke für zwei Klaviere (1976)', in *Gesammelte Schriften*, vol. 2, pp. 110–11 and 277–80.

Example 26 Ligeti, *Continuum*, beginning

Prestissimo *

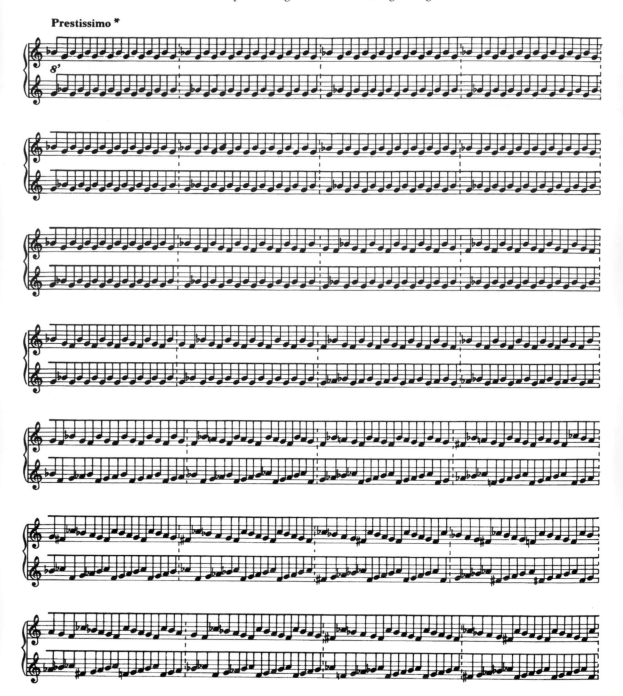

instance for the weather on earth, and yet what we observe appears random or devoid of order. Small variations can have unexpected effects for the observer. A mathematical law and an algorithm are practically the same and Ligeti's works are often thought of as being algorithmic compositions. That this is not so is obvious from the following quote:

Somewhere underneath, very deeply, there's a common place in our spirit where the beauty of mathematics and the beauty of music meet. But they don't meet on the level of algorithms or making music by calculation. It's much lower, much deeper – or much higher, you could say.[7]

Still it is possible to connect Ligeti's ideas, for instance in *Désordre*, to the discovery of deterministic chaos. Their common base lies in the deterministic character of chaos, as opposed to chaos in the sense used by Xenakis, whose compositions owe more to the traditional concept of chance and stochastic phenomena.

Fractals: the geometry of chaos

Before concluding let us mention one last point, which brings us back to the beginning of this essay. Ligeti was just as fascinated by the discovery of deterministic chaos as he was by Benoît Mandelbrot's fractal geometry. He was particularly fond of one of the images I had produced, which is the reason I dedicated it to him in one of my books. Figure 2 shows the Ligeti fractal, a so-called Julia set, named after the French mathematician Gaston Julia, whose mathematical investigation at the beginning of the 20th century I pursued at the beginning of the 1980s with the help of computer graphics.[8]

Figure 2 The Ligeti Fractal

[7] Richard Steinitz, 'Music, Maths & Chaos', *Musical Times* 137/1837 (March 1996), pp. 14–20, at p. 14.

[8] I would like to thank Hartmut Jürgens for once again reconstructing this image as a printable copy. The only copy I had was an illustration from one of my books from 1986. Five years are a long time in the computer age, and not everything which was possible then is better today. In order to mathematically capture this image so magnificently, he had to come up with quite a few very good ideas.

What are fractals and why did they impress and influence Ligeti so deeply? Just as all man-made things have a form, which can be described by Euclidean geometry (line, square, rectangle, circle, cube ...), so does nature also have its own geometry. A cloud, a coastline in Croatia, an oak tree, or a vasculature in the liver, all have a geometry which cannot be grasped, described or measured by Euclidean geometry. In the 1970s Benoît Mandelbrot expanded classical geometry in such a way as to render it possible to describe and measure forms from nature as easily as to describe man-made objects by the means of Euclidean geometry.

The secret of trees

Hardly anything seems more familiar to us than trees: deciduous trees, fir trees, vascular trees, but we also think of the trees in a flowchart, or what comes to mind can be the tributaries of a river like the Elbe or lightning in the sky. Botany defines trees as perennial, woody seed plants with a single main dominating trunk, whose secondary growth, in the form of branches, increases its girth. Mathematics also has its trees: these are connected graphs in which any two vertices are united by only one path. In this way all trees can be brought down to a common denominator. It becomes more difficult, however, when one has to describe the structural difference between an oak and a fir tree. Even more difficult is when we have to explain in a split second how we perceive the difference between an oak and a beech. And very difficult to understand is how the hepatic portal vein, the tree in the liver, can reach all the liver cells.

It took a long time before the relevant areas of mathematics (geometry, graph theory, topology, statistics) were able to contribute anything of use on this subject, but fractal geometry has fundamentally changed this. In one model, that of self-similarity, the whole can be dismantled in parts that look like small copies of the whole. If this feature is present, even only approximately, one speaks of statistical self-similarity, as for example in an oak tree. The Sierpiński triangle in Figure 3 is a striking example of exact self-similarity: the whole is made out of three parts which are reduced copies of the whole. A beautiful example from nature would be comparing a leaf taken from a fern to the whole plant, as seen in the mathematically generated figure of the Barnsley Fern, also shown in Figure 3.

The whole thing becomes more difficult if we ask ourselves why a tree is shaped the way it is. On the one hand, nature seems to play with variants, that is, it prefers a bit of chance. On the other hand, trees are highly optimized organisms. For instance, their geometric structure is organized in such a way that as many leaves as possible are turned towards the sun to insure photosynthesis. Only recently have we understood that the particular geometry of trees also reduces its susceptibility to snapping under a gust of wind. But how does a tree grow? Is everything carefully encoded genetically in a seed which grows according to an unchangeable programme or should we maybe forget this predominant interpretation of genetics? Many growth processes in organic and inorganic nature follow similar laws and mechanisms of self-organization, and self-similarity is typical of models of self-organized processes.

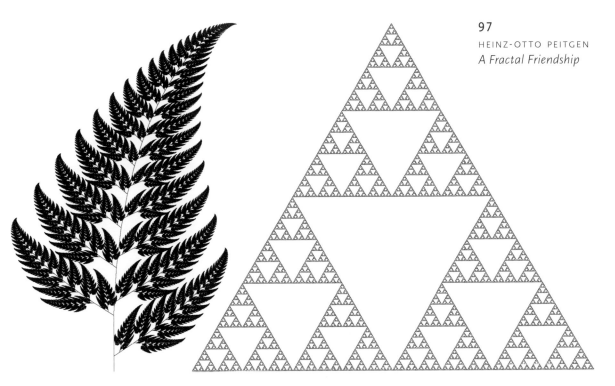

Figure 3 Self-similarity in the Barnsley Fern (*left*) and the Sierpiński Triangle (*right*)

New elements of geometry

Unlike Euclidean geometry, fractal geometry has no elements such as lines, circles, ellipses and the like. Instead, fractal geometry has iterative[9] or recursive processes, which is our link to chaos. The following simple process was the forerunner of the discovery of chaos:

$$\begin{cases} x_{n+1} = ax_n(1-x_n) \\ n = 0,1,2,3,\ldots \end{cases}$$

The number for a is chosen arbitrarily, for instance $a = 2$. A starting number x_0 is then chosen, for instance $x_0 = 3$, which is placed on the right side of the term, and finally $2 \cdot 3(1-3) = -12$ is calculated. Thus, the first step of the iteration has been carried out and the result is transferred to the right side. Then $2 \cdot (-12)(1-(-12)) = -312$ is calculated and this completes the second step. The result of the third step is -195312. The following sequences are obvious: the outcome of each last step is inserted and results in the next step. This is the meaning of the numbers n and $n+1$, which are annexed to the numeric values x. Although there is hardly a simpler iterative process, we have discovered that the process for $a = 4$ and starting numbers x_0, chosen between 0 and 1 (thus for instance $x_0 = 0.3356987\ldots$), is chaotic. Today this process is considered *the* prototype for chaos. In his ground-breaking work Edward Lorenz was able to show that the mechanisms for the formation of weather had something to do with this process, which is actually so chaotic that one could very well lose faith altogether in calculating anything with computers. Let us compare it now with the following process:

[9] Iteration or recursion means repetition. See also Heinz-Otto Peitgen, Hartmut Jürgens and Dietmar Saupe, *Chaos and Fractals* (New York, 1992).

$$\begin{cases} x_{n+1} = ax_n - ax_n^2 \\ n = 0,1,2,3,\dots \end{cases}$$

One immediately sees that we only expanded what was in parentheses in the first term. The new process is therefore mathematically identical with the old one, only the order of the operations has been changed. Just to make sure let's take our example $x_0 = 3$, this time with $a = 4$:

$$4 \cdot 3(1-3)$$
$$4 \cdot 3 - 4 \cdot 3^2$$

And now let's look at what a computer does with these calculations when we carry the iteration much further, for instance, by calculating 79 iterative steps and then comparing them, when we start with $x_0 = 0.3$ and choose $a = 4$.

Process 1 (with parentheses)

1	0.3	21	0.941784606	41	0.755660148	61	0.207807201
2	0.84	22	0.219305449	42	0.738551554	62	0.658493472
3	0.5376	23	0.684842276	43	0.772372624	63	0.899519277
4	0.99434496	24	0.863333332	44	0.703252615	64	0.36153739
5	0.022492242	25	0.47195556	45	0.834753498	65	0.923312422
6	0.087945365	26	0.996854038	46	0.551760383	66	0.283226373
7	0.32084391	27	0.012544262	47	0.989283451	67	0.812036779
8	0.871612381	28	0.049547612	48	0.042406818	68	0.610532194
9	0.447616953	29	0.188370585	49	0.162433919	69	0.951130536
10	0.989024066	30	0.611548432	50	0.544196564	70	0.185924957
11	0.043421853	31	0.950227789	51	0.992186655	71	0.605427469
12	0.166145584	32	0.18919751	52	0.031009187	72	0.955540195
13	0.554164917	33	0.61356309	53	0.12019047	73	0.169932523
14	0.988264647	34	0.948413698	54	0.422978883	74	0.564221843
15	0.046390537	35	0.195700621	55	0.97627099	75	0.98350222
16	0.176953821	36	0.629607551	56	0.092663775	76	0.064902415
17	0.582564664	37	0.932807531	57	0.336308798	77	0.242760365
18	0.972732305	38	0.250710565	58	0.892820762	78	0.735311082
19	0.10609667	39	0.751419111	59	0.382767396	79	0.77851478
20	0.379360667	40	0.747153723	60	0.945026066	80	0.68971807

Process 2 (expanded, without parentheses)

1	0.3	21	0.941784606	41	0.755660148	61	0.207882282
2	0.84	22	0.219305449	42	0.738551554	62	0.658668955
3	0.5376	23	0.684842276	43	0.772372624	63	0.899296651
4	0.99434496	24	0.863333332	44	0.703252614	64	0.362248737
5	0.022492242	25	0.47195556	45	0.834753499	65	0.924098358
6	0.087945365	26	0.996854038	46	0.55176038	66	0.280562331
7	0.32084391	27	0.012544262	47	0.989283452	67	0.807388438
8	0.871612381	28	0.049547612	48	0.042406813	68	0.622049393
9	0.447616953	29	0.188370585	49	0.162433902	69	0.940415783
10	0.989024066	30	0.611548432	50	0.544196519	70	0.224135753
11	0.043421853	31	0.950227789	51	0.992186671	71	0.695595668
12	0.166145584	32	0.189179751	52	0.031009125	72	0.846969338

13	0.554164917	33	0.61356309	53	0.120190235	73	0.518449114
14	0.988264647	34	0.948413698	54	0.422978169	74	0.998638521
15	0.046390537	35	0.195700621	55	0.97627055	75	0.005438503
16	0.176953821	36	0.629607551	56	0.092665451	76	0.021635701
17	0.582564664	37	0.932807531	57	0.336314262	77	0.08467039
18	0.972732305	38	0.250710565	58	0.892827917	78	0.31000526
19	0.10609667	39	0.751419111	59	0.382744912	79	0.855607995
20	0.379360667	40	0.747153723	60	0.945004977	80	0.494171815

Both charts show 80 numerical values. The first chart starts with 0.3 as starting value and calculates the following

$$4 \cdot 0.3(1-0.3) = 1.2 \cdot 0.7 = 0.84$$

The second chart also starts with the starting value 0.3 and calculates

$$4 \cdot 0.3 - 4 \cdot 0.3^2 = 1.2 - 4 \cdot 0.09 = 1.2 - 0.36 = 0.84$$

As anticipated, the result is the same in both cases. The computer now continues to calculate the iteration in both charts and if we compare both left columns we see that each step results in the same decimal number. This was to be expected because the calculations use two formulae that are mathematically equivalent. Also the second columns in the charts are the same. In the third column, however, we observe some alarming events: in the 44th position, the first process (after 43 steps) generates value 0.703252615, whereas the second process in the same position results in value 0.703252614! Nearly the same result, but not exactly the same! At the ninth digit after the decimal point there is a difference of 1, that is, the results differ from each other by one-billionth. We have nearly yet not exactly the same result. This is the point where chaos is setting in.

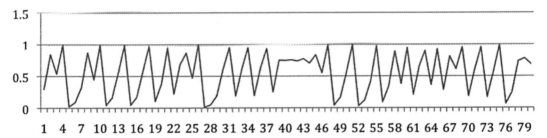

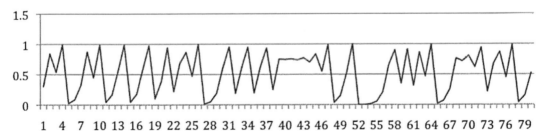

Figure 4 Differences in results of mathematically equivalent formulas depicted in a time series. One notices immediately that both processes are identical up to a bit past the middle where they then deviate more and more from each other. This result is amazing given the fact that, in the computer calculations, we only replaced the formula $4x(1-x)$ by the mathematically equivalent formula $4x - 4x^2$.

If we compare positions 45 to 69, we see that this minute difference continues to grow. At position 69 the difference has reached the second digit after the decimal point, that is, the difference between the two processes (iterations) has grown to about one-hundredth and this is equivalent to a growth factor of 10 million! Again, between step 45 and step 69, or just 14 iterations, the difference has increased by a factor of 10 million, while between steps 2 and 44 everything looked tame, or like expected: the two mathematically equivalent processes generate the same results. What follows gets stranger and stranger. If we compare both positions at 75, we have 0.98350222 in the first process and 0.005438503 in the second! Now, if we consider that all results have to fall between 0 and 1, we have reached almost the greatest possible difference. Which of the two processes is correct and which is faulty? It is not possible to say for sure[10] because chaos has struck. How can we explain this? One of the reasons why this can happen lies in the way computers calculate. They calculate pretty exactly, but not entirely exactly, and they do not accept decimal numbers with many digits, let's say, not more than 16. All numbers that need more digits are drastically rounded off at 16. This may sound extreme but you really don't notice it in everyday use because the difference is so tiny. And remember, chaos means that the smallest differences can cause the greatest impact. But why does the iteration produce more and more digits after the decimal point? Let's have a look at the first column: we start with a number that has one digit after the decimal point. The first step produces 2, then 4 and 8 digits after the decimal point. Each step practically doubles the number of digits and very soon a tiny inaccuracy occurs, because the computer starts to round off the numbers. Even if both processes are mathematically equivalent, the result of the calculations is a different sequence. In combination with the rounding off, somewhere along the line a tiny difference occurs and chaos takes its course.

How difficult it is to tell if a process is chaotic or not becomes clear when we notice that the process for $a = 4$ is chaotic and, for instance, the one for $a = 2$ not at all. And in this case, when $a = 2$, they will both always give the same answer even if we let both processes run parallel to each other endlessly. This means that the rounding off and the doubling of the digits alone do not explain the chaotic behaviour: it is not the cause of chaos, it only helps chaos to occur. Chaos lies much, much deeper, hidden in the process. If this was not the case, it would have been discovered a long time ago and not just very recently.

If chaos can exist in such a simple computing process one must suspect that this is not an isolated case, it can happen anywhere. As a matter of fact, iterative processes can easily slip into chaos. For instance, let's take the weather: powerful computers and extremely intertwined computing processes help us forecast next week's weather based on the observation of today's weather. How does that work? Let's say the computer begins with today's weather at noon. Instead of forecasting tomorrow's weather and the weather for the day after tomorrow straight away, the computer takes a different course. It virtually proceeds in tiny time steps of a few seconds, the process is iterative and runs through an incredible number of steps till

---

[10] In any case not on a computer which cannot calculate more exactly.

it reaches tomorrow. And if the process is chaotic, the tiniest inaccuracies, precisely the butterfly effect, can have a great impact on the results.

One can imagine how our conversations and the discoveries they allowed him to make fascinated Ligeti. His enthusiasm, however, did not end there. Here I must add one of the most beautiful discoveries of recent mathematics. As inquisitive as he was, Ligeti had tapped into this during our conversations and its trace can be found in the fourth movement of the Piano Concerto.

One can also follow the process

$$\begin{cases} x_{n+1} = 4x_n(1-x_n) \\ n = 0, 1, 2, 3, \ldots \end{cases}$$

in another way. As we have seen in the beginning, for $x_0 = 3$, for instance, the process always runs further in the minuses. For x_0 between 0 and 1, however, the resulting values are between 0 and 1. We can check that, in fact, for initial values x_0 smaller than 0 and x_0 bigger than 1 the iteration always drop in the minuses. Accordingly, we have two types of behaviour: for x_0 taken from the interval [0,1], the iterated values stay within [0,1]; one could say, they are *imprisoned*, and for x_0 taken outside of [0,1], the iterated values tumble down into the minuses, one could say, they are *escaping*. The set of all such initial values is called the escape set. The set of the initial values x_0 for which the iteration remains imprisoned is called the prisoner set. The set of points which separates the escape and prisoner set is called the Julia set.[11] But we are in for another surprise if we change a, for instance, to $a = 4.2$. We agree that there are still initial values x_0 for which the iteration remains imprisoned in the Julia set, and others for which the iteration continues to fall into the minuses, for example, when $x_0 = 1$, then the iteration will not escape, while for $x_0 = 0.5$, the iteration will escape. Whereas the prisoner set for $a = 4$ was the interval [0,1], it is now, for $a = 4.2$, endlessly fragmented, and here the prisoner set and the Julia set coincide. Mathematicians speak here of a Cantor set (see Figure 5), a historical example of a fractal. The iteration stays imprisoned on this set and behaves chaotically; that is, the smallest inaccuracies can cause big deviations. As long as a is greater then 4, the situation remains the same: the Julia set is fractal and the iteration on it is chaotic. This situation seems very special and it is the simplest example of one of the fundamental discoveries in mathematics at the end of the 20th century: an image pattern which is generated by a chaotic process is typically a fractal. Fractal geometry is the geometry of chaos and self-similarity, and the replication of a greater whole in its smaller parts is a typical attribute of chaos.

Let's look again at the example for $a = 4$. Here the prisoner set was the interval [0,1]. But is it also self-similar? Indeed it is, a degenerated fractal maybe, but still a self-similar object because one can divide the interval in two parts, for instance [0, ½] and [½,1], which look like the whole only smaller.

We have nearly reached our goal, which will at least hint at what Ligeti found so fascinating with the Julia set and especially with Figure 2. Let's take another look at the iteration

[11] Named after the mathematician Gaston Julia who examined these phenomena at the beginning of the twentieth century, still without a computer naturally.

$$\begin{cases} x_{n+1} = ax_n(1-x_n) \\ n = 0,1,2,3,\ldots \end{cases}$$

this time from a new angle. Instead of using normal numbers we will now iterate with so-called complex numbers. Through a system of coordinates every point of a plane can be described as a pair $z = (x,y)$. To calculate with complex numbers is nothing more than doing arithmetic with these pairs of numbers. Likewise, we can extend the value of a to a complex number.

$$\begin{cases} z_{n+1} = az_n(1-z_n) \\ n = 0,1,2,3,\ldots \end{cases}$$

The iteration now describes the motion of a point in a plane and we can observe again two patterns of behaviour: either the iteration moves further and further to the outside – the iteration *escapes*, or it doesn't – the iteration remains *imprisoned*. In this way, for any choice of a we have again the escape set and the prisoner set, and the Julia set is the set separating the escape and prisoner set (more precisely, the Julia set is the boundary of the escape set). Depending on how a is chosen, the Julia set either is a dust – that is, a Cantor set – or it is not (more precisely, a connected set). When it is a dust, the iteration on the Julia set is chaotic, and so fractals and chaos come together again. In fact, in the last decades, mathematicians and scientists have learned that chaos and fractals form a twin pair: if a process is chaotic it typically leaves a fractal trace, and the process behind a fractal is often chaotic.

Our many conversations helped Ligeti to work out for himself these dimensions in great depth and his fascination was comparable to that of those who had first made the discoveries in the 20th century.

Figure 5 The step-by-step development of a Cantor set: one begins with the interval [0, 1], divides it in three equal parts and takes the middle part out. That leaves the parts [0, ⅓] and [⅔, 1]. Then you once again take the middle parts out and are left with the intervals [0, ⅑], [²⁄₉, ⅓], [⅔, ⁷⁄₉] and [⁸⁄₉, 1]. This procedure is repeated several times: the middle parts are always taken out of the remaining intervals of the previous step. In the fifth step we already have $2^5 = 32$ parts, and if one carries on the iterative process, there are, at the end, an infinite number of parts, which then make up the Cantor set. The iterative process depicts a systematic fragmentation, leaving at the end only a 'dust' of points.

If we look at Bauhaus architecture, we see the concept standing naked in front of us and we can describe it using the elements of Euclidean geometry. The structure of a classical composition is also more or less easy to describe. A Ligeti Étude or the *Poème symphonique* is barely analysable with traditional elements of description. Here it is the process itself which is defining, and it is not a coincidence that the structure of many of Ligeti's works resembles the structure of chaos. If the Ligeti fractal (Figure 2) made a strong impression on him it was not just because of its apparent beauty but rather that it was obtained from an extremely simple mathematical process! Let's remember that the generative process for this pattern is encoded in the formula $az(1-z)$ for $a = (0.111, 1.222)$. This is nearly unbelievable and sheds a new light on the complexity of nature. We are used to thinking that a complex pattern needs a complex process for its generation. And what we see here is an image whose complexity and also appealing beauty is unequalled, and still the process which engendered it could not be simpler. Ligeti also understood this, he always asked probing questions and dared to venture towards the most difficult mathematical heights. He called the picture I had dedicated to him 'the maelstrom' (Figure 6). It inspired him to musical processes which played a fundamental role in the composition of the fourth movement of the Piano Concerto. But the correspondence is by no means superficial and should not be understood as programme music.[12]

I knew Ligeti as a probing inquirer, who was rooted in music history as well as in his own time. It is not necessary to know that mathematics – especially chaos and the fractals, and other sciences, particularly the psychology of perception – fascinated him in order to fall under the spell of his music. However both were for him more than a stimulus. He felt like someone who, through his work, participated and contributed in his own way to these exciting fields, and I think he succeeded in an inimitable way.

When I think of the *friend* Ligeti, I think with immense gratitude of the wonderful gift that binds me to him forever. He once phoned me on my birthday and surprised me with the news that he wanted to dedicate to me his 17th Étude for Piano. Also smaller gifts are cherished. As we were walking back to our hotel after a joint appearance at the music festival in Huddersfield, I admired his magnificent umbrella. 'It comes from Harrods in London and now it's yours,' he said succinctly. Of course, it was impossible not to accept the gift: 'If it makes you feel any better, you can explain to me how Mandelbrot found the term self-similarity.' That's the way he was, my friend György Ligeti.

Translated by Louise Duchesneau

Figure 6 *(overleaf)* Excerpt from the Ligeti Fractal – the maelstrom

[12] Ligeti on the fourth movement of his Piano Concerto: 'The whole structure of the piece is self-similar and the impression we get is that of a giant interconnected web ... This vast self-similar maelstrom can be traced back – indirectly – to musical ideas which had been unleashed by beautiful fractal images of the Julia and Mandelbrot sets ... Not that I used iterative calculations when I composed this piece ... rather, it originated out of an intuitive synesthetic correspondence on a poetic level.' György Ligeti, 'Zu meinem Klavierkonzert (1988)', in *Gesammelte Schriften*, vol. 2, p. 299; translated by Louise Duchesneau.

Simha Arom and Pygmy performers rehearsing for a concert to celebrate Ligeti's 80th birthday in Vienna (2003)

6 A Kinship Foreseen: Ligeti and African Music

SIMHA AROM IN CONVERSATION[1]

Meeting Ligeti I

Wolfgang MARX Shall we try to go back to when you met Ligeti for the first time, I think it was in 1984? Do you remember that meeting?

Simha AROM I didn't remember exactly when it had taken place so I had to look it up. At the time, I was involved in a joint project of the CNRS (Centre National de la Recherche Scientifique) and the Centre for the Study of Jewish Music which is part of the Hebrew University of Jerusalem and whose director was professor Israel Adler. I was working with a small group of young researchers on the plurivocality of Yemenite Jewish liturgy and we were sitting in a seminar room when suddenly – it was about 11 o'clock – someone knocked on the door. I opened, Professor Adler came in and said, 'Simha, may I disturb you for a moment, I am here with maestro Ligeti and he would like to meet you.' I was very surprised, I wondered why he wanted to see me and after telling my group to wait a minute I went outside in the hall, where Ligeti said to me, 'I've heard your records and would very much like to know more about your work. Do you think we could meet?' I said, 'With pleasure', and since I had a small pied-à-terre in Jerusalem I invited him to come over that afternoon. Ligeti then asked if he could come with his wife and his son and I answered that, of course, they were also welcome. They came at two in the afternoon, and stayed until seven o'clock ...

What had happened was that Ligeti had been chatting with Adler in his office when he mentioned polyrhythm. Israel then said to him: 'Oh, if you are interested in polyrhythm, you have to meet Simha Arom.' 'Do you know him?', Ligeti asked. 'Of course, he is a very old friend of mine,' Adler answered. So Ligeti asked how he could meet me and Adler said that I was presently one floor above them. That's how this first meeting came about. In the afternoon, Ligeti said that he only knew some records of mine but none of my theoretical work. We had a good discussion and I played many examples for him, especially examples of re-recording.

Re-recording

This is a recording method, which I conceived in order to be able to understand the very complex Central African polyphonic music. It allows to isolate each constituent part of a polyphonic or polyrhythmic piece without causing it to become desynchronized in relation to the other parts. It is then possible to transcribe and analyse the piece.

To carry out a *re-recording* all you need to do is to connect two portable stereo tape recorders together. A previously made recording of the polyphonic piece one wants to analyse is played on the first tape recorder and transmitted through a headset to the first musician who will perform. He is asked to play his part again while he listens to the original recording. His performance is picked up by a microphone and recorded, *on its own*, on the left track of the second tape recorder while the piece, played by the whole

[1] This interview was conducted in Paris by Louise Duchesneau and Wolfgang Marx on 19 November 2008.

ensemble of musicians, is simultaneously re-recorded on the right track of the second tape recorder. Consequently, the first musician's part is on the left track, completely separate from the rest. Then we rewind the tapes and switch them. Following this principle, the whole piece is synthetically reconstructed, always with the same procedure: the first musician's part is transmitted to the headset of the second musician; this part is re-recorded on the right track of the second tape recorder while the left track will feature the part played by the second musician who is listening to his predecessor through the headset. The resulting recording allows one to listen simultaneously, but also singly, to the perfectly synchronous parts of the two musicians. One only needs to repeat the procedure with each musician in as many sequences in order to obtain, two by two, the separate and synchronous recordings of all of the parts. (That is, the first musician plays along with the entire piece, the second musician follows only the first musician, the third musician plays with the second musician, and so on.) At the same time, the Elders, who have been given a number of headsets, accept or reject the successive recordings. At the end of this operation we have each voice separately but also in combination with another (1 + 2, 2 + 3, 3 + 4, etc.). But there is still one very important thing missing: how can we synchronize this in time? what is the common beat to all these parts? In Africa, most music is without a materialized beat, that is, the beat is inside the performers – they know where it has to be. After I have finished the whole process of recording and re-recording, I just ask someone to put headphones on and to clap to the music of each isolated part. This gives me what I call an *organic* metronome, which is inherent to the music we have just recorded. I can then draw vertical bars through the parts and put together an authentic score of the piece.[2]

Louise DUCHESNEAU That's very clever because the beat is not obvious to us. I heard many of Simha's lectures when he had musicians with him and he would ask the audience to clap to the beat. The audience would try to find it but nobody ever knew where the beat was. So this method of finding it is really very clever.

AROM One of the main things I discovered while working with this music is that I was often wrong. I learned many things: for instance, that Africans don't feel co-metric, that is, they don't go with the beat as we do. The accents in African music mostly come against the beat, as off-beats. So you are misled because you listen to accents and you tell yourself 'That has to be a strong beat.' But the music has neither strong nor weak beats, it only has beats which are all equal, a continuum of regular pulses which are in the mind of the performers.

MARX Now, if they play that a second time, would it be exactly the same?

AROM Exactly the same.

MARX There is no element of improvisation in it?

AROM Not in the least. I worked on this because an experiment has no value if the results are different the second time around. I went from village to village, in the same ethnic group where all speak the same language and

---

[2] Simha Arom, 'The Use of Play-Back Techniques in the Study of Oral Polyphonies', *Ethnomusicology* 20/3 (1976), pp. 483–519.

have the same music, and I played one track. 'What you will hear belongs to a piece of yours, could you please clap to it?', I would ask. Meanwhile I had headphones on and was listening, on the other track, to the clapping that was already recorded. And it was always exactly the same, except if someone made a mistake, so this validated the results I had found. I came back to the same villages one year later and the first thing I always did was to check what I had done the time before. I would say, 'Please, clap to this', and there was never any problem. But why should this be so? It took me some years to understand this. I always asked myself: 'How can they know when to clap if they don't usually clap when the music is playing? What is the cognitive clue for this?' And the answer is so simple that I am ashamed to think about it even today. I found it, I will always remember, while I was shaving. Suddenly I had the answer: in Africa, music is almost always connected to dance so the beat they were clapping is the materialization of the basic dance step. When you ask someone to clap, in 95% of the cases he immediately gives you the pulse of the basic dance step. It can happen that the musicians don't understand when I ask them just to clap. Sometimes they confuse just clapping a regular beat with a rhythmic pattern. So I would say to the musician I had asked to clap the beat to 'Listen through the headphones and dance on the spot where you stand by moving only your feet.' This way you got a regular pulse. Then I said 'Now clap to your feet', and he clapped synchronously, and so I said 'Now stop moving your feet and go on clapping.' And there it was.

You know, in this profession one has to use lots of small things such as this. When my students come back from the field and say they have found a wonderful piece they would like to transcribe, the first thing I ask them is: 'Did you record the clapping?' When they say 'No', I send them back. Why? Because, if you don't have the clapping you cannot accurately transcribe a piece of African music and so your transcription would only be speculative. If you want to transcribe it correctly you must have the beat, the pulse those people use because, if not, you betray the music, you don't have *their* conception of how the music should be. Look, if you have a piece whose period has 12 beats and each beat – or pulse – is divided on a ternary basis into three small values – i.e. 36 – you have seven theoretical possibilities to place the beat, but only one is the right one. This is very important. My colleagues here in Paris at the Musée de l'Homme would laugh at me and say, 'Ah, Arom, he pulses.' But nowadays, everyone pulses. In the '70s, when I was a beginner, no one understood why I did this. All of a sudden, 30 years later, everyone writes about pulsation – then nobody was talking about it. Why was this so important to me? Because I was a musician before becoming an ethnomusicologist. This made all the difference.

But let me now finish the story about Ligeti.

Meeting Ligeti II

Ligeti was very astonished when he listened to the examples of re-recording I played for him during our meeting in Jerusalem because he had not expected anything like this. He asked me what I had written about this and I gave him copies of some articles I had with me. He read these and we began to exchange letters. You know, Ligeti's letters were always very funny. He would send typed letters on which he had added comments by hand.

He would begin to write on one side of the page and continue around it, all in different colours.

So that was the beginning of our acquaintance. Then, in early 1988, I received a letter from Manfred Stahnke in which he wrote that he was a pupil of Ligeti's and that they were organizing a symposium for his 65th birthday at the Hamburg Musikhochschule.[3] He also wrote that Ligeti had insisted that I be invited to give a talk. I was very honoured and I answered that if I came to give a lecture, which I would very much like to do because I knew that Ligeti was interested in polyrhythm, I would propose that they also invite a group of four African drummers I sometimes worked with, so that I could give a live demonstration. This was Gamako, a group living in Nantes, and they were invited. I remember that after we finished, Ligeti came on the podium and kissed all of us.

After that, every time he was invited to a festival of his music, he would ask that I also give a workshop or a lecture. 'Bring me Simha,' he would say. He would sometimes come to Paris and once he came to my laboratory. There he met my advanced students and we talked about the interactive experiments we were conducting on the often very complex African scales. We also showed him videos we had made on these experiments.

African scales

Our aim was to understand how Africans conceive their anhemitonic pentatonic, non-temperate scales. An African traditional musician cannot verbalize about this out of context, you can't ask him if it's the D that is too sharp or the E that is too flat, so we had to find an experimental way of doing this. It so happened that when I came to Hamburg in 1988, I was sitting in a bistro with John Chowning, Louis Dandrel and Jean-Claude Risset. We were discussing this problem and I asked them what solution they could offer. 'There is only one,' they answered, 'the Yamaha DX7 II.' In fact, this synthesizer can be pre-programmed with different timbres as well as with different pitches. You have a cursor and many knobs by which you can modify the pitch and timbre as you wish.

When I left Hamburg I went to Cologne. The next day, while I was taking a walk, I happened on a music shop which had synthesizers on show. I went in and asked if they had a Yamaha DX7 II. They did and I asked if I could see how it worked. After I came back to Paris I thought: 'Well, that's wonderful, but I cannot ask African xylophonists to play on a synthesizer.' I didn't sleep for two nights just thinking about this, and I finally found a solution. You take a sheet of plywood and cut it up so that it goes in the place of certain keys of the synthesizer (thereby neutralizing all the other keys) and you attach the pieces on the keyboard with Velcro.

You put as many of these plywood keys as you need to simulate a xylophone on the synthesizer. And since the DX7 II could memorize different timbres, we pre-programmed it according to a certain number of

---

[3] The colloquium, entitled 'Bilder einer Musik', took place at the Musikhochschule in Hamburg, 12–14 November 1988. A selected number of contributions are published in Constantin Floros *et al.*, eds., *Für György Ligeti: Die Referate des Ligeti-Kongresses Hamburg 1988*, Hamburger Jahrbuch für Musikwissenschaft 2 (Laaber, 1991).

xylophones whose tuning we had already recorded in Africa. All this we did at IRCAM (Institut de Recherche et Coordination Acoustique/Musique) in Paris so that when we came to the villages we could ask the musicians, 'Look, we have remade your instrument on this. Do you want to try to play it?' And the moment they began to play they could not stop. I asked them if this was the timbre, the colour of their instrument, if it sounded like their instrument. We showed them that they had the possibility to change the timbre and how they could do it themselves. The key idea was that everything should be interactive. They could push this knob and play, and then push another one till the resulting timbre was to their liking. Since they don't know how to read, we had put little stickers of different colours on the knobs and with that they managed. So it became easy for them to play on the synthesizer with their own mallets. After that, we asked them if the synthesizer sounded like their xylophone. One of them answered that it was like 'the twin' of his instrument. We then showed them the cursor on the Yamaha and said, 'If you don't like the pitch of one of the keys, you can change it, you can just go up or down here.' And they immediately did it and did it well. When they would say, 'This one is not good,' about one of the bars we would tell them to go ahead and change it with the help of the cursor. And they did it. We had a Macintosh with a generator because there was no electricity there so, in order to use the information later on, we recorded all their adjustments in the memory of the computer. We proceeded like this in five different ethnic groups with 12 types of xylophones. In a photo you see an ensemble of four xylophones where two musicians (whose parts were in different ranges) first started to play on the synthesizer and right after that were joined by the two *real* instruments. This was the validation that our experiment worked because it meant that the other musicians also accepted the synthesizer. And something else was significant. There were always a few people sitting around the player with the synthesizer. When the tuning was good, these people began to sing a few seconds after he began to play. So we understood right away that if they didn't sing a short while after the music started there must be something wrong with the tuning. We gathered a lot of information, which would have been inaccessible any other way, with this experimental method by just giving the musicians the opportunity to do it themselves. That was in 1989, 20 years ago, and we filmed it all on video. It is now almost an historical document.

Meeting Ligeti III

So to come back to Ligeti, he came to our laboratory because I wanted to show him the videos we had made on the African scales. We met many times after that and wrote each other often. In the beginning there were things he did not understand, and I explained them to him in letters. Then we met again and so on.

MARX This at the time he started experimenting with different intonations, different tuning systems?

DUCHESNEAU No, I think what mainly interested him was polyrhythm. He had already experimented with different tuning systems in *Ramifications, Passacaglia ungherese* or *Clocks and Clouds,* for instance.

AROM One of the things which interested him was polyrhythm and the other one was the effect of polyrhythm – ambiguity. In this play with ambiguity he was a master. He did not say it explicitly but it is what he was looking for. And this has nothing to do with the illusory patterns which Gerhard Kubik says he found in African music. Ligeti liked to quote this but I never agreed with Kubik's theory that the superimposition of different rhythms produces illusory patterns.[4] It may be right for Ligeti and that was maybe his intention, but it does not come from African music, I am convinced of that. We have it in Western music since the Baroque, for instance in the Bach chaconne for solo violin. There, it's exactly the same phenomenon: the musician plays a lot of broken chords, and what you hear are different melodic lines, which unfold in different registers. That's precisely the same principle.

MARX Perhaps it's different in your case because you bring together five, ten people, each playing their own layer. The result is something not a single one of them could have produced, only the group. However, Ligeti writes his Piano Études for one pianist who has to play three or four or five of these layers on his own. Is this perhaps where the difference lies?

AROM This was another of his preoccupations, to give the impression of having different tempi with only one pianist. He also included pitch classes, for example, in *Désordre*, which was his first piece influenced by African music. As such, it is based on equal periods, like in African music. The periodicity doesn't move, what changes is the time interval between the emergence of the high pitches, which are distributed in non-similar ways in the different periods. So, every time you think you've perceived it correctly you are baffled because it doesn't come back at the moment you expect it ... This is very interesting because it means he constructed rhythmic configurations just by displacing pitches.

Accents, tension and release

For me this was quite familiar because when I came to Africa I tried to understand where the beat was. All of a sudden I was hearing a high pitch in the melody, then low pitches and a high pitch again, and the time interval between the high pitches was never the same. At first I thought the high pitches must be the strong beats because I was in the Western frame of mind at the time. Then I began to understand that a rhythmical effect can be caused by the higher pitches when they are perceived as being stronger. They aren't stronger by any means, they are just higher, and what we perceive as higher we immediately assume is accented. That was one thing. The other was the polyrhythmic effect when accents, produced by different instruments of an ensemble, 'cross' each other, i.e. when they are antagonistic to each other.

MARX But the pulse is quite clear, isn't it?

---

[4] See in particular: Gerhard Kubik, *Zum Verstehen afrikanischer Musik, ausgewählte Aufsätze* (Leipzig, 1988), and many articles in Artur Simon, ed., *Musik in Afrika*, Veröffentlichung des Museums für Völkerkunde Berlin, Folge 40, Abteilung Musikethnologie IV (Berlin, 1983), for instance, Gerhard Kubik, 'Die Amadinda-Musik von Buganda', pp. 139–65.

AROM In African music, the pulse is mostly inherent, i.e. it is not materialized. That is one of the things which fascinated Ligeti. In Western classical music you have two basic notions: tension and release. In African music you have no release. Polyrhythm stems from the antagonism between, let's say, three drums. And if you clap on top of that, you have four parts: three drums, the accents of which are in contradiction with each other and the clapping, which is in contradiction with all of them, because they are offbeat – and you never have rests. This produces a continuous tension, which ends only when the piece ends. Ligeti immediately noticed this and he writes about it in the foreword to my book. What was also interesting for him was that he had discovered music that was all tension and no release.

MARX When does an African piece end? Is there some point where things come together again, for instance, or is there a decision made to stop at a certain point?

AROM Exactly. I would say they stop when they are tired.

MARX So it's not like Steve Reich's music, in which one part goes out of phase, and when it comes together again it stops. For instance, there may be a pulse of eight in the left hand and seven in the right hand, the whole thing lasts for 56 beats and when it all comes together again, the piece is over.

African and medieval music (and Ligeti is never far away)

AROM That is the principle of African polyrhythm, which Steve Reich learned in Ghana. For him, there is a reason why it stops where it stops but in Africa it doesn't work like that. For instance, this music is functional, so when people dance to music, they dance for a reason. Because they don't have electricity, they rejoice in the light of the full moon and dance. There are ceremonies, for instance when someone is critically ill or when someone dies, that oblige you to dance the whole night long. The music never stops. The drummers replace each other: when one is tired another one jumps in. I have been in villages where I couldn't sleep all night because someone had died …

And the tension is always present: when you try to find the pulse, which throbs through the music, you think you have it and ten seconds later you say no, it's not right. You can listen to many performances and unless you have a clue you cannot find it. The only clue you have is the basic step of the dancers' feet. Only then can you organize mentally what you hear. This is the kind of thing, which interested Ligeti, because he was looking for the smallest unit – what he called the fast pulsation – on which to build his layers of different tempi. This fast pulsation, which results from subdividing the pulse – i.e. the inherent beat – was something he found in my writings. I told him once that he would have found it eventually by himself. He had more than the necessary intellectual equipment, such a memory, such a mind, culture and curiosity. It would just have taken him a bit more time, that's all. He would also mention how attracted and fascinated he was by the time of Philippe de Vitry, Guillaume de Machaut and Johannes Ciconia – the *ars subtilior*, which is exactly what Africans do. African music only seems more complex than the music of *ars subtilior* because its tempo is faster. You have no time to organize your perception. You see that there is a *Gestalt* there, but you cannot find it, you don't have the time to seize it. In *ars subtilior* we can have pieces with six voices. The principle of *tempus perfectum* and *tempus imperfectum* ruled here. It's exactly like the absence of strong and weak beats, Ligeti knew this. Strong and weak beats were first introduced in dance music in the 18th century. Before that it was *tactus* and then *tempus*. Both were even beats, there was no 'measure', and African music is exactly the same. I wrote an article about this, 'Une parenté inattendue', an unforeseen kinship between African music and medieval music.[5] We can find much in medieval music which exists in African music, such as the principle of hocket, or the principle of harmony, for instance, which is based on octaves, fifths and fourth, All this existed in both cultures although they never had any contact.

MARX Also, there is no release in isorhythm. You can have a part running in two, the other in three, so the one in two is always behind and the piece ends at some point without the parts having caught up.

AROM In isorhythm you always have a residue, something left over that you don't know what to do with. In African music you have periods and what I call macroperiods. A macroperiod is a construct in which everyone starts and ends together but within which the parts present different periodicities. Everyone plays till they all meet at the same junction point. Before that all the layers are asymmetrical. And since this period is much bigger than any period played by any part, I call it the *macroperiod*.

MARX And that is where Steve Reich says the piece can stop. But do Africans have this in mind, does reaching this point play a part in their music? Would Africans realize they have reached this point and that this is a special point? Or does it not matter?

AROM That's not a type of question you can ask because they cannot answer. What is important is not so much that they have in mind 'Here we are and here we begin' but that they know exactly what the relationship between the parts has to be.

Meeting Ligeti IV

MARX I see, it's not teleological. This is what minimal music was accused of and some pieces by Ligeti could fall into that category as well: the process is not teleological. There is no reason why it ends where it ends. And some people say the same thing about much of Western contemporary art music: it stops, but there is no obvious reason why it stops there, it could go on or could have stopped somewhere else.

AROM You have just described contemporary music. When I listen to a contemporary piece of what seems to me to be of lesser quality, and this happens quite often, I sometimes ask myself why the composer shouldn't have stopped right there, why did he go on? I don't hear anything new,

[5] Simha Arom, 'Une parenté inattendue: polyphonies médiévales et polyphonies africaines', in *Polyphonies de tradition orale: histoire et traditions vivantes, Actes du Colloque de Royaumont 1990*, ed. Michel Huglo and Marcel Pérès (Paris, 1994), pp. 133–48.

the treatment of the material is absolutely imperceptible. It's then that I switch off.

MARX Well, sometimes there is something but it's inaudible. If you take serial music, for instance, there is something there but few can actually follow the rows, it is rather music to be read, analysed.

When Ligeti wrote the pieces which were influenced by African music, did he contact you, were you in touch with him, did he ask you about some detail on rhythm?

AROM No, he used principles, most of which he found in my publications. I don't think he used any African rhythms, he used the principles and ideas, and they fired his imagination. Then he put everything in a pot and let it simmer like a soup on the stove. He did not quote African music and he was not consciously imitating African music. For my 65th birthday some colleagues and my students offered me a *Festschrift*. They had asked Berio, Boulez and Ligeti to contribute, and Ligeti sent a sketch from the Violin Concerto. After examining it closely I said to him, 'I wonder if you are conscious of the fact that everything on this page is the so-called pan-African standard pattern 2–2–3–2–3?' He answered, surprised, 'Really? No!' I recently found by chance on the web a study by a young man named David Isgitt, who did his Master of Music at the University of Texas in 2002. It's a very good analysis of periodic rhythmic structure in the music of Steve Reich and György Ligeti. He quotes Ligeti about *Désordre*: 'Another fundamental characteristic of African music was significant to me: the simultaneity of symmetry and asymmetry.' That was another important fact, which Ligeti found in my writings. Isgitt continues quoting Ligeti: 'The cycles are always structured asymmetrically (e.g. twelve parts in 7+5).'[6] That's exactly what I have described, and I didn't know that Ligeti had used it in *Désordre*. To my mind, however, he searched for new ways of fabricating rhythms without being consciously influenced. And what is also interesting here is that the tension thus created is never ending.

Aksak, the Balkans (and Ligeti always ...)

MARX But Ligeti found some of these rhythms in Eastern Europe as well, did he not?

AROM I think that by this you mean *aksak* rhythms, which always result from grouping together short binary and ternary values (such as 2–2–3–2). I wrote a long article on *aksak* some years ago, in which I tried to form a theory about this phenomenon.[7] I established the following typology: first, there is true *aksak*, which is built on prime numbers (adding up to 5, 7, 11, 13 etc. of such short values); then quasi-*aksak*, that is, rhythms which give rise to an *odd* number but are divisible into equidistant pulsations (such as 9 or 15); and finally pseudo-*aksak*, which is based on even numbers (such

[6] David Isgitt, 'An Analysis of Periodic Rhythmic Structures in the Music of Steve Reich and György Ligeti' (Master of Music thesis, University of North Texas, 2002), p. 57; quoted from booklet notes to György Ligeti, *Works for Piano*, György Ligeti Edition 3, Sony Classical 62308 (1997).

[7] Simha Arom, 'L'aksak: principes et typologie', *Cahiers de musiques traditionnelles* 17, 'Formes Musicales' (2005), pp. 11–48.

as 8 in 3–2–3, or 12 in 2–2–3–2–3, or 16 in 2–2–2–3–2–2–3) and whose rhythms are thus globally symmetrical. Here in *Désordre*, 7 and 5 is a pseudo-*aksak*. If you ask Africans to clap to this figure, they will divide it into four regular ternary beats (since $4 \times 3 = 12$). A figure of 7 and 5 illustrates a fascinating African principle, which I named 'rhythmic oddity', i.e. globally symmetrical figures that you can never segment into two equal parts. The result will always be 'half plus one / half minus one': $8 = 5+3$, $12 = 7+5$, $16 = 9+7$, and $24 = 13+11$. And that creates tension. It's brilliant. How did the Africans find it? Nobody knows.

MARX But Ligeti came from the Balkans and had studied this music, therefore I think it possibly made him more open to or interested in this kind of music. He was familiar with it – unlike Messiaen, for instance, who added an extra note to a rhythmic pattern because he didn't like symmetry and regularity (the 'rhythms with added values'). The result was something like $8+1$, which of course still means he thinks in terms of what is normal and what is not. In this case, $8+1$ is not normal. That's not what Ligeti would have thought.

AROM No, because to have a rhythmic pattern you need at least either two different values, or some mark – like an accent – on one of them. There has to be a contrast between the two. However, I don't believe Ligeti would have thought that this was a combined *aksak* which gave him overall symmetry because 7 and 5 is 12 (thus producing a regular 123–123–123 or 1234–1234–1234). The reason for this is that *Désordre* was inspired by African music as he says in the foreword to the English translation of my book: 'I also began to sense a strong inner tension between the relentlessness of the constant, never-changing pulse, coupled with the absolute symmetry of the formal architecture on the one hand and the asymmetrical internal divisions of the pattern on the other.'[8] The fact that you are always floating between groupings of 2 and of 3, but in a symmetrical framework, is fascinating. You don't have that in normal *aksak*.

MARX The other thing, of course, is that at some stage in Ligeti's music the regularity most often starts to break down. You have wonderful mottos at the beginning of your book. One of them is by Jacques Chailley who says 'There is no music in the proper sense unless man imposes some kind of order.'[9] And *Désordre*, for instance, starts in a very ordered way with these patterns running against each other. After a while, however, Ligeti deliberately destroys the regularity by adding a note or taking one out. We have that much earlier in *Continuum* as well. As he says himself it starts like a machine but he doesn't want it to run periodically forever, so he takes a cogwheel out and it starts to auto-destruct. Is this not the breaking down of order?

AROM This is exactly what we are talking about. At that time, Ligeti was acquainted with the work of Steve Reich and Terry Riley, and in Reich's dephasing similar principles apply. After the dephasing another pattern begins, with another periodicity, because if it didn't, we would fall asleep ...

---

[8] György Ligeti, 'Foreword', in Simha Arom, *African Polyphony and Polyrhythm: Musical Structure and Methodology* (Cambridge, 1991), pp. xvii–xviii, at p. xvii.

[9] Ibid., p. xv.

MARX So would you say that this is a kind of meta-order, or is it just an apparent breakdown of order?

AROM I think it is a kind of meta-order. Let me quote Ligeti on this. 'What we can witness in this [African] music is a wonderful combination of order and disorder which in turn merges together producing a sense of order on a higher level.'[10] He said so many things in this short text, it is so condensed and still important for me today. And it really answers your question. If you have no disorder at a lower level, it's boring because it sounds mechanical. And so, what he did – and that's exactly what he liked in African music – was to combine disorder at a lower level with order at a higher level.

Meeting Ligeti V (with Cage and Stravinsky)

MARX When did you meet Ligeti for the last time?

AROM It was in Vienna for the Wien Modern concerts in the fall of 2003. Pierre-Laurent Aimard was there with his wife Irina and their children, I came with my wife Sonia and Ligeti came to the concert in a wheelchair.

MARX We talked about order and disorder. Just as an aside, what do you make of Cage's indeterminacy in music, which tries to be 'unordered' from the very beginning? Is that music?

AROM I personally am not a fan of this, as you can imagine, because by pushing things to this extreme the whole thing just becomes a joke.

MARX It's making a philosophical point ...

AROM I understand but I'm not a philosopher, I'm a musician and as a concert-goer, I want to hear music, not 4′ 33″ of silence ... Of course things happen around you, but they happen whether you sit in a church without saying a word, in a mosque or in a synagogue. There is something there, of course, but is this creating something new? It seems that today everything has to create something new. It's terrible.

MARX It's postmodern.

AROM Yes, but are we not already in 'post-postmodernism', because what else can we do after postmodernism? I'm not a fan of these things and I'm quite conservative in my tastes. Ligeti said to me once, 'Simha, you don't like my music.' (He could be very nasty when he was in a bad mood.) I said, 'Why do you say that? What makes you think that?' To me he was one of those rare composers, maybe the unique one, who in every work created something new, something which had not been there before. Of how many composers in the second half of the 20th century can we say this? Of course, there are pieces I like more than others and some about which I was not absolutely enthusiastic, but that's my private opinion ... I was utterly fascinated by the richness of this man's musical imagination, by his 'know-how', by his virtuosity and also by his courage. Take the second movement of the Violin Concerto, it's not even postmodern, it's post-romantic with its huge melody that goes back to Sibelius. Who would dare to do something like that today? But that's the way he felt, how he expressed himself.

MARX And that's what he was criticized for.

[10] Ibid., p. xvii.

AROM But I think it's very courageous. He said in his music what he felt he wanted to say. And it did not matter to him how people reacted. I did not know he was criticized – by whom?

DUCHESNEAU Well, he was criticized by the avant-garde who were responsible for keeping the faith. 'You betrayed us, you went retro on us, you became post-romantic, all these octaves.' He was criticized very much for the Horn Trio, and he was criticized for the Piano Concerto – a famous conductor said it was just a bit more complicated than Gershwin.

AROM This is interesting. Maybe what I will say now is not very exact, but thinking about this brings to my mind that his itinerary was quite similar to Stravinsky's. Stravinsky had periods – from neo-classicism to atonality to serialism – finally he always did what he really wanted to do. And I think both of them probably went through different manners, abandoned them when they did not believe in them anymore and then turned to something else.

MARX That is a very good comparison because there are three Stravinskys and to me there are three Ligetis as well – the micropolyphonic one, the polyrhythmic one and the microtonal one. And I feel that, in a way, they all come together at some point.

AROM I agree. Both Ligeti's and Stravinsky's paths were similar. Most composers just find one way of writing and then keep to it. Maybe a third composer who continuously renewed his own work, but in a different way, was Luciano Berio.

DUCHESNEAU And all three made great use of folk music and folk songs.

AROM It seems that Stravinsky invented the folk music he used.

DUCHESNEAU Sometimes he did, sometimes he heard melodies on the street and borrowed them. Ligeti did the same thing, taking the tunes from known folklore and also composing folk tunes.

MARX But again, it is an allusion, it would be 'in the style of' rather than authentic quotations.

AROM I once wrote a short article about the relationship between traditional music and composers of the 20th century, and I call this 'faux folklore', 'fake folk music', imaginary folk music.[11]

DUCHESNEAU That's what Ligeti called it too – imaginary folk music.

AROM That's interesting because he was influenced by Bartók in many ways, and Bartók used real melodies.

MARX Yes, Bartók collected them.

DUCHESNEAU Ligeti also collected folk music in Romania in the 1950s. Besides he transcribed folk music from wax cylinders, among these some of Bartók's. He filled little booklets with his transcriptions and would refer to them when composing.

MARX As you said before, it is interesting to note that he used the principle and would not quote exactly. I often compare that to Charles Ives because Ives always quotes. You have many different rhythmic layers in different

[11] Simha Arom, 'Musiques traditionnelles et création contemporaine', in *Catalogue de l'exposition André Jolivet – 'Les objets de Mana'* (Paris, 2003), pp. 27–32.

instruments – one plays in 3/2, the other in 3/4, another one in 4/4, and a fourth in 12/8. And if you look closely, you can recognize the hymns he quotes. Ligeti, on the other hand, is a bit like Mahler in a way. Mahler's melodies sound Bohemian or Hungarian ...

AROM ... or Jewish. Berio also quoted many times, and he did it in a very clever manner. What he did with Central African Banda-Linda horn music in *Coro* is quite impressive. However, in this case, he did not quote. Rather, he used the African principle of hocket in a very sophisticated way.

MARX I sometimes find it easier to listen to Ives' Fourth Symphony if it is well played because you can actually recognize something you know, you can follow it and take it as a guideline while trying to put the rest in context, whereas it is more difficult initially to find your way into a piece if it's a stylistic quote. Once you have it, it is fine, but it's this initial approach which is difficult.

AROM How do you know when you have it?

MARX When I feel comfortable with it, I think.

AROM I ask this question, because there are types of African music which can be listened to in different ways. What you hear is an amalgam of sounds out of which you choose a melodic line – if you know the available ones.

MARX So you create some imaginary leading part that is your own. It is a little bit like the *Poème symphonique for 100 Metronomes* where I always – and I think most people do – pick one of the metronomes and I follow its beat. There is no reason for choosing this particular one, it's just the one I pick and then relate everything else to it.

AROM David Isgitt writes of three types of music in Ligeti's work: the mechanical music of *Continuum*, the minimalist music à la Reich and Riley and the African-influenced music. And he only mentions three composers: Reich, Ligeti and Messiaen. He also writes some very interesting things about Messiaen's musical notation. For instance, that he was a foregoer of both Reich and Ligeti, because Ligeti at a given time wrote everything in the same metric framework.

MARX So did Stravinsky. Stravinsky does not write in polymetric bars. He changes the time signature in every bar but this applies to all the parts. I like to play for my students the wonderful interview that Stravinsky gave 50 years after the famous scandal with the première of the *Rite of Spring* at the Théâtre des Champs Élysées. Stravinsky said that he was there, standing in the wings during the performance, shouting 1231212312312, otherwise the dancers would not have gotten it right.[12]

AROM I have a project which I would like to realize with a musicologist because my vocabulary of classical music is not good enough. I would like to make a periodic analysis of the 'Dance of the Augurs of Spring' from the *Rite of Spring* in terms of time units or pulses, however, from an ethnomusicological rather than from a musicological point of view. The result would be something totally different, because I think that's the way Stravinsky built the piece. He writes bars, but the bars have no meaning

---

[12] *Igor Stravinsky 1882–1972, Vol. IV: Symphonies, Rehearsals and Talks*, Sony Classical SM2K 46294, CD 1/11.

because the accents one perceives are all over the bars; there is no strong beat, no weak beat. So you have to group other things together, i.e. use other criteria, and when you do this, you realize that the metric structure of this piece is based on perfectly regular pulses – like most African music – and that the melodic content is only made up of *ostinati*, which wander from one instrument (or group of instruments) to another.

MARX And it is interesting to see how this is actually notated, because Stravinsky always puts the strong beat on one. He therefore has to change the time signature in every bar to make sure that the instruments know where the strong beat is. Whereas Ives, for instance, uses polyrhythm, so he has to give each instrument a different time signature. So you have one who plays in 7/8, another in 5/3 and so on. And then you have Ligeti where, although you don't have a regular metre, you still have a straightforward regular metric organization. This is for the convenience of the players, it's a way of keeping everybody together. In a similar way, Messiaen had different time signatures for different parts, because he was using Hindu rhythms with a regular pattern, which would recur every 11 beats or so, but he also had bird songs that were completely irregular, with no metric pattern.

AROM How did he write the bird songs, in regular notation?

MARX Yes, but he would occasionally also use different time signatures in different parts. Since these were other players, they would only see their own part and play their own music till everybody came together again after a certain number of bars.

AROM It looks like a type of macroperiodicity.

Postmodernism redux

MARX Let me come back to something we mentioned a while ago. As we have said, Ligeti was accused of being postmodern. I personally have a rather neutral definition of postmodernism, which is neither good nor bad. I would like to know whether you would say that Ligeti was postmodern?

AROM I must confess that I never really understood what the term means.

MARX My understanding is that when the term was first widely used in the '60s it described a kind of eclectic style in architecture, whereby elements of former styles were mixed together in new ways. My question is whether something new results from this or are we just left with a mix of things we already know.

AROM If you mean a collage, then my answer is definitely 'no'. Each piece of Ligeti presents something new. Even the Études, for instance, are all different and always introduce distinctive new elements. Nor are the other, bigger pieces, collages.

MARX Of course, it's more than that. But in my personal definition – and there are so many different ones – I would call him postmodern, but not in a derogatory sense. The classic postmodern composer is probably Schnittke. You hear where the music comes from when he writes a concerto grosso, or *Moz-Art à la Haydn*, and you see that although there is something new, it stays very close to the original. Ligeti's music is much more complex, you can pinpoint two or three stylistic features, but there is always so much more.

AROM Ligeti never wrote collages. There is always invention; there are always new colours in the orchestration. 'Postmodern' is a very strange term because your definition applies to different domains. People talk about postmodernism in anthropology, but there it means something totally different. In anthropology, postmodernism means that what your informant says is more important than everything else. This is, of course, ridiculous. I know from experience that it is a lot if 10 per cent of what informants in Africa tell you is correct. It's not because they are liars, but because it is not their way of expressing things. It is our way. You ask a question and they answer about something totally different. This makes communication very difficult. I don't like this kind of terminology. It is significant to note that Ligeti was criticized because he did not write as he should have. Some people need to pigeonhole strong personalities, but some artists cannot be pigeonholed because they are too rich.

Meeting Ligeti VI

DUCHESNEAU I have a question about Ligeti's interest for music from other cultures, his curiosity towards what is foreign. Do you think that being a Jew, that is, a member of a group who was persecuted for no reason, shaped his view and made him more open towards non-European music, be it African, Asian, American, or anything else apart from traditional Western art music?

AROM I don't think I have the means to answer this question. When I met Ligeti I didn't know he was a Jew. Being Jewish in the 20th century was our common past – a parallel past as Jews who were hunted by the Nazis and whose parents were sent to Auschwitz. In my case, you immediately know that I am a Jew when you first hear my name. Ligeti never talked about this, but it goes without saying that being a Jew in this century means something and defines your identity. And this stays with you always even if you don't go to the synagogue, because being a Jew had consequences. Although Ligeti felt this in his flesh, he began to talk about it very late and never mentioned his parents' deportation. He never even said he was Jewish and that has an importance. I cannot answer this question but I know how it was for me. When I first came to Africa I was shocked by the way Western people spoke about Africans, as if they were 'Untermenschen' because I immediately identified with my younger self some 20 years before that.

DUCHESNEAU But that is exactly what I felt when Ligeti spoke of the Roma, of the Gypsies he had heard when he was a young child. He was very interested in Gypsy music, but he said that, as a child, he was afraid of them because of all the bad things he had heard the adults say about them.

AROM Yes, your own past makes you more sensitive. The last paragraph in my book *African Polyphony and Polyrhythm*, expresses my desire that after one has read what I have tried to show in it, one cannot consider Africans as some people do.[13]

---

[13] 'The principles underlying African polyphony and polyrhythm testify admirably to the ingeniousness of their inventors and to the people who still make use of them today. For many outsiders, however, "African music" means no more than a stereotype with half-clothed perspiring men beating wildly on

DUCHESNEAU You said that when you came to Africa you had this feeling that the people there were being seen as *Untermenschen*. Is that one of the reasons you started being interested in their music?

AROM No, I did it by curiosity.

DUCHESNEAU Because you were a horn player?

AROM Because I was a musician. At first, I was shocked by the way Western people – mostly the French – talked about the Africans. The first thing I did when I began to work there was to put together a choir of young Africans. They wanted to sing French and Hebrew songs, but it wasn't very successful because they could not sing half-tones. I then said to myself, 'This is ridiculous. Why should they sing French or Hebrew songs? Let them sing their own songs.' The choir then sang only traditional African music, and it had an enormous success because – and I understood this only later – of the three hundred experts from all the countries you can imagine who were there, I was the only one not trying to show them how to drive a tractor, how to plant their fields or how to dig a sewage. I was the only one trying to make them aware of their own culture. Only after that did I discover how fascinating this culture and its music were. And that ended my career as a horn player.

DUCHESNEAU Well, I think you had a very good second career even though we might have lost a good horn player.

drums and other percussion instruments in supposedly 'improvised' fashion. This pejorative 'tom tom' image implies some sort of entirely spontaneous music with no rational organisation. I would hope to correct this attitude by showing how coherent and complex this music actually is; by formulating its rules and underlying theory; by reporting how it is conceived and classified in the terminology of the native languages; by making clear how much creativity and subtlety it involves; and by describing how various musical categories are intrinsically related to social and cultural circumstances. I hope thereby to have made a contribution in some way to fostering greater recognition of the value of the culture of the Others through increased interest, more equitable appraisal, and better understanding. No less importantly, this is also one way, and perhaps not the worst way, of combating the blind discrimination of racism.' Simha Arom, *African Polyphony and Polyrhythm: Musical Structure and Methodology* (Cambridge, 1991), p. 659.

Ligeti listening to music at home
(Hamburg, 9 November 1989)

7 'Play it like Bill Evans': György Ligeti and Recorded Music

LOUISE DUCHESNEAU

György Ligeti did not own a television set in Hamburg. He did not want to be distracted when he was working and was afraid that an 'addiction' to television would be detrimental to his composition. However, he did own very expensive, high-quality stereo equipment and loved to listen to music. If he had a hobby at all this had to be it. Ligeti had his favourite hi-fi shops in Hamburg and Vienna and was well known in these cities' many record shops. A trip could always be combined with a long shopping spree to Tower Records in London or New York or to the FNAC[1] in France. In fact, it was during one of these visits to Paris, in 1980, that he discovered recordings of music by Conlon Nancarrow: 'Last Summer, I found in a Paris gramophone shop the records of Conlon Nancarrow's music (Volumes One and Two). I listened and became immediately enthusiastic.'[2] After buying a number of records in that Parisian shop he came back to Hamburg in a friend's car. Because of the distance they stopped for the night in a hotel where the car was left in the indoor parking, the records safely stored in the boot. What a surprise to find in the morning that the car had been broken into, and all the records had been stolen except for the two Nancarrow discs: Ligeti owed his discovery of Nancarrow to a music-loving but, in his musical tastes, unadventurous thief.

In his small Hamburg flat Ligeti had a great number of LPs, CDs, also tapes and cassettes of every imaginable type of music.[3] When he wanted to take a break from his daily chores of checking his mail, proofreading texts, or other mildly boring activities, or when, in the middle of work on a new piece, he felt the need for a change of scenery he either went out on his bicycle or listened to music. He would make himself a tea, usually Earl Grey, put on a record or a CD, sit down in his comfortable Eames chair with the record's liner notes and put his feet up. He would often use this free time to make cassette copies of the music that was playing for students, friends or anybody who had expressed an interest. This is how he relaxed.[4]

---

[1] FNAC is an acronym for 'Fédération Nationale d'Achats des Cadres'. With its numerous outlets, it is an institution in France.

[2] Quoted in a letter to Charles Amirkhanian from 4 January 1981, in Conlon Nancarrow, *Studies for Player Piano*, vols. I & II, Wergo WER 6168–2 (1999), CD liner notes, p. 23.

[3] Ligeti started buying CDs after an initial protest: 'I don't need a CD-player and I certainly don't need CDs since I have everything I want on my LPs.' He soon noticed that some new recordings only appeared on CDs and that most of his favourite LPs were being reissued as CDs. As the production of LPs gradually slowed down and stopped altogether he finally bought a CD-player and started his collection of CD recordings, keeping his valuable turntable, however, to continue listening to his favourite LPs.

[4] So as not to forget to whom he had promised which cassette, Ligeti would make notes in his 'little book', a pocket agenda, or would scribble something on a piece of paper. An example of this is a short note in one of the many sketches for the fifth movement of the Violin Concerto: 'Schneider AFRI xylophon cassette'. This was probably a reminder to make a cassette of (most

The Paul Sacher Foundation in Basel holds a number of LPs from Ligeti's collection. Having known it in Hamburg, my first idea was to write up an annotated list of these records which, I hoped, would be useful to Ligeti scholars. However, the 242 LPs which are now in Basel make up but a small part of Ligeti's large collection.[5] These include 32 LPs of European folk music, 62 of music from the Middle-East, Asia and Oceania, 44 records of African music, 8 of jazz and pop music, 91 of miscellaneous new music: 41 records of Ligeti's own music and 50 of other contemporary/ modern composers' music – Conlon Nancarrow, Pierre Boulez, John Cage, Karlheinz Stockhausen, Charles Ives, Edgar Varèse, Arnold Schoenberg, Harry Partch, etc. – and finally one each of music by Johann Sebastian Bach, Joseph Haydn, Jean-Philippe Rameau and Johannes Brahms (which seem to have been included here by mistake).

While I was in Basel, I also had a look at Ligeti's sketches and noticed that very often, under the heading of a work or a movement, there was an impressive listing of words which could refer to any style of music and often to a certain record: for instance, he would write down the name of a country ('Cameroun', no. 117),[6] of a musical genre ('Kecak': the Balinese Monkey Dance, no. 84, here written 'Ketjak') or the title of a track ('Miss Mabry' from Miles Davis's *Filles de Kilimanjaro*). These indications certainly meant something to the composer, but what exactly? Wouldn't it be interesting to try to match these cues to a particular record? I soon noticed, however, that the sketches, the scores, Ligeti's own texts and interviews contained so much interesting and colourful material that I soon found myself drowning in a sea of innumerable accounts of innumerable occurrences that were directly, indirectly or only very barely (and this with much power of imagination) connected with the subject at hand. Ligeti wrote a great many texts: there were radio texts with which he would earn a bit of money in the 1950s and 1960s, introductory notes for his own works which would be demanded by the concert organizers, articles on music in general and countless interviews in many different languages. Besides, a great number of his sketches often consist only of words without musical notation.[7]

In the end, I did have to temper my desire to communicate all of the information I had gathered (how I admire Paul Griffiths' virtuoso and bewildering abridgment of the Western history of music into a slim book of 348 pages!)[8] and chose to outline the importance recorded music had in Ligeti's life and work, refering to the annexed LP list when a correspondence to a particular record could be found. Ligeti became acquainted with

likely) African Amadinda music for Albrecht Schneider, a friend and professor of musicology/ethnomusicology at Hamburg University.

[5] The greater part of these LPs, which I would estimate at over a thousand, are still in Vienna.

[6] These numbers correspond to the records in the list of LPs at the end of this essay.

[7] Ligeti's articles and texts have been published in two volumes by the Paul Sacher Foundation and Schott Music International: *György Ligeti: Gesammelte Schriften*, ed. Monika Lichtenfeld (Mainz, 2007). An English translation of these texts would be very helpful for research as would also a publication of his collected interviews.

[8] Paul Griffiths, *A Concise History of Western Music* (Cambridge, 2006).

recorded music in his early childhood and records continued to fascinate him all through his life. His impassioned curiosity towards anything and everything new was only matched by his attachment to tradition, its forms and devices. It is between these two poles that his powerful musical personality developed and matured.

Jazz in Romania

Around the middle of the 1920s the only 'musical instrument' the Ligeti family had at home was a rather modern wind-up gramophone, on which was played the collection of 'schlager',[9] some jazz records (the husky sound of the muted trumpet delighted the young boy; his parents, however, felt that this music was not for children), opera arias, overtures and movements of symphonies. Ligeti loved to listen to these records and his favourite piece, at the age of three, was the 'March of the Dwarfs' from Grieg's *Peer Gynt Suite*, closely followed by Beethoven's Fifth Symphony[10] and, later on, Wagner's 'Feuerzauber' music from the end of *Die Walküre*.[11]

Stravinsky in Budapest

After the war, there were no records left in Budapest because all the 78s had been shattered along with the glass window panes. It was possible, however, to get records sent from abroad even if the customs duty was very high. Also, one could buy, on the black market, American records which were produced for the soldiers. It was on one of these records that Ligeti heard, in 1954 and 1955, Stravinsky's *Symphony in C* and *Symphony in Three Movements*, albeit only on a 'pseudo record player'. There were no needles, so a thorn from an acacia bush had been screwed in instead and the old gramophone had been slowed down from 78 rpm to 33 rpm. There were neither headphones, amplifiers or loudspeakers. Nevertheless the gramophone functioned with electricity and Ligeti could hear Stravinsky very softly.[12]

Ligeti and tradition I

Ligeti grew up in a Hungarian-speaking environment in Transylvania (a region which was part of Hungary and the Habsburg Empire till 1918, then belonged to Romania till 1940, when it reverted back to Hungary, and was

[9] These are mainly easy-listening vocal ballads popular in German-speaking countries. The German verb 'schlagen' means 'to hit', the noun 'Schlager' is thus 'a hit', a popular song.

[10] It would be some while before Ligeti realized that he had been merely listening to the exposition of the first movement because at that time only three minutes of music would fit on one side of a record.

[11] Reinhard Oehlschlägel, "'Ja, ich war ein utopischer Sozialist' – György Ligeti im Gespräch mit Reinhard Oehlschlägel (1978 and 1988)', *MusikTexte – Zeitschrift für neue Musik*, 28–9 (March 1989), pp. 85–102, at p. 85; *'Träumen Sie in Farbe?'* – György Ligeti im Gespräch mit Eckhard Roelcke* (Vienna, 2003), p. 16; György Ligeti, 'Musikalische Erinnerungen aus Kindheit und Jugend (1972)', in *Gesammelte Schriften*, vol. 2, pp. 11–18, at p. 12; Denys Bouliane, 'Stilisierte Emotion: György Ligeti im Gespräch mit Denys Bouliane', *MusikTexte– Zeitschrift für neue Musik* 28–9 (March 1989), pp. 52–62, at p. 60.

[12] Ligeti and Roelcke, *Träumen Sie in Farbe?*, pp. 73–4.

finally given back to Romania in 1945) and first encountered Romanian folk music at the age of three (nos. 25–32). What he heard then, a Romanian alpenhorn called 'bucium', certainly sounded completely different from 'normal' music, as did the wild Gypsy musicians (no. 24), playing violin and cimpoi (bagpipe), who filled the town with music.[13] Their bands played at weddings and funerals, in taverns and on the streets.[14]

Ligeti composed his first piece at the late age of 14, immediately after he started taking piano lessons. It was 'a waltz in the style of Grieg, because one of the very easy *Lyric Pieces* is a waltz'.[15] In 1941 Ligeti entered the music conservatory in Cluj where he started his composition studies with Ferenc Farkas. After the war, in Budapest, Ligeti continued his studies with Sándor Veress and, after Veress fled to the West in 1949, again with Ferenc Farkas. With these exceptional teachers Ligeti learned Palestrina-style counterpoint, formal analysis and the technique of writing pastiches in any given style, a solid craft which would be of great use to him throughout his life.[16]

For a young Hungarian composer of the time, Bartók was perfection and since Bartók had based his music on folk music, Ligeti would do the same.[17] As may be expected, the folksongs Ligeti collected or transcribed left traces in his music. He mentions that he wrote the first of the four *Wedding Dances* in the same spirit as the folk music he had heard in the Szék area (nos. 26–8),[18] and that some of the Romanian melodies he transcribed later in the Bucharest Folklore Institute found their way in the *Baladă și joc* (Ballad and Dance) which was written first for school orchestra (1949–50), then arranged for two violins (1950) to finally become the first two movements of his *Concert Românesc* (*Romanian Concerto*) from 1951. Ligeti admits that not everything is genuinely Romanian in this piece, as it also contains 'invented elements in the spirit of the village bands'.[19] How perfectly Ligeti could imitate this uninhibited music can be heard in the fourth movement's spellbinding 'Gypsy' violin solo.[20]

[13] György Ligeti, 'György Ligeti on his Orchestral Works', in *György Ligeti: The Ligeti Project II*, Teldec Classics 8573-88261-2, 2002.

[14] György Ligeti, 'Musikalische Erinnerungen aus Kindheit und Jugend (1972)', in *Gesammelte Schriften*, pp. 11–12, at p. 11.

[15] Paul Griffiths, *György Ligeti* (London, 1997), p. 4.

[16] György Ligeti, 'Between Science, Music and Politics', *Kyoto Prizes & Inamori Grants 2001* (Kyoto, 2002), pp. 231–65, at pp. 251–5. This is the original English language text of the 'commemorative lecture' which Ligeti gave in Kyoto in November 2001. To my knowledge the English text has never been reprinted elsewhere since. A copy of this publication can be consulted at the Paul Sacher Foundation and a German translation was published in *Gesammelte Schriften*, vol. 2, pp. 33–50.

[17] Pierre Michel, 'Entretiens avec György Ligeti (1981)', in *György Ligeti: compositeur d'aujourd'hui* (Paris, 1995), pp. 149–202, at p. 129.

[18] Ligeti and Roelcke, *Träumen Sie in Farbe?*, p. 126.

[19] Ligeti, 'György Ligeti on his Orchestral Works'.

[20] Ligeti long withheld the publication of this work mainly out of fear that, were it known, this exhilarating fourth movement would become his most popular piece.

New music for the bottom drawer

At the same time that Ligeti was writing official music based on folk music, he was also trying to develop a personal musical style. Numerous obstacles lay in his path: in the post-1949 Communists years, modern music as a whole was banned in Hungary, even Bartók's important works were removed from concert hall and theatre. Stravinsky, Debussy, Bach and Handel (the last two because of clerical tendencies) went unheard, and even studying or teaching a banned work could be dangerous.[21] Nonetheless, the scores of Schoenberg's Second Quartet and Berg's *Lyric Suite* were available in the library of the Music Academy and Ligeti could hear recordings of Schoenberg's Third and Fourth String Quartets as well as Webern's *Five Movements for String Quartet*, op. 5. Twelve-tone music was modern and so, for a short while, Ligeti tried to write music using rows but in a style that was not serial in the sense of Boulez and Stockhausen. He wrote an orthodox 12-tone *Chromatic Fantasy* for piano and also began a twelve-tone requiem in 1956.[22]

An important source of information about the music of his contemporaries in the West were the new music programmes of West German radio stations which could be heard in Budapest. Although the broadcasts were jammed because of the news reports, it was still possible to hear the higher frequencies, mainly piccolo and xylophone. Cologne's programme was broadcast on the West German Radio on Thursdays at 11 pm and from Munich came the 'Musica Viva' programme on Mondays, also at 11 pm, on Bavarian Radio.[23] Ligeti also read *Melos*, a West German periodical published by Schott, which was available in the rooms of the Musicians' Union and for which he wrote three articles.[24] During the revolution, on 7 November 1956, he was able to hear, this time without interference, Stockhausen's *Gesang der Jünglinge* and *Kontra-Punkte* which made a strong impression on him. Books were also banned, but Ligeti managed to receive, through his wife Vera, a copy of Thomas Mann's *Doktor Faustus* and Adorno's *Philosophy of New Music*, both of which had an 'enormously liberating influence' on him.[25]

At the same time, Ligeti was experimenting with what would later become the 'Ligeti-style': a static music with no perceptible rhythm, metre or melody. Written in 1956 in Budapest, the totally chromatic orchestral piece *Víziók* (Visions) became the first version of *Apparitions*, Ligeti's first orchestral work written in the West. The impulse for this new direction

---

[21] Ligeti relates that, in 1952, the Communists had wanted to dismiss him from his teaching post because he had analysed Stravinsky's *Symphony of Psalms* in class. See Marina Lobanova, 'Interviews (1991)', in *György Ligeti: Style, Ideas, Poetics* (Berlin, 2002), pp. 357–98, at p. 388.

[22] Griffiths, *György Ligeti*, pp. 12–14.

[23] Ligeti and Roelcke, *Träumen Sie in Farbe?*, p. 75.

[24] Written in German, the articles are 'Neue Musik in Ungarn', from 1946, 'Neues aus Budapest: Zwölftonmusik oder 'Neue Tonalität'?', from 1948 and 'Neues aus Budapest: Von Bartók bis Veress', from 1949. The first two articles are reprinted in *Gesammelte Schriften*, vol. 1, pp. 51–5 and pp. 56–60, but not the third one, which is mentioned in Friedemann Sallis, *An Introduction to the Early Works of György Ligeti* (Cologne, 1996), p. 226.

[25] Ligeti, 'György Ligeti on his Orchestral Works'.

did not stem, however, from any 'modern' music he knew or could guess at. While still in Budapest, he was fascinated by the music of Johannes Ockeghem which, as a teacher of counterpoint, he knew very well. In the 15th century Ockeghem had also written a 'music like a constant stream, a continual flow in which there are no climaxes, only an unchanging tension'.[26] *Apparitions, Atmosphères* and later his *Requiem* were triggered by this music, in which 'one wave follows the other and where the individual parts move while the overall picture is static.'[27] Still, although he could *hear* the music he imagined, he did not yet possess the *technique* of putting it on paper.[28]

The Cologne–Darmstadt avant-garde

Ligeti fled from Hungary during the revolution in 1956 and, all of a sudden, he was free to write any music he pleased. 'Maybe the most crucial occurrence of my life was the short four-month scholarship I received in February 1957 from Herbert Eimert, who was the head of the modern music programs at the West German Radio (WDR) in Cologne.'[29] It was in the WDR's electronic music studio that he met Karlheinz Stockhausen, Gottfried Michael Koenig, Franco Evangelisti, Hans G Helms[30] and Mauricio Kagel. Because he knew next to nothing of the music of his contemporaries, he spent his first weeks in Cologne listening to hundreds of pieces the WDR had on tape in their archive. It was all a shock for him, maybe the best shock of his life.[31] All at once, Stockhausen and Boulez replaced Bartók and Stravinsky as his new ideals: Boulez' *Le marteau sans maître* and Stockhausen's *Gesang der Jünglinge* and later *Gruppen* became model works.[32] In the electronic music studio he learned the technique 'of putting pieces together layer by layer' which helped him realize the 'idea of micropolyphonic webs' that he had conceived in Budapest. His work in the electronic studio[33] finally gave him the technique to write, this time for living musicians, the static music he had imagined.[34]

---

[26] Lobanova, *György Ligeti: Style, Ideal, Poetics*, p. 365.

[27] 'György Ligeti und Manfred Stahnke: Gespräch am 29. Mai 1993', in *Musik – nicht ohne Worte: Beiträge zu aktuellen Fragen aus Komposition, Musiktheorie und Musikwissenschaft*, ed. Manfred Stahnke, Musik und 2 (Hamburg, 2000), pp. 121–60, at p. 141.

[28] 'György Ligeti talking to Péter Várnai (1978)', in *György Ligeti in Conversation with Péter Várnai, Josef Häusler, Claude Samuel and Himself* (London, 1983), pp. 13–82, at p. 33.

[29] Ligeti, 'Between Science, Music and Politics', p. 261.

[30] Hans G Helms insists that his middle initial be written without a dot. This mysterious 'G' stands either for Günther (*The New Grove Dictionary of Music and Musicians*, ed. Stanley Sadie (London, 1980), vol. 8, p. 468) or Georg (The National Library in Berlin, website: staatsbibliothek-berlin.de).

[31] György Ligeti, 'Mein Kölner Jahr 1957 (1993)', in *Gesammelte Schriften*, vol. 2, pp. 29–32, at p. 31.

[32] Ulrich Dibelius, 'Gespräch über Ästhetik', in *György Ligeti: Eine Monographie in Essays* (Mainz, 1994), pp. 253–73, at p. 260.

[33] In Cologne Ligeti wrote three works of electronic music, of which only *Artikulation* (1958) remains in his catalogue.

[34] Griffiths, *György Ligeti*, p. 18.

Ligeti took an active part in the intellectual and musical life of the avant-garde from the late 1950s to the early 1970s, participating, for instance, in the International Summer Courses for New Music in Darmstadt, first as a student, later as a teacher. Still he sometimes felt a bit like an outsider. The exhilarating newness of the beginnings wore off, the models Webern, Boulez and Stockhausen were pushed into the background and a 'gradual infiltration of traditional elements' into Ligeti's music took place.[35]

Ligeti and tradition II

Ligeti had always considered himself a traditionalist. Models for pieces like *Atmosphères* can be found in the Prelude to *Rheingold*, in Debussy, also in Bartók and even the extremely avantgardistic *Volumina* is, in many ways, linked to Bach's organ music. Asked if *Lontano* could be considered an 'Hommage à Mahler', he answers 'of course, but also to Bruckner.'[36] In the same way, his Second String Quartet owes much to Bartók's Fourth and Fifth String Quartets, Berg's *Lyric Suite*, late Beethoven string quartets, Mozart's 'Dissonance' Quartet in C major,[37] Webern's *Bagatelles* ... and even includes a slight allusion to Stravinsky's *Le sacre*.[38]

These allusions to tradition were well understood by the finger-wagging champions of the avant-garde.[39] In an effort to make a clear break with avant-garde aesthetics Ligeti composed his opera *Le Grand Macabre* (1974–7), which, with its collage technique, was completely different and more radical than anything he had previously written.[40] However, another work would mark the real beginning of a new 'Ligeti-style': the conservative Horn Trio from 1982.

1972: California

For five months in 1972, his first time ever in the United States, Ligeti was composer-in-residence at Stanford University in California. By this time, however, he had heard the music of Charles Ives, had met John Cage at Darmstadt in 1958, and had befriended Morton Feldman in Berlin in the early 1970s. But it was in the music library of Stanford University that he discovered two records which would have an incredible impact on his

---

[35] Dibelius, 'Gespräch über Ästhetik', p. 260.

[36] Bouliane, 'Stilisierte Emotion', p. 54.

[37] See György Ligeti, 'Konvention und Abweichung – Die 'Dissonanz' in Mozarts Streichquartett C-Dur KV 465 (1990)', in *Gesammelte Schriften*, vol. 1, pp. 271–8. This analysis of 'dissonance' in Mozart's C major quartet was based on an analysis Ligeti had made while still a teacher in Budapest.

[38] 'György Ligeti talking to Josef Häusler (1968/69)', in *György Ligeti in Conversation*, pp. 83–110, at p. 106.

[39] Martin Zenck speaks of the 're-romanticizing timbre-composition *Lontano*' ('re-romantisierenden Farbkomposition *Lontano*') in '"Die ich rief, die Geister / Werd ich nun nicht los." – Zum Problem von György Ligetis Avantgarde-Konzeption', in *György Ligeti: Personalstil – Avantgardismus – Popularität*, ed. Otto Kolleritsch, Studien zur Wertungsforschung 19 (Vienna, Graz, 1987), pp. 153–78, at p. 157.

[40] Dibelius, 'Gespräch über Ästhetik', p. 266.

imagination: Terry Riley's *In C* and Steve Reich's *It's gonna rain* and *Violin Phase*. After returning to Germany he met Steve Reich in Berlin in 1973 and heard a performance of *Drumming*. The same year, Ligeti wrote *Clocks and Clouds* for female voices and orchestra, which was strongly influenced by Steve Reich, and in 1976 he dedicated to Steve Reich and Terry Riley the second movement of his *Three Pieces for Two Pianos*, 'Self-Portrait with Reich and Riley (with Chopin in the Background)'.[41]

It was also in California that Ligeti first heard the microtonal music of Harry Partch (with its well-known 43-microtone scale) and saw his instruments ('his Diamond Marimba, which I had the chance to play, was for me an important stimulus').[42] One of Partch's most beautiful pieces, *Oedipus* (no. 163), reminded Ligeti of the declamation of medieval troubadours, while *Delusion of the Fury* (no. 162), Ligeti felt, was inspired by Indonesian music.[43] For Ligeti, Harry Partch's music was like folk music, 'the folk music of a people which consists of a single individual, simply of Harry Partch'.[44] Partch's microtonal tuning became very important to Ligeti who was seeking alternatives to the tempered system: Ligeti credits Partch for guiding him in the Horn Trio, 'not so much his music but rather his tuning system and its application in his instruments'.[45]

1973: Hamburg, pop music, jazz and Latin American music

Immediately after his stay in California, in 1973, Ligeti accepted a professorship to teach composition at the Music Academy in Hamburg. While at Stanford he had met John Chowning and Jean-Claude Risset, two pioneers of computer-generated music, and he was very eager to establish in Hamburg a similar computer music institute to the one in Stanford. He even thought of going back to composing electronic music, something he had given up in the late 1950s because, then, the equipment had been too primitive to realize his musical ideas. To Ligeti's great disappointment, however, this project did not materialize. At the same time, the dominating influence of avant-garde aesthetics on the imagination of young composers was beginning to loosen, and some of Ligeti's students turned to pop music as a point of departure for a new kind of music. Ligeti did not take kindly to this post-romantic, retrospective trend in his class and in the midst of the debate which ensued (debates which could often be very heated) he wrote the two short harpsichord pieces *Hungarian Rock* and *Passacaglia ungherese* (both 1978), 'as musical arguments in a discussion I was having with my students, especially Hans-Christian von Dadelsen who was deeply influenced by British and American pop music'.[46] However exasperating

---

[41] György Ligeti, 'Begegnung mit Steve Reich (2002)', in *Gesammelte Schriften*, vol. 1 (Mainz, 2007), pp. 520–1.

[42] Louise Duchesneau, 'György Ligeti on his Violin Concerto', *Ligeti Letter* 2 (Hamburg, 1993), pp. 1–7, at p. 5.

[43] György Ligeti, 'Tendenzen der Neuen Musik in den USA: Steve Reich – Terry Riley – Harry Partch (1972)', in *Gesammelte Schriften*, vol. 1, pp. 456–68, at pp. 465–6.

[44] Ibid., p. 466.

[45] Duchesneau, 'György Ligeti on his Violin Concerto', p. 5.

[46] Lobanova, *György Ligeti: Style, Ideal, Poetics*, pp. 396–7.

these exchanges were, they did introduce Ligeti to a completely new musical world.

At that time, Ligeti already knew and loved the music of the Beatles. He writes that the most beautiful example of multitrack recording can be found in *Sgt. Pepper's Lonely Hearts Club Band*, 'when the music suddenly stands still on a long major chord which seems to unfurl into infinity'.[47] In the sketches for the *Nonsense Madrigals* (1988–93), there is a reference not only to 'Eleanor Rigby' (from the album *Revolver*, 1966) and to the song 'I want you' (from the album *Abbey Road*, 1969), but also to 'Dufay/Beatles' and 'Dufay-Stravi (for Stravinsky)-Beatles'. One should not forget that Ligeti wrote the *Nonsense Madrigals* for the King's Singers and that he knew their recording of Beatles songs (no. 148). Therefore, any mention of the Beatles in a sketch of the *Nonsense Madrigals* could refer not only to the Beatles' music but also to the King's Singers' rendering of it.

Ligeti was also impressed by the pop group Supertramp and its record *Breakfast in America*.[48] Both *Breakfast in America* and another well-known Supertramp album *Crime of the Century* are mentioned in sketches for *Alice in Wonderland*. Ligeti must have had a very special vision of this work since, beside the name 'Alice' he wrote: 'Los Papines, Kecak, Supertramp: Crime of the Century, Breakfast in America', a mix of salsa, Balinese dance theatre and pop music! Among the sketches for *Alice* is also a newspaper clipping[49] on the subject of arranging pop music. Ligeti underlined the words 'syncopation' and 'flat leading-note in a major key' and wrote in capitals in the margin: 'SLÁGER ALICE?'. Was he thinking of composing some kind of light, pop-like music (a schlager?) for the character of Alice? Maybe, why not, at that time he certainly enjoyed listening to such 'schlagers' as the very popular *Ballade pour Adeline*, a catchy tune played by the pianist Richard Clayderman.

Jazz also had an enormous influence on the music Ligeti composed from the early 1970s onwards. He liked 'all the greats of jazz from King Oliver, Louis Armstrong and Duke Ellington to Ornette Coleman'[50] and the elegance of this music, at once simple and complex, fascinated him. However primitive the form might appear, Ligeti thought that records such as Miles Davis's *Kind of Blue* and *Filles de Kilimanjaro*, were as graceful, carefree and elegant in their manner, and just as unaffected as music by Mozart.[51] Among his favourites were 'the jazz record on which Herbie Hancock and Chick Corea improvise the most intricate polyrhythms on two pianos, and Thelonious Monk's well-known jazz standard *Round Midnight* with its romantic harmony ...'[52]

Ligeti's great love of jazz is reflected in many of his works. He writes, for instance, that jazz pianism played an important role in the Piano Études,

---

[47] Ligeti, 'Tendenzen der Neuen Musik in den USA', in *Gesammelte Schriften*, vol. 1, p. 461.

[48] Dibelius, 'Gespräch über Ästhetik', p. 266.

[49] *Die Welt*, Nr. 224, 26 September 1975.

[50] Dibelius, 'Gespräch über Ästhetik', p. 266.

[51] Ibid., p. 266.

[52] 'György Ligeti und Manfred Stahnke: Gespräch am 29. Mai 1993', pp. 146–7.

'above all the poetry of Thelonious Monk and Bill Evans',[53] transforming the fifth Étude, *Arc-en-ciel*, into a kind bridge between Chopin and jazz.[54] Or, in the score of his Viola Sonata, Ligeti writes that the second movement, 'Loop', should be played 'in the spirit of jazz: elegant and relaxed'. One can only sympathize with the soloist who has to play all the notes at the breakneck speed required by the composer, while at the same time trying to appear 'relaxed'.

Countless names of musicians, song titles and jazz genres are mentioned in Ligeti's many texts and sketches. In an interview he refers to Dizzy Gillespie, Bebop, Charlie Parker and Eric Dolphy[55] and in different sketches (for the Violin Concerto, Viola Sonata, *Nonsense Madrigals* and *Hamburg Concerto*), he writes: Elliot Sharp, Oscar Peterson, *52nd Street Theme* (a song written by Thelonious Monk in 1944), Charlie Parker, Django Reinhardt, 'Round Midnight', Blues, 'Miss Mabry', Stanley Clarke: Light as a Feather (written by Stanley Clarke, this is the title track of Chick Corea's album *Light as a Feather*, which came out in 1972) and 'So What' (the first track of *Kind of Blue*). Unfortunately the list of those jazz records held in Basel is very short, it contains only six LPs, three of negro spirituals, one of boogie-woogie, one of Miles Davis (*In a Silent Way*), and one of crossover jazz (Dave Brubeck playing music by Leonard Bernstein).

Commercial Latin American music became very important to Ligeti in the 1980s mainly because of its polyrhythmic complexity. Already in the 1970s Ligeti had a particular fondness for the rhythmic drive of Latin American music,[56] he loved the Brazilian samba, the Puerto-Rican salsa (Richie Ray, the virtuoso salsa pianist is mentioned in a sketch for *Alice in Wonderland*) and the Cuban rumba (the name of a famous Cuban rumba band, 'Los Papines!', appears in a sketch for the *Nonsense Madrigals*). Ligeti used Latin American rhythms in the second movement of the Horn Trio, where 'the asymmetrical rhythms such as 3{+}2{+}3 and 3{+}3{+}2 stem for the greater part more from samba and rumba as from music of the Balkans.'[57] There are no LPs of Latin American music in our list; however, because of the many remarks in texts and sketches, we must assume that he knew this music very well.

Beyond jazz, pop and Latin American music, Ligeti was mainly interested in the multitude of diverse ethnic and folk music, all of which were conveniently available on records. For Ligeti, composing was a bit like the work of a scientist: musical works were problems which required

[53] György Ligeti, 'Works for Piano', in *The Ligeti Project* 3, p. 11, translation: Annelies McVoy and David Feurzeig. In a score of *Arc-en-ciel*, which is kept at the Paul Sacher Foundation, Ligeti wrote in the margin of the first page: 'Play it like Bill Evans'.

[54] Bouliane, 'Stilisierte Emotion', p. 60.

[55] Dibelius, 'Gespräch über Ästhetik', p. 266.

[56] György Ligeti, 'Rhapsodische, unausgewogene Gedanken über Musik, besonders über meine eigenen Kompositionen', *Neue Zeitschrift für Musik* 1 (1993), pp. 20–9, at p. 25.

[57] Detlef Gojowy, 'György Ligeti über eigene Werke – Ein Gespräch mit Detlef Gojowy aus dem Jahre 1988', in *Für György Ligeti: Die Referate des Ligeti-Kongresses Hamburg 1988* (Laaber, 1991), pp. 349–63, at p. 361.

a solution.[58] In that sense, the treasure trove of exotic music was there to help him find answers to those musical questions which interested him the most. These were first, the question of tuning, and second, complex polyphony.

The problem of non-tempered tuning

'When I look back, I realize that I have always been, consciously or unconsciously, looking for an alternative to the twelve-tone temperament.'[59] As far back as 1961, in *Atmosphères*, Ligeti sought to find something that lay between noise and musical sound, and when he wrote *Ramifications* (1968), his only work in quarter-tones, what he was again searching for was the irisating, 'dirty' sound, the shimmering quality of *Atmosphères* and the *Requiem*. By the time Ligeti had thought up the tuning scheme of the Horn Trio – the piano is tempered, the violin is tuned to perfect fifths and the horn plays like a natural horn with natural sevenths and 11ths – he was already trying to solve the 'problem of intonation by ... listening to a great deal of ethnic music'. For the Violin Concerto he drew on 'the music of the Iatmul,[60] a people who live on the Sepik River in New Guinea and whose musical system is built on pure overtones ...',[61] as well as on the 'unbelievable music ... of the Solomon Islands and the Bismarck Archipelago (no. 91, Manus and Bougainville are both islands in the Bismarck Archipelago).'[62] This is the reason why Ligeti included in the orchestra of the Violin Concerto, '... along with the 'normal' orchestral instruments, a scordatura (irregularly tuned) violin and viola, as well as many instruments with imprecise pitch such as ocarinas, a recorder and slide-whistles'.[63] The more he listened to ethnic music, the less he could stand tempered scales: 'it almost hurts', he writes.[64] In the Violin Concerto, where he was 'very consciously looking for a new kind of way of building a melody', he incorporated certain 'aspects of melodies from the Far-East, ... Thailand (nos. 75–6) and Cambodia' (nos. 73–4).[65] Scattered among many pages of sketches for the Violin Concerto and the *Hamburg Concerto* are the comments: 'BURMA!, Cambodia, Laos (no. 72), Vietnam (nos. 66–71), Thai Court' and 'Iatmul, Middle Sepik, Bougainville, Melanesia, Papua (nos. 90–3)'. When asked about the melodies in his Violin Concerto, Ligeti answers that he listened to a great number of recordings of music

---

[58] 'György Ligeti und Manfred Stahnke: Gespräch am 29. Mai 1993', p. 122.

[59] Duchesneau, 'György Ligeti on his Violin Concerto', p. 5.

[60] There are no recordings of the music of the Iatmul nor of the Solomon Islands in the Sacher LP list. I know however that the following LPs were in Ligeti's Hamburg collection: (1) *Music of Oceania, Papua Niugini: The Middle Sepik* (Bärenreiter-Musicaphon BM 30 SL 2700, 1981); (2) *Music of Oceania: The Iatmul of Papua Niugini* (Bärenreiter-Musicaphon BM 30 SL 2701, 1981); *Flûte de pan mélanésiennes 'Are'are, Malaita, Solomon Islands*, recorded by Hugo Zemp, Collection Musée de l'Homme (Disques Vogue, vol. 1: LDM 30104, vol. 2: LDM 30105, vol. 3: LDM 30106, 1971).

[61] Duchesneau, 'György Ligeti on his Violin Concerto', p. 5.

[62] Ligeti and Roelcke, *Träumen Sie in Farbe?*, p. 138.

[63] Duchesneau, 'György Ligeti on his Violin Concerto', p. 4.

[64] Gojowy, 'György Ligeti über eigene Werke', p. 355.

[65] 'György Ligeti und Manfred Stahnke: Gespräch am 29. Mai 1993', p. 128.

from Thailand, from the Khmer culture, also from Laos because he was deliberately looking for new ways of constructing melodies.[66] He adds that other tunings than the tempered system can also be found in the music of the Chokwe and Lunda people from Angola (no. 121), or in the Baulé music of Ivory Coast (nos. 106–7) with its neutral thirds and that listening to Pygmy music (nos. 124, 128) also helped him to hear certain deviations from the tempered system, for instance their wider major seconds and smaller minor thirds.[67] His own Romanian/Hungarian folk heritage also provided many an idea for non-tempered tunings. 'Hora lungă' (no. 28), the first movement of the Viola Sonata 'evokes the spirit of Romanian folkmusic' and bears in its predilection for natural intervals 'a striking resemblance to the 'Cante jondo' in Andalusia and also to the folkmusics of Rajastan'.[68]

Harry Partch's microtonal tuning was also certainly a model for Ligeti, but the rarity of his custom-made instruments made it difficult for anyone to follow his lead. The music of Syzygys (no. 149), which is based on Partch's 43-tone scale, remains an individual case. Although the invention of the Yahama DX7 II (a tunable synthesizer developed by John Chowning at Ligeti's request)[69] opened the doors to every imaginable tuning, it was still an electronic instrument.[70] What Ligeti really wanted was to apply new types of tuning to acoustic instruments, and for inspiration he turned to the music of many ethnic cultures, especially from Africa and South-East Asia.[71]

The challenge of complex polyphony

Complex polyphony fascinated Ligeti, whether it was African polyrhythmic and polymetric music, the irregular rhythms of Eastern-European folk music, or the polyrhythmic complexity of Nancarrow's player-piano studies.

The influence of African polyphony on Ligeti's music is well documented in numerous books, articles and interviews. It all started in 1982, when Ligeti first heard music of the Banda Linda tribe from the Central African Republic from an LP his student Roberto Sierra had brought to class.[72] Ligeti had never heard such 'marvelous polyphonic,

---

[66] Ibid.

[67] Ibid., p. 136.

[68] Text printed in the score of the Viola Sonata.

[69] Ligeti, 'Rhapsodische, unausgewogene Gedanken über Musik', p. 29.

[70] Both Syzygys and the Yamaha DX7 II are mentioned in a sketch for the Violin Concerto: 'Mikroton: Syzygyzys [*sic*] (DX7 II) Face B Faun Grotesque'. The B side of this odd record contains the eery and predictably out-of-tune track 'Fauna Grotesque' which interested Ligeti. One can hear an excerpt of this piece on the website www.syzygys.jp, accessed on 15 August 2011.

[71] Ligeti, 'Rhapsodische, unausgewogene Gedanken über Musik', pp. 28–9.

[72] *Banda Polyphony, Central African Republic*, recorded by Simha Arom, Musics & Musicians of the World, Auvidis-Unesco, International Music Council, LP 1976, reissue: The International Institute for Comparative Music Studies and Documentation (IICMSD) Berlin, CD 1992. Ironically, this well-known recording is not included in our list of LPs. There are, however, many recordings of Central African music: see nos. 124–9, especially nos. 125, 128 and 129, recorded by Simha Arom.

polyrhythmic music'[73] and was deeply impressed. By chance, a few years later he discovered Gerhard Kubik's world of 'inherent patterns', the illusionary musical shapes which can be found in many African musical cultures.[74] Here Ligeti found parallels to his own music, for instance to the 'super-signals' in *Continuum* for harpsichord (1968) or *Monument* for two pianos (1976) but warns the listener that one will not find folk music in his pieces, 'as these influences are exclusively technical.'[75] European folk music was also a source of polyrhythmic complexity: the second movement of the Horn Trio, for instance, is 'a very quick polymetric dance inspired by the various folk music of non-existing peoples, as if Hungary, Romania and the entire Balkan region were situated somewhere between Africa and the Caribbean.'[76]

For Ligeti, Conlon Nancarrow's polyrhythmic pianola studies (no. 161) remained an absolute milestone in the music of the 20th century.[77] With his extremely intricate music Nancarrow had established a standard of what could be achieved in polyrhythmic-polymetric complexity. Without Nancarrow there would not have been a Piano Concerto nor any Piano Études.[78] Not without a note of triumph, Ligeti writes that in his sixth Piano Étude, *Automne à Varsovie*, he tried for the first time 'to write many simultaneous tempi for one pianist' and succeeded in what Nancarrow had done for mechanical piano, namely to 'create the illusion of many simultaneous tempi on a conventional piano.'[79]

Concluding thoughts

It is rather amusing to look through Ligeti's sketches and try to disentangle what he could have meant with these long lists of miscellaneous comments and quotes. One has the impression he was enjoying himself. His sketches are filled with such mentions as 'Balkans' (nos. 5–12, 21–2, 25–32), 'DAN MASQUES' (nos. 104–5), 'Georgia' (nos. 13–15), 'Gagaku' (no. 34), 'LP-Szardinia!' (no. 17), 'Sierra Leone LP!' (no. 100), 'Gabon LP!!' (nos. 118–20), 'Bali: Anthologie' (nos. 80–2), 'Cameroun' (no. 117), 'Tibet' (nos. 44–8), 'Eskimo' (no. 96) or 'Grisey' (no. 158). Asked if there were

[73] György Ligeti, 'Foreword', in Simha Arom, *African Polyphony and Polyrhythm: Musical Structure and Methodology* (Cambridge, 1991), pp. xvii–xviii, at p. xvii. This book was originally published in French in 1985.

[74] Artur Simon, ed., *Musik in Afrika*, Veröffentlichung des Museums für Völkerkunde Berlin, Folge 40, Abteilung Musikethnologie IV (Berlin, 1983), 2 music cassettes. Ligeti mentions elsewhere ('Paradigmenwechsel der achtziger Jahre', in *Gesammelte Schriften*, vol. 2, pp. 116–18, at p. 116) that, for him, the most important article in this publication was Kubik's 'Kognitive Grundlagen afrikanischer Musik', pp. 327–400.

[75] György Ligeti, 'György Ligeti on his works: *Melodien*, Chamber Concerto, Piano Concerto, *Mysteries of the Macabre*', in *György Ligeti – The Ligeti Project I*, Teldec Classics 5873-83953-2, 2001.

[76] György Ligeti, 'Trio for Violin, Horn and Piano', trans. Sid McLauchlan, booklet to *Ligeti: Études pour piano – 1er livre, Trio pour violon, cor et piano; Donatoni: Tema, Cadeau*, Érato, ECD 75555, 1990, p. 21.

[77] Ligeti, 'Rhapsodische, unausgewogene Gedanken über Musik', p. 25.

[78] Dibelius, 'Gespräch über Ästhetik', p. 267.

[79] Denys Bouliane, 'Geronnene Zeit und Narration – György Ligeti im Gespräch', *Neue Zeitschrift für Musik* 149/5 (1988), pp. 19–25, at pp. 22–4.

any musical cultures at all which did not interest him, he answered: 'Yes, technically, I haven't paid much attention either to Chinese, Korean or Vietnamese music.'[80] This may be true; however, one cannot imagine that he listened to his many records of Chinese (no. 39–42) and Vietnamese (nos. 66–71) music with anything less than his complete attention. These impulses and ideas all fell into a 'melting pot', in which all kinds of unrelated elements were mixed together and from which he could take what fit his musical needs of the moment.[81] As the work on a piece progressed and it began to take shape, some ideas and inspirations were abandoned or combined with others, thus obscuring their origins.

> Often I'll write the name of a composer in a sketch or scribble something with one of my coloured pencils. For instance, at some point, somewhere in Scriabin I hear a chord which interests me. I then only need to write down the word 'Scriabin', whereas I'm not thinking about this particular chord, but about something similar. It's the 'scent' of Scriabin, if you wish.[82]

The writings, remarks and notes of a composer are easily misunderstood. It meant something for him but what does it mean to us? Does it bring us closer to his intentions or does it just satisfy our curiosity by providing us with a simplistic view of inspiration? Ligeti would speak of a piece of music as a pot of soup in which he would add a bit of this and a bit of that. He would say about a piece which wasn't quite finished: 'It's not cooked enough.' It is the music itself that reveals the true complexity of the work of art, not any of its identifiable ingredients. Combined together in the secret world of the composer's imagination, these elements only serve to nourish his creativity and provide a favourable atmosphere in which he can work.

List of recordings in the Paul Sacher Foundation

The following list of LPs is complete as far as European folk music, music from the Middle East, Asia and Oceania, African music, and jazz and pop music are concerned. As to contemporary music, I chose to make a selection of those recordings which I found of interest. Finally, no recordings of Ligeti's music are included, as these are generally well known.

Always an attentive listener, Ligeti would also read the record's liner notes carefully. Some records show these signs of use, a worn-out cover (no. 125), tea stains (no. 91) or remarks notated in the liner booklet (nos. 28, 66).

Ligeti loved to spend time in record shops and would always come out with armfuls of new records. The first thing he did, however, when he stepped into a shop was to go straight to the contemporary music section and see what the shop had stocked of his own music. It was only once he had established his place in the store's inventory that his hunt to discover something new began.

---

[80] Ligeti and Roelcke, *Träumen Sie in Farbe?*, p. 138.

[81] Denys Bouliane, 'György Ligeti im Gespräch mit Denys Bouliane', in *Neuland – Ansätze zur Musik der Gegenwart* 5 (Cologne, 1984/85), pp. 72–90, at p. 84.

[82] Ligeti and Roelcke, *Träumen Sie in Farbe?*, p. 168.

European folk music

1 **La Flûte Indienne, Los Calchakis, Los Guacharacos**, Barclay 820-054, Série Panache, 1967

2 **The Happy Family of Folk**, LP 1: South America, LP 2: A Mexiko, B Spain, LP 3: A United States, B Ireland, Scotland, England, LP 4: A Russia, Greece, LP 5: France, B Italy, Zeit Magazin, LSP 14 501

3 **Music in the Andean Highlands, Bolivia**, recorded by Max Peter Baumann, Museum Collection Berlin (West), MC 14, 1982

4 **Équateur, rythmes indiens et afro-américains**, recorded by Xavier Bellenger, Édition Az LD 5905 (800 994 320), 1975

5 **Chants des Albanais de Calabra, Groupe Arbëreshë di Lungro**, Arion ARN 33714, 1982

6 **Marcel Cellier présente L'Albanie folklorique**, recorded by Marcel Cellier, Disques Cellier N° 010, 1979

7 **Yugoslavian Folk Music of Macedonia**, Olympic Records, The Atlas Series, Music from around the World, 6130

8 **Chants et danses de Yougoslavie**, Le chant du monde, LDX 74384

9 **Grèce, Musique Populaire de Tradition Orale, Chants des Akrites (VIIIème au XIIIème siècle)**, recorded by Domna Samniou, I. Musiques de tradition orale, Ocora 558 600, 1982

10 **Songs of Thrace (Part 1)**, Society for the Dissemination of National Music, Volume 6, SDNM 106, 1973–4

11 **Chants et Danses de Grèce**, Le chant du monde, LDX 7 4411, 1968?

12 **Musik der Pontos-Griechen, Nordgriechenland**, recorded by Christian Ahrens, Museum Collection Berlin (West), MC 5, 1974

13 **The Music of Georgia I, Songs of Oral Tradition from the Georgian Soviet Socialist Republic**, recorded by the Tbilisi Conservatoire and Yvette Grimaud, UNESCO Collection, A Musical Anthology of the Orient, Bärenreiter-Musicaphon, BM 30 L 2025, *c.* 1974

14 **Géorgie, Chants de travail**, recorded by Yvette Grimaud, Musiques traditionelles vivantes, V. Musiques populaires, Ocora 558 513, 1977/1982

15 **Géorgie Vol. 2, Chants religieux**, recorded by Yvette Grimaud, Musiques traditionelles vivantes, II. Musiques rituelles et religieuses, Ocora 558 544, 1979/1982

16 **Religious Music of Oral Tradition from Risiu, Corsica**, recorded by Jacques Cloarec, UNESCO Collection, Musical Sources, Sources of European Polyphony XIII-1, Auvidis/Philips 6586 033, 1978

17 **Sardaigne – Sardinië, Polyphonies**, recorded by Jos Gansemans and Thomas Gallia, Musiques traditionelles vivantes, I. Musiques de tradition orale, BRT/Ocora 558 595, 1981/1983/1986

18 **Portugal, Tras-os-Montes, Chants du blé et cornemuses de berger**, Musiques traditionelles vivantes, I. Musique de tradition orale, Ocora 558 547, 1980

19 **Folk Music in the U.S.S.R.**, edited by Henry Cowell, Ethnic Folkways Library FE 4535 A/B, 1960

20 **Russian Hymns, 'Dedicated to the 75th Jubilee of His Holiness Patriarch Pimen of Moscow and all Russia'**, recorded at the Assumption Cathedral of the Trinity St. Sergius Laura, C90 23389 000, 1985

21 **Liturgies de l'Orient, Chœurs des Moines Bénédictins de l'Union de Chevetogne**, Chœurs Bulgares, Harmonia Mundi, HM 520, *c.* 1965

22 **A Harvest, a Shepherd, a Bride: Village Music of Bulgaria**, recorded by Ethel Raim and Martin Koenig, Nonesuch Explorer Series H-72034, 1970

23 **Folk Music of Hungary**, recorded in Hungary under the supervision of Belá Bartók, Folkways Records FM 4000, Monogram Series of the Ethnic Folkways Library, 1950

24 **Folk-Songs by Hungarian Gipsies (Szabolcs-Szatmár County)**, recorded by Rudolf Víg, Hungaroton SLPX 180 82, 1984

25 **Roumanie-Roemenië, La vraie tradition de Transylvanie**, recorded by Herman C. Vuylsteke, Musiques traditionelles vivantes, I. Musiques de tradition orale, BRT/Ocora 558 596, 1981

26 **Transylvanian Wedding Music**, recorded by László Kürti, Ethnic Folkways Records FE 4015, 1983

27 **Roumanie, Musiques de mariage de Maramures**, Musiques traditionelles vivantes, V. Musiques populaires, Ocora 558 506, 1976

28 **Folk Music of Rumania, Brauls, Bocets, Wedding Dance, Sarba bin brau, Folk Dances, Doinas, Horas**, from the collection of Belá Bartók, Ethnic Folkways FE 4419, 1950/1961

29 **The Romanian National Collection of Folklore, A. The Traditional Folk Music Band, I. Oltenia (1)**, recorded by Constantin Brăiloiu, Tiberiu Alexandru, Harry Brauner and Emilia Comişel, Institute for Ethnological and Dialectological Research, Electrecord EPE 02095, 1977

30 **The Romanian National Collection of Folklore, A. The Tradtional Folk Music Band, II. Bucovina**, recordings collected in 1936 and between 1954 and 1956, Institute for Ethnological and Dialectological Research, Electrecord EPE 02164, 1984

31 **Roumanie, polyphonie vocale des Aroumains**, recorded by Bernard Lortat-Jacob, Le chant du monde, CNRS Audio Visuel, LDX 74803, 1983

32 **Roumanie, Le Monastère de Putna**, Musiques traditionelles vivantes, II. Musiques rituelles et religieuses, Ocora 558 505, 1982

Music from the Middle-East, Asia and Oceania

33 **Music of Japan I: Sokyoku**, A Musical Anthology of the Orient, UNESCO Collection, Bärenreiter-Musicaphon BM 30 L 2012, 1962

34 **Music of Japan II: Gagaku**, A Musical Anthology of the Orient, UNESCO Collection, Bärenreiter-Musicaphon BM 30 L 2013, 1962

35 **Music of Japan III: Music of the Edo Period (1603–1867)**, A Musical Anthology of the Orient, UNESCO Collection, Bärenreiter-Musicaphon BM 30 L 2014, no year

36 **Music of Japan IV: Buddhist Music**, A Musical Anthology of the Orient, UNESCO Collection, Bärenreiter-Musicaphon BM 30 L 2015, 1953–7

37 **Music of Japan V: Shinto Music**, A Musical Anthology of the Orient, UNESCO Collection, Bärenreiter-Musicaphon BM 30 L 2016, 1953–7

38 **Music of Japan VI: No-Play/Biwa and Chanting**, A Musical Anthology of the Orient, UNESCO Collection, Bärenreiter-Musicaphon BM 30 L 2017, 1962

39 **Chine: Musique du Foukien**, Musiques & Traditions du Monde, CBS 65574, 1973

40 **Chine Populaire: Musique classique**, Musiques traditionelles vivantes III, Musiques d'art, Ocora 558519, 1977

41 **Chinese Opera: Songs and Music**, Folkways Records FW 8880, 1960

42 **Chinese Masterpieces for the Erh-Hu (Lui Man-Sing and his group)**, Lyrichord LLST 7132, 1969

43 **Mongolian Folkmusic**, recorded by Lajos Vargyas, UNESCO Cooperation, Hungaroton LPX 18013-14, 1972

44 **The Music of Tibet: The Tantric Rituals**, A Musical Anthology of the Orient, An Anthology of the World's Music, recorded by Huston Smith, Anthology AST-4005, 1970

45 **The Music of Tibetan Buddhism I**, recorded by Peter Crossley-Holland, A Musical Anthology of the Orient, UNESCO Collection, Bärenreiter-Musicaphon BM 30 L 2009, 1961

46 **The Music of Tibetan Buddhism II**, recorded by Peter Crossley-Holland, A Musical Anthology of the Orient, UNESCO Collection, Bärenreiter-Musicaphon BM 30 L 2010, 1961

47 **The Music of Tibetan Buddhism III**, recorded by Peter Crossley-Holland, A Musical Anthology of the Orient, UNESCO Collection, Bärenreiter-Musicaphon BM 30 L 2011, 1961

48 **Songs and Music of Tibet**, recorded by Howard Kaufman, Ethnic Folkways Library FE 4486, 1962

49 **Songs and Dances of Nepal**, recorded by Caspar Cronk, Ethnik Folkways Library FE 4101, 1964

50 **Afghanistan, Music from the Crossroads of Asia**, recorded by Peter Ten Hoopen, Nonesuch Explorer Series H-72053, 1973

51 **Musik aus Afghanistan: Nuristan**, recorded by H. D. Preßl, Adevaphon 001, 1976

52 **Musique folklorique de Pamir**, recorded by Liouba Berger, Melodia M30-1182/M30-41183, 1997

53 **Turquie: Musique Soufi Vol. 1**, Musiques traditionnelles vivantes, II. Musiques rituelles et religieuses, Ocora 558522, 1977

54 **Musik in Asien I: Indien und der Vordere Orient**, recorded by Josef Kuckertz, Musik Aktuell Klangbeispiele, UNESCO Collection, Bärenreiter Musicaphon BM 30 SL 5130, 1981

55 **Inde du Nord: Mithila/Chants d'amour de Vidyapati**, recorded by Georges Luneau, Musiques traditionnelles vivantes, V. Musiques populaires, Ocora 558 516, 1974

56 **Inde du Nord: Chant Dhrupad et Dhamar**, recorded by Hubert de Frayssaix, Musiques de l'Asie traditionelle Vol. 9, Playasound, PS 33513, 1976

57 **An Anthology of North Indian Classical Music Vol. I, Vocal Music: Alap-Dhamar-Khyal-Thumri**, recorded by Manfred Junius, UNESCO Collection, Bärenreiter-Musicaphon BM 30 SL 2051, 1975

58 **An Anthology of North Indian Classical Music Vol. II, Vocal Music: Bhajana-Tappa, String Instruments: Vina-Sarangi, Drums: Pakhavaj-Tabla**, recorded by Manfred Junius, UNESCO Collection, Bärenreiter-Musicaphon BM 30 SL 2052, 1975

59 **An Anthology of North Indian Classical Music Vol. IV, String Instruments (Sarod – Dilruba), Wind Instruments (Flute – Shahnai)**, recorded by Manfred Junius, UNESCO Collection, Bärenreiter-Musicaphon BM 30 SL 2054, 1975

60 **Music of South India (in Kerala and Tamil Nadu)**, recorded by Wolf-Peter Stiftel, Lyrichord LLST 7358, 1981

61 **A Musical Anthology of the Orient, India III**, recorded by Alain Daniélou, UNESCO Collection, Bärenreiter-Musicaphon BM 30 L 2018, 1968

62 **Jnan Prakash Ghosh, Drums of India**, Vol. II, EMI ECSD 2583, 1979

63 **Sri Lanka: Kolam – The Masked Play**, recorded by Cyril de Silva Kulatillake, An Anthology of South-East Asian Music, Bärenreiter-Musicaphon BM 30 SL 2569, 1979/1982

64 **Musique populaire traditionelle d'Iraq**, recorded by Vaclav Kubica, Harmonia Mundi France, Ocora OCR 55, no date

65 **Israël, Traditions Liturgiques des Communautés Juives, I/Les jours du Kippour**, recorded by Olivier Bernager, Musiques traditionelles vivantes, II. Musiques rituelles et religieuses, Harmonia Mundi/Radio France, Ocora 558 529, 1977

66 **Musique du Viêt-Nam, Tradition du Sud**, Nguyên Vinh Bao et Trân Van Khê, Radio France, Ocora 68, 1994

67 **Music of Viet Nam, Tribal Music of the Highland People, Traditional Music, Folksongs**, selected by Pham Duy with the collaboration of Stephen Addiss and Bill Crofut, Ethnic Folkways Library FE 4352, 1965

68 **Musiques de l'Asie traditionelle Vol. 10, Vietnam, Musique traditionelle et chants populaires**, Tran Quang Hai et Bach Yen, Playasound PS 33514

69 **A Musical Anthology of the Orient, The Music of Viet-Nam I**, recorded by Trân Van Khê and Nguyên Huu Ba, UNESCO Collection, Bärenreiter-Musicaphon BM 30 L 2022, 1968–9

70 **A Musical Anthology of the Orient, The Music of Viet-Nam II**, recorded by Trân Van Khê and Nguyên Huu Ba, UNESCO Collection, Bärenreiter-Musicaphon BM 30 L 2023, 1968–9

71 **Viêt-Nam, Nouvelle Musique Traditionelle**, recorded by Geneviève Nguyen, programme notes by Trân Van Khê, Musiques traditionelles vivantes III, Musiques d'art, Ocora 558 512, 1973

72 **A Musical Anthology of the Orient, The Music of Laos**, recorded by Alain Daniélou, UNESCO Collection, Bärenreiter-Musicaphon BM 30 L 2001.

73 **Musiques de l'Asie traditionelle Vol. I, Cambodge**, recorded by Jacques Brunet, Playasound PS 33501, *c.* 1970

74 **Cambodia: Ceremonial, Folk and Court Music**, edited by Alain Daniélou, A Musical Anthology of the Orient, UNESCO Collection, Bärenreiter-Musicaphon BM 30 L 2002.

75 **Les Môns de Thaïlande**, recorded by Hubert de Fraysseix, Musiques et Traditions du Monde, CBS 81398, 1976

76 **Music of Thailand**, recorded by Howard Kaufman, Ethnic Folkways Library FE 4463, 1959

77 **The Music of Malaysia, A Musical Anthology of the Orient**, recorded by Jacques Brunet, UNESCO Collection, Bärenreiter-Musicaphon BM 30 L 2026, 1972

78 **Music of Indonesia: Sumatra, Ambon, Bali**, recorded by Phil and Florence Walker, Ethnic Folkways Library FE 4537, 1961

79 **Barong, Drame Musical Balinais**, recorded by Louis Berthe, Collection Musée de l'Homme, Disques Vogue 500 764, VG 403, 1971

80 **Ritual Music from Bali I, The Annual Cycle in Tatulingga: The Usaba Sumbu**, An Anthology of South-East Asian Music, recorded by Dieter Mack, Danker H. Schaareman and Tilman Seebass, Institute for Musicology of the University of Basel, Bärenreiter-Musicaphon BM 30 SL 2570, 1972

81 **Ritual Music from Bali II, Cross-section through the Music of the Annual Cycle in Tatulingga**, An Anthology of south-East Asian Music, recorded by Dieter Mack, Danker H. Schaareman and Tilman Seebass, Institute for Musicology of the University of Basel, Bärenreiter-Musicaphon BM 30 SL 2571, 1972–3

82 **Ritual Music from Bali III, The Gong Gĕdé from Sulahan**, An Anthology of South-East Asian Music, recorded by Danker H. Schaareman, Barni Palm and Monika Nadolny, Institute for Musicology of the University of Basel, Bärenreiter-Musicaphon BM 30 SL 2573, 1987

83 **Bali, Divertissments musicaux et danses de transe**, recorded by Gilles Fresnais, Musiques traditionelles vivantes, Ocora OCR 72, 1973

84 **Scintillating Sounds of Bali: Gabor, Gamelan Anklung, Gamelan Gong Kebjar, Gamelan Bebonangan, Topeng, Baris, Ketjak**, recorded by Doreen Powers, Lyrichord LLST 7305, 1976/1974

85 **Bali éternel: Legong, Baris, Ramayana, Kriss transe a kuta**, recorded by François Jouffa, Arion ARN 33544, 1980

86 **Indonesia I: Java Court Music**, A Musical Anthology of the Orient, recorded by Jacques Brunet, Bärenreiter-Musicaphon BM 30 SL 2031, 1972

87 **Java, 'Langen Mandra Wanara', Opéra de Danuredjo VII**, recorded by Jacques Brunet, Musiques traditionelles vivantes, III. Musiques d'art, Ocora 558507/9, 1976

88 **Gendang Karo, Nordsumatra**, recorded by Artur Simon, Museum Collection Berlin MC 13, 1987

89 **Sunda, Musique et chants traditionnels**, recorded by Jacques Brunet, Musiques traditionelles vivantes, V. Musiques populaires, Ocora 558 502, 1976

90 **Traditional Music of Papua and New Guinea**, recorded by Frédéric Duvelle, Lyrichord LLST 7370, 1976

91 **Papouasie Nouvelle-Guinée, Manus Bougainville**, recorded by Charles Duvelle, Musiques traditionelles vivantes, Radio France/Ocora OCR 86, 1984

92 **Music of Oceania: The Kaluli of Papua Niugini, Kaluli Weeping and Song**, recorded by Stephen Feld, Bärenreiter-Musicaphon BM 30 SL 2702, 1985

93 **Music of Oceania: The Abelam of Papua Niugini**, Bärenreiter-Musicaphon BM 30 SL 2704, 1983

94 **Music of Oceania: Samoan Songs, A Historical Collection**, Bärenreiter-Musicaphon BM 30 SL 2705, no year

95 **Current Music of Tonga**, recorded by Ad and Lucia Linkels, Lyrichord LLST 7400, 1987

96 **Inuit Games and Songs**, recorded by Nicole Beaudry, Claude Charron, Denise Harvey and Jean-Jacques Nattiez, UNESCO Collection, Musical Sources, Philips 6586 036, 1978

Music from Africa

97 **Musique Toma Guinée**, recorded by Pierre-Dominique Gaisseau, Jean Fichter and Tony Saulnier, Disques Vogue LDM 30107, 1972

98 **Kora Music from the Gambia, Foday Musa Suso**, recorded by Verna Gillis with Ramon Daniel Perez Martinez, Folkways Records FW 8510, 1978

99 **African Flutes**, recorded in the Gambia by Samuel Charters, Ethnic Folkways Records FE 4230, 1978

100 **Sierra Leone**, recorded by Jean Jenkins, Musiques traditionelles vivantes, Musiques de tradition orale, Ocora 558 549, 1979

101 **Musique Guéré, Côte d'Ivoire**, Collection Musée de l'Homme, recorded by Hugo Zemp 1965–7, Disques Vogue 500 764, VG 403

102 **Chants & Danses d'Afrique, Kanté Facelli / Keita Fodéba**, Le chant du monde, LDX 7 4 381, 1954

103 **Musik der Senufo, Elfenbeinküste**, recorded by Till Förster, Museum Collection Berlin MC 4, 1987

104 **An Anthology of African Music, The Music of the Dan**, recorded by Hugo Zemp, UNESCO Collection, Bärenreiter-Musicaphon BM L 2301, 1965

105 **Masques Dan, Côte d'Ivoire**, recorded by Hugo Zemp, Ocora 52, 1971

106 **Music and Dances of Occidental Africa, Music of the Malinke, Music of the Baoulé**, recorded by Gilbert Rouget, Music from around the World, Olympic 6110, 1974

107 **The Baoulé of the Ivory Coast**, recorded by Donald Thurow, Ethnic Folkways Library FE 4476, 1956

108 **Ghana, Music of the Northern Tribes: Mamprusi, Grunshi, Fra Fra, Kasena, Dagarti, Kusasi**, recorded by Verna Gillis with David Moisés Perez Martinez, Lyrichord LLST 7321, 1978

109 **Ghana, musica cerimoniale et celebrativa**, Original Ethnic Music of the Peoples of the World, recorded by John Tanson, Albatros, VPA 8400, 1978

110 **Togo, Music from West Africa**, recorded by Dan Kahn and Bill Nowlin, Rounder Records 5004, 1978

111 **Togo, Musique Kabiye**, Musiques traditionelles vivantes, I. Musiques de tradition orale, Ocora 558 640, 1984

112 **Ceremonial Music from Northern Dahomey, Ceremonial, Ritual and Magic Music**, recorded by Simha Arom, UNESCO Collection Musical Sources, Philips 6586-022, 1975

113 **An Anthology of African Music, Nigeria – Hausa Music I**, recorded by David Wason Ames, UNESCO Collection, Bärenreiter-Musicaphon BM 30 I. 2306, no year

114 **An Anthology of African Music, Nigeria – Hausa Music II**, recorded by David Wason Ames, UNESCO Collection, Bärenreiter-Musicaphon BM 30 I. 2307, no year

115 **An Anthology of African Music, Nigeria III – Igbo Music**, recorded by David Wason Ames, UNESCO Collection, Bärenreiter-Musicaphon BM 30 I. 2311, 1975

116 **Musiques du Nigeria Central, Benue-Plateau, State, Idoma, Alago, Lindiri, Eggon, Chamba, Junkun**, recorded by Benoît Quersin, Institute of African Studies, University of Ife, Ocora 85

117 **Musique du Cameroun (Bakweri, Bamileke, Bamoun, Beti, Bafang, etc.)**, Ocora 25, 1965

118 Gabon, Musica da un microcosmo equatoriale, Musica Fang Bwiti con esempi musicali Mbiri, recorded by James W. Fernandez, Original Ethnic Music of the Peoples of the World, Albatros, VPA 8232

119 Le Gabon Éternel, recorded by Michel Montésinos, Arion ARN 33-487, 1979

120 Musiques du Gabon, recorded by Michel Vuylsteke, Ocora 41, 1968

121 Mukanda Na Makisi (Circumcision school and masks), Angola, recorded by Gerhard Kubik, Museum Collection Berlin (West) MC 11, 1981

122 Zaïre, Musique des Salampasu, recorded by Jos Gansemans (1973), Musiques traditionelles vivantes, I. Musiques de tradition orale, BRT/Ocora 558597, 1981

123 Musique Kongo, ba bembé – ba-congo – ba-congo-nséké – ba-lari, recorded by Charles Duvelle, Musiques traditionelles vivantes, Ocora 35, 1966

124 Anthologie de la Musique des Pygmées Aka Centrafrique, recorded by Simha Arom, Musiques traditionelles vivantes, I. Musiques de tradition orale, Ocora 558 526/27/28, 1978

125 Rondes et jeux chantés banda-linda, République Centrafricaine, recorded by Simha Arom, Selaf Orstom, CETO 745, 1973

126 Empire centrafricain, Musique Gbáyá/Chants à penser, recorded by Vincent Dehoux, Musiques traditionelles vivantes, I. Musiques de tradition orale, Ocora 524 558, 1977

127 Musique Centrafricaine, Azandé, recorded by Charles Duvelle, Ocora 43, 1963/68

128 An Anthology of African Music, Central African Republic, recorded by Simha Arom and Geneviève Taurelle, UNESCO Collection, Bärenreiter-Musicaphon BM 30 I. 2310, 1983

129 Musiques Banda, République Centrafricaine, recorded by Simha Arom, Collection Musée de l'homme, Disques Vogue VG 404, 1971

130 An Anthology of African Music, Music from Rwanda, recorded by Denyse Hiernaux-L'hoëst, UNESCO Collection, Bärenreiter-Musicaphon BM 30 I. 2302, 1956

131 Music of the Sudan, The Role of Song and Dance in Dinka Society, Burial Hymns and War Songs, recorded by Francis Mading Deng, Ethnic Folkways Record FE 4303, 1976

132 Musik der Nubier, Nordsudan, recorded by Artur Simon, Museum Collection Berlin (West) MC 9, 1980

133 Dikr and Madih, Islamic Customs in the Sudan, recorded by Artur Simon, Museum Collection Berlin (West) MC 10, 1982

134 Ritual Music of Ethiopia, recorded and edited by Lin Lerner and Chet A. Wollner, Ethnic Folkways Records FE 4353, 1973

135 An Anthology of African Music, Ethiopia II – Cushites, recorded and commentary by Jean Jenkins in 1965, UNESCO Collection, Bärenreiter-Musicaphon BM 30 I. 2305, no year

136 Musik der Hamar, Südäthiopien, recorded by Ivo Strecker, Museum Collection Berlin MC 6, 1977

137 Éthiopie, Polyphonies et techniques vocales, recorded by Jean Jenkins, Musiques traditionelles vivantes, Ocora OCR 44, 1985

138 **Vokale Mehrstimmigkeit in Ost- und Südostafrika, Multi-Part Singing in East- and South-East Africa**, Tondokumente aus dem Phonogrammarchiv der Österreichischen Akademie der Wissenschaften, Verlag der Österreichischen Akademie des Wissenschaften, Ethnische Gruppen: Wagogo, Wakisi, Ashirima, Uamakonde, etc., recorded by Helmut Hillegeist/Gerhard Kubik, PHA LP 2, 1989

139 **Africa, Shona Mbira Music**, recorded in Mondoro and Highfields, Rhodesia by Paul Berliner, Nonesuch Explorer Series H-72077, 1977

140 **The Soul of the Mbira, Traditions of the Shona People of Rhodesia**, recorded by Paul Berliner, Nonesuch Explorer Series H-72054, 1973

141 **Africa Djolé, Percussion music from Africa**, Free Music Production SAJ-19, 1978

Jazz and pop music

142 **The Complete Library of Congress Boogie Woogie Recordings of Albert Ammons, Pete Johnson and Meade Lux Lewis**, recorded 24 December 1938, The Jazz Piano JP 5003, no year

143 **The Golden Gate Quartet's Greatest Spirituals**, EMI Columbia, C 063-10 516

144 **Negro Spirituals, Golden Gate Quartet**, EMI Columbia, IC 062-10 514

145 **Negro Religious Music, Sanctified Singers**, Part One, Vol. 1, Blues Classics 17, BC LP No. 17, *c*. 1960

146 **The Dave Brubeck Quartet Plays Music from West Side Story and Wonderful Town** etc., CBS Jazz Masterpieces, CBS 4504101, 1962

147 **Miles Davis: In a Silent Way**, CBS Jazz Masterpieces, CBS 4509821, 1969

148 **The King's Singers: The Beatles Connection**, EMI Electrola / 495561, 1986

149 **Syzygys**, Hitomi Shimizu (43-microtone organ) and Hironi Nishida (voice and violin), Café Disc, 1987

Contemporary music

150 John Cage, **The First Meeting of the Satie Society, the Socie Satiety the Sozi Sattität the Socie Satiety the Sozi Sattität**, Edition Michael Frauenlob Bauer, MFB 014-015, 1988

151 John Cage, **John Cage liest Empty Words Part IV**, MFB 003-004, 1987

152 **Music before Revolution:** John Cage: **Credo in US, Imaginary Landscape No. 1, Concerto for Piano and Orchestra, Solo for Voice I and II, Rozart Mix**, Earle Brown: **Four Systems**, Christian Wolff: **In Between Pieces for Three Players, Electric Spring 2**, Morton Feldman: **For Franz Kline, The Straits of Magellan, Between Categories**, Toshi Ichiyanagi: **Sapporo, Life Music, Conversations with John Cage**, C. Wolff, Hans G. Helms, M. Feldman, E. Brown and Heinz-Klaus Metzger in discussion, Ensemble Musica Negativa, conducted by Rainer Riehn and Earle Brown, 4-LP box, EMI C 165-28 954/57, 1972

153 Elliott Carter: **Syringa, Concerto for Orchestra**, New York Philharmonic Orchestra, Leonard Bernstein, CRI 469, 1969

154 Elliott Carter: A **Symphony of Three Orchestras, A Mirror on Which to Dwell**, New York Philharmonic Orchestra, Pierre Boulez, Columbia Masterworks, M 35171, 1980

155 Ruth Crawford Seeger: **String Quartet**, George Perle: **String Quartet No. 5**, Milton Babbitt: **String Quartet No. 2**, The Composers Quartet (Matthew Raimondi, Anahid Ajemian, Jean Dupouy, Michael Rudiakov), Nonesuch H-71280, 1973

156 Morton Feldman, **Three Voices**, Beth Griffith: Soprano, MFB 002, 1982

157 Morton Feldman: **The Viola in my Life, False Relationships and the Extended Ending**, CRI SD 276, 1971

158 Gérard Grisey, **Partiels, Dérives**, Musique française d'aujourd'hui, Ensemble Ars Nova, conductor: Boris de Vinogradov, Orchestre national de France, conductor: Jacques Mercier, Erato STU 71 157, 1981

159 Charles Ives, **Die vier Sonaten für Violine und Klavier, Largo für Violine und Klavier**, Martin Mumelter, Herbert Henck, MFB 011-012

160 György Kurtág: **Chamber Music: String Quartet, Wind Quintet, Eight Piano Pieces, Eight Duos for Violin and Cimbalom, Játékok**, Hungaroton SLPX 11846, 1977

161 Conlon Nancarrow: **Complete Studies for Player Piano, Volume Four**, 1750 Arch Records S-1798, 1984 (Dedication: 'For György Ligeti, with profound admiration and affection – Conlon Nancarrow')

162 Harry Partch, **Delusion of the Fury, A Ritual of Dream and Delusion** (first recording), 2 record-set, Columbia Masterworks M2 30576, 1971 (with four pages of colour photos of the instruments)

163 Harry Partch: **Oedipus (excerpted)**, Gate 5 Records, Issue D, 1954

164 Pierre Schaeffer, **études aux objects, étude aux allures, étude aux sons animés, étude de bruits, l'oiseau RAI, suite quatorze**, Prospective 21° siècle, Philips 6521 021, 1971

165 Arnold Schoenberg: **Pierrot Lunaire**, Anton Webern: **Zwei Lieder op. 8, Fünf Canons op. 16**, Pierre Boulez: **Improvisations sur Mallarmé I–III**, conductor: András Mihály, Hungaroton SLPX 11385-a, 1971

166 Edgard Varèse: **Hyperprisme, Octandre, Intégrales**; Arnold Schoenberg: **Suite op. 29**, conductor: Pierre Boulez, Présence de la Musique Contemporaine, Les concerts du domaine musical, Véga C 30 A 271, 1959

167 Edgard Varèse: **Density, Intégrales, Offrandes, Hyperprism, Octandre, Ionisation**, Die Reihe, Friedrich Cerha, Candide CD 31028, 1971

168 Edgard Varèse: **Déserts, Hyperprism, Intégrales, Densité 21,5**, Ensemble Instrumental de Musique Contemporaine de Paris, conductor: Konstantin Simonovitch, EMI Electrola 1 C 063-10 875, 1971

169 Kurt Weill: **Die Sieben Todsünden**, Lotte Lenya, CBS S 62646, 1956

170 Iannis Xenakis: **Metastasis, Pithoprakta, Eonta**, Le chant du monde, musique de notre temps LDX 78 368, 1965

Ligeti whispering with Louise Duchesneau during a rehearsal in London
(October 1989)

8 Rules and Regulation: Lessons from Ligeti's Compositional Sketches

JONATHAN W. BERNARD

From the time of Nottebohm's work on Beethoven's *Nachlass*, the study of compositional sketches has grown to become part of standard musicological practice. The study of later 20th-century composers' sketches, however, is still in its infancy – or, at most, early childhood – for several reasons. One of them is obvious, of course: the sketches themselves haven't been around for very long, and if they have been made available for researchers' perusal at all, this has happened, at earliest, only within the last few decades – in many cases much more recently than that.[1] Another is that it is a well-established tradition among musicologists not to take much interest in very recent music, preferring to wait until the work in question has passed into the realm of the safely historical.[2]

But probably the most significant reason for the relative neglect of sketch study in music composed since World War II is that, for much of the repertoire of Western art music in that period, one often doesn't have a very good idea, in an initial encounter with primary documents such as sketches, just what one is looking at – and this is owing to the fact that one often doesn't have a very good idea of what might be worth looking *for*, either. The 20th century saw a great fragmentation of compositional practice; to be sure, the widespread dissemination of dodecaphony and serialism during the 1950s and 60s did indicate a consensus of a kind, but our lengthening perspective on that era shows that it was a consensus of relatively brief duration, and one of limited scope at that. Far more numerous than the 'committed' serialists were composers who never subscribed to such methods, or who at most showed only a tentative interest in them – and, as time has gone on, this group has taken on much greater importance than any observer might have predicted even half a century ago. But the researcher who seeks to infer details of compositional process or practice from the sketches of a late 20th-century (or, by now, early 21st-century) composer faces challenges that extend considerably beyond the sheer proliferation of non-serial methods. For many of these composers seem to have done something different in each new piece, or at least to have taken up new approaches in more or less rapid succession. Thus having deduced anything about – even something central to – the workings of one particular piece might well represent relatively little progress, if one were to have to start the discovery process all over again that yielded this insight, for some other piece by the same composer.

---

[1] For example, the sketches of Edgard Varèse (d. 1965) did not become accessible until 2004, when the Sacher Foundation purchased them for its archive in Basel.

[2] This tendency (which may very well be changing now) has left sketch study of music since 1950 wide open for researchers from other subdisciplines in music. Theorists, in particular, are not necessarily trained in the standard methodologies of historical musicology but, encouraged by the prospect of making a new kind of contribution to the study of music that is already regarded as a legitimate specialization within their own field, have proved willing and able to educate themselves in the requisite skills.

It should come as little surprise that the compositional sketches of György Ligeti are subject to the same constraints imposed by these circumstances. In early 2002, when I first undertook study of these sketches, they were largely *terra incognita*, having been acquired by the Paul Sacher Foundation only about a year previously: no one had yet worked with the contents of the entire collection in any depth.[3] Bearing in mind the great changes in style and technique that Ligeti had brought to his work over the duration of his long career, I expected to see at least small differences in method exhibited even between pieces composed only a few years apart – to say nothing of the big differences that could be foreseen when comparing pieces in one of the major stylistic periods to those in another. My initial reconnaissance, by and large, confirmed these expectations, leading me to consider how best to spend the necessarily finite time I had available to devote to this project.

To keep the prospective task manageable, one viable plan would have been to concentrate on materials pertaining to just a few compositions, in order to gather some especially pertinent examples of ways in which sketch study informs analysis of Ligeti's music. As I became immersed in the project, however, over the course of two separate visits to the collection, it began to seem essential to look closely at almost everything it contained. This change of strategy arose partly out of sheer curiosity, impossible to restrain; partly as the result of discovering that the collection was not quite as large as it first seemed;[4] and partly also because it soon became obvious that I would not be able even to begin forming hypotheses about Ligeti's working methods without the benefit of such a comprehensive overview.

It will hardly astonish anyone to learn that, despite this effort, many aspects of Ligeti's compositional process remain quite mysterious. Nevertheless, I can vouch for the fact that there are important lessons to be drawn from the substantial body of sketch material that is now available for study. The pages that follow provide an outline of some of these lessons, ranging from the very broadest sort – those pertaining to his entire œuvre, or at least very large stretches of it – to others that have emerged from examination of just a few bars.

✦ ✦ ✦

Ligeti's sketches fall into five basic types, any or all of which may be found among the sketches for a particular piece. The first part of this essay introduces the reader to each of these types, by way of examples selected from work that Ligeti accomplished at different points during his long career; the second part shows how all five contribute to our understanding of a single work.

---

[3] This is not to say that none of the sketches had been available to any scholars before their acquisition by the Sacher Foundation. Two authors of early monographs on Ligeti's music, Erkki Salmenhaara and Ove Nordwall, had benefited from Ligeti's willingness to place in their hands certain documents pertaining to his work, as long-term loans; and photocopies of some of this material are reported to have circulated from time to time.

[4] This circumstance is a decidedly mixed blessing: for several works, including some important ones in Ligeti's œuvre, the sketch record in the Sacher Foundation's archives apparently has some major gaps – to the point (in a few extreme cases) of containing almost nothing at all – for reasons that have not yet been adequately explained.

For presentational convenience, these sketch types have been arranged in an order roughly general to specific: corresponding, that is, to the kind of compositional 'information' one can extract from them. It should be kept in mind, however, that one cannot necessarily infer from such an order the actual, chronological order of creation for any single work. For one thing, Ligeti's sketches hardly ever bear dates of any kind (even approximate ones); for another, some types may conceivably recur at different points in the compositional process.

Jottings

Sketches of this first type involve no musical notation, or even substitute musical notation, of any kind, being strictly prose descriptions of what Ligeti envisions a piece in its early stages – or perhaps even before a single note is actually set to paper – will eventually turn out to be like. One quite significant aspect of such jottings is that they are almost always in Hungarian. German was Ligeti's second language – as it was, one would imagine, for most Hungarians of his generation – and German became especially important as a means of communication with the larger musical world once he had emigrated. But in these jottings he is talking only to himself. They consist largely of lists of qualities, usually section by intended section (or movement) – sections which, to judge by tentative (and sometimes repeatedly revised) timings placed alongside, are sometimes destined to be quite brief. Below is a partial transcription of one of the more extensive sets of jottings that I have come across, for Ligeti's first major success, the orchestral work *Atmosphères*, premiered in 1961. These are so detailed, in fact, that they could almost be called a continuity draft, and translate roughly as follows:[5]

1. Broad, soft, low; entirely static   – 48"

2. Broad, soft, low; gradual variation in colour and dynamic shading; strings dominant; disturbances resembling waves expanding from the individual voices:

in patterns like so: – 29"

3. Broad, soft low; layers emerging from and vanishing [into] the depths (wavelike disturbances as above); a few layers begin and end suddenly ◁f, cluster–harmony–cluster alternations, alternation of harmonies also   – 55"

4. Broad, soft, low; trill-tremolo (strings arco, with winds); other instruments alternate in large rocking motions; simultaneous projection of quiet and accelerating layers as well   – 37"

5. Broad, coarse, very soft trill-tremolo colour variation (alternating rocking motions as above)   – 6"

---

[5] While I cannot claim to be fluent in Hungarian, I have found that a good translating dictionary is adequate to the task of deciphering most of these jottings, since there are usually no syntactical puzzles to be solved in lists or brief annotations of this kind. All translations into English in this essay, unless otherwise noted, are my own.

6. Figural variation, dynamic variation as well (trill-tremolo at beginning, then smooth). Complex, proliferating variations in figures. Gradually into 7. [next] – 23″

7. Gradually developing outward, with a massive crescendo: big, shrill, high, loud, sharp (4 picc., 1 or 2 E♭ clarinets; several more clarinets too). Perhaps high strings here and there; perhaps glockenspiel, crotales. Suddenly breaks off as 8. enters unexpectedly. – 33″

8. Very deep, very massive, very loud. Begins abruptly, directly connected with 7. as it breaks off. After a while, becomes softer; meanwhile, 9. enters; as it does so, 8. gradually slows, then dies away. – 14″

[This series of numbered descriptions continues to 21.]

There are at least two reasons to believe that such jottings are more than preliminary exercises for Ligeti, the sort of thing that one might set aside or discard as soon as more 'musical' work has begun. For one thing, this particular set of jottings, like several others for other pieces, is typed. Furthermore, such sketch leaves (and this is particularly true of the ones for *Atmosphères*) often bear many signs of having been referred to again and again. Section-by-section descriptions are reordered; some are crossed out, others inserted; projected timings, as mentioned, are often revised, sometimes several times over. Often these pieces of paper are in an extremely limp and oxidized state, even by comparison to many of the other well-worn sketch pages, which seems to indicate that they were among the most frequently handled of all the sketch materials.

Ligeti followed this procedure at least into the early 1970s, after which point he seems gradually to have abandoned it – although it is difficult to be certain of this, since the sketch record is notably incomplete for many pieces from the late 1960s until the early 1980s, where more abundant documentation resumes. For pieces from the 1980s on, a different kind of jotting appears in the sketches: many, sometimes a great many, handwritten lists for each work, often on tiny pieces of paper, which indicate the intended character of individual movements but do not break them down further than that. Usually these lists reflect Ligeti's wide-ranging interests in music from all styles and periods within the Western 'art-music' tradition, as well as many from ethnic sources and/or other cultures. Here is one particularly exuberant example, intended for the fifth movement of the Piano Concerto:

Presto: loud and soft. Fragmented. Nancarrow [Study] 41b dense, 'Caribbean-Bulgarian' rhythm, with Central African [rhythm], 'hyper-major' [scale], jazz-pianistic gleam and sparkle. Coda: 'Liszt' prestissimo, with infinite speed disappearing into the high register

Lists of this kind do not bear the same signs as the earlier ones of having been worked over and repeatedly referred to. They are usually so numerous for each work or movement thereof, and so different from one another, that it seems reasonable to conclude that they really were preliminary exercises, 'thinking on paper', with little or no function to perform once the actual business of composition was under way.[6]

Drawings

Drawings, the second category of sketches, are Ligeti's projections, as visualizations, of how the music is to 'go'.[7] Often they take on the general aspect of pitch-time graphs, with pitch displayed from low to high on the vertical axis, time elapsing from left to right on the horizontal. These drawings vary greatly in degree of precision, and also of scale: sometimes an entire movement or work is outlined, sometimes only a short section. Brief discussions of two examples follow.

The first example (Colour plate 1) is one (probably the first) of three sheets devoted to outlining the orchestral work *San Francisco Polyphony* (1974); the handwritten notations perform some of the same functions as do the jottings, but here they are inseparable from the visual depiction. Although it is clear that many of the details have yet to be fully worked out, all the basic features of the shape that the piece ultimately took (excluding the coda, which is not depicted on this sheet) are already reflected here. Ligeti's own description of *San Francisco Polyphony*, taken from an interview conducted in 1978, is an excellent guide to this drawing:

> [T]he exposition of the musical material creates a chromatic space that is filled up with heterogeneous tunes which are different from, and stand in contrast to, one another. The space then gets less dense, as if someone went through it with a comb, thinning it out; the introduction ends on a high note ..., then follows the middle section, the longest part of the work, where twisting ostinatos whirl around long, expressive melodies. Gradually the musical texture gets polarized between the higher and lower registers; at the two poles density increases, leaving an expanding empty space in the middle. Ultimately the melodic texture is squashed to the ceiling and the floor and it all ends on a C across several octaves; every tune has been eliminated, as if ironed flat, reduced to one note.[8]

---

[6] Richard Steinitz, in 'À qui un hommage: Genesis of the Piano Concerto and the Horn Trio', the next essay in this collection, considers the role of these multitudinous jottings in Ligeti's compositional process for two of his post-*Grand Macabre* works.

[7] Or, in some cases, actually does go, for some of these drawings are so neatly concise that they could almost be summaries of work that has already been done. To put all such drawings into the category of *compositional* sketches, then, might well be jumping to conclusions – yet most of them do differ in at least a few plainly evident ways from the finished music. See also the interview cited in n. 11 below.

[8] Ligeti, interview with Péter Várnai ('Bészelgetések Ligeti Györgyyel', 1978), trans. Gabor J. Schabert, in *György Ligeti in Conversation with Péter Várnai, Josef Häusler, Claude Samuel and Himself* (London, 1983), pp. 13–82, at p. 44. The timings (both original and revised) across the top margin of the sketch suggest that Ligeti at first had in mind an appreciably shorter duration for this part of the piece, which may explain why the subsequent pages seem to outline a continuation far longer than one would expect for a coda that, in the finished composition, accounts for just over one-fourth of its total length.

The second drawing (Colour plate 2) is of much smaller scope, concerned as it is with a few bars of *Atmosphères*. In this one it is clear that the overall design in space is of paramount importance: note the octave designations in the left margin. On a grid formed by the octaves (in the vertical dimension) and the barlines (in the horizontal), the activity of the many-voiced divisi of the string section plus woodwinds is depicted: some parts moving downward in pitch and disappearing from the texture at the end of bar 33; others moving upward and either fading out or continuing to the end of the drawing in bar 39. The musical activity illustrated here, in fact, corresponds directly to numbers 7 and 8 from the jottings quoted above. Again, as in the first drawing, the essential qualities of the passage are in place, even if some of the details (such as orchestration in this case) remain to be worked out.[9]

Perhaps we should not be all that much surprised that drawings play such a significant role in Ligeti's sketch process. Many of his descriptions of specific works (such as *San Francisco Polyphony*, as quoted above) and of his compositional process in general have a strong visual component: 'In general,' Ligeti has said, 'my works abound in images, visual associations, associations of colours, optical effects and forms'; he has admitted to being 'inclined to synaesthetic perception'.[10] Even more revealing is a comment he made on one occasion about his compositional process: that after first imagining a new work from beginning to end ('ten times, perhaps 100 times'), 'the next step is always to have a drawing – no notes. I am never writing directly scores [*sic*]. They are very similar to what is called graphic notation,' which he then noted that he had carried directly over to the form of the published score in only one case: *Volumina*, a work for organ dating from 1961–2.[11] Other evidence of the importance of the visual to Ligeti comes in the form of the creations he calls his doodlings, some of which have been widely reproduced.[12]

Charts

In this, the third type of sketch, individual pitches are specified but are usually not displayed in staff notation. Instead, Ligeti uses German pitch names, arranged in vertical stacks. Like the drawings, charts emphasize construction in pitch space; in fact, charts occasionally emerge quite explicitly as realizations of drawings. One particularly clear example of

---

[9] Along with indications of violins and winds in the upper right corner of the drawing, crotales, glockenspiel, and celesta are listed, none of which feature in the percussionless orchestra of *Atmosphères*. This sketch is also reproduced and discussed in Richard Steinitz, *György Ligeti: Music of the Imagination* (London, 2003), pp. 109–10.

[10] *György Ligeti in Conversation*, pp. 57, 58.

[11] 'Ligeti Talks to Adrian Jack', *Music and Musicians* 22/11 (1974), pp. 24–30. The interview was conducted in English; its published form preserves various idio-syncrasies of Ligeti's speech in that language.

[12] One spectacular example of Ligeti's talents as a 'doodler' was reproduced on the cover of a five-LP box set of Ligeti recordings issued by Wergo in 1984 (WER 60095). Dating from 1967 and rendered in coloured pencil and oil crayon, it is entitled (evidently in Ligeti's own hand) 'Die Bevölkerung in den Wolken' [The Inhabitants of the Clouds].

such realization is a chart that seems to proceed from the drawing of the *Atmosphères* passage previously shown in Colour plate 2. In Colour plate 3, a small part of the music sketched in this drawing is worked out in detail: the second violins in bars 30–2. The numerals refer to the individual parts in this divisi of 14; all such numerals except the ones denoting the initial positions of parts 1–9, the only ones sounding at the beginning of the passage, are written in red, with arrows (also in red) showing the successive relocation of individual parts in the stack as they leapfrog upwards. (The isolated pitches in staff notation are evidently provided to serve as reminders of registral position.)[13]

Another example from the 1960s, the construction of the vocal parts in bars 65–74 of the Introit movement of the *Requiem* (Colour plate 4), shows intensive attention to the divergence from an initial unison attack (a regularly recurring feature of this movement) and, once again, a working with the results in actual pitch space. The circled numbers 3 and 5 in the left margin refer to triple and quintuple divisions of the beat, respectively, in individual parts (parts without a number are divided duply). Notice that Ligeti seems to be mainly interested in the relative placements of notes in the various parts, not in any exact resultant rhythm. This is perfectly in keeping with his general attitude at that time, often expressed in his writings and interviews, that although the notation of a score should be as precise as possible, the performance of the music need be only as near to exact as the players or singers can manage – and that the little discrepancies that arise from this effort are not only tolerable but actually part of the composer's desired effect.[14]

Tables

The fourth type of sketch is different from the others in that it is not directly compositional; nevertheless, it has an important role to play in many of Ligeti's works. The table is a kind of running account of pitches, rhythms, or durations as they are used in the compositional process – almost as though Ligeti were keeping statistics on his own usages. Judging from the form in which these tables are left, he does not seem to have made an effort to arrange for the totals to come out exactly the same in any of these categories, pitch or rhythm; it does seem plausible, however, that he tried to keep things more or less even as the process went along. An example of a rhythmic tabulation appears as Colour plate 5. A reasonable surmise is that it pertains to the Introit of the *Requiem*, since this is one of the two movements the text of which appears on the same sheet. (The other movement whose text is here, the Kyrie, does not make the same use of these rhythmic 'cells', as one might call them.) In practice, it is quite

[13] In 'À qui un hommage' Richard Steinitz refers to such charts as 'matrices' – not to be confused, however, with the 12×12 pitch-class squares employed in 12-tone composition that are also often called matrices. See p. 172–3.

[14] For a particularly clear enunciation of this philosophy, see *György Ligeti in Conversation*, p. 53. It holds true, of course, mainly for the music Ligeti composed between the late 1950s and the late 1970s. For pieces in the newer style, from about 1980 on, Ligeti's charts often incorporate the rhythmic aspect of the music as it takes shape, with the polymetres and polyrhythms precisely aligned on sheets of graph paper.

difficult to trace these totals back (or, more properly speaking, ahead) to the finished score, although my own attempt at making a parallel tabulation did yield results that approximate those shown here. The reader will notice that although patterns involving septuplet divisions of the beat are shown, no totals are registered for them. A plan involving the use of such septuplet divisions evidently belonged to an earlier stage of work on the Introit – and, indeed, some sketches for this movement, rather remote from the finished product, do exhibit such divisions. (There are none in the Introit as published.) The idea of performing this kind of tabulation may well have sprung from Ligeti's exposure to 1950s-style serialism, although one could hardly call such an approach to regulation serial in itself. It would be more accurate to say that by doing this Ligeti sought to achieve (what he saw as) one of the chief desiderata of the serial method, but by a different means altogether.[15]

Musical notation

The fifth type of sketch, finally, encompasses work in conventional musical notation, and can be divided further into two subtypes. First, there are sketches that consist either of pitches in staff notation with no rhythm or duration indicated, or of rhythms with no assigned pitches – the latter much more common after 1980. Rhythmic sketches differ from the rhythmic charts shown earlier in that their contents correspond to specifically worked-out passages or sections of pieces, as opposed to general or generic metric/rhythmic situations. As for pitches in staff notation, there are two basic varieties of sketch. An illustration of the first of these, the pitch map, is given (in transcription) in Colour plate 6. In this excerpt from a sketch for *San Francisco Polyphony*, an initial sonority undergoes gradual metamorphosis, as one pitch at a time is altered. A little horizontal bar situated at or near the middle of each chord (marked in red ink, just barely visible in Plate 6) seems intended to track the upper and lower constituents of the evolving vertical structure: in each chord, there are nine parts below, nine parts above this marker. Together with similar usages in sketches of earlier pieces in which such a midpoint is literally marked 'symm' or 'asymm', this example serves to an extent as independent corroboration of the empirical findings of several researchers, who have found various analytical techniques based strictly in pitch to be particularly revealing of salient qualities in Ligeti's music, symmetry among them.[16]

---

[15] Ligeti speaks briefly of this possibility in 'Metamorphoses of Musical Form', *Die Reihe* 7 [Form–Space] (Bryn Mawr, PA, 1965), pp. 5–19, at pp. 13–14; and at greater length in 'Fragen und Antworten von mir selbst', trans. Geoffrey Skelton, in *György Ligeti in Conversation*, pp. 124–37, at p. 131.

[16] See, for instance, Jonathan W. Bernard, 'Inaudible Structures, Audible Music: Ligeti's Problem, and his Solution', *Music Analysis* 6 (1987), pp. 207–36; Jonathan W. Bernard, 'Voice Leading as a Spatial Function in the Music of Ligeti', *Music Analysis* 13 (1994), pp. 227–53; Jonathan W. Bernard, 'Ligeti's Restoration of Interval and its Significance for his Later Works', *Music Theory Spectrum* 21 (1999), pp. 1–31; Jane Piper Clendinning, 'The Pattern-Meccanico Compositions of György Ligeti', *Perspectives of New Music* 31/1 (Winter, 1993), pp. 192–234; Jane Piper Clendinning, 'Structural Factors in the Microcanonic Compositions of György Ligeti', in *Concert Music, Rock, and Jazz since 1945*, ed. Elizabeth W. Marvin and Richard Hermann (Rochester, NY, 1995), pp. 229–56;

Another variety of pitch-based sketch (Example 27a) pertains to the second movement of the Chamber Concerto, a substantial work completed in 1970. Here we see a single line of pitches that is marked with each of the first five pitches corresponding to a particular instrument: an outgrowth of Ligeti's well-known practice involving many-voiced canons in close stretto, which he worked out during the late 1950s and the 1960s. In this later practice, all five voices start at the same point in time and follow the same strand of pitches in rhythmic unison, but begin at different pitches in that strand. Example 27b shows the beginning of the 'resolutio' of the sketch in Example 27a, as it stands in the published work.

The second subtype comprises sketches in more complete musical notation, with notes actually in rhythm – and it is at this point, of course, that the documents in question start looking less like sketches and more like finished pieces. Not that they are less interesting to study, of course, for many of them bear evidence of continued revision and working out, as well as 'analytical' features that clearly relate to the tables discussed earlier. Also to be included in this category, at least nominally, are the occasionally encountered passages that to all appearances have been set down in definitive form, to the last detail, yet are not to be found in any of Ligeti's finished compositions. One spectacular example is the first version of the Violin Concerto, dating from 1990: there are three complete movements and an incomplete fourth movement, all copied out painstakingly in Ligeti's usual fashion, none of which bears more than a fleeting and tenuous relation – and mostly none at all – to the five-movement final version of 1992.

✦ ✦ ✦

In light of this five-part classification of his sketches, Ligeti might well seem at first to be a composer to whom words and pictures mattered almost as much as music. But while it is true that both the verbal and the visual played important roles in his creative process, and in his creative life in general, Ligeti was actually quite traditional in the meticulous way in which he worked out the *sound* of his pieces. The visual elements do not signify a conceptual bent; Ligeti was no philosopher-composer of the John Cage type. He did have a brief flirtation with aleatory at one time, but it left no traces other than in a few highly atypical works of the early 1960s, notably *Volumina*, written (as mentioned earlier) in a graphic notation, and the famous *Poème symphonique* for 100 wind-up metronomes, the 'score' for which is simply a set of instructions.[17] In all his other works, Ligeti's notation is essentially a direct and accurate representation of a specifically envisioned sonic realization. It may be that the jottings and drawings had a kind of catalytic role to play, and thereafter served as contextual guides, helping him keep the larger dimensions and intentions of his piece in

Michael Hicks, 'Interval and Form in Ligeti's Continuum and Coulée', *Perspectives of New Music* 31/1 (Winter, 1993), pp. 172–90; Miguel Roig-Francolí, 'Harmonic and Formal Processes in Ligeti's Net-Structure Compositions', *Music Theory Spectrum* 17 (1995), pp. 242–67.

[17] The *Poème symphonique* in particular has been referred to as a product of Ligeti's 'Fluxus' period, although Ligeti himself denied having any strong aesthetic affinity with the Fluxus group. See Eric Drott, 'Ligeti in Fluxus', *Journal of Musicology* 21 (2004), pp. 201–40.

Example 27 Chamber Concerto, II: (a) canonic strand;
(b) corresponding score excerpt

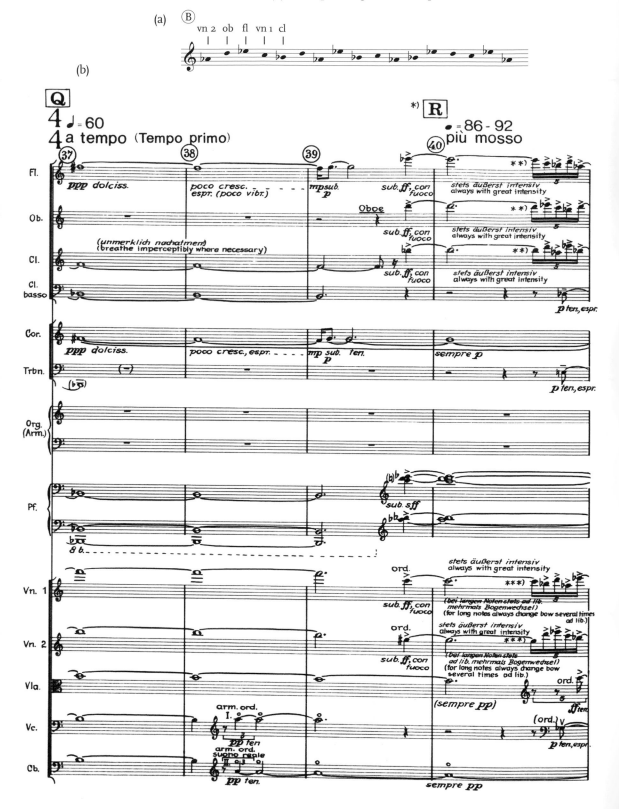

mind as he worked out the details of the score. Thus these documents remain interesting even as the intricacies of notes and rhythms emerge from study of the other sketches.

Turning now to the sketch record for Ligeti's *Requiem*, specifically the second movement (Kyrie), we find many different kinds of sketches corresponding to the five basic types already enumerated.[18] The *Requiem*, a very large work in four movements which Ligeti began composing in 1963 and did not finish until early 1965, comes at the end of his so-called 'cluster-composition' period. Although the final movement shows some signs of a new tendency to focus periodically on 'clear' intervals, a characteristic that has much to do with the music he wrote from the mid-1960s on,[19] in the first three movements the vocal and instrumental textures exhibit the kind of maximum vertical proximity of parts already familiar from his earlier orchestral works *Apparitions* and *Atmosphères*: with semitones dominating, that is, in the harmonic sense. In the Kyrie in particular (see Example 28), this style takes the form of 'bundles' of voices, as Ligeti called them, treated polyphonically, each bundle a group of four parts subdividing the soprano, mezzo-soprano, alto, tenor, and bass sections of the choir: thus 20 parts in all.[20]

One thing readily evident from the sketches for the *Requiem* is that Ligeti, in the early planning stages for this piece, was not sure just how many movements there would be. It is safe to assume, however, that he tried hard from the beginning to make the entire conception very different from that of an earlier requiem, begun in the 1950s before leaving Hungary, which he failed to carry beyond a few pages of score. For this new attempt, a page of jottings titled 'Missa pro defunctis' outlined seven movements projected to last about 35 minutes. In the end, a planned Part II, encompassing movements four through seven (Offertorium, Sanctus, Agnus Dei, and Communio), was discarded in favour of a single, short, epilogue-like fourth movement, the 'Lacrimosa'. Compared to the practically moment-by-moment jottings for *Atmosphères* displayed earlier, those for this overall plan for the *Requiem* are far less detailed – although there is a good deal more for the third movement, Sequentia, than for any of the others, eventually supplemented by many more jottings for that movement alone. For the Kyrie, however, there is only a brief (typed) text that translates roughly as follows: 'A large unending web ("polyphonic", indeed, incidentally, quasi-canonic), flowing, rather soft, never pausing. Chorus and instruments intertwined (braided). Lengthy.' Supplementing this typescript are some handwritten notations in the margins and between the lines, some of which are legible: 'Small intervals, scale-like. "Bach-Motet" – cantus firmus within?'[21] Other, partly legible jottings suggest

---

[18] Some of what follows about the Kyrie was previously published, in much briefer form, in Jonathan W. Bernard, 'A Key to Structure in the Kyrie of György Ligeti's *Requiem*', *Mitteilungen der Paul Sacher Stiftung* 16 (2003), pp. 42–7.

[19] György Ligeti, 'Auf dem Weg zu Lux aeterna', *Österreichische Musikzeitschrift* 24 (1969), pp. 80–8.

[20] Ibid. Ligeti uses the term 'Stimmbündel' in this essay.

[21] Earlier composers, styles, genres, or even names of famous works set in quotation marks, like 'Bach-Motet' here, always signify allusion in a very general, remote, or fleeting sense – *not* quotation, but something more like the *idea* of that earlier music.

Example 28 *Requiem*, Kyrie: first page of score

that at this point Ligeti was thinking of casting the movement either for ten to 15 solo voices or for ten solo voices with a 20-voice accompanying texture. Thus the general conception of this movement is already in place at this point, even if the specifics are not (for instance, the movement is certainly not 'rather soft' all the way through, and not all the voice-leading is scale-like, either). But it does flow unceasingly and polyphonically; the concept of voice bundles is already present; and it is second only to the Sequentia in length. As for the cantus firmus, in a sense there is one, as the ensuing discussion will show.

At this point, one might wish to see a reproduction of the drawing of the Kyrie that is to be found among the sketches for this work. Unfortunately, this does not happen to be one of Ligeti's more beautiful or evocative drawings. It's rather blurry, in fact, and consists mainly of shaded, overlapping, elongated hillocks or (perhaps) waves, portraying the passage of time from left to right, evidently intended to convey the idea of continuous motion with the bundles of voices overlapping in their entries and durations. One interesting feature of the drawing, though, is the fact that the hillocks are labelled 'Kyrie' and 'Christe' along with their choral-part designations (soprano, alto, and so forth), in a fashion consistent with the contrapuntal design of the movement..

Before displaying more sketches – including one especially revealing chart – it will be worth outlining the general characteristics of Ligeti's Kyrie movement. The two text phrases are kept aurally distinct from one another by being set to radically contrasting melodic material. The words 'Kyrie eleison' are always set to the same melody (to within strict pitch transposition and strict pitch inversion). This melody moves solely by melodic adjacencies of whole tones and semitones, and in durational values that gradually diminish through a range extending from somewhat longer than a beat to as short as nonuplets, then gradually lengthen back again. The settings of the text 'Christe eleison', on the other hand, are much more diversely and more angularly constructed. They vary considerably in length (that is, in terms of sheer number of bars) and involve a larger range of possible melodic adjacencies, all generally conforming to expanding and contrasting wedge designs; they exhibit a more angular pattern of durations too, selected from a range extending from shorter than a beat to much longer. The 'voice-bundle' feature mentioned earlier, however, does enforce a general similarity between the two types of material, as does the consistent stretto-canonic feature.

Example 29 displays the pitch sequences of some of the melodies, so that some of the other differences between Kyrie and Christe material may be appreciated. It is the wedgelike design of the Christe melodies that lends them their general tendency to run through all 12 of the pitch classes in fairly short order – a feature not shared at all by the Kyrie melody. In fact, there are two occurrences of the Christe melody (both included in Example 29: sopranos entering at bars 40 and 102) that each consist of exactly 12 pitches, corresponding to the 12 pitch classes, and thus could be read as *series*, in the strict 12-tone sense. Do they have actual 12-tone significance, though? One would think not, since this work otherwise exhibits no affinity to dodecaphonic or serial procedures, and since it is well known that Ligeti explicitly turned away from serialism very early on.

162

Example 29 *Requiem,* Kyrie: melodic material for 'Kyrie eleison' and 'Christe eleison'

Yet it bears keeping in mind that Ligeti, like many of his contemporaries in post-War Europe, had developed a deep fascination with the music of Webern – especially, it would appear, the 12-tone works. Articles about Webern dominated Ligeti's bibliography from the late 1950s until the mid-1960s, a period during which he wrote more for publication than he ever did thereafter. He also found Webern important enough to make his music the subject of a ten-part series of lectures that he delivered over Southwest German Radio in 1963–4.[22]

Is it just a coincidence that the version of the *Christe* melody at bar 102 begins with the same two pitches, B_4 and Bb_5 in that order, that end the version at bar 40, and that the latter could therefore be regarded as the retrograde inversion, at T_{11}, of the former? The sketch record contains other evidence, not simply that this relationship was carefully worked out, but that it is the basis for a single scheme, extending over the entire movement, that governs the order of all entries of the Kyrie and Christe melodies. The first hint of this basis comes in a sketch labelled *Grundtypus*, or fundamental type, that is equivalent to the series at bar 40 at T_5, or, equivalently in this case, transposed down a perfect fifth. This Grundtypus, paired with its RI_{11} (thus also transposed down a perfect fifth, compared to the series at bar 102), is the basis for a further sketch, displayed in Colour plate 7. It's not very easy to read, but still it is worth the effort required to understand the scheme as outlined in Ligeti's own hand. Here the two series are dovetailed, in Webernian fashion, to form a 22-pitch sequence. Above each note appears an indication of correspondence to the order of entries of Kyrie and Christe material. For the first note, for example (Bb), the legend 'A Kyr O + T Chr UK' signifies that the 'Kyrie eleison' melody is given to the altos, in its original (uninverted) form ('O'), while simultaneously the tenors sing a version of the 'Christe eleison' melody in its inverted retrograde form (*Umkehrung Krebs*, hence 'UK'). At the second note, A, we read 'B Kyr U', which means the basses project Kyrie material in inversion; at $G\sharp$, the mezzos sing Christe material in original form; and so on. Ligeti revised the order of pitch classes in the basic scheme in two places, as shown by arrows drawn on the chart: it's not very easy to make out, but G and $F\sharp$, which should have been the 15th and 16th notes of this double series respectively, have been swapped; and at the end the sequence B–Bb–A is circularly permuted to Bb–A–B. This, then, is the 'cantus firmus' to which Ligeti referred in his jottings.

Even more interesting than the Webernian allusions is the idea of using such a series as a kind of master control mechanism to regulate a composition that is decidedly neither 12-tone nor serial in its note-to-note organization. Such a scheme is at the heart of one of Karlheinz Stockhausen's great works of the 1950s, his *Gruppen* for three orchestras. In this work, the intervals between adjacent notes of a series are used to define precise ratios between the tempi of consecutive brief sections; the intervals of the series are also used to define the vertical (pitch) spaces, or 'fields', within which these brief sections

---

[22] Four of these ten lectures by Ligeti have been published as 'Aspekte der Webernschen Kompositionstechnik', in *Musik-Konzepte, Sonderband: Anton Webern II*, ed. Heinz-Klaus Metzger and Rainer Riehn (Munich, 1984), pp. 51–104.

operate.[23] In this connection, it is worth recalling that one of Ligeti's first close-up glimpses of musical composition as it was being practised in the West was almost certainly of this piece, at Stockhausen's house in Cologne, where he stayed for a time as a convalescing guest in early 1957: Ligeti was put up, in fact, in Stockhausen's own studio! At this time Stockhausen was exclusively occupied with writing out the full score of *Gruppen* from the elaborate scheme that had taken him over a year to put together.[24] Clearly, this exposure induced no particular desire on Ligeti's part to write in a style like Stockhausen's; his own music from that time on could hardly have been more different. Yet the general, procedural parallel, at least, is striking.

This scheme provides us with an idea of one aspect of regulation in Ligeti's compositional method. And of course a cantus firmus, or a structure analogous to one, is also a *rule* of a sort. But it isn't the only kind of rule alluded to in the title of this essay. The prevalence of imitation in this Kyrie movement brings to mind another part of the legacy of Western musical practice: voice-leading rules. Ligeti often affirmed the existence of such rules in his part-writing, although he never disclosed for publication exactly what they were. As he commented in one interview: 'I have retained melodic lines in the process of composition, they are governed by rules as strict as Palestrina's or those of the Flemish school, but the rules of this polyphony are worked out by me.'[25] As it turns out, the sketches, along with another interesting document that has surfaced in the Sacher collection, are enlightening in this regard as well.

The document in question is a letter, or perhaps the draft of one, written in German and dated 10 August 1965, from Ligeti to Erkki Salmenhaara, at the time a doctoral student at the University of Helsinki and one of the first researchers anywhere to become seriously interested in Ligeti's music. It was evidently meant to accompany a shipment of materials pertaining to the *Requiem*, which Ligeti had agreed to lend to Salmenhaara. In this lengthy letter, Ligeti lays out very specifically the rules for the third movement, the Sequentia or 'Dies irae'. Some of the more significant excerpts are quoted in translation below:

> Voice leading proceeds predominantly in leaps; all leaps are possible from minor third up to major ninth, except the octave. Concerning the proportional distribution of intervals in each voice, the major and minor sevenths, major and minor ninths are dominant, the small intervals occur less frequently.
>
> The rules for series of leaps are slightly different for the chorus than for the soloists. For the chorus, consecutive leaps in opposite directions are permitted without limit, but two in the same direction are not permitted at all. For the soloists, however, two in the same direction are admissible as long as they do not form a major or minor triad. Stepwise rules are the same for both: two steps in the same

---

[23] See Jonathan Harvey, *The Music of Stockhausen* (London, 1975), pp. 55–76.

[24] The story is told in a text of Ligeti's, 'Meine Kölner Zeit' (1993), published in *Neue Musik in Köln, 1945–1971*, for the exhibition at the MusikTriennale, Cologne, 1994. The original typescript is in the György Ligeti Collection at the Sacher Foundation.

[25] *György Ligeti in Conversation*, p. 14.

direction are not allowed, and one step may follow another in the opposite direction only when they are two different kinds of seconds. After two such steps, a leap must follow.[26]

As for pitch usage, the same pitch [class] should as far as possible not recur again soon. At least three new tones should intervene. This rule is flexible, though, and may be overruled by some more important consideration, such as harmony – in which case the same pitch could recur with only two other tones intervening. There are also rules for sequences, prohibiting direct repetition of the same interval and discouraging its re-use after only one intervening tone; the same goes for longer sequences of intervals.

With regard to harmony: unisons are possible only rarely, at certain high points of the movement. Otherwise, separation of parts by at least a second is required. In places where the voice-leading remains stationary for a short time, a 'chordal feeling' can arise, predominantly m2 + TT + P4 or P5. In more active regions, all vertical combinations are possible.

Finally, Ligeti refers to 'twelve-tone economy' in this movement, by which he means that there are no rows, yet 'vertically-horizontally' the tones are distributed such that no tone is heard, insofar as possible, any more frequently than the others, ensuring as even a distribution of the 12 tones as possible. Again, there is flexibility here, and harmonic considerations may override this desideratum in specific instances.

Ligeti then says (to paraphrase): So much for the third movement. For the other movements, similar rules apply, *mutatis mutandis*. Some you will easily discover yourself, such as those governing the Kyrie settings in the second movement. And he concludes: Thus are the rules different for every movement; however, the principle of strict regulation is always fundamentally the same.

Did Salmenhaara ever take up this implicit challenge from Ligeti, and attempted to derive the Kyrie rules empirically, simply from the evidence of the score – once Ligeti had told him what sort of thing he considered a rule to be? There is no evidence of his having done so in his dissertation, so I thought that I might give it a go, 40 years on – with just what degree of success to be detailed below. First, however, it will be useful to peruse some of the sketches that evidently led to the version of the Kyrie melody that he eventually adopted. Colour plate 8 displays one version – evidently constructed fairly early in the process – which is written out in full with the *Original* line paralleling the *Umkehrung*. It resembles the final version in its general contours, but it will be noticed that it is composed exclusively of semitones: not a whole tone to be found anywhere. The key to this version,

---

[26] Ligeti also provides quite thorough and exacting rules, not included in my abridged quotation of this letter, governing leaps after steps and vice versa. Especially at this juncture, his method of outlining rules closely resembles that employed by Knud Jeppesen in his well-known study of Palestrina, *Der Palestrinastil und die Dissonanz* (1925). Ligeti himself has confirmed the importance of Jeppesen's influence: speaking of his own educational background, he commented that 'Without the Palestrina exercises I learned through Jeppesen I would never have been able to work out intricate micropolyphonic textures.' *Györgi Ligeti in Conversation*, p. 71.

which turns out to be an important way-station, is to be found in a tabular sketch transcribed as Figure 16a.

In this series of numbers, with some arithmetical calculations below, each number stands for a phase of the contour, and counts the consecutive

(a)   2 2 2 3 4 2 3 4 3 5 3 3 3 5 2 2 3 2 6 3 2 4 2 5 2 2 4 4
      2 3 5 3 2 4 3 4 3 2 2 4 4 3 4 3 2 2 4 3 2 2 3 2 4 2 2

$$2 \times 22 = 44$$
$$3 \times 16 = 48$$
$$4 \times 12 = 48$$
$$5 \times 4 = 20$$
$$6 \times 1 = 6$$

(b)

6	10	12	12	10
6	5	4	3	2
	5	4	3	2
		4	3	2
			3	2
				2

Figure 16 *Requiem*, Kyrie: (a) number tables; (b) number tables (2)

tones that either ascend or descend before a change of direction occurs. At each change of direction there is an overlap: thus, for example, the first members of the series, 2 2 2, correspond to Bb–A–Bb–A, so that the first A is the last member of the first 2 and the first member of the second 2 – and so forth. The calculations simply reveal how many notes in all are involved with spans of 2, how many with spans of 3, etc. Which came first, the melody or the calculation? It is difficult to tell, but one can say, at least, that the design revealed by the numbers does seem to have kept the totals for 2, 3, and 4 nearly even, with those for 5 and 6 markedly lower. It also seems that this design was itself a revision of a prior one, never even fully realized, which was more symmetrical, giving the same total of notes to spans of 2 as to spans of 5, and the same to spans of 3 as to spans of 4 (Figure 16b).

At any rate, once he had the all-semitone melody, Ligeti was evidently not satisfied with it and sought to open it up a bit by injecting whole tones at certain points. A (probably slightly later) sketch, displayed in Colour plate 9, shows him doing just that, but something is clearly not quite right, since the effort is soon broken off and the inversion is not even begun. One possible surmise as to what happened at this point was that he drew up an explicit set of rules for placing whole tones: rules which led to the result we know in the finished piece. They can be summarized as follows:

1. All successive intervals are tones and semitones, the latter by far predominant. No direct repetitions of tones are allowed.

2. Consecutive semitones may occur in the opposite or the same direction. No more than two may occur consecutively in the same direction.

3. A whole tone may occur only after two consecutive semitones in the same direction, and must continue in that same direction. (However, see Rule 5.)

4. A whole tone may be followed only by a semitone, in either the same or the opposite direction. By far the more common continuation is the latter.

5. If two semitones follow a whole tone in the same direction, the next interval must be a semitone in the opposite direction.

To help explain the application of these rules, Example 30 reproduces the pitches at the beginning of the first Kyrie melody (sopranos), with numbered brackets each illustrating one of the rules as enumerated above.

Earlier I said that the whole tones were injected; a more accurate way of putting it would be that each whole tone simply replaces a semitone from the earlier version. Thus the contour remains the same, and the melody ends only a semitone away from where it originally did. But the finished melody is much more interestingly variegated, while remaining very strictly controlled in its behaviour.

Example 30 *Requiem*, Kyrie: pitch succession in altos, bars 1–8, illustrating hypothetical rules of voice leading

✦ ✦ ✦

Even this relatively small selection of sketches should serve to make it clear that Ligeti finds his particular compositional voice along that sometimes rather hazy boundary between freedom and stricture: freedom on the one hand to make up his own rules, the obligation on the other to obey their constraints. More significant than the voice-leading rules just discussed, however – which constitute one extreme of Ligeti's approach to obtaining a result that is both consistent and musically interesting – is the overall tendency to regulate by principle rather than precept. The idea of keeping things *more or less even*, which comes out in his self-direction to keep the 12 tones in steady circulation without binding them to rows as such, is one example of a not-so-rigid approach to control that is nonetheless very effective; his methods of guaranteeing that all possibilities of combination will be exhausted (such as with rhythmic cells), even in the absence of a specific algorithm for doing so, constitute another example. Although the method or methods in use will change from piece to piece, or even from section to section (and sometimes radically at that), it is this approach to regulation (as Ligeti said himself) that can be counted on – and it is surprising just how much difference that sort of footing can make. For this researcher it has helped sort out what would otherwise be a bewildering sea of documents and has made these compositional sketches, if not exactly easy to study, at least somewhat more tractable.

*Ligeti studying his sketches during an exhibition in Güterlsoh
(1990)*

9 À qui un hommage?
Genesis of the Piano Concerto and the Horn Trio

RICHARD STEINITZ

Writer's block

Some artists enjoy lives of unbroken productivity, even those who – like Goya and Stravinsky – execute major stylistic changes during the course of a career. Others encounter times of doubt and indecision when little is produced. The rapidity of stylistic change in the 20th century left composers particularly vulnerable to self-questioning. One thinks of Walton unable to complete his Symphony no. 1 (first performed without its finale), of Copland labouring five years over his *Piano Fantasy*, of Sibelius running irredeemably into the creative buffers. Ligeti, too, after the première of his opera *Le Grand Macabre* in 1978, struggled with deep uncertainty, completing only two brief harpsichord pieces later that year and then nothing until 1982.

This apparently fallow period provoked speculation which the composer did little to illuminate. He was 'gravely ill',[1] or he 'was not'[2] – according to his own contradictory self-diagnoses. He was approaching 60, which 'is in itself an illness'.[3] He had reached a point of profound 'compositional crisis'. But it was not, as he later explained, only 'a personal crisis', rather 'a crisis of the whole generation to which I belong'.[4]

Whatever the reasons, the impasse lasted on and off for seven years. Ligeti's most pressing obligation was to compose a piano concerto. It had been commissioned in the early 1970s by the American conductor Mario di Bonaventura at a time when, without any permanent appointment, Ligeti badly needed income. On 25 November 1968 di Bonaventura wrote to inform the composer that he would programme the Cello Concerto with Siegfried Palm at the Hopkins Centre in Dartmouth, USA.[5] A year later he wrote of its great success and invited Ligeti to write a work for the Centre for a fee of $1,500, perhaps 'a horn concerto for the gifted English artist, Barry Tuckwell'.[6] 'There would be no date imposed', but he hoped it would be for the Congregation of the Arts in summer 1971 or 1972. Ligeti had other commissions to fulfil, and anything else would have to await completion of his opera. Nevertheless a commission was agreed, although for a piano concerto rather than one for horn, to be played by Mario di Bonaventura's brother Anthony.

---

[1] Ligeti, interview with István Szigeti broadcast by Budapest Radio, 29 July 1983; reprinted as 'A Budapest Interview with György Ligeti', *New Hungarian Quarterly* 25/94 (Summer 1984), pp. 205–10, at p. 209.

[2] 'I wasn't seriously ill 78–82, it was a stylistic crisis': postcard to the writer, November 1996.

[3] Szigeti, 'A Budapest Interview with György Ligeti'.

[4] Ligeti, interview with Monika Lichtenfeld in *Neue Zeitschrift für Musik* 142 (1981), pp. 471–3.

[5] Letter in the Ligeti archive, Paul Sacher Foundation.

[6] Di Bonaventura letter to Ligeti, 3 November 1969, Paul Sacher Foundation.

But when, after the opera's première, Ligeti began to work on the Concerto, he found it impossible to compose even an opening to his satisfaction. In the six years between his first jottings in the summer of 1980 and the rush of inspiration from which flowed the Concerto's first three movements in 1986, he tried over and over again to start the piece, writing innumerable versions of its first page, all abandoned. These abortive beginnings tell a remarkable tale of trial and error.

Ligeti's sketches

During three days I spent with Ligeti in Hamburg in February 2000, he said that he had made 'hundreds of attempts' to compose the Concerto's first page, and in answer to my question 'Where are they?' gestured to a sprawling pile under his grand piano. I assumed that it would stay there, to be explored only after his death. His early manuscripts were already available for study at the Paul Sacher Foundation in Basel. In the years after Ligeti's dramatic escape from Hungary in 1956, they had been secretly retrieved by the Swedish musicologist Ove Nordwall from the cellar of his mother's apartment in Budapest. Ligeti had allowed Nordwall to retain them in order to write his monograph on the composer,[7] and later agreed that Nordwall should keep the proceeds of their sale to the Foundation, provided it coincided with the purchase of all the manuscripts in his own possession. Despite protracted negotiations, however, Ligeti refused to accept Sacher's offer, and Nordwall proceeded without him. Ligeti was angry that the condition had not been observed and, in 2000 when I visited him, was still withholding from the Foundation all the sketches and autographs he had written in the West.

In October 2001, near to completing my own book on the composer,[8] I visited Basel to look at his early scores, and was surprised to find that virtually all the later manuscripts had just arrived. Unfortunately, there remained little time to examine them, and, regarding the Concerto, I refer in my book only to a set of photocopied 'first pages' whose originals Ligeti had given to di Bonaventura.[9] Subsequent visits to Basel have revealed more than 50 successive 'beginnings' spread over six years, plus three preliminary 'plans' (in words) – one projecting a seven-movement Concerto, one four movements, the other five. It was, of course, the five-movement concept that prevailed, although the last two movements proved almost as difficult to write as the first. So that the di Bonaventuras need wait no longer, having finished the first three movements Ligeti allowed them to be premièred in Graz on 23 October 1986, and the complete Concerto was first performed in Vienna 16 months later on 29 February 1988.

During the early 1980s Ligeti was absorbed in new interests, ranging from medieval counterpoint to the music of Central Africa, from Nancarrow's studies for mechanical piano to molecular biology and computer-generated fractals. These 'discoveries' would feed into his music, but how was far from clear. Ligeti's only major work completed in the seven years after the opera was the Trio for Violin, Horn and Piano, composed

---

[7] Ove Nordwall, *György Ligeti: eine Monographie* (Mainz, 1971).

[8] Richard Steinitz, *György Ligeti: Music of the Imagination* (London, 2003).

[9] Ibid., pp. 315–21.

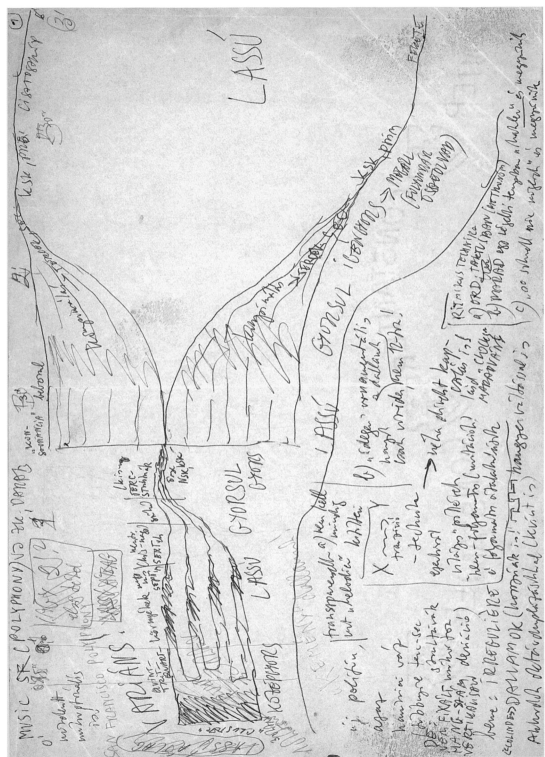

1 *San Francisco Polyphony*: first page of drawing

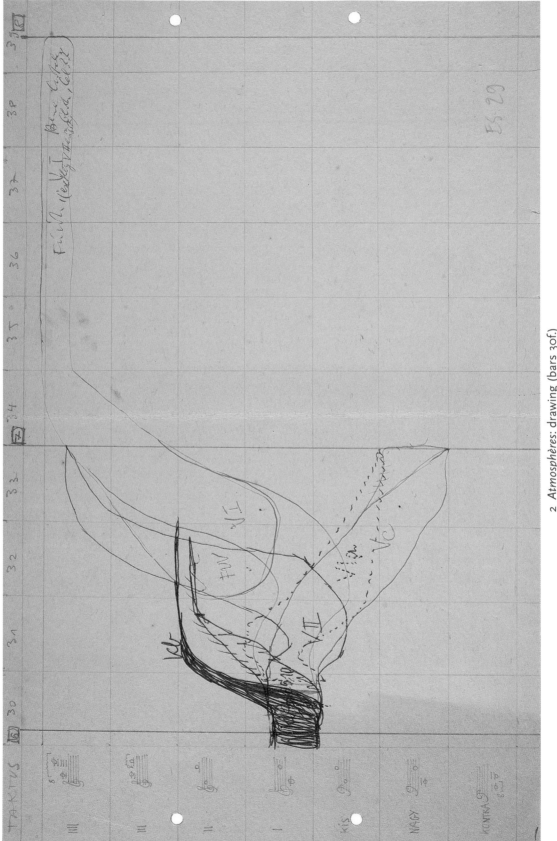

2 *Atmosphères*: drawing (bars 30f.)

3 *Atmosphères*: chart for bars 30–3, violin II

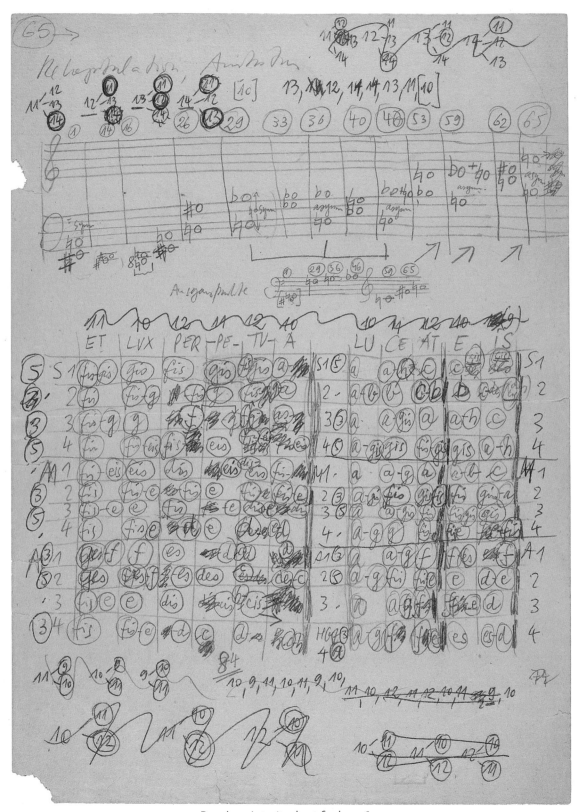

4 *Requiem*, Introit: chart for bars 65–74

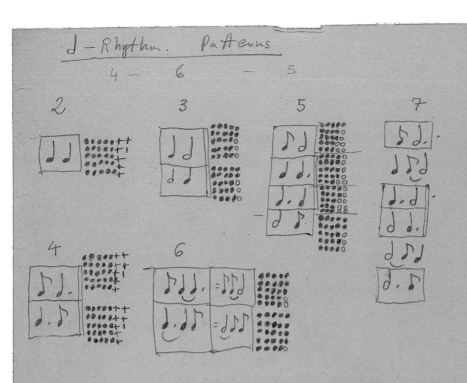

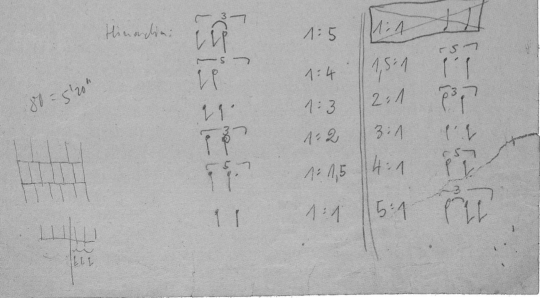

Requiem aeternam dona eis Domine: et lux perpetua luceat eis.

Te decet hymnus Deus in Sion, et tibi reddetur vorum in Jerusalem:

exaudi orationem meam, ad te omnis caro veniet.

Requiem————eis.

Kyrie eleison (iij) Christe eleison (iij) Kyrie eleison (iij).

5 *Requiem*, Introit: table of rhythmic patterns

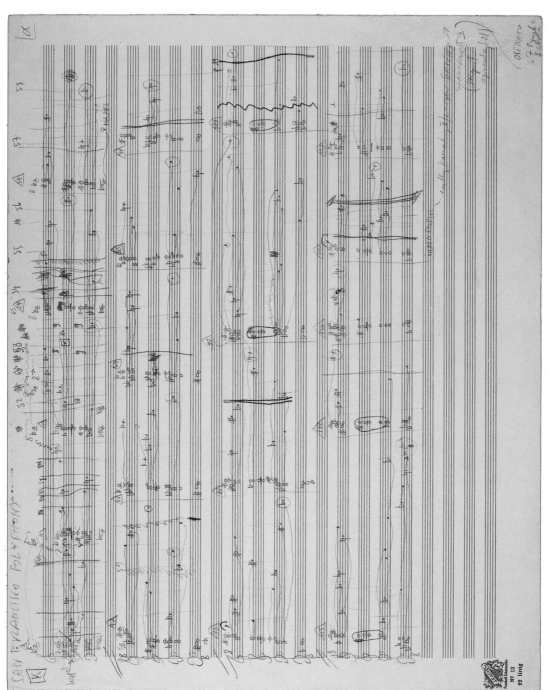

6 *San Francisco Polyphony*: pitch-change graph

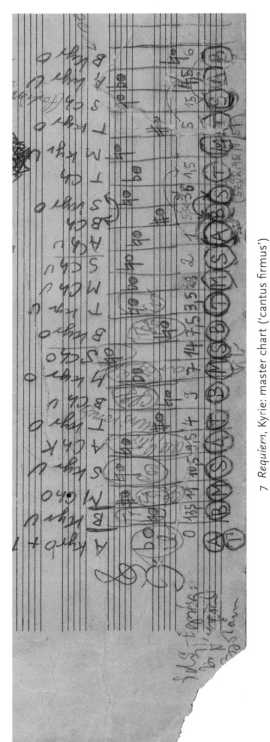

7 *Requiem*, Kyrie: master chart ('cantus firmus')

8 *Requiem*: all-semitone first version of Kyrie melody

9 *Requiem*: new attempt at Kyrie melody, injecting whole tones

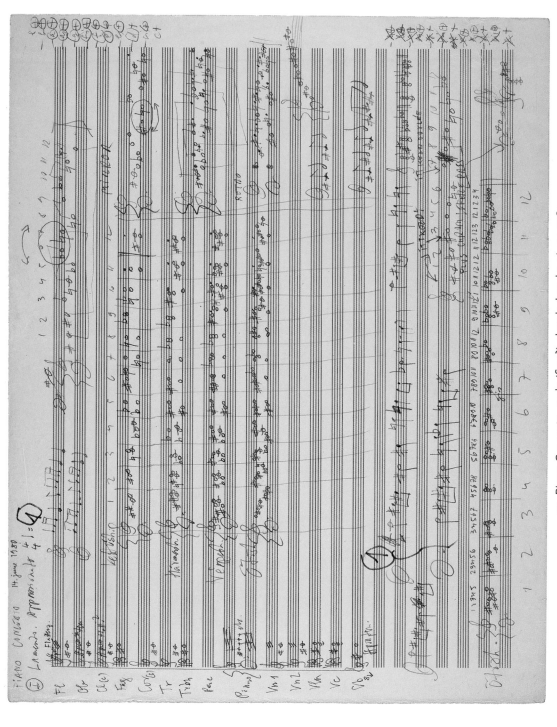

10 Piano Concerto, early (first?) sketch dated 14 June 1980

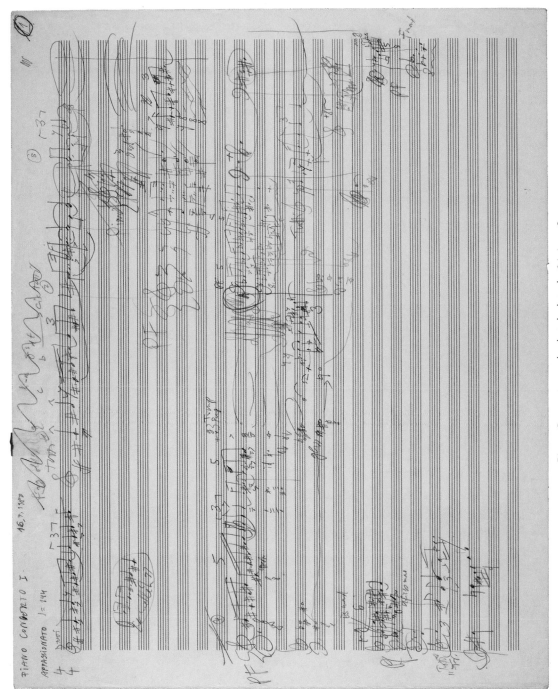

11 Piano Concerto, early sketch dated 16 July 1980

12 Piano Concerto, first movement, a linear idea

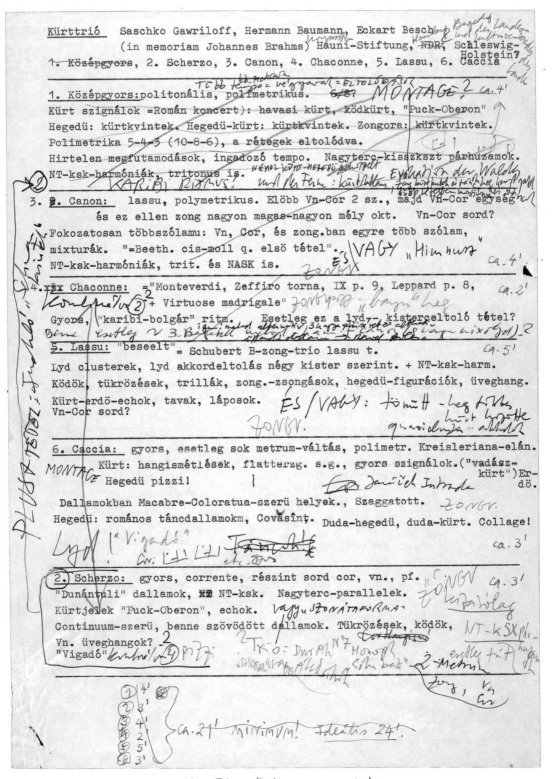

Kürttrió   Saschko Gawriloff, Hermann Baumann, Eckart Besch
     (in memoriam Johannes Brahms) Hauni-Stiftung, NDR, Schleswig-
                                                          Holstein?
1. Középgyors, 2. Scherzo, 3. Canon, 4. Chaconne, 5. Lassu, 6. Caccia

1. Középgyors:politonális, polimetrikus.   6/8? MONTAGE ca.4'
Kürt szignálok =Román koncert): havasi kürt, ködkürt, "Puck-Oberon"
Hegedü: kürtkvintek. Hegedü-kürt: kürtkvintek. Zongora: kürtkvintek.
Polimetrika 5-4-3 (10-8-6), a rétegek eltolódva.
Hirtelen megfutamodások, ingadozó tempo. Nagyterc-kisszkszt párhuzamok.
NT-ksk-harmóniák, tritonus is.
     KARIBI RITMUS!

3. 2. Canon: lassu, polymetrikus. Elöbb Vn-Cor 2 sz., majd Vn-Cor egységn
          és ez ellen zong nagyon magas-nagyon mély okt.   Vn-Cor sord?
Fokozatosan többszólamu: Vn, Cor, és zong.ban egyre több szólam,
mixturák. "=Beeth. cis-moll q. elsö tétel". VAGY "Himnusz"
NT-ksk-harmóniák, trit. és NASK is.   ca.4'

4. Chaconne: ="Monteverdi, Zeffiro torna, IX p. 9, Leppard p. 8, ca.2'
          + Virtuose madrigale"
Gyors, "karibi-bolgár" ritm.   Esetleg ez a lyd - kisterceltoló tétel?

5. Lassu: "beseelt" = Schubert B-zong-trio lassu t.   ca.5'
Lyd clusterek, lyd akkordeltolás négy kister szerint. + NT-ksk-harm.
Ködök, tükrözések, trillák, zong.-zsongások, hegedü-figurációk, üveghang.
Kürt-erdö-echok, tavak, láposok.   ES/VAGY:
Vn-Cor sord?

6. Caccia: gyors, esetleg sok metrum-váltás, polimetr. Kreisleriana-elán.
     Kürt: hangismétlések, flatterzg. s.g., gyors szignálok.("vadász-
     Hegedü pizzi!   kürt")Er-
                                                                   dö.
   Dallamokban Macabre-Coloratua-szerü helyek., Szaggatott.
Hegedü: románoss táncdallamokm, Covâsînţ. Duda-hegedü, duda-kürt. Collage!
                                                        ca.3'

2. Scherzo: gyors, corrente, részint sord cor, vn., pf.   ca.3'
"Dunántuli" dallamok. NB NT-ksk. Nagyterc-parallelek.
Kürtjelek "Puck-Oberon", echok.
Continuum-szerü, benne szövödött dallamok. Tükrözések, ködök,
Vn. üveghangok?
"Vigadó" pizzi

①4'
②3'
③4'   ca.21' MINIMUM! Ideális 24'
④2'
⑤5'
⑥3'

13 Horn Trio preliminary movement plan

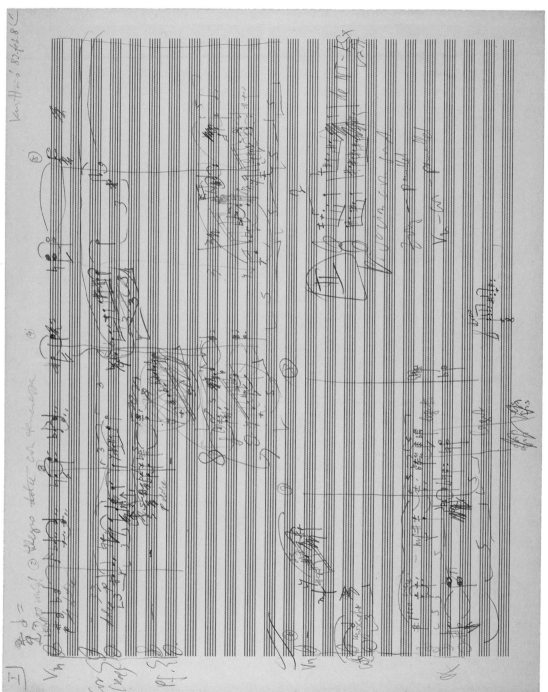

14 Horn Trio, first movement sketch, 8 February 1982

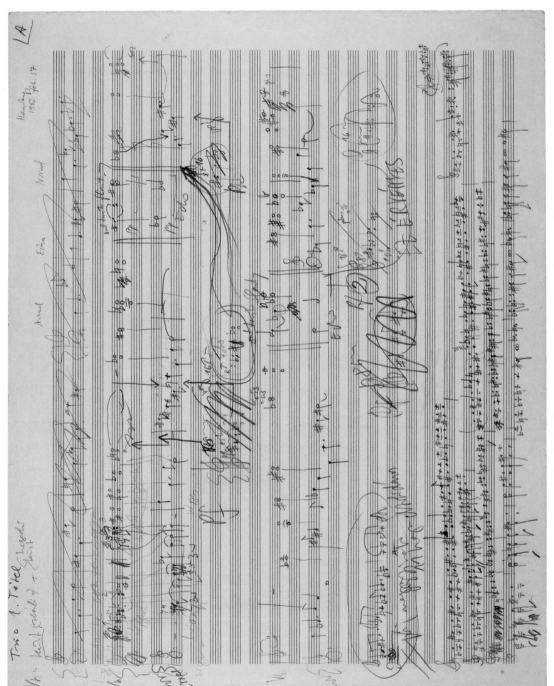

15 Horn Trio, first movement sketch, 17 February 1982

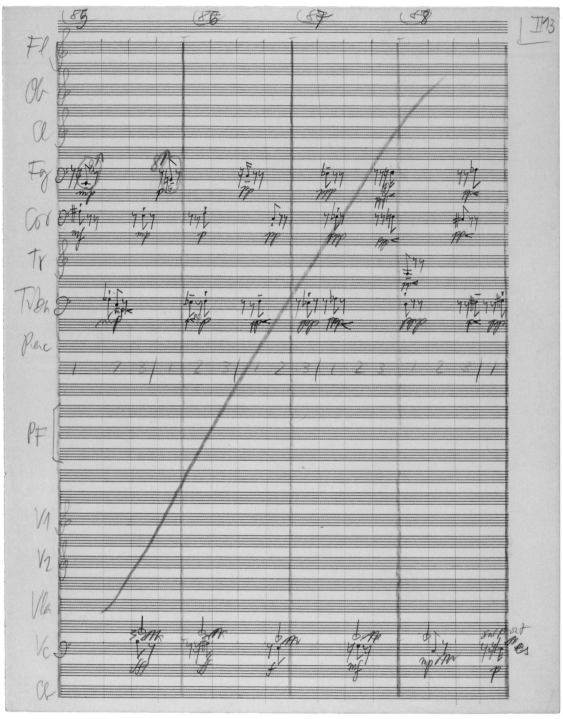

16 Piano Concerto, a page from the second movement, first version

171

RICHARD STEINITZ
*Genesis of the
Piano Concerto
and the Horn Trio*

with apparently little difficulty during the first half of 1982 and premièred in Hamburg on 7 August. Stylistically, the Trio owes much to Ligeti's habit of playing chamber music with students of the Hamburg Hochschule für Musik und Theater, a practice dating from soon after his appointment as professor of composition in 1973. Writing it allowed him to sidestep the intractable problems of the Concerto by indulging his deep regard for the classical canon. It was a level of involvement unique among his avant-garde colleagues, to some of whom the Trio's retrospective stance signified a betrayal. Ligeti himself was aware of the danger, and beat a retreat via two unaccompanied choral pieces whose structure and style were governed by their texts: *Drei Fantasien nach Friedrich Hölderlin* composed immediately after the Trio, and *Magyar etüdök* composed in 1983. Then he returned to the Concerto. But the search for a viable beginning remained problematic, and without establishing an opening to his satisfaction, he could write no other part. There can surely be few composers who, with such success behind them and at the height of their game, laboured quite so long and hard to begin a composition.

Not all of Ligeti's sketches are in Basel; indeed, the whereabouts of some of them appears to be unknown. For the Double Concerto and *Lontano* Basel has relatively few, for *Melodien* only two sheets. Some pages of *Apparitions* and *Atmosphères*, which Ligeti gave to the Webern expert Hans Moldenhauer, are now in the Library of Congress. In May 1984 Ligeti sold three sketches for the Horn Trio at Sotheby's in London. The following year he contributed eight sketches for the Piano Études to an auction organized at Sotheby's to raise money for the Aldeburgh Foundation.[10] Both lots were purchased by Northwestern University Library in Evanston, Illinois which, in 2008, also acquired the autograph score of the Piano Concerto. Ligeti had given this to Maria di Bonaventura 'in token of their friendship'. But now in his 80s and suffering poor health, di Bonaventura decided that it should go to the institution which had presented the American première.

The Paul Sacher Foundation was disappointed not to have obtained the manuscript, but had an unexpected acquisition of its own. In the summer of 2009 Ligeti's autograph score of *Atmosphères*, long considered lost, turned up for auction at Christie's. The Foundation purchased it along with Ligeti's performance notes and two printed copies of the score. The autograph might add little to research, but as one of Ligeti's most iconic compositions, notated on exceptionally tall 88-stave paper, its elegance and clarity make it both historically interesting and visually something to treasure.

Ligeti wrote numerous sketches for the Concerto, fewer apparently for the Horn Trio. Taken together, however, they afford a fascinating insight into the creative process. The Paul Sacher Foundation has also Ligeti's 'plan' for the Trio, projecting six or even seven movements and citing 'models' by seven other composers – although curiously not by Brahms, to whom the Trio is ostensibly 'un hommage'. His three plans for the Concerto allude to even more diverse stimuli.

---

[10] Louise Duchesneau thinks that these were the only occasions Ligeti sold anything at auction.

In the years after their premières, Ligeti acknowledged specific influences on both compositions. That some he repeatedly emphasized was due, no doubt, to the clarity of hindsight, added to which, like other prominent people frequently interviewed, he developed a store of stock answers. During the protracted process of composition his thoughts naturally were more diverse and exploratory, including gambits with no useful outcome. In what follows I attempt to illuminate the sometimes circuitous evolution of both works primarily as revealed in their sketches, and the role and range of Ligeti's 'models'. To put these in context, let us first consider his practice in previous compositions.

The creative process

With a few exceptions (as noted above), the Paul Sacher Foundation now owns sketches for all of Ligeti's compositions completed in the West, many of them in considerable quantity. For a number there are preliminary 'plans' or 'drawings' – sometimes both – which Ligeti occasionally labelled 'forma' (i.e. 'form', 'shape', but also 'mould' and 'model' in Hungarian). The 'plans' are mostly typed lists of movements or sections, with notes about their intended character and techniques, including relevant guide works or models. Less specific are hundreds of scraps of paper on which Ligeti recorded ideas as they occurred to him – almost always in words, rarely in musical notation. From the early 1960s until the end of his life they provide a mine of information about his creative ideas. Relevant to the last two decades is also a leather-bound, loose-leaf notebook, maintained from the mid-1980s to 1995, in which Ligeti refined his plans for a second opera (on *Alice*), an orchestral piece to be called *Labyrinths*, a third string quartet intended for the Arditti, and other works – although, disappointingly, only in words.[11] The 'drawings' or 'maps' date from earlier and are hand-drawn graphic projections of the music he was about to compose. To work out voice-leading he also wrote detailed tables and matrices, especially during the 1960s, for although never a committed serialist, like other members of the avant-garde he wished to organize pitches, durations and dynamics systematically.[12]

At first the approach suggests a combination of the mathematical and sculptural – primarily abstract, although never without dramatic and emotive import. Like many composers, Ligeti worked best within the discipline of self-imposed limits. This was already evident in *Musica ricercata* (1951–3) in which, to exorcise the Bartókian language of his upbringing, he resolved to start again from basic ingredients. Twelve years later, to construct the far more sophisticated 20-part edifice of the Kyrie in the *Requiem*, he set himself such exacting contrapuntal

---

[11] On the night of 23/4 August 1986, Ligeti had 'a Mozart dream' which he recorded after waking up, writing down on two staves what he had 'heard' (four bars for piano in E♭ major). It is the only fully notated music in the notebook!

[12] In 'Rules and Regulation: Lessons from Ligeti's Compositional Sketches' pp. 149ff. in this volume, Jonathan W. Bernard defines five basic types: 'jottings' (i.e. prose descriptions), 'drawings' (i.e. 'visualizations'), 'charts', 'tables', and actual 'musical notation' ranging from pitch maps to fair copies.

173

RICHARD STEINITZ
*Genesis of the
Piano Concerto
and the Horn Trio*

rules[13] that its completion took nine months, and the whole work much longer.[14] But by the 1980s, when he began writing the Piano Concerto and the Horn Trio, Ligeti had largely abandoned pitch charts and matrices. Some of their many sketches are fragmentary; but they are 'normally' notated, even when dealing only with pitch, their purpose being to 'try out' possible ideas, techniques and styles.

During our conversations, Ligeti said that he had also written many 'beginnings' for *Apparitions* (1957–9), his first major composition in the West. This seminal orchestral score originated in an earlier piece, *Víziók*, which Ligeti had partly composed in the weeks before leaving Hungary, but of which only half a page survives. The change of perspective after his arrival was as marked as that of the early 1980s, except that Ligeti's admission into the Western avant-garde provided a benchmark for what he wanted to achieve. None of his first attempts at *Apparitions* appear to have survived, although the Paul Sacher Foundation has some pages of a draft full score, and a folder containing matrices and mathematical calculations on scraps of card and paper. Most are in fractions and look as if they are serially ordered. Some project durations into realms of astronomical fantasy: in one case 3/2, 9/4, 27/8, 81/16, 243/32, continuing in 12 steps to 531441/4096! By the time Ligeti began the Piano Concerto he had left such unrealistic game-playing far behind.

Among the sketches for *Atmosphères* (1961) are more tables and matrices, plus a drawing of the registral flow between bars 30–9 (see Colour plates 2 and 3). Although a visual representation of just one event, Ligeti's drawing is a foretaste of the notation adopted in *Volumina* for organ, composed immediately after *Atmosphères*, in which he used graphic notation without any specific pitches throughout the printed score. Appropriate to the unique (in Ligeti's œuvre) concept of *Volumina* and the mechanical attributes of the organ, he never used such notation again.

For the Cello Concerto (1966) a single sketch fragment and a sheet of tables survive. But a hand-drawn structural 'map' and detailed preliminary notes tell us more about the progress of its composition. Cut up into small strips of paper are typed descriptions of the 27-section single movement work which Ligeti originally planned. Another sheet shows their later compression into 'one big movement', described by Ligeti (in Hungarian) as 'wandering E. T. A. Hoffmann-like (rather like Sindbad):[15] romantic, mysterious, extremely fantastic'. With a nod in the direction of *Aventures* and *Nouvelles Aventures*, he notes that it could be an 'Aventures sans paroles', or even 'avec paroles'. At an intermediate stage Ligeti allocated the 27 sections to four movements, and wrote the numbers 'I → II → III → IV' in ballpoint at the top of the page, adding durations in minutes, and noting that II and III would be the equivalent of a scherzo and slow movement. The Concerto that emerged was, as we know, neither in one, nor four, but

---

[13] Influenced by Ligeti's study of 16th-century counterpoint as a student, and by such models as Ockeghem's mensural canons, Frescobaldi's *oblighi* technique and the serial rigour of Nono's choral writing in *Coro di Didone* and *Il canto sospeso*.

[14] Conversations with Richard Steinitz in Hamburg, February 2000.

[15] Not the Sinbad of *The 1001 Nights*, but the alter-ego of Hungarian novelist Gyula Krúdy – a traveller through time, memory and imagination.

two movements. Section 1 – much drawn out – became the first movement, and the remaining 26 sections the second, following each other in rapid succession and 'glued' together 'like a collage'. At this stage Ligeti considered the second movement to be an expanded variant of the first: a view confirmed by his structural drawing, in which the same graphic symbols are deployed in both.

Evidently the 27 sections were originally typed on a single sheet and the scissors used later. But, whatever their order, it is well-nigh impossible to relate the 27 sections to the finished composition – a timely caution against reading too much into Ligeti's preliminary plans. Yet the process illustrates the fluidity and openness with which Ligeti sought viable structures at a time when precedent had been rejected, and his reliance upon literary analogy to underpin musical narrative. Despite the abstract nature of what we hear, his preparatory thinking was not just technical, but broadly allusive. In his descriptions of the individual sections are references to a 'Bosch portrait (Mahler variants)', 'Miró, Steinberg-signature', 'baroque-concerto-allusions ... *René Clair – Picabia, continuous – Chaplin ... March – Ives*'.[16] Section 14, labelled 'Idyll', is to have a 'golden-rose, dreamlike string melody' with 'bitter-sweet Schubertian/Mahlerian harmonic relationships (as in the Schubert String Quintet, *Siegfried Idyll* and the *Adagio* (coda) of Bruckner's eighth symphony)'. Under section 3, following 'EGYHANGÚ lassú' ('MONOTONE slow'), Ligeti has typed 'Scelsi-kettősfogások' ('Scelsi double-stoppings').

This last reference is surprising, since one would not have expected Ligeti to have heard of Scelsi at this time. Years later, in a birthday message to his friend Friedrich Cerha, Ligeti recalled showing each other their early scores (Cerha's *Fasce* and Ligeti's *Apparitions*, both completed in 1959), surprised at how alike they were. 'We couldn't know then that another older composer in Rome was doing something similar, independently from us', he wrote, 'that was Giacinto Scelsi, whose existence we only heard of twenty years later, in the '80s.'[17] Ligeti made a similar assertion in conversation with Ulrich Dibelius,[18] saying that he first heard about Scelsi in the journal *Musik-Konzepte* edited by Metzger and Riehn (no. 31) in 1983.

How, then, do we explain the reference in Ligeti's plan for the Cello Concerto written in the mid-1960s? To type 'Scelsi double-stoppings' in relation to 'MONOTONE' seems nothing if not aware. Although reclusive and little known, in the previous 15 years Scelsi had composed his second, third and fourth string quartets, the hour-long *Trilogy* for solo cello (1956–65) and a handful of larger works. There were even occasional performances. In 1950 the cantata *La Naissance du Verbe* received a sensational première, followed in December 1961 by the extraordinary *Quatro Pezzi (su una nota sola)*, both in Paris. By then Ligeti had already been living in the West for five years and, with his ever-alert antennae, may have learnt indirectly of Scelsi's existence, perhaps from Siegfried Palm, a

---

[16] The words printed here in italics Ligeti added by hand.

[17] György Ligeti, 'Fritz Cerha, herzlichst, zum siebzigsten Geburtstag', trans. Louise Duchesneau, in *Gesammelte Schriften*, ed. Monika Lichtenfeld, vol. 1 (Mainz, 2007), pp. 473–8, at p. 475.

[18] Ulrich Dibelius, 'Gespräch über Ästhetik', in *György Ligeti: Eine Monographie in Essays* (Mainz, 1994), p. 260.

175

RICHARD STEINITZ
*Genesis of the
Piano Concerto
and the Horn Trio*

leading exponent in the development of cello technique for whom he was composing his own concerto. Did Ligeti type the reference after being told about Scelsi's unusual *scordatura* double stoppings[19] and then forget that he had ever heard of the composer? Whatever the answer, Ligeti has the last laugh. Other than a pair of open harmonics, the solo part contains no double stopping at all.

It would seem that these precisely itemized sections – subsequently cut up so that they could be shuffled – amounted eventually to little more than an *aide-mémoire*. None of the references appear in his programme notes, which eschew everything extra-musical. Writing such detailed plans appears to have been partly a warm-up exercise to stimulate momentum, partly a receptacle for ideas which might or might not be relevant to the finished piece. But they were not insignificant. Jonathan W. Bernard suggests that Ligeti's many jottings and drawings had 'a kind of catalytic role',[20] adding that evidence of frequent handling suggests that he referred to them 'again and again'.[21]

That the Concerto's impetus was referential, and its structure episodic, may have been a consequence of Ligeti having just composed *Aventures* and *Nouvelles Aventures*. But the practice had also been 'sanctioned' by the première of Bernd Alois Zimmermann's opera *Die Soldaten* in 1965, with its mixture of existing genres and real quotations, a precedent not lost on Ligeti when he composed *Le Grand Macabre*.

A very different picture is presented by a drawing, on three sheets of paper, outlining the course of *San Francisco Polyphony* (1973–4). This is basically a topological 'map' – a 'visualization' in Jonathan W. Bernard's terminology (see p. 153, and Colour plate 1 for the original of Ligeti's first sheet). As well as representing the intended shape of the music, it is peppered with descriptions of harmonic, textural and contrapuntal attributes. There are no references to works by other composers, nor to anyone else – except in one place to 'Mahlerian' tempo, and in another to Ligeti's own *Melodien* whose techniques *San Francisco Polyphony* expands. Instead we find (translated) such things as 'new polyphony (mainly third-second structures) ... microtone derivation ... more transparent than *Melodien*, no need to fill out all the time ... Compression ... getting cloudy ... . cluster and consonance alternating ... everywhere melodies ... SURPRISE! Stormy, humming ... TUMULT ... getting thinner ... perpetuum mobile'.[22] Essentially the music is propelled by its own internal logic, but for the première Ligeti wrote an uncharacteristically descriptive programme note evoking 'clouds sailing slowly from the ocean', even 'the turning of the cable car'. He quickly suppressed it, and his liner notes for the exemplary Teldec recording, written near the end of his life, are succinctly technical:

[19] In 'Ygghur', the final part of *Trilogy*, Scelsi has the cello retuned so that a unison can be played on all four strings simultaneously. Quartet no. 4 requires all the instruments to be tuned *scordatura* and the multiple stoppings in each part are notated on up to four staves.

[20] See p. 157 in this volume.

[21] See p. 152 in this volume.

[22] I am grateful to Rachel Beckles Willson for translating Ligeti's often unclear handwriting.

'I worked with dramatic contrasts ... the dilation and compression of the range and the idea of contour and "filling" with countless teeming figures.'[23]

For the Three Pieces for Two Pianos (*Monument–Selbstportrait–Bewegung*), composed for the Kontarsky brothers in 1976, there is no drawing. Instead we have a typed movement plan far more detailed than for any work hitherto. Surprisingly, it projects not three but six movements, as does the later plan for the Horn Trio. And it similarly contains many references to other composers and their works, in this case piano repertoire ranging from Scarlatti to Stockhausen. There is no reference to Reich and Riley, two of the three composers mentioned in the subtitle of *Selbstportrait*. But the third of them, Chopin, *is* listed – indeed five times. The citation could hardly be more relevant, for Ligeti's 'transformed' version of the Presto from Chopin's Sonata in B♭ minor actually ends *Selbstportrait*.

As we might expect, his typescript of the libretto for *Le Grand Macabre* is saturated with references to operatic repertoire, and the music is intentionally allusive. Indeed, the opera is Ligeti's most referential work, and we know that he considered it a stylistic rag-bag that it would be unwise to revisit. But by the time of its première, most of the techniques he had used during the previous 20 years he considered to be exhausted. Tired of clusters and micro-polyphony, disenchanted with an avant-garde 'that has become academic' and a Darmstadt 'transformed into political discussions about progressivity',[24] the problem was how

> not to go on composing in the old avant-garde manner that had become a cliché, but also not to decline into a return to earlier styles. I've been trying deliberately in these last years to find an answer for myself – a music that doesn't mean regurgitating the past, including the avant-garde past.[25]

As for 'the retrograde, neo-Romantic movement that had spread through Europe and the United States' and was seducing his students, to join it would be anathema.[26] He needed 'a third way: being myself, without paying heed either to categorization or to fashionable gadgetry'.[27]

Few of Ligeti's contemporaries shared this sense of crisis. During the early 1980s Boulez, Nono and Stockhausen built on what they had achieved to create works of spacious summation: *Répons*, *Prometeo*, *Licht*. In his preface to Boulez's collected writings, Jean-Jacques Nattiez suggests that *Répons* is 'the true completion of earlier works unfinished ... the single, total work which, in a sense, cancels all the others and makes the completion of the unfinished ones pointless'.[28] For Ligeti, always wary of repeating himself, this was not an option. *Le Grand Macabre*

[23] György Ligeti, *Atmosphères, Chamber Concerto, Etc.*, György Ligeti – The Ligeti Project II, Teldec Classics 8573-88261-2 (2002).

[24] Conversations in Hamburg.

[25] Lichtenfeld interview.

[26] Although, after the appearance of the Trio, he was accused of doing so.

[27] Ligeti in conversation with Claude Samuel in 1981: English translation in *György Ligeti in Conversation with Péter Várnai, Josef Häusler, Claude Samuel and Himself* (London, 1983), p. 123.

[28] Pierre Boulez, *Orientations: Collected Writings*, ed. Jean-Jacques Nattiez (London, 1986), pp. 23–4.

177

RICHARD STEINITZ
*Genesis of the
Piano Concerto
and the Horn Trio*

had already been a summation, although also transitional, pointing forward.

But forward to what? Ligeti's perennial curiosity and self-doubt were his undoing. Writing about Ligeti's demeanour with his students, Manfred Stahnke recalls his 'profound self-questioning, his constant scepticism and his boundless intellectual searching', arguing that Ligeti's hyper-nervous, prima donna-ish behaviour in the concert hall was primarily 'because he feared his music would fail'.[29] The tension this generated in their classes was mitigated by the 'discoveries' he invited his students to introduce, and to which 'nobody listened more eagerly nor enjoyed ... better than Ligeti himself'.[30] Unlike some composers, Ligeti never ring-fenced his aesthetic position by closing his mind to other ways. If his openness and receptivity to ideas and criticism temporarily undermined his confidence, as a means of enrichment and renewal they were rare and invaluable strengths.

A real impediment to starting the Piano Concerto, after the completion of *Le Grand Macabre*, were the invitations to attend performances, festivals, summer schools and to receive awards, which burgeoned alongside Ligeti's growing reputation. One of the most agreeable was a return to Budapest in November 1979 for a festival featuring his own music and that of Kurtág. But the reawakening of Hungarian loyalties posed another question: where exactly were his roots? More troubling were further productions of the opera, all of them different. Following its Stockholm première in February 1978, there were productions in Hamburg in October, Saarbrücken and Bologna in May 1979, Nuremberg in February 1980, Paris in 1981 and London in 1982. These required translation of the libretto into four languages and dealing with seven stage directors. No wonder composition was difficult.

Then there was Ligeti's ill-health. To say that he was 'seriously ill' was probably an exaggeration. But he was a habitual hypochondriac. Louise Duchesneau, his assistant for many years and co-editor of this volume, explains that 'Ligeti was always "seriously ill" and at various points in his life mentioned it to every journalist he met.'[31] In the early 1980s more specifically Ligeti had high blood pressure and related kidney problems, which made him anxious and for a while unable to fly. His ailments did not impede teaching but must have induced a degree of lassitude.

Fundamentally, however, the problem was stylistic. Dissatisfaction with repeated attempts to begin the Concerto meant that few went beyond a handful of bars, or at the most five pages. Ligeti's determination to quit the avant-garde on the one hand and shun neo-romanticism and minimalism on the other was unshakeable. But what was the alternative? The search for a solution exposed an older reflex – the Bartókian language of Ligeti's youth from which he had turned away in *Atmosphères* and to which he now felt reconnected.[32] But to be over-influenced by Bartók certainly would not do.

---

[29] See p. 226–7 in this volume.

[30] See pp. 226–7 in this volume.

[31] Email to the writer, 24 February 2010.

[32] 'It is only natural that I set out from Bartók's music, since we didn't know anyone else. For my generation, the era of Hitler, followed by the years of Stalin's rule, meant complete isolation ... In Budapest in the early 1950s

Tentative beginnings of the Piano Concerto

It was in Hamburg on 14 June 1980 that Ligeti wrote what appear to be his first ideas for the Piano Concerto – not now in words, but on an A3 22-stave landscape sheet filled with musical notation (Colour plate 10). We see at once the intention to write for a sinfonietta-size ensemble as employed in the Chamber Concerto, rather than the larger orchestra of *San Francisco Polyphony*. There is a *ff* tremolo on a unison C♯ with the instruction '*Lamento. Appassionato*'. Not much of a beginning, but '*Lamento. Appassionato*' will prove durable.

The centre of the page is taken up with tables of intervals and chords derived from a 12-note series on the top stave. For Ligeti, establishing such chord banks was an important starting point. The series itself recalls the fan-shaped note-row used by Nono in *Il canto sospeso*, and by Ligeti himself in the 'Christe' motif of the *Requiem*. Hardly new, then – any more than a second 12-note series (lower right) from which he generates 12 chord clusters along the bottom of the page. More surprising is the plaintive strand of melody top left, whose folk-like modality would have been unthinkable in the 1960s. And still in 1980 maybe, since a circled '1' directs us to a derivative lower down, where the phrase is reshaped and extended to include all 12 pitch classes. The tonal ambivalence thus acquired is attractive, but it is still essentially a melody. One might have expected that, at this stage of his career, Ligeti would have had no truck with serial methodology, despite the mirror and retrograde noted on the right-hand side of the sketch. Quasi-tonal melodies occur frequently in the finished Concerto where they have no serial allegiance. Nevertheless, the dominant technique of the mid-century had become an ingrained instinct, and Ligeti's continued use of 12-note material in subsequent sketches suggests that it was not easily eradicated.

Fortunately, he had at his fingertips any number of starting points. A two-bar fragment dated 'Hamburg, June 21, 1980' explores rhythmic syncopation, taking its cue from the C♯–D–C♯–D motif at the end of the 13th stave of the first sketch (Colour plate 10). Ligeti tosses its ingredients around in six variants, like a dog worrying a bone. Despite their brevity, they are meticulously headed: '*Appassionato*', '*Agitato con fuoco, molto ritmico*', finally '*APPASSIONATO, LAMENTOSO. Agitato con fuoco, molto ritmico*' – a somewhat fulsome directive, one might think, for only two bars. But, then, character and tempo were among the first things he felt he had to define. One version extends to three bars (Example 31). Another combines piano in 12/8 with a bar for orchestra (high bassoon and pizzicato violins) syncopated in 4/4 – a momentary hint of the simultaneous metres that characterize the eventual first movement. But in all of these versions the ostinato appears to be stuck. Five years later the octaves reappear in the sixth Piano Étude, *Automne à Varsovie*, in a far more fluid context.

I was beginning to move away from Bartók as an exclusive ideal .... When I first conceived that completely static kind of music which eventually took form in *Atmosphères* in 1961, that was already a "rebellion against Father" ... . But Bartók was always there as an ideal ... . Ever since the early 1980s I have experienced a kind of return to Bartók, especially as far as the Piano Concerto is concerned.' Tünde Szitha, 'A Conversation with György Ligeti', *Hungarian Musical Quarterly* 3/1 (1992), pp. 13–17.

Example 31 Piano Concerto, first movement, a possible beginning

On 16 July Ligeti turned to the motif on the 15th stave in Colour plate 10, and wrote an extended version employing all 12 pitches of the second series (C♯–D♯–F♯–G–E –C B A G♯–D–F–B♭), with some cells repeated and one cell (G–E–C–B–A) twice transposed. Shared between orchestra and piano, it lasts for seven and a half bars (Colour plate 11). Ligeti thought well enough of this to make a fully scored fair copy, adding the dedication to Mario di Bonaventura.[33] But he probably felt uncomfortable with its declamatory rhetoric, and during the next few months repeatedly reworked it.

A revision dated July–September 1980 breaks up this sketch into a series of three-note cells treated to three transpositions, three different rhythms and three different scorings. What had previously sounded Bartókian now recalls the opening of Webern's Concerto, op. 24 – although its abrupt, detached phrases also anticipate the Piano Concerto's fourth movement. This version Ligeti also wrote out in fair copy (Figure 7) but he then did nothing further with it. Instead, a variety of undated sketches explore other ideas.

Early in 1980 Ligeti had learnt of the existence of the émigré American composer Conlon Nancarrow, living obscurely in Mexico City, and in the autumn he came across two recordings of Nancarrow's studies for player piano. Their impact Ligeti described to Charles Amirkhanian in a letter dated 4 January 1981:

This music is the greatest discovery since Webern and Ives ... something great and important for all music history. His music is so utterly original, enjoyable, perfectly constructed, but at the same time emotional ... for me it's the best music of any composer living today.[34]

[33] The fair copy is reproduced in Steinitz, *György Ligeti: Music of the Imagination*, p. 317. This is the first of more than twenty versions of the opening page which Ligeti later gave to Mario di Bonaventura.

[34] Quoted in Kyle Gann, *The Music of Conlon Nancarrow* (Cambridge, 1995), p. 2. Amirkhanian had travelled to Mexico City in 1977 to interview Nancarrow, after which he began issuing recordings of Nancarrow's studies for player piano on the Arch label.

Figure 7 Piano Concerto, fully scored opening, starting with tutti Db–Eb–Gb

181

RICHARD STEINITZ
*Genesis of the
Piano Concerto
and the Horn Trio*

Could Nancarrow's combination of breath-taking speed, rhythmic intricacy and unrelated metres be replicated by a human pianist? Ligeti pondered the challenge.

Despite appearances, he was not inactive. A folder in the Paul Sacher Foundation contains numerous fragments and jottings for the Concerto, as well as more substantial sketches. Some are dated 1981 and most or all may belong to that year. They include metrical grids and tables of intervals (harking back to his practice in the 1960s), sequences of descending thirds, collections of four-note chords (one headed '*Ostinato*', another harmonizing the motif B–A–C–H), and an '*Energico*' theme for piano in upward-rising dyads and dotted rhythm, doubled in each hand. Ligeti wrote such fragments on any handy bits of paper. Few connect with the final composition, and some chains of thirds and sixths are more relevant to the Horn Trio – as they also recall the opera's final Passacaglia. There are also slowly descending chromatic lines like those in the Trio's fourth movement.

Amongst the most interesting sketches is a melody dated '1981 Nov. 26' which continues without a break for 92 bars covering three pages (Colour plate 12). Unusually it is headed '*Zongverseny I*' (a contraction of the Hungarian 'Zongoraverseny' meaning piano concerto) – for Ligeti normally wrote 'Piano Concerto' in English, in deference to its American commissioner. This sketch, however, was not amongst those given to di Bonaventura, probably because Ligeti never scored it. Nevertheless, he wrote several versions that day, all in asymmetric rhythm with variable bar-lengths. One uses the pitches of the second series, whilst this facsimile starts with its transposition on G, followed by transpositions on E♭, B, D etc. In both, the first three pitches are heard three times and the melody constantly recoils on itself in order to repeat a segment before continuing. All versions explore the same concept, in which chains of irregular bar lengths are defined by how many notes there are in each bar.

This sketch runs the gamut from three to 12 notes per bar, with the total written over each bar. One is reminded of Messiaen's 'Danse de la fureur pour les sept trompettes' in the *Quartet for the End of Time*, although there are neither 'added values' nor 'non-retrogradable' rhythms. But the strongest influence would seem to be Nancarrow. Although there is only one line of music, that it is intended to be a canon is evident from a description preceding the first bar. That it is also a mensural canon is shown by some of the other versions, to which canonic entries in different tempi are added. If Ligeti doubted whether such a relentless melody, even in canon, was suitable for the piano concerto, there was a more pressing reason for taking it no further. He had just agreed to a new and very different project, and wanted to begin it.

The Horn Trio

The Trio for Violin, Horn and Piano was instigated by a colleague at the Hamburg Hochschule, the pianist Eckart Besch, who suggested that if Ligeti composed a companion piece to the Brahms Horn Trio, he would arrange for its commission to mark the 150th anniversary of the composer's birth in Hamburg in 1833. Ligeti was attracted to the proposal on several counts. As he told István Szigeti later, 'I was just in the mood because I am very fond of the horn.'[35] He had long been drawn to the instrument, ever since as a child he had been fascinated by alphorns in the Carpathian mountains. And thoughts of writing a concerto for Barry Tuckwell had been in the air since the suggestion made by di Bonaventura in 1969, although for various reasons it had not materialized.

Besch's proposal of a trio was timely. For nearly a decade, since his appointment as professor of composition, Ligeti had been playing chamber music with students from the Hamburg Hochschule.[36] This weekly immersion in classical repertoire had undoubtedly influenced him; possibly even accelerated his disenchantment with the avant-garde. Furthermore, Besch promised to engage for the work's première two outstanding musicians: Germany's finest horn player at that time, Hermann Baumann, and a violinist whom Ligeti already admired, Saschko Gawriloff, to whom he would later dedicate the Violin Concerto.

The earliest sketch for the Horn Trio appears to be a torn off scrap of paper containing a few chord clusters, in the corner of which is written 'KÜRT [horn] III 1, 81 – 12 – 9'. Two days later Ligeti filled an A3 landscape sheet with ideas. Amongst them is a short melody in 3/4 (Example 32a), and next to it a similar phrase labelled '*ELLENMENET*' ('counter-march'). The unvaried crotchets are very different from the ideas he had been pursuing in the Concerto, and directly anticipate the *Più mosso* middle section of the Trio's third movement. Their rhythmic simplicity, along with the ternary import of the label 'counter-march', are early indications that Ligeti intended to pit his skill against classical norms (Example 32b).

Nevertheless, a request from the president of one of the commissioning foundations for Ligeti to quote actual themes by Brahms he firmly rejected, promising 'as a compromise' to accept the subtitle 'Hommage à Brahms'.[37] In reality, as he soon made clear, the work is more of a homage to Beethoven, indeed to the whole mind-set of classical structure – to proportional symmetry, motivic and harmonic logic, and recapitulations virtually identical with their expositions. Unusually amongst Ligeti's mature works, the Trio is composed in four movements.[38] To audiences familiar with his previous work its classical attributes must have come as a huge surprise, as they also angered the hard-line avant-garde. But, in fact, Ligeti never lost his contemporary adventurousness and the music is characteristically multi-faceted, coloured by a growing interest in non-tempered tunings. Brahms had designed his Trio to be played on the natural horn, although for comfort players today mostly use the valve horn. Ligeti specifies the valve horn, but increasingly asks for 'natural' harmonics differently tuned from the tempered scale. This allows him to appropriate traditional forms without sounding regressive. There is a constant strangeness. The music, as he says, 'has odd angles and trick floors'.[39] Never is it mindless pastiche.

[35] István Szigeti, 'A Budapest Interview with György Ligeti', *New Hungarian Quarterly* 25/94 (Summer 1984), pp. 205–10, at p. 209.

[36] Only after his appointment to the Hamburg Hochschule in 1973 could Ligeti afford to buy a grand piano – indeed any piano.

[37] Conversations in Hamburg; see also Ulrich Dibelius, 'Ligetis Horntrio', *Melos* 46/1 (1984), pp. 44–61, at p. 45.

[38] Apart from the *Requiem*, the only other is the Chamber Concerto.

[39] György Ligeti, *Chamber Music*, György Ligeti Edition 7, Sony Classical 62309 (1998).

Example 32 Horn Trio: (a) an idea from an early sketch;
(b) third movement, middle section;
(c) sketches, trying out dyads; (d) sketches, towards a 'two-part chorale'

The classical poise of the first movement is skewed by an astringent relationship between horn melody and violin dyads, whilst their non-metrical durations remove any sense of equal beats. But the subtlety of this balance took time to achieve, as the sketches show. Those of 9 and 11 December establish little other than the melody in Example 32a. In an undated sketch, probably also from December, Ligeti begins with six dyads using 12 different pitches; and the rest of the page contains chord banks or scales of chords in contrary motion. One, for example, is a descending chromatic scale of 12 first-inversion minor triads above an ascending chromatic scale of 12 second-inversion major triads.

'... a kind of two-part chorale'

It is the dyads, however, that are significant. We recall that the two-bar motif of *Passacaglia ungherese* is built entirely of dyads. Equally consonant, although tonally more ambivalent, are the 24 dyads that constitute the passacaglia theme at the end of the opera. And double-stopped dyads, with an occasional open string below, are the essence of the violin part in the opening section of the Horn Trio. Clearly, in his search for a new ambivalent multi-tonality, Ligeti found that these simple intervals could be interestingly juxtaposed.

The evidence is contained in two A5 landscape sketches, neither of them dated, but probably written in early 1982. One is in the Paul Sacher Foundation, the other in the Library of Northwestern University, although viewable online.[40] Together they contain over a dozen chains of dyads, all in 3/4 crotchets, but different harmonically, and lasting anything up to eight bars. Their purpose seems to have been to tease out one particular idea: what Ligeti describes in his programme note for the première as the violin playing 'a kind of two-part chorale'. The majority of intervals are major thirds, minor sixths, perfect fifths, and tritones, but juxtaposed to sound multi-tonal. The phrases move freely between treble and bass clefs, and at this stage there is no indication that any will eventually be entrusted to the violin.

Most (but not all) of the phrases begin with three descending dyads which, either directly or obliquely, recall the traditional sequence known as 'horn fifths'. In tonal harmony the term 'horn fifths' denotes a particular instance of voice-leading to and from a perfect fifth, so named because it was a characteristic progression for a pair of natural horns. Its three intervals are a major third, perfect fifth and minor sixth (e.g. E♭–G, B♭–F and G–E♭), which in German-speaking countries were associated with the mail coach and the postillion's post-horn. Ligeti, however, either lowers the third interval by a semitone (E♭–G, B♭–F, F♯–D) or raises it (E♭–G, B♭–F, G♯–E), or makes other alterations, all of which introduce a degree of tonal ambivalence.

One phrase, written half-way down the sketch in Basel, reappears at the top of the sketch in Northwestern University, proving that they are connected (Example 32c). There are four versions, all beginning with a major third followed by a perfect fifth. Below these are several more chromatic sequences; whilst along the bottom two of the latter are joined together to create an eight-bar phrase of continuously descending dyads (Example 32d). This is written in heavier pencil with the bars prominently numbered, suggesting that Ligeti considered it definitive. Perhaps so, for its further modification of the 'horn fifths' in bar 1 produces the three dyads with which (when transposed to begin on G and B) the Trio's first movement actually begins.

Some conclusions can be drawn. The first is that these processions of dyads were being groomed to fulfil Ligeti's notion of 'a kind of two-part chorale'. The second, that they are probably conscious extensions of the 'horn fifths' sequence. The third, that Ligeti had not yet decided how to score them. The fourth, that we should not infer from the continuous crotchets that he was unconcerned with rhythm, merely that he preferred to determine first the pitches, then their durations. Finally, at this stage Ligeti was more interested in harmonic possibilities generated by the 'horn fifths' sequence, and no direct allusion to Beethoven's 'Les Adieux' Sonata was yet intended.

Unlike the two pages of dyads, the dated sketches from around this time are scored. A sketch written on Christmas Eve starts with violin double-stopping and adds a bar for horn, all in crotchets and minims (Example 33a). A sketch headed '1981' is structurally prescient regarding the disposition of the instruments, but rhythmically conventional (Example 33b). It is noteworthy that neither Example 33a nor Example 33b contains the

---

[40] http://nucat.library.northwestern.edu/cgi-bin/Pwebrecon.cgi?BBID=4205000, accessed on 10 August 2010.

185

RICHARD STEINITZ
*Genesis of the
Piano Concerto
and the Horn Trio*

intervallic sequence of the eventual opening. This we find in a sketch dated 3 January 1982, where it is transposed to begin on G and B – the germinal motif, as it turns out, of the entire Trio. In other respects this sketch is surprisingly naïve: rhythmically bland and attended by embarrassingly clichéd horn arpeggios (Example 33c).

Example 33 Horn Trio, first movement, three early sketches

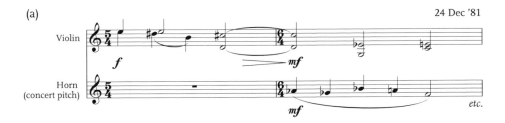

The Horn Trio's movement plan

For the Trio Ligeti drew no 'maps'; indeed, they would have been superfluous for a work using traditional structures. But his preliminary movement plan is fascinating. Typically, he typed it on the back of a discarded sheet that happened to be lying around: an announcement from Peters Edition about forthcoming performances in February and March 1980. Ligeti must have typed the plan somewhat later, and probably not before New Year 1982. Then, as was his habit, he scribbled additions in pencil, blue biro, black ink and pens of assorted colours (Colour plate 13). Like the earlier plan for the Three Pieces for Two Pianos, it projects more movements than Ligeti actually composed: six, indeed – or even seven if one includes an afterthought added by hand. Seven works by other composers are cited and two by Ligeti himself. One of the latter is the *Romanian Concerto* typed after 'Kürt szignálok' ('horn signals') amongst ideas for the first movement, included no doubt because of its use of untempered horn harmonics. But it is the citations of other composers' works that are more revealing, adding much to our understanding of the Trio's provenance.

The projected movements are: 1. *Középgyors (medium fast)*, 2. *Scherzo*, 3. *Canon*, 4. *Chaconne*, 5. *Lassú (adagio)* and 6. *Caccia*. Ligeti must have decided to add the *Scherzo* after he had typed the *Chaconne* and then amended the numbering. Later, the March in Schumann's Piano Quintet triggered the idea of an 'extra movement' which he added vertically up the side. In the actual Trio, the description of *Középgyors* correlates with the first movement; *Canon* – originally numbered 2, then 3 – becomes a model for the fourth; whilst aspects from more than one of the planned fast movements may have influenced the Trio's second movement.

The cited compositions are:

Beethoven: C♯ minor quartet (first movement)
Janáček *Intrada*
Ligeti: *Romanian Concerto*
Ligeti: Bagatelle no. 3
Monteverdi: *Zefiro torna*,[41] IX p. 9, Leppard p. 8
Ravel *Bolero*
Schubert B♭ piano trio (slow movement)
Schumann: *Kreisleriana* spirit
Schumann: Piano Quintet 'March' (second movement)

Among the list of musical ingredients we find 'horn signals, horn fifths, alpine horn, foghorn, "Puck-Oberon", Romanian dance melody, Covasînt,[42] bagpipe, mists, reflections, trills, piano murmurings, horn-forest-echoes, lakes, marshes, "Caribbean-Bulgarian" rhythm, "Trans-Danubian" melody, "Merry-making", Macabre-Coloratura-like passages ...' More specifically technical are 'Lydian chordal aggregates, major thirds–minor seconds, polytonal, polymetrics 5–4–3, clusters, Collage' and – significantly – 'Sonata Form'.

---

[41] Ligeti uses the alternative, less common spelling *'Zeffiro'*.
[42] A town in Romania where Ligeti collected folk music in 1949.

187

RICHARD STEINITZ
Genesis of the
Piano Concerto
and the Horn Trio

At some stage Ligeti crossed out the top three movements. This may seem curious, for their descriptions chime most closely with movements in the Trio (although in a different order). But his practice on earlier occasions, particularly when using pitch and rhythmic matrices, had been to cross out guidelines as he applied them, like someone in a supermarket ticking off items on a shopping list. This would suggest that the plan was more than a generalized collection of preliminary ideas put aside when Ligeti began to compose; rather that he continued to refer to it. On the other hand, qualities like 'Lydian' harmony and polytonality infiltrate all four movements, as they do subsequent works.

Schumann, if we count the 'March', is cited twice. Interviewed by Petér Várnai in 1978, Ligeti spoke of the composer's increased importance for him, and how

> I am trying to change the course of my music, give up the cool, distanced music, or rather a music that is observed from afar; I want to get it closer to the current, give it immediacy, and in this Schumann's influence on me is considerable. Technically speaking I am fascinated by Schumann's internal ornamentation. In his piano music you always find meandering lines embedded in the texture. There was nothing like that before him … Schumann's internal weaving of lines, both very dense and unsystematic … consists of figures and ornaments run wild. It is very original … (and) gives the impression of a musical form that has overflown the banks.[43]

In contrast to Schumann, Ravel and Janáček ('Intrada' is the orchestral conclusion of his *Glagolitic Mass*) have little perceptible influence. Of far greater importance are Ligeti's typed citations.

Monteverdi's madrigal *Zefiro torna* may seem an unlikely model for a piece of quasi-classical chamber music, but in relation to the Trio's second movement it is surprisingly apt and illuminating, as I argue below. No less significant is the first movement of Beethoven's String Quartet in C♯ minor, op. 131. Listed under '*Canon*', along with other ideas (e.g. 'slow, polymetric', 'very high-very low octaves', 'gradually polyphonic … increasingly in multi-part clusters') it can only relate to the Trio's final *Lamento. Adagio.* True, the *Lamento's* impassioned climax has the piano right hand, and then the horn and violin, doubled not in octaves but in disconsolate major sevenths. But the relevance of the Beethoven fugue (Example 34) is underlined by an earlier sketch for the Trio's *Lamento*, in which the entries are more consistently fugal than in the completed composition.

Example 34 Beethoven, String Quartet in C♯ minor, op. 131, opening

Adagio, ma non troppo e molto espressivo

[43] English translation by Gabor J. Schabert in *György Ligeti in Conversation*, p. 78.

György Ligeti:
Of Foreign Lands
and Strange Sounds

Both sketch and published movement begin with the germinal motif, but with its opening major third now minor. With the addition of two more dyads, this becomes a five-bar passacaglia starting in the violin and descending through the piano. Above it in the sketch are six statements of a seven-note phrase treated as a quasi-fugal exposition (Example 35).

Example 35 Horn Trio, fourth movement, early sketch

189

RICHARD STEINITZ
*Genesis of the
Piano Concerto
and the Horn Trio*

The entries alternate with text-book precision as 'subject' and 'answer': three beginning on F (bar 6 in the piano, bars 11 and 16 in the violin) and two beginning a perfect fourth higher on B♭ – respelled as A♯ (bars 10 and 16 in the piano) – followed by a sixth entry starting another perfect fourth higher on D♯ (bar 15 in the piano). There is an expressive empathy between the two fugue subjects as well as similarities of shape – albeit Beethoven's wider intervals are at the beginning of his subject, Ligeti's at the end.

Yet, rather than continue the fugal discipline, in which the horn has so far taken no part, prompted Ligeti to extend and enhance his seven-note theme by repeating segments, as he had done in sketches for the Piano Concerto. He starts again, this time composing a longer three-phrase melody. It, too, commences in bar 6 and uses the same pitches (F E♭ D), but then recoils to restart on F and descend one note lower (F E♭ D D♭). Then it recoils again to state the original seven-note phrase, but starting with a dissonance (F/E) and continuing slightly altered with D D♭ C B♭ D and B. Example 36 shows this longer melody as introduced by the piano in the published score. Its salient features are those of the '*lamento*' formula as it occurs in Ligeti's later compositions: three phrases beginning at or near the same pitch, each longer and descending further than before, the third intensified with a dissonance.[44]

Example 36 Horn Trio, fourth movement: the 'lamento motif' as it first appears

In the Trio itself this embryonic formula is treated loosely. After the piano comes a complete statement from the violin starting on A. Another begins in the piano, but its second phrase is altered and its third phrase missing. During the rest of the movement others begin but are freely developed both rhythmically and melodically. The fugal rigour of the sketch gives way to heightened drama, as the music builds to a climax of extraordinary intensity. Nevertheless, aware of the sketch and its model, one can hardly disassociate the profoundly contemplative mood of the Beethoven from Ligeti's bleak *Lamento* – plumbing, as it does, emotional depths he had scarcely touched before.

Les Adieux

Considering the potency of these citations, it is odd that the music which is often thought to haunt the Horn Trio is not mentioned in the plan: i.e. the 'Lebewohl' (farewell) motif at the beginning of Beethoven's 'Les Adieux' Piano Sonata, op. 81a. Nor is it mentioned in Ligeti's programme note for the first performance, although he spoke frequently of it afterwards and

---

[44] For examples see Steinitz, *György Ligeti: Music of the Imagination*, pp. 296–7.

acknowledged it in his liner notes for the Sony CD recording of 1998. This is less significant than it might be, since the note for the première is entirely technical (except for the disclaimer that 'there are neither quotations nor influences of Brahms's music in my piece'), whilst the CD liner note is more polemic, casting the Trio, with – as Ligeti then acknowledged – its 'false quotation from Beethoven', 'as a sort of rebellion against the established conventions of the avant-garde'.

The reason is surely that, when Ligeti compiled his plan, no overt allusion to 'Les Adieux' had occurred to him, although he knew the sonata well and had referred to it long before in 'Metamorphoses of Musical Form' published in *Die Reihe* 7 in 1960.[45] In his note for the Trio's première he writes of the opening 'melodic-harmonic germ – major third, tritone and minor sixth – as an 'oblique' variant of the traditional sequence for two horns'. But the sketches reveal that even this concept emerged gradually, settling in its final form only around 17 February, ten weeks after he began the composition. Two years after the première, Ulrich Dibelius published an extended analytical article on the Trio in *Melos*,[46] to prepare for which he interviewed Ligeti the previous July. Like the composer, his discussion of the opening motif and its treatment refers only to its derivation from the traditional 'horn fifths'. The article does contain a mention of 'Les Adieux'. But it is not in relation to the Trio, instead to the eighth movement of the *Ten Pieces for Wind Quintet* which Ligeti describes as a miniature 'concerto' for the horn, 'full of atmospheric allusions to former epochs like a yellowing picture album'.[47]

A composition, like a novel, develops its own momentum in the course of being written. Personalities, motifs and situations pursue trajectories whose outcome cannot be predicted. A composer may have no idea how a work is going to end; even, as in the case of Ligeti, how many movements it will contain. So it is unlikely that he foresaw the further change he would make to the germinal motif in the last movement whilst he was composing the first; or, perhaps, that he would use it at all. By making a further change, he had now altered the intervals of the traditional sequence in three respects: (1) by lifting the third dyad a semitone, (2) by changing the perfect fourth to a tritone, and (3) by changing the opening major third to minor, as can be seen in Example 35. At the start of the 'Les Adieux' Sonata Beethoven also treats the sequence unexpectedly, by using an interrupted cadence in bar 2 and the much greater surprise of Cb major in bars 7–8. It is the strangeness of their harmonic treatments that connects Beethoven and Ligeti, a strangeness that is absent from his early dyadic experiments. I conjecture that, because the analogy between their transformations actually deepened during the Trio's composition, Ligeti came fully to acknowledge its significance only after he had finished.

---

[45] English translation by Cornelius Cardew (Pennsylvania, 1965), pp. 5–19.
[46] Dibelius, 'Ligetis Horntrio', pp. 44–61.
[47] Ibid., p. 46.

191

RICHARD STEINITZ
*Genesis of the
Piano Concerto
and the Horn Trio*

The first movement

Naturally, the first movement is the focus of the early sketches; so it would be reasonable to expect that's its description will be reflected in the music. Here (translated) is how Ligeti first envisaged the movement (for Ligeti's original see Colour plate 13):

1. <u>Medium-fast</u>: polytonal, polymetric. 6/8 (crossed out)   c. 4'

Horn signals = Romanian concerto): alpine horn, foghorn, 'Puck-Oberon'

Violin: horn fifths. Violin-horn: horn fifths. Piano: horn fifths

Polymetrics 5–4–3 (10–8–6), in dislocated layers

Suddenly running away, unstable tempo. Major third-minor sixth parallels.

M3-m6 harmony, also tritone.

Later he added in red: 'several different tempi = SHIFTING', and in black: 'MONTAGE?'; and below in red: 'IN SOME PLACES HORN–VIOLIN muted, CARIBBEAN RHYTHM! In the distance: horn melody, Evocation of the forest ... multi-layered collage dances'.

Few of the handwritten additions occur in the Trio's first movement: no 'Caribbean rhythm', 'shifting tempi' or 'multi-layered collage dances', although the horn and violin are muted 'for some of the time'. More pertinent is Ligeti's typed projection. The movement is indeed polytonal, polymetric and 'medium-fast' (*Andantino*), although without any sudden 'running away'. The horn echoes played off stage in the *Romanian Concerto* are replicated here by hand-stopping, and the use of natural harmonics could at times suggest an alphorn. The 'horn fifths' ('kürtkvintek' in Hungarian) assigned first to violin, then violin and horn, and thirdly to the piano, correctly map the structure of the opening paragraphs of music.

Polymetre one might judge to be absent, if guided only by the ear. But in the score the meaning of '5–4–3' becomes clear.[48] These are the units (quintuplets, quavers and triplets) which Ligeti uses to measure durations in the piano, violin and horn parts, and which turn the workaday rhythms of the early sketches into something infinitely more subtle. Ligeti had used such durational layering before (e.g. in *Lux aeterna* and *Lontano*) and would do so in future sketches for the Piano Concerto.

The polymetrics (as Ligeti calls them) first occur in an A5 landscape sketch dated 8 February 1982 (Colour plate 14). Here the durational layers are easily visible, despite crossings out: 5 in the piano, 4 in the violin and 3 in the horn. This is also the first sketch to convey the essence of the movement's opening section. The horn plays an asymmetric melodic line similar to that in the published Trio, whilst the violin plays dyads, first answered, then taken over by the piano. The upward arpeggios in all three instruments are a distinct improvement on the dominant sevenths in Example 33c. But in the final score they are more effectively withheld until

---

[48] The 10–8–6 subdivisions do not appear in the music.

bar 41, where upward sweeps in all three instruments enhance the codetta that ends the first part of the ternary structure.

Although the violin dyads are the familiar major third, tritone and minor sixth, in this instance they do *not* mirror the shape of the descending sequence. 'Horn fifths' are prominent on the plan, but so are their constituent intervals – 'Nagyterc-kisszkszt párhuzamok' ('major third–minor sixth parallels')[49] and 'NT-ksk-harmóniák, tritonus is' ('M3–m6 harmony, also tritone') – which are listed in such a way as to imply no fixed order.

Only on 17 February is Ligeti's 'oblique variant' firmly established, and in a sketch in which we can watch the music actually taking shape (Colour plate 15). The page begins with a line for the horn, which is twice reworked. In the second version Ligeti alternates normal and echo phrases (i.e. hand-stopped). Then he decides that the echo should be delayed and given to all three instruments. This happens in the third version, to which violin (now playing the three-interval sequence as it appears in the Trio) and piano are added. At this point the horn pitches also achieve their final order, but triplets are only applied to the first two bars. Thereafter, Ligeti only outlines the rhythms of the horn, and abandons them entirely in the violin to concentrate on pitch relationships. Between the horn and violin these are exactly those of the finished movement; as indeed they are in the piano after a premature entry has been deleted and the next three dyads moved to their eventual position in the score.[50]

Establishing pitch content was key, and doing so to Ligeti's satisfaction ensured that 17 February was an exceptionally productive day. Before the end of it he had replaced this sketch with another in order to define the rhythms of the first 11 bars. Wanting to revise these further, he then began again, altering some durations until he had what is more or less the final version of the Trio's first 48 bars. It fills two A5 pages, but that there is no third or subsequent page is no proof that they did not exist, because, as I have suggested, the available sketches appear to be incomplete.

Even at this stage some of the durations are not those in the final score. But they are close, and the phrase relationships clearly established. From this moment the composition takes wings, moving in a single day from yet another tentative beginning to an unstoppable flow. From now on Ligeti composes almost entirely in score. Rarely stumbling, apart from occasional bars crossed out and restarted, the manuscript exudes some of that purposeful assurance which distinguishes the autographs of Bach and Handel.

Chronology

It would be interesting to know more precisely when Ligeti made the plan. It surely cannot have been after 17 February, when he wrote a third or more of the first movement virtually in its final form; for he would hardly have included 'Caribbean rhythms, shifting tempi and multi-layered collage

[49] 'Kisszkszt' is short for 'kisszekszt'.

[50] In the lower section of the sketch Ligeti has written chromatic scales of parallel intervals (including major thirds and minor sixths as listed on the plan). One wonders why he needed to write out such commonplace material.

193

RICHARD STEINITZ
*Genesis of the
Piano Concerto
and the Horn Trio*

dances' already knowing that they had no part. Nor can it have been much before 3 January, the date of the first sketch based on 'horn fifths'. Before that Ligeti floats other ideas, like those in Exx. 33a and 33b, and a sketch dated 31 December that contains 11 bars of fluid *tremolandi* – atmospheric, attractive, but never used in the Trio. If he had written the plan in December, would not more of its projected ideas have been incorporated into these early sketches?

The pages of dyads were probably written in early January. If their purpose *was* to evolve 'a kind of two-part chorale', then – had the plan been typed afterwards – the 'chorale' would surely have been alluded to? The word 'Choral' does appear, but in faint pencil and attached to the *Scherzo*. Of course, the idea of calling the violin phrases a 'kind of chorale' may also have occurred in retrospect when Ligeti had to write a programme note. Lacking further evidence, I venture that the plan was made in early January, and the two pages of dyads were sketched soon after to explore possible treatments of the 'horn fifths'.

In these two sketches Ligeti was concerned only with pitch; indeed rhythmic relationships are strangely neglected in all the early sketches. In February they received his full attention and, through successive refinements, attained the wonderfully fluidity of the finished composition, whose lines flow unfettered yet with a deeply satisfying symmetry. Violin and horn phrases follow each other in the classical manner of 'antecedent' and 'consequent' and are gathered in three similar paragraphs whose cadences ('*quasi eco*') coincide rhythmically and end together on a concord. At this point the piano enters, on each occasion playing a transposition of the violin's opening dyads – the altered 'horn fifths' or 'false quotation from Beethoven'. Meanwhile the hand-stopped horn ('*quasi eco*') and *flautando* violin impart their strangeness. The central B section is slightly faster: stylized, graceful, rhythmically together, except when halted (three times) by recollections of the A section. It seems miraculous that, from the seeming naïvety of some of the early sketches, the finished composition attains such sophistication.

The influence of Monteverdi

The plan describes three fast movements ('gyors' in Hungarian): *Chaconne, Caccia* and *Scherzo*. Any of their ideas may have influenced the second (and only really fast) movement of the Trio: *Vivacissimo molto ritmico*. But for a direct model we must look to the *Chaconne*. Under *Caccia* Ligeti describes 'sok metrum-váltás' ('many metrical changes') and 'Macabre-Coloratura-like passages' – hardly the stuff of the *Vivacissimo*. Some of the *Scherzo* description could be applicable, but not '*Continuum*-like', nor sonata form. The *Vivacissimo*, on the other hand, with its persistent ostinato, is a chaconne, albeit fast in the manner of the Italian Baroque. The fusion of Caribbean and Bulgarian rhythms ('"karibi-bolgár" ritm.') is explained further in Ligeti's programme note. Introducing the *Vivacissimo* for the première, he writes of a 'national music belonging to non-existing nations, as if Hungary, Romania and the entire Balkan peninsula were situated somewhere between Africa and the Caribbean', whilst in the CD liner notes he refers to 'an imaginary, synthetic folklore of Latin American and Balkan elements'.

More enigmatic is the citation of *Zefiro torna*, since Ligeti seems never to have referred to it again – at least, not in relation to the Horn Trio. What, then, is it's relevance? And what is meant by 'Virtuose madrigale'? This, it transpires, was the title of an Archiv LP of Monteverdi madrigals containing *Zefiro torna*, issued by Deutsche Grammophon in 1971 and which Ligeti possessed. The volume and page numbers of the complete edition are printed in the notes for the LP, differentiating this setting of a paraphrase by Rinuccini from Monteverdi's earlier setting of the original Petrarch sonnet, both of which are recorded on the disc. Rightly celebrated, the later setting in the ninth book of madrigals (1651) is an airy, dancing piece above a springy ground base, a 'Ciaconna' as Monteverdi calls it (Example 37a). Although separated by 330 years, the vocal duet and *Vivacissimo* have a similar effervescence. And 'virtuoso' the *Vivacissimo* spectacularly is.

Example 37 (a) Monteverdi, *Zefiro torna*, bars 5–9; (b) Ligeti, a sketch for *Hungarian Rock*; (c) Ligeti, *Hungarian Rock* (Chaconne), bars 1–4

Ligeti may have had *Zefiro torna* in mind when he composed *Hungarian Rock* in 1978; for amongst his sketches for the two harpsichord pieces is a page filled with ground basses, one of which, fully harmonized, is a pastiche of the madrigal both in rhythm and harmony (Example 37b&c). Its very title, *Ciaccona*, suggests the Italian Baroque. *Hungarian Rock* itself may reek more of a salsa bar than Monteverdi, but it, too, is subtitled

195

RICHARD STEINITZ
*Genesis of the
Piano Concerto
and the Horn Trio*

'Chaconne', and its first three bars are as consonant as *Zefiro torna*, which is consonant almost throughout.[51]

Tracing such parallels is not incompatible with Ligeti's view of the harpsichord pieces as 'ironic remarks to my students who always wanted this kind of "retro" music'.[52] That a variety of ingredients should come together in these two intentional parodies is typical of the composer. Their hybrid nature is indicated by the alternative titles he tried out in the sketches: *Tango con Passacaglia* and *Passatango* amongst others for *Passacaglia ungherese; Amero-Hungarian Rock-Chaconne* and (delightfully) *Les Folies d'Hongrie (Chaconne)* for *Hungarian Rock.*

A further connection between *Hungarian Rock* and the second movement of the Trio is that they have the same tempo indication. But, in the Trio '*Vivacissimo molto ritmico*' is followed by 'fresh, sparkling, light, gliding, dancing' in German and English (a description even more applicable to the madrigal, one could say). 'A hint of overkill?' asks Richard Toop in his book on the composer.[53] But Toop also reminds us of the movement's neo-Bartókian aspects. For if *Zefiro torna* is one progenitor, it is Bartók who provides a template for the ostinato. We find it in the first of the *Six Dances in Bulgarian Rhythm* which conclude volume 6 of *Mikrokosmos*. Here Bartók has a similarly dynamic one-bar ostinato, an ascending scale of $4+2+3$ quavers repeated for 13 bars – then, starting on a different pitch, for a further seven. The last of Bartók's *Six Dances* is conjured half way through the Trio movement, where Ligeti clones its chordal theme in unequal beats of $3+3+2$ quavers. Was he knowingly kleptomaniac? Almost certainly. But, if so, surely without guilt, for Ligeti's treatments are as original as they are inventive.

Ligeti's scrawled additions to the plan are hard to decipher. But below *Chaconne* one can make out '3. Bagatelle' and, further to the right, 'Ravel Bolero' and 'mixolyd' (i.e. mixolydian). '3. Bagatelle' must be the third of Ligeti's own Six Bagatelles for Wind Quintet, adapted from *Musica ricercata* for solo piano. It is an interesting youthful precedent, for its revolving folk-like melody, floated over an unchanging pentatonic ostinato, has an Arcadian, Monteverdian gracefulness.

It could be that Ligeti was doing no more than listing analogous pieces as they occurred to him. Yet all confront the technical issue of a short repetitive ostinato above which, to avoid tedium, extended melodies must be spun. In *Zefiro torna* Monteverdi achieves this with such skill that, above its ostinato, the two tenors launch into effortless phrase extensions and alternating roulades that keep the music constantly alive. In the second movement of the Trio, Ligeti's shifting stress patterns and ever changing phrase lengths are more complex, but similarly light-footed. Accepting that Bartók's influence was paramount, may we also imagine Rinuccini's dancing zephyrs, whose notes are 'tempered by love and joy', wafting across the centuries to inspire them?

In answer to this question, Louise Duchesneau offers a caution:

---

[51] So, of course, is the Passacaglia at the end of *Le Grand Macabre*.

[52] Conversations in Hamburg.

[53] Richard Toop, *György Ligeti* (London, 1999), p. 188.

Ligeti had all of Monteverdi on LPs, duplicated by a few CDs. He loved that music and listened to it continuously. Often however, the music he loved, played on the piano and listened to only functioned as a mood-giver or distant inspiration. The piece he was writing would have ended up with a 'faint smell' of something which would maybe be a mixture of many different things, not only music, just everything he had come in contact with recently as well as long ago. And so he wrote down many words just to 'remind' himself of a particular mood. I think the Monteverdi would have been in this category.[54]

Ulrich Dibelius's *Melos* article provides an interesting footnote. Dibelius asserts that: 'with two Monteverdi madrigals, as well as with the final lament of Purcell's *Dido and Aeneas*, Ligeti underwent even quite close relationships', claiming that *Lamento della ninfa*, may have been a 'distant inspiration' as he composed his own *Lamento*. Ligeti's fascination with the other madrigal the composer himself explains, although without linking it to a particular movement:

> In *Zefiro Torna* – which is a *Ciaccona* on a 2-bar model – there exists a Monteverdian trick, in that the return of the six bass notes is always asymmetrically open. The contrapuntal flights in the three parts have an entirely different periodicity yielding constantly new asymmetries above the same chord sequence as it continues to rotate.

The available sketches for the second movement throw no light on these issues, since they show only bars 45–109 at a stage when Ligeti was sure of their direction. At bar 53 he takes a wrong turn, deletes two attempts at the next four bars, then confidently resumes. His fluency owes something to a familiar prop. For at least part of the movement a 12-note series generates the melodic flights both above and below the ostinato (see the piano right hand from bar 15, the left hand from bar 40, and the violin part from bar 27).[55]

The last two movements

A late addition to the plan was the March from Schumann's Piano Quintet. But it is, if at all, only a distant model for the third movement of the Trio. Ligeti acknowledged a closer connection with the second movement of Beethoven's Piano Sonata in A major, op. 101.[56] Both Beethoven's movement and the second movement of the trio are marked *Alla Marcia* and are similar in tempo (unlike the Schumann). The detached, jerky rhythms of the Trio movement recall the dotted rhythms of the Beethoven, and their fluid legato middle sections provide comparable contrasts. In the outer sections of the Trio movement, however, Ligeti deploys a distinctly contemporary technique – the phase-shifting of Steve Reich; whilst the addition of the horn to an otherwise exact recapitulation, playing

---

[54] Email to the writer, 24 February 2010.

[55] Ligeti's treatment of the same ostinato in the Piano Étude *Fanfares* is completely different, and apparently without any trace of serialism.

[56] Conversations in Hamburg.

197

RICHARD STEINITZ
Genesis of the
Piano Concerto
and the Horn Trio

untempered overtones bell in air and 'very loud', takes the music into a quite different domain. It is, writes Ligeti mysteriously, 'the riddle of a *non-manifest* musical language'.[57]

There is only one sketch page for the *Alla Marcia* in Basel, containing bars 237–72 virtually as published. Northwestern University has two covering the whole of the *Più mosso*. These, too, are more or less as printed, although far from being a fair copy. Some bars are indecipherable, but the issues are mainly to do with notation and we learn little about compositional choices. Basel's three sketches for the opening of the fourth movement are more revealing. One begins with deep, sustained and very soft chords, through which descends a chromatic pitch sequence: B–Bb–A–Ab–G. After nine bars the music ceases, but Ligeti continues to write the pitch names of this potential passacaglia below the empty staves. The heading is 'lassú (slow) chaconne'. In the top right he has written 'Ives "Serenity"' (Ives being a perennial fascination), and one wonders whether he was considering a similarly static but more sombre music. The second sketch is insubstantial. In the third we find Ligeti's penultimate version of the last movement with its fugal exposition inspired by Beethoven's C♯ minor Quartet which I have already discussed (see pp. 187–9).

Taken as a whole, the sketches for the Trio seem to support the view that any relationship with Beethoven's 'Les Adieux' Sonata occurred to Ligeti relatively late. It would appear that the germinal motif at the start of the Trio emerged from Ligeti's dalliance with a two-part quasi-chorale; that it formulated in his mind as a variant of the 'traditional sequence for two horns'; that it's wider implications as a 'false quotation from Beethoven' dawned on him much later; and that the idea of a darker variant to begin the last movement emerged only when he recast its opening. Which is why, perhaps, when I asked Ligeti what led him to employ the 'Les Adieux' motto in the Trio, he replied, 'I don't know.'[58]

Resuming the Piano Concerto

To the Concerto we now return. Ligeti, however, had two new commissions to compose: *Drei Fantasien nach Friedrich Hölderlin* for Swedish Radio, and *Magyar etűdök* for the Schola Cantorum of Stuttgart. *Magyar etűdök* was due for performance on 18 May 1983, but only two of its three pieces were finished in time and the première of the third had to await the autumn.

In September 1983 Ligeti also attended the 33rd annual Berlin Festival, where four concerts were given in honour of his 60th birthday. Reviewing the event for *Current Musicology*, Jeffrey Bossin reported that Ligeti introduced the Horn Trio in 'a decidedly defensive tone'.[59] Mindful no doubt of the criticism it had attracted, Ligeti decried the assessment of compositions according to the position they were deemed to occupy in the development of post-war music, instead of for intrinsic aesthetic qualities. Interviewed for the radio, he expressed again his aim of 'trying to develop a harmony and melody which are no genuine return to tonality, which are

---

[57] Liner notes to György Ligeti, *Chamber Music*, György Ligeti Edition 7, Sony Classical 62309 (1998), trans. Annelies McVoy and David Feurzeig.

[58] Conversations in Hamburg.

[59] Jeffery Bossin, 'Report from Berlin', *Current Musicology* 37/8 (1984), pp. 237–78.

neither tonal nor atonal but rather something else, above all in connection with a very high degree of rhythmic and metric complexity'.[60] These were his aims as he resumed work on the Concerto.

When he did so is not clear. A new attempt at its first page is broadly labelled '1982–83' (Figure 8). Fully scored, and using pitch material from earlier sketches, it develops a counterpoint of durational units in the ratio 3–4–5 and lasts for 16 bars. The durational layers may have been prompted by their use in the Horn Trio, but here the intention is to compose a more dynamic hocket, as Ligeti had used very effectively in 'Spiegelkanon' from *Magyar etűdök*, and before that in *Monument*, the first of the Three Pieces for Two Pianos. Both *Monument* and 'Spiegelkanon' combine simple and compound time divisions: 4/4 and 6/8 in *Monument*, 2/2 and 6/4 in 'Spiegelkanon'. The latter is both a mensural and a mirror canon: 'extremely constructivistic', according to the composer.[61] Sung by 12 solo voices, it depicts the drip, drip of a thawing icicle. His new sketch for the Concerto is also a mensural canon, but in three metrical layers whose hocketing rhythms so nearly coincide that they could be mistaken for ragged ensemble. On 22 December 1983 Ligeti tried a simpler version in two layers, in which duple rhythms in the strings are set against triple in the wind. But neither sketch includes the piano.

Further planning

Although Ligeti devised three different movement plans for the Concerto, none are so relevant to the finished work as is his single plan for the Horn Trio. Nor can any of them be dated. But the mention (or at least implication) of canon, and of polymetric layering, points to their being made during 1982–3. What appears to be the first is a handwritten list:

1. 5' Appassionato – 12 tone – Collage form
2. 6' Fluid – Schumann C major Fantasy (surging, fiery ardour) [?[62]]
3. 6' Slow = passacaglia – repeatedly chromatic etc
4. 4' Trans-Danubian scherzo, Presto
        Peterson-Nancarrow   the end of Nancarrow 40

'Appassionato – 12 tone' succinctly sums up his previous efforts to compose the first movement. The rest could describe the Horn Trio, except for the reference to Nancarrow. Ligeti had discovered Nancarrow's music in 1980; but, as we have seen, his growing interest seems to have had relatively little bearing on the Trio, for which stimuli mainly came from elsewhere.[63]

This changed in the autumn of 1982, when Ligeti joined Nancarrow and his wife in Graz, where, at Ligeti's instigation, the 70-year-old composer had been invited for the annual ISCM World Music Days. From there the party continued to Innsbruck, Cologne and Paris, where Boulez welcomed them

---

[60] Ibid., pp. 234, 238.

[61] Liner notes, György Ligeti *Works for Piano*, György Ligeti Edition 3, Sony Classical 62308 (1997), trans. Annelies McVoy and David Feurzeig.

[62] Ligeti's handwriting is difficult to read here.

[63] Except perhaps on the 5–4–3 durational layering of the Trio's first movement.

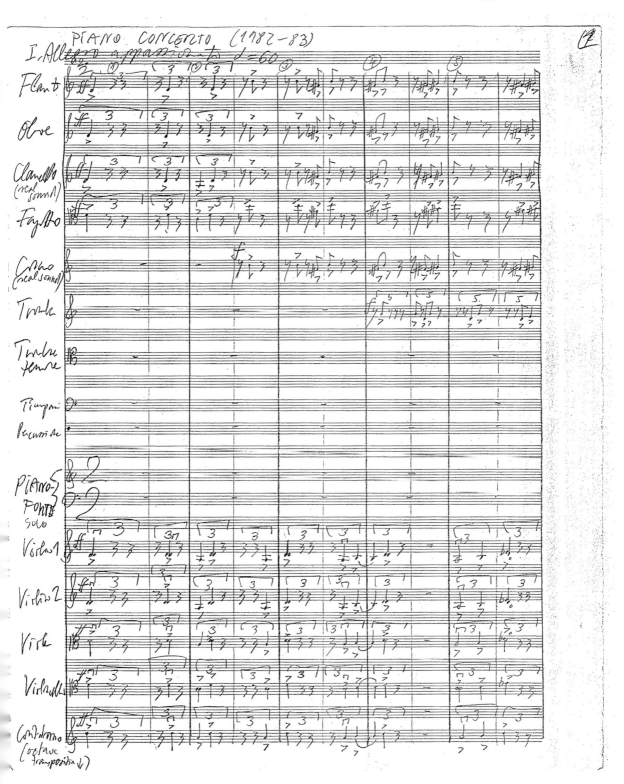

Figure 8 Piano Concerto, first movement sketch dated 1982–3,
scored for the orchestra mainly in triplets, but with quintuplets in the trumpet

to IRCAM. Lacking a mechanical piano, Nancarrow had to demonstrate his works on tape, but it was sufficient to deepen Ligeti's regard. His reference to 'the end of Nancarrow 40' probably refers to Study no. 40, a canon based on the mathematical constants e and π. It was Nancarrow's first use of irrational tempo relationships, and he may well have played a recording of it during the tour.

The second plan is typed in greater detail and projects seven movements. The first (*Appassionato*) is to be 'canonic and row-based'; the second (*Lamento*) a 'chromatic passacaglia'; the third a breathless *Toccata*; the fourth something 'fifth–fourth based, medium fast', and 'part canonic, like Nancarrow'; the fifth a *Scherzo*; the sixth a 'gamelan-like' *Adagio;* and the seventh a 'swinging' *Prestissimo*. At some stage Ligeti drew a circle around the third and fourth movements, and added an arrow pointing to the words 'Horn Trio'. This could have occurred whilst he was composing the Trio, or before, or even afterwards. Whenever it was, it led to the making of a third more substantial plan – now for a work in five movements, as Ligeti would indeed compose.

In the third scheme the projected movements are *Appassionato, Lamento, Scherzo, Adagio* (or *Lento*) and *Prestissimo*. This time the *Prestissimo* is conceived as a 'Hommage à Conlon Nancarrow', which becomes 'faster and faster, ragged and metallic sounding ..., a twisting maelstrom ..., with drive and a big swing!' Jazz references include: 'disco rhythm', Charlie Parker's *Ornithology* and *Yardbird*, and Oscar Peterson's *52nd Street* theme. And there is something else. Despite a determination to be himself, without recourse 'to categorization or to fashionable gadgetry', Ligeti was evidently still susceptible to the enthusiasms of his students. Who but they can have introduced him to *Breakfast in America*, the highly successful album by the British progressive rock band Supertramp, released in 1979, which reached no. 3 in the UK charts and no. 1 in America?

This was hardly a blueprint for a finished piece: more a Joycean assemblage of associations to be dipped into at will. In the years before the fifth movement was written other 'discoveries' would become influential. Foremost was that of the Banda-Linda pipe orchestra of the Central African Republic, introduced to Ligeti by his student Roberto Sierra, whose polyrhythmic polyphony Ligeti studied in detail. (See the conversation with ethnomusicologist Simha Arom elsewhere in this book.) It would be African polyrhythmic music, as much as anything else, that finally rekindled his creative fire.

Mensural canons

In early 1984 Ligeti addressed himself to the Concerto with renewed energy. Most of his sketches from this period concentrate on a three-part polymetric (or mensural) canon, employing the familiar 5–4–3 durational units. He tried several versions, all using different transpositions of the second 12-note series from Colour Plate 10. Some are loosely canonic, others more or less strict, and, as in earlier sketches, segments are frequently repeated. The difference between them is mainly in how the rhythms interlock, entries and rests being readjusted to explore different relationships. Figure 9 shows a version led by the piano in 4/4 quavers, followed by a bass clef entry in triplet crotchets, and (in bar 12) a treble clef entry in quintuplet

Figure 9 Piano Concerto, first movement sketch in 5–4–3 layers
beginning with reiterated A–C quavers in the piano

quavers. The rhythmic units in each layer are grouped in $3+3+2$ and, since stresses fall on the first of each group, the result is an irregular interplay of cross-accents. The pitches commence with a reiterated minor third taken from a different segment of the respective transposition. In the bass they are pitch-classes 12 and 1 from the series beginning on E. The piano has pitch-classes 2 and 3 from the series beginning on G. The treble is not, as might be thought, an inversion, but begins with pitch-classes 3 and 4 (sounded together) and 5 from a transposition beginning on F.

In these attempts Ligeti came closer than before to the polymetric character of the eventual first movement. During the next few months, he tried to reconcile the dogged rigour of the canons with a more spontaneous and colourful concerto texture. One version, for example, re-scores the piano opening for the more vigorous sonority of unison strings, and the bass clef entry for woodwind and brass in *ff marcato* octaves. Another lasts for 29 bars fully scored, taking its cue from Figure 9. It is more substantially orchestrated and transposed up a semitone to start on B♭–D♭. The first piano entry is thickened out and its character more flamboyant and improvisatory. Later it branches into four- and five-note chords doubled *marcato* in each hand. But contrapuntal logic is compromised and ten bars later the sketch breaks off.

In Figure 10 Ligeti thickens the whole texture by adding dyads and chords to each layer. The pitches are those of the second series, commencing with pitch classes 12, 1, 2, 3 and 4 in the middle, followed by transpositions in the bass and treble. The three layers again contrast quaver units in the middle, triplets in the bass, and quintuplets in the treble; with the connecting beams in each part conforming to a basic pattern of $3+3+2$. Although strict regarding pitch, the mensural canon is allowed leeway regarding rests to make alternations between the parts more effective. The sketch is unscored but apparently intended it for instruments, until, in a change of mind, Ligeti transferred the treble entry to the piano to lend it more weight.

Other sketches start with the piano. Ligeti tries at least nine versions, all with the same opening gesture (Example 38), but with different continuations in an attempt to integrate the piano convincingly. One sheet contains three attempts, each five bars long, two of which have a second piano interjection interrupting the canon – one in bar 4, the other in bar 3. In most of the others the piano parades its four chords, then plays no more.

Example 38 Piano Concerto, first movement, starting with the piano

Figure 10 Piano Concerto, first movement, polymetric (mensural) canon with thicker texture

The order of undated sketches

Only one of these sketches is dated. But there are clues to the order of others. Close scrutiny reveals that, in Figure 10, Ligeti wrote 'I/1' in the top right-hand corner (i.e. first movement, first page) over a partly erased 'I/4'. Evidently, to start writing this new attempt, he took an unused page 4 (with its bar-lines pre-ruled) from a version recently discarded. But which? The answer lies in his habit of numbering every bar. One can see that bars '1, 2, 3, 4, 5' have also been written over previous numbers ('39, 40, 41, 42, 43') which have been only partly erased. Ligeti's practice was to pre-rule several pages, with three systems per page and five bars per system (totalling 15 bars per page). So page 4 should have begun with bar 46. Why it does not is explained by another sketch – one of those that begins with chords in the piano. Seven bars into this, Ligeti crossed out what he had just written and began again. He then renumbered the bars to exclude the false start, and consequently sheet 4 begins at bar 39.

This is strong evidence for the order in which the two versions were written; although, curiously, from their musical content one might have concluded the opposite: i.e. that the sketch starting with the arresting piano chords followed, rather than preceded Figure 10, in which a thickening of the piano part is first explored. Whatever the order, Ligeti's repeated difficulty in reconciling the piano flourish with the linearity of the canon is evident. Having reached another impasse, on 11 November 1984 he put the Concerto aside yet again and began sketching the Piano Études.

With the benefit of knowing the completed Concerto, we may conclude that none of the beginnings so far composed enjoy the airiness of the published first movement. Three simultaneous transpositions of the series, with their minor thirds and semitones, generate an acidic tonal climate. If anything it sounds Bartókian – hardly the 'third way' for which Ligeti professed to be looking and which he would eventually discover through the Piano Études. In the Concerto's actual first movement, the crabby mensural canons are replaced by the polarity of white and black note scales, similar to those in the first Étude. Their character is more tonal or pentatonic than chromatic, whilst the combination is aerated by 'open' intervals (perfect fourths and fifths, major thirds and tritones). The superimposed melodies of chords are built in triads, sevenths, ninths and 11ths – all tonally familiar, but when combined sounding piquant and other-worldly. Until these enter, Ligeti has two, not three polymetric layers, one in 12/8 quavers, one in 4/4 quavers. Each dances to a different pattern of unequal beats. Their pairing is graceful and adroit; and, when he adds the chordal melodies in their own rhythmic units, they are combined with effortless élan.

Studies in black and white

Polymetre and tonal differentiation are the focus of Ligeti's first sketches for the Piano Études, as indicated by their titles: 'PULSATION 7/5', and in brackets '(NOIR ET BLANC)' or '(BLANC/NOIR)'. These simply mean that the pairing of a seven-note scale on the white keys with a pentatonic scale on the black is matched by a 7:5 relationship between the metrical layers. The second sketch includes the dedication: 'Étude polyrythmique I – pour

205

RICHARD STEINITZ
*Genesis of the
Piano Concerto
and the Horn Trio*

Pierre Boulez'. Boulez had conducted a wonderful concert for Ligeti's 60th birthday in 1983, and Ligeti reciprocated by writing the first three Études for Boulez's 60th birthday in 1985.

Ligeti's other sketches for the Études cannot be considered here. Sufficient to say that, whereas the first Étude, *Désordre*, retains the black and white note distinction, its pulsation processes are not based on 7 and 5. Nevertheless, it was the twin techniques of polymetre and complementary tonality in *Désordre* that pointed the way forward for the Concerto. The Étude's predetermined parameters and implacable process of compression challenged his ingenuity. 'I have a tendency always to make technical gadgets,' Ligeti has said, adding disarmingly, 'I know that this is ridiculous.'[64] On the contrary, it seems often to have been beneficial. Yet the lesson of *Désordre* did not at once provide a solution; and, when Ligeti returned to the Concerto on 21 December 1985, the four-pages he wrote that day revert to the gestural manner of earlier sketches. They are basically motivic, starting with a horn call on the pitches G–E–C–B–A (notes 4–8 of the series) answered by its transposition on muted trumpet. The next sketches explore ostinati and *lamento*-style melodies in the manner of *Automne à Varsovie*, with similar *taleae* defining their durations. In one, after eight bars of a regular ostinato in 6/4, a melody enters in which each note lasts three crotchets and a semiquaver (to clarify which Ligeti writes 13 13 13 written above each step). Another melody has a durational pattern of 9 3 3 9 9 3 3 semiquavers.

There are two versions on one sheet (both subsequently crossed out) of a mysteriously dark, undulating texture marked *Appassionato funebre* and *pppppp* (Figure 11). In the first a double bass makes a fleeting appearance; otherwise both are for piano alone. Arrows pointing down show that both hands are to be played an octave lower than notated. More significantly, their lines are cautiously polymetric, based on a simultaneous division of 6/4 into three minims and four dotted crotchets, indicated top left. The concept is more effectively realized in the second attempt halfway down the page, where triplet quavers in the left hand accompany a chromatic melody of dotted semiquavers in the right. This consists of six phrases of (successively) 5 6 7 8 7 and 6 dotted quaver units (see the numerals written on the sketch). Ligeti had used a similar expanding and contracting durational scheme in *Monument*, the first of the Three Pieces for Two Pianos and a technical precursor of both the Études and Concerto.

His love of numerical patterns had been revived by Douglas Hofstadter's book *Gödel, Escher, Bach*,[65] published in 1979, and then by the new art of computer-generated fractals developed by the Bremen mathematicians Heinz-Otto Peitgen and Peter Richter, whom Ligeti met in 1984. Pulse and pattern led usefully away from the linearity of canons, series and conventional rhetoric. Cast aside were the '*Appassionato agitato*' indications of earlier sketches, to be replaced by the urbane suavity of '*molto ritmico e preciso*' as in the eventual first movement.

---

[64] Conversations in Hamburg.

[65] Douglas R. Hofstadter, *Gödel, Escher, Bach: An Eternal Golden Braid* (Hassocks, 1979).

Figure 11 Piano Concerto, first movement, a later sketch from 1985–6

207

RICHARD STEINITZ
Genesis of the
Piano Concerto
and the Horn Trio

An undated sketch charts the transition. It begins with a bar in which the descending melodic semitones of Figure 11 (see the second phrase of the second version) are lifted several octaves higher and doubled in both hands. The three descending quavers are beamed like a triplet; and under a sustained B♮ faster triplets embrace a minor third (Example 39). The next sketch is not only the penultimate, but effects the most significant change so far (Example 40). There are still triplets and an open texture – indeed, the triplets are continuous. But in other respects this is startlingly unlike previous sketches and clearly influenced by *Désordre*. The first bar begins with minor thirds, but then the harmonic climate shifts. The opening has no key signature; and the notation in flats, plus a rogue G♮, suggest that Ligeti began without intending to use complementary scales. By the end of the first bar he has adopted them: white keys in the right hand excluding E♭, black plus E♮ in the left. On the second page of the sketch (second system in Example 40) he adds a key signature in the left hand only. Buoyed by the tonal ambivalence, the music takes off, left and right hands soaring and diving together like a pair of birds in flight.

Example 39 Piano Concerto, first movement,
link to the penultimate sketch

Curiously, although written on sheets prepared for the whole ensemble, Example 40 is a duet for piano and glockenspiel. The tempo (crotchet = 144) is close to the 138 of the actual score. Asymmetric dance-like rhythms emerge from a durational scheme, in which triplet quavers are organized in groups of 3 10 3 3 7 3 10 3 10 3 10 3 3 7 3 10 3 3 7 3 10 3 3 3 7 3 3 – each group beginning with an accent. The groups are further emphasized by the glockenspiel, which doubles both accents and anacruses.

Example 40 Piano Concerto, first movement, penultimate sketch

Example 40 *continued*

The eureka moment

What is absent from Example 40, but present in the Concerto, is polymetre. Was it the arrival of cross-accentuation in bar 12 that triggered the addition, or were the polymetric cogs already revolving in his mind? Breaking off at bar 12, Ligeti starts again – and for the last time (Figure 12). Seemingly written at speed,[66] here finally is the first movement of the Piano Concerto exactly as we know it. The triplets are retained, now notated in 12/8, but the pitches, melodies and accentuation are all new. A contrasting metrical layer in the strings has jaunty off-beat pulses in 4/4. The music displays a fecund and inventive ingenuity earlier attempts had lacked. New ideas fit effortlessly into already intricate textures and the sketch continues to the end of the movement with remarkably few corrections. A vital component of its success is Ligeti's decision frequently to reinvent the metrical relationships. Beginning with 12/8 against 4/4, they are so daringly varied that by the end of the movement there has been no dominant metre.

In conversation with the Hungarian musicologist Tünde Szitha in 1990, Ligeti spoke of the value of numerical relationships in giving 'solidity' to a structure: 'It matters a great deal to me that the joints are tight, the cogwheels revolve smoothly and the construction is stable.'[67] Since returning to the Concerto's composition in 1983, he had tried many polymetric and mathematical constructs. None had provided an adequate foundation, and the first movement in its final form shows why they failed. So right does it sound, so assured and felicitous, one could wonder why Ligeti did not compose it before. In reality, many things needed to come together, others to be dropped, and the vital polymetric and harmonic components discovered. The result is a polyphony of finely balanced layers – defined by pulse, pattern, timbre and intervallic character – dazzlingly combined in a democratic collective of independent metres and multi-tonal harmony.

[66] This sketch also begins on what Ligeti had pre-ruled as page 5 of its predecessor.

[67] 'A Conversation with György Ligeti', *Hungarian Music Quarterly* 3/1 (1992), p. 17 (first published in *Muzsika*, 1990).

Figure 12 Piano Concerto, first movement, the final sketch

211

RICHARD STEINITZ
*Genesis of the
Piano Concerto
and the Horn Trio*

The Concerto's other movements

'The spontaneous is the fruit of conquest.' So wrote the poet Paul Valéry, who suffered a much longer creative block than Ligeti's, lasting all of two decades. Having recovered his own spontaneity, Ligeti worked fast. For the Concerto's second and third movements he spent little time on preliminary sketches. The second came so easily that he wrote two completely different versions, both fully scored. The first has an explosive, fragmented opening followed by loud, but declining bass drum strokes. Its first 19 bars are a hocket between unpitched percussion, cello and double bass. Melodies are added and the music becomes richer and more contrapuntal, but with only isolated single or pairs of chords from the piano. After 72 bars of increasingly diverse ensemble, there is a sudden return to the disjointed character of the opening: at this point a hocket for bassoon, horn, trombone and cello (Colour plate 16). There appear to be number series operating as in *Monument*. But the evolving textures in the middle of the movement and the dogged persistence of the hocket are strangely unmatched. At bar 108 the sketch tails off and seems to have been entirely discarded.

For 69 bars the second version is close to the published score, but with some bars crossed out and rewritten. After that there are more erasures and over-writing, not always easy to read. Ligeti's working-out is interestingly exposed, and differentiated using colour, although honed to the eventual character of the movement. The third movement is also preceded by two sketches: one of 11 pages taking the music to bar 78 virtually as published; the other explosive and melodramatic – but abandoned after seven bars.

The fourth and fifth movements were mainly composed only after the first three had been premièred, in 1987. A preliminary sketch for movement four contains most of the initial gestures, but relatively compressed and less dramatic than in the published score. It opens with the strings' snap pizzicato but without the side drum rim shot. There is no $f\!f$ piano entry in bar 4, nor its two interjections in bars 4 and 8. The piano enters in bar 9, but at that point the sketch breaks off and Ligeti begins again. This time the gestures are more dramatically juxtaposed and punctuated by silence. Until bar 45 the music is almost as published, then becomes sketchy. The overall shape is discernible, but durations are left to be worked out later. The final pages are particularly thin and quite unlike the published score. Ligeti described this as 'a fractal piece', the principle of its construction being 'a certain geometric vortex' in which 'the ever-decreasing rhythmical values produce the sensation of a kind of acceleration'.[68] His additional notes could reveal how the process was assembled; but, being handwritten in sometimes illegible Hungarian, are unfortunately beyond the scope of this study.

There is a similar sketch for the fifth movement, partly detailed and precise, partly in outline, with durations and rhythms left to be defined later. Most of the work on this movement probably took place in August 1987. By the early autumn all was done, and the first performance of the completed Piano Concerto took place the following February.

[68] Szitha, 'A Conversation with György Ligeti', p. 16.

It had been an extraordinarily drawn-out gestation, but the reward is in the finished piece. The more intimately one knows the Concerto, the more one marvels at its originality, audacity and technical bravura. Nor is it unduly serious. Reviewing the Teldec CD for *The Hungarian Quarterly* in 2001, Paul Griffiths describes the Concerto as 'One of music's great comedies and magic shows, full of funny, strange and wonderful feats of imagination: surges of harmony, beautifully orchestrated, that disappear like coloured smoke.' There is also poignancy, as 'the glorious bustle of the first movement trails away to leave a low string-bass note, ominously sustained'. And in the following lament 'the instruments step forward cautiously in this lonely world, subject to shock. And what they say ... is haunting and touching.'[69]

Conclusion

The key to the breakthrough was not only polymetric. Polymetre, after all, had been an occasional component of Ligeti's earlier music (not least the famous metronome piece); it had underwritten the rhythmic fluidity of the Horn Trio, and was implicit in the mensural canons attempted when he resumed sketching the Concerto in 1982–3. True, the actual first movement is more ingeniously polymetric than anything Ligeti had composed before. But crucially it is supported by something else: the layers are also differentiated harmonically.

The long gestation of the Concerto had another outcome, for it was also a process of spring-cleaning during which Ligeti discarded techniques no longer useful (clusters, micropolyphony, serialism) and established those which were (polymetre, passacaglia, alternative temperaments, melody). The natural horn harmonics used in the Trio lead to the complex non-tempered textures of the 1990s. Permissions Ligeti restored to himself in the Trio and Concerto legitimatize the eloquent melody in the Violin Concerto's second movement, which surprisingly turns out to be the Arcadian quasi-folk melody from *Musica ricercata* dropped two octaves and much slowed down. The lovely 'Keserédes', whose melody we hear four times over in *Síppal, dobbal, nádihegedűvel* is another example. What melodic charms might Ligeti have brought to *Alice*, one wonders, had he ever composed his long-planned second opera?

Along with these melodies, the pared-down poignancy of the Concerto's second movement and intensity of the Trio's *Lamento* assert a primacy of feeling over technique. There is a similar liberated expressivity in the Piano Études – *Automne à Varsovie* and *L'escalier du diable* for example: a directness of emotion which the Three Pieces for Two Pianos do not display. Above all, it was the partnership between polymetre and Ligeti's unique brand of multi-tonality that emphatically secured the ground for the achievements of his final years. He was too inclusive a composer wholly to jettison the past. But the renewal was dazzling, securing for Ligeti's late works an exceptionally wide following amongst the general public.

---

[69] Paul Griffiths, 'Music's Magic Show', *Hungarian Quarterly* 42/162 (Summer 2001) pp. 146–9, at p. 149.

Ligeti at home scratching his head
(Hamburg, 9 November 1989)

10   Craft and Aesthetics – The Teacher György Ligeti

WOLFGANG-ANDREAS SCHULTZ

I worked with György Ligeti from 1975 till his retirement in 1989, first as a 'special student' as it was then called in Hamburg (I had already finished my diploma in composition) then as his assistant. We were always in perfect agreement on matters of compositional craft, it was in questions of aesthetics that we differed quite a bit. As we remember the teacher Ligeti, this discrepancy is perhaps a good starting point to reflect about the relationship between craft and aesthetics.

It must have been 1976. Ligeti and his class were having lunch, as they often did, in the Café Bohème near the Music Academy. 'In fact,' he said, 'I should teach you all counterpoint, strict Bach-style, the way I learned it in Farkas's class in Budapest because it is very useful for composition. But, unfortunately, I don't have time for each of you individually which is why I was guaranteed an assistant when I was appointed professor, someone who will teach my future students counterpoint. Would one of you like to do this? This will mean a very hard two-year apprenticeship and no time for your own composition. Afterwards, I will work out the necessary teaching hours with the Academy.' To this day I don't understand why I was the only one who volunteered. Of course, I do come from a family of church musicians, grew up with Bach's music and felt I knew the style pretty well. Furthermore, thanks to my first teacher Ernst Gernot Klussmann, I had a good base in counterpoint, albeit not in Bach-style.

My period of training with Ligeti was very intense. Whereas the composition class nearly always took place in a group, this was private tutoring. Ligeti had an incredibly keen ear when it came to stylistic inconsistency, whether it was a modulation in the dominant key that had been going on too long or the occurrence of a stylistically questionable six-four chord. He was, however, unable to offer concrete suggestions for improvement because his practical experience with Bach-style was too far in the past – I had to do that myself. After I had written a three-part fugue on a chromatic theme which could, as a whole, be mirrored following the model of *The Art of Fugue*, a five-part chorale prelude with a cantus firmus in canon and a three-part chorale arrangement with the cantus firmus in the bass and two descant voices in canon he shook my hand and pronounced me 'Master of Counterpoint'. The apprenticeship lasted only 15 months, and I even composed my 'Concerto for Viola da Gamba and Orchestra' on the side.

In 1977 I was given a teaching post in music theory at the Hamburg Musikhochschule, which included Ligeti's composition class. Apart from teaching counterpoint to all his new composition students (some of whom came from abroad for a year while others had already finished their studies) I soon began teaching music theory in general (harmony, Bach and Palestrina counterpoint, classical instrumentation, modulation, cadences, etc.) to all diploma students at the Hochschule.

In order to keep in touch with Ligeti and to follow the compositional development of my counterpoint students, I continued to take part in the composition classes on an irregular basis and would take advantage of these visits to present my newest works. Sometimes Ligeti would ask for my advice, for instance in the case of a student who had submitted an incredibly complex orchestra piece and stubbornly insisted that one could hear everything he had written. Ligeti did not agree with this and asked me to explain why the score was so opaque. I tried to explain to the student that one should combine events together in layers and compose hierarchical processes and developments. Ligeti was obviously very happy with my explanation and the performance showed that we were both right.

Although Ligeti demanded absolute professionalism in matters of craft, it was obvious that he had his doubts about its universal validity. He was just as fascinated by the idea – or should one say: the phantom? – of the untrained original genius. For him Mussorgsky was such a genius and he stood in opposition to Rimsky-Korsakov, the at times academic professional. He was always attracted to the American West Coast, unencumbered as it was by European culture and standards. Even so, he couldn't take the step to trade Hamburg for Los Angeles, because he knew all too well that he needed the European cultural soil in which he was rooted. Nevertheless the question 'Can a composer also be handicapped by a solid craft?' was always present.

Now, the notion of 'craft' consists of a whole series of levels. The bottom level is the mastery of certain compositional techniques of one's own tradition, for example, the technique of counterpoint, how to deal with several simultaneous events, but also the grasp of harmony and the classical form idioms. And it is true that craft harbours a danger in this sense because it tempts the composer into relying on tried and true traditional solutions, especially if he has a good command of these. Seen this way, craft can be 'conservative' and something in Ligeti rebelled against this. Ligeti was not only a cultured specialist of Bach-style but also one who gladly broke taboos, destroyed conventions and transgressed the boundaries drawn by good handiwork.

However, a composer who wants more than just to break taboos and destroy tradition has to have a certain higher level of craft at his disposal so that he can draft vivid ideas, bring them to a head and develop a feeling for conciseness. On this level, the composer is no longer bound to the rules and conventions of the lower, purely technical level – well-known examples of this are the 'Puccini fifths' and Debussy's mixtures made of parallel-lead sounds. Craft in the sense of producing concise figures is anything but conservative because the willingness to break conventions and rules is not an end in itself but a way of creating a vivid new image. As a composer one should have a very developed feeling for conciseness because it is exactly this quality which is lacking in those composers who deliver works which are just technically well-made (in the sense of the lower craft level), be they 19th-century Mendelssohn epigones or 20th-century Ligeti imitators. Ligeti once said about a technically well-written piece: 'But it doesn't blossom.' This beautifully describes the missing step on the way towards a concise, clear-cut form. At the same time, however, one must master the lower level of craft to a certain extent in order to move freely on the higher level. And this is why, as far as Ligeti was concerned, Hamburg always won over Los Angeles.

Because this higher level of craft was so important to Ligeti, he rejected the clichés and conventions of contemporary music. I was to feel the full brunt of his aversion when, immediately after his appointment to the class in 1973, my first attempt fell through. I had presented a 'Concert Piece for Piano and Chamber Orchestra' which began with the minor second E–F and then built up to a cluster similar to that in the first movement of Ligeti's Cello Concerto. I'm not even sure he looked at the rest of the piece because with that gesture my work was dismissed. Following this ill-fated cluster was a figured A♭ major dominant-seventh chord and then, with every new beginning, notes were filtered away which did not belong to D♭ major until the piece ended on a D♭ triad. It was a very original idea but I must admit that even so the piece is not really good …

Later on his scathing judgement would often boil down to a simple: 'This sounds like modern music!' Not only did he hate the conventions of the new music, which filled the programmes of music festivals, but he expected a personal signature, originality even, and seemed to have forgotten that he himself had only found his own style after first imitating Bartók. There was little place in his teaching for learning through imitation or for a slow and gradual development of originality. This could be terribly dramatic for very young students who were thrown in severe crises or even gave up composition altogether. It was therefore advisable to have at least started or, even better, to have finished studying somewhere else and then to enter Ligeti's class at an age where one's own path was at least already drawn. The discussions in the class were very hard. Ligeti seemed to take pleasure in making spiteful and offending remarks which, because of his linguistic genius, often hit the mark. Out of rivalry and a need to distinguish themselves, the students would then pounce on the reviewed piece and the discussion would dangerously escalate further. In later years Ligeti became more lenient, very much to the displeasure of a student from the first years who had dropped in and launched into a vigorous attack in the style of earlier times. The group then followed in this crushing critique, the victim of which was my own piano trio *Elegien und Capricci*. When the piece was later performed and broadcast on the radio, however, most of them suddenly found it good and one even said disarmingly: 'We just can't read score.'

Seldom did the discussion heat up around problems of craft or about technical details of composing (except sometimes on questions of instrumentation technique) but nearly always about questions of aesthetics. Postmodernism had entered in music in the late 1970s, and with it appeared a 'new simplicity' which, coupled with a new romanticism, lead to the question: What can one compose today? To what extent can one fall back on tradition when it comes to harmony and formal language? It is interesting to note that melody was not even discussed then.

Even if he criticized the avant-garde and the old hardened conventions of new music, Ligeti refused to yearn for the past even though his own work was marked by reminiscence. Once, we tried to point out that *San Francisco Polyphony* was actually a rather romantic piece – he shrank more and more in his chair … In fact, this ambivalence coloured his own works: on the one hand, he looked for new ways and wanted to be totally open, on the other, he stayed linked to tradition. This is the reason why his Trio for Violin, Horn and Piano was massively criticized at a symposium in 1984.

Ligeti found himself now on the defendant's bench where he had so readily placed some of his students.

What was unique in Ligeti's class was its cosmopolitanism, first of all thanks to the students who came from other countries and cultures (Japan, Korea, China, Central America). Usually they came to Hamburg with the hope of deepening their knowledge of the Western avant-garde – and were encouraged by Ligeti to look into the roots of their own culture. They were not to learn the Esperanto of the international avant-garde he disapproved of; rather, they should engage in a dialogue with their own tradition's musical language. Here Ligeti's teaching really made a difference and actually gave rise to some interesting developments.

Beyond this, Ligeti was incredibly curious about any type of music. He always brought something new to class for us to hear. It could be works by Harry Partch, Conlon Nancarrow, or music from Indonesia, Africa or Mongolia. The discussions could focus on jazz and pop, or centre on music of the late Middle Ages known as *ars subtilior*. All this widened our horizon beyond what is, in the narrowest sense, known as classical tradition and avant-garde. At some point Ligeti relocated the class to his flat, which was for us students a clear benefit because all his scores and recordings were right there at hand. What interested him the most, however, were alternative tuning systems, microtonality and different ways of structuring rhythm. It became clear that Ligeti, too, was looking for something, and it was this common search and a constant feedback which made these class meetings so productive. Ligeti often mentioned that he learned from his students, and he also accepted suggestions from them. Each and every point of view would be open to criticism. This could be hard but if you stood your own, you would become more alert and confident in the pursuit on your goals. Composers who came out of Ligeti's class possessed a higher degree of awareness and a greater depth of reflection on music.

The older Ligeti became, the more he included his own earlier works in this critical discourse. However, to criticize Ligeti's music was difficult, as he could be very touchy. He said so himself when some of us made fun of the incredible number of annotations, and the very few notes, written on a page from a piece which was about to be performed. When he was working on the opera *Le Grand Macabre* he showed me some pages, which he had just finished. I dared to point out what I thought was a problem with the dramatic form. He wanted to integrate closed sections into the loose recitative texture, and I called his attention to the fact that a uniform structure does not guarantee a closed form, that more had to come from the inner structure of the form. A uniform structure only breaks off and does not prevent the music from scraping by from one detail to the next. And exactly the impression I had from the score was confirmed when one listened to the piece. Later Ligeti mentioned that he had given my criticism a lot of thought. Maybe this is one of the reasons why Ligeti finally thought of the opera as a failure.

'Quality always conveys the impression of a well-ordered, intact world', as Michael Braunfels pointed out.[1] Although this sentence stems from a conservative point of view, might it nonetheless contain insights worth considering? Is quality in the highest sense unreachable for a composer who expresses his chaotic and disordered world in his music?

In an interview he gave to Ulrich Dibelius in 1994 Ligeti linked the *ars subtilior*, which particularly interested him, to the plague, the Hundred Years' War and to the Papal Schism (with two popes, one in Rome and one in Avignon).[2] Had he ever established a correlation between the music of his generation, his own, and the experience of the Second World War, the sufferings of persecution and the ordeals of the Cold War? To my knowledge, he never mentioned this, but he himself suggested that there are parallels between the 14th and 20th centuries. The relationship between craft and aesthetics in the second half of the 20th century could hence be seen in a new way.

Perhaps one finds that the values and ideals of a culture are encoded in the highest level of craft, such as embodied by Bach and Mozart for instance, that is, in the balance between emotion and reason, in the relation between the parts and the whole (such as the idea of individual and society interpreted by Schiller), also in the richness of relationships, in the interdependence of the parts, in the question of musical time (as an attempt to establish a coherent succession of events) and so in the meaning of form, indeed the big form. Ligeti was honest enough to avoid the big form and he regarded my own attempts in this direction with a certain ironic scepticism, as if I was pursuing a completely outdated ideal. I can't even remember that questions of form, formal development and formal balance ever came up in the class discussions. More important for Ligeti were vivid ideas, one's own voice, originality – the best was when it was 'crazy', eccentric and, in some way, spectacular.

He made a comment after having read my score of *Abendländisches Lied* for English horn and orchestra, which I not only found moving but which preoccupied me a long time. He said: 'You must be a happy person.' At first, I wanted to protest but then I left it at that. In fact, happiness is not what one commonly associates with 20th-century artists. Still this remark shows that he was aware of the aesthetic gap between us. Ligeti probably saw himself more as a 'musicien maudit' – or maybe a 'poète maudit', a type first personified by Baudelaire and Rimbaud, the artist who feels himself outside of society, has broken asunder and feels torn from the world which replenishes his creative energy. Cynicism and self-hatred also came naturally to Ligeti.

'Coolness' was the prevalent attitude in the class during my first years and it applied not only to jazz but also to contemporary music. It was very strange to me that many aspired to being 'cool'. Ligeti saw himself in the tradition of the 'cold' composers, hence his affinity to Stravinsky. In *Cool Conduct: The Culture of Distance in Weimar Germany*, a study which had then not yet been published, the German scholar Helmut Lethen describes a type of personality, predominant in anthropology and literature,

---

[1] Michael Braunfels, *Die Krankheit der verwalteten Musik* (Zurich, 1975), p. 79.

[2] Dibelius, *György Ligeti: Eine Monographie in Essays* (Mainz, 1994), p. 256.

who is unattached, always wide awake and constantly on the alert, and who protects himself with an armour of coldness and distance.[3] This type of person wants to appear invulnerable and distances himself from everything that makes him vulnerable and excludes him: primarily the world of emotions and expression. This attitude in music lead, right after the First World War, to neoclassicism and to the dodecaphonic works of the 1920s.[4]

Bound in this 'aesthetics of coldness', music somehow suffers from an energy blockage, its powers of melody, harmony, rhythm and form do not flow, they cannot unfold, they do not embrace the listener but rather exclude him. A certain distance results, it is perceived as coolness and exudes a lack of emotions and frozen feelings. Walter Benjamin spoke of the importance of shocks in connection with Baudelaire and the directive 'Stop suddenly, as though torn off', which is often found in Ligeti's scores, could point to a context of traumatic shocks.[5] In connection with this, one often comes across the inability to express feelings, this very typical coldness of 1920s modernism.

It may very well be that the connection between musical structures which suffer from an energy blockage, and a composer who experienced the 20th century is inevitable. Even if it is important as an artistic option, as a general attitude, however, it is problematic. It should be possible to transcend the limits of the 'aesthetics of coldness' if we keep an attitude of active openness and view craft in the highest sense as the ability to allow the musical forces of melody, harmony, rhythm and form to go where they want to go (to paraphrase Adorno). I have the impression that Ligeti was always perched on a sort of borderland – in certain works (such as *Melodien* for example, which is a work that I still admire very much) he succeeded, in his own way, to write very beautiful, flowing music.

On the other hand, the opera *Le Grand Macabre* (after Michel de Ghelderode) seems to have been written from the position of the 'musicien maudit' – and probably failed because of it. The breaking of real or alleged taboos, the pubertal pleasure taken at perverse and infantile behaviour, and the time structure's almost programmatic regression to the here and now, all this exacts revenge on the music, be it when it disintegrates into unconnected individual moments, even when they are as 'crazy' as you want taken for themselves, or when the music becomes boring, which admittedly can be reversed because *Le Grand Macabre* is, of course, a dazzling piece of theatre.

This opera is an example of how an aesthetic position can damage musical craft. On the other hand, the opposite is shown in the *Hölderlin*

---

[3] Helmut Lethen, *Cool Conduct: The Culture of Distance in Weimar Germany* (Berkeley, 2001). The original German-language work was entitled *Verhaltens-lehren der Kälte – Lebensversuche zwischen den Kriegen* (Frankfurt am Main, 1994)

[4] Wolfgang-Andreas Schultz, 'Avant-garde and Trauma – 20th-Century Music and the Experiences from the World Wars', http://www.wolfgangandreasschultz.de/schultz_avantgarde_en.pdf, accessed on 15 August 2011.

[5] See Walter Benjamin, 'On Some Motifs in Baudelaire', in *Illuminations*, trans. Harry Zohn, ed. Hannah Arendt (New York, 1968), pp. 155–200.

Phantasies for choir, which is of a masterly texture, wonderfully precise and sensitively composed. Each aesthetic question has a pendant in the realm of craft because aesthetics – often unconsciously and rarely accessible to the composer – contains, encoded in it, the secret goal of the work, which will be realized with the help of craft. Ghelderode and Hölderlin, it was between these two poles that Ligeti played out his artistic tug-of-war, between his love for crazy sensational details and the knowledge that an ideal, coherent and multifaceted whole is encoded in perfect craft.

In his later years, Ligeti's increasingly showed his admiration for Mozart. Had he ever yearned for such a wonderfully balanced, perfect music, perhaps for a 'happy' music? The Piano Étude which later became *L'escalier du diable* was originally going in that direction, only to turn out 'very, very dark'.[6] Was it really so important that Ligeti had witnessed appalling poverty in California, as he said himself, or had he met here his aesthetic and technical limits?

The experience of war, persecution and loss of his family in the Holocaust clearly traumatized Ligeti. It is therefore admirable that he succeeded, by avoiding the serial avant-garde, in freeing his music from traumatic torpor to lead it back to liveliness, a powerful imagery and expressiveness. There was a certain boundary, however, which he was not able to cross: that of tradition with its many-layered meanings and that of melody and tonality. The class continued to meet occasionally at Manfred Stahnke's house after Ligeti retired from the Musikhochschule. It was at one of these meetings that I presented my dance poem *Shiva*. This work, in which the evolution of consciousness is depicted as the Hindu god dances in the Wheel of Life, naturally contains a multitude of references to several levels of tradition. And again, as so often, my piece was torn apart: 'I've heard all that somewhere before!' As we said goodbye, however, he shook my hand and said: 'But your piece impressed me very much!'

It had often been that way. While he recognized a technically well-written piece, he always had to add the disparaging remark: 'But why do you have to write such old-fashioned music?' We can take different directions and perhaps those who go one way cannot really see what there is really new to be found in the other direction. Today, with much distance and after having given these music philosophical questions much thought, I would answer: 'Because these particular aesthetics, encoded as they are in the highest notion of craft, are for me still up-to-date.'

Translated by Louise Duchesneau

---

[6] Dibelius, *György Ligeti: Eine Monographie in Essays*, p. 270.

Ligeti during a rehearsal of his Cello Sonata at home
(Hamburg, 9 November 1989)

11 The Hamburg Composition Class

MANFRED STAHNKE

Both Ligeti and his way of thinking as a teacher were, to say the least, quite complex: often extremely exciting, he could also be vicious and unfair not only towards other, well-known composers, but towards his own students as well. Remarkable, though, was the fact that he would often include himself in the thrashing. Ligeti detected the 'new music' clichés, which originated in Schoenberg's and Webern's wake (generally the periods of serialism and post-serialism), and unmasked their heavy ideological bent. Much was discussed in the class about the first 'serial' masters' capacity for self-judgment, mainly Stockhausen and Boulez. We were aware, of course, that Boulez' *Le marteau sans maître* and Stockhausen's *Gruppen* were masterpieces in their own time. Yet what had changed in the ensuing, 'post-serial' generation? Ligeti often saw here a political ideology which used music only as a vehicle and this although he would have been in complete agreement with one basic tenet of modernism, as we can see from the following quotation by Helmut Lachenmann.

> One should participate in art as an experience and as a test of one's own abilities, not from its unknown gothic depths but by progressing from an apparent sense of security to a real sense of danger. It is necessary to be able to understand and to cope with the rich possibilities of this experience as well as with the contradictions of its values. Art would then be a social learning process and an artistic pleasure in one. The composer who follows this ideal has a chance of being understood if he directly opposes the rules of the communication game and society's expectations towards expression. By consequently blocking society's preferred path to the work, his music, born in the free space it has forced open for itself, addresses society in an unmistakable way.[1]

Why then did Lachenmann become one of Ligeti's 'favourite enemies' ('Lieblingsfeinde'), as he liked to put it? Ligeti would never have accepted to place artistic creation and artistic experience completely into the realm of society. He would have presumed that the opposition – or rather dualism – of artist and society was obvious, and he would have moved on to deal with music for its own sake. Had he ever had a discussion with Lachenmann about this, he might have stressed the incredible heterogeneity of 'society' and 'the listening experience'. He absolutely abhorred any of these fashionable catchphrases. Smiling, he would have concluded by pointing to Lachenmann's raised finger that he who accuses 'society' of being a dumb school class validates in a patronizing manner his own existence as a teacher: that is what is 'unmistakable'.

It is surprising how relative points of view can be. Ligeti did not perceive the 'Lachenmann style' as a 'progression from an apparent sense of security to a real sense of danger'. Once it was established, this style seemed to him

---

[1] Helmut Lachenmann, 'Die gefährdete Kommunikation', in *Musik als existentielle Erfahrung: Schriften 1966–1995*, ed. Josef Häusler (Wiesbaden, 1996), pp. 99–103, at p. 100.

to be overburdened with theory and to become self-perpetuating over the years. Ligeti did not see that it put itself in question. That indeed is the tragedy of composition: if the composer has finally found a functioning language which is defined by continuously putting itself in question, it should be included in this process. Otherwise there results what Lachenmann also has to avoid: the apparent sense of security. Ligeti broke out of this sheltered position again and again, and this escape became the main subject of his teaching.

As soon as I joined Ligeti's class in 1974, Ligeti asked me what I thought of the aesthetic positions of my former teachers. I had studied first with Wolfgang Fortner until 1973, and, after that for a year in Freiburg with Klaus Huber and Brian Ferneyhough. I was 22 years old then and accepted Fortner's, Huber's and Ferneyhough's very different positions because I had heard good pieces from all three of them: Fortner's chamber opera, *In seinem Garten liebt Don Perlimplin Belisa*, which in my opinion remains one of his strongest pieces because of its complete tenderness, Huber's Violin Concerto and the first of Ferneyhough's *Time & Motion Studies*.

In 1974, an interesting situation had developed in Ligeti's class: Wolfgang von Schweinitz and Detlev Müller-Siemens were experimenting with tonality (the points of reference were Mahler, Schumann or Schubert), and were using traditional forms; Schweinitz worked with symphonic form, while Müller-Siemens adapted *Ländler*. Hans-Christian von Dadelsen brought Bob Dylan songs to the class and music by the pop group Supertramp. In the middle of the 1970s I felt like I was on another planet and, after some tonal experiments, I threw myself into extreme microtonality: the result was my 12th-tone (not 12-tone!) orchestral piece *Metallic Spaces*, with a title coined by Ligeti. This work was premièred in 1978 at the Gaudeamus Festival in Hilversum using tone generators which produced six different concert pitches a twelfth-tone apart from each other. The very 'abstract' patterns I had created in this way had nothing to do with Harry Partch's 'just intonation', however. (Ligeti had visited Partch in California in 1972 and had brought back some of his recordings to Hamburg.) At the same time I was analysing Pierre Boulez' music, especially his partially finished Third Piano Sonata from 1956. As a result, much of my work moved me far away from the discussions on pop music and tonality which then prevailed in the Ligeti class. It was only later, after my year of study in the USA with Ben Johnston, Harry Partch's friend and supporter, that I began to understand Ligeti's dictum of the 'dead avant-garde'. I tried to find my own answer to 'tonality', first by including a retuned harp (influenced by Partch) in my chamber opera *Der Untergang des Hauses Usher* (The Fall of the House of Usher, 1980). Later, in 1985, I wrote the *Partota* for solo piano in the Vallotti temperament while Ligeti composed his first Piano Études. These commentaries on traditional patterns of pitch and rhythm allowed me to indulge in my childhood love of retuning keyboard and string instruments. Ligeti helped and supported me most sympathetically in this. I mixed music of the Middle Ages and the Renaissance, discovered for the most part during my musicology studies, with that of Nancarrow, Partch, jazz or African music. In my orchestra piece *Mandelbrotbaum*, for instance, I retuned the whole orchestra, thus creating a rhythmically pulsating, quasi-tonal language, which was in strong contrast to the *Metallic Spaces* of 1978. In the 1980s several students of Ligeti's class were combining very different kinds of music in their works, albeit each in their own very personal style. Some of them, Unsuk Chin, Michael Daugherty, Roberto Sierra, Benedict Mason, Xiaoyong Chen, Sidney Corbett and Mari Takano, have in the meantime become quite well known.

In my view, Ligeti managed to keep his personal language of the 1980s from influencing the works of most of his students. The group, on the other hand, did influence itself mutually from within and Ligeti took part in these discoveries. In his class, everybody had to find his or her own respective musical style without copying the teacher or other contemporary music masters. Did Ligeti help to find one's 'own' style? Yes, but this was achieved only indirectly, I believe, by playing a lot of music, by discussing practically all fields of thought, by putting false security into question – and there we once again come close to Lachenmann's thoughts quoted above!

Question upon question: there is no simple explanation of the phenomenon 'Ligeti', let alone of 'Ligeti as a teacher'. Spontaneously I would say first of all that Ligeti was not a real teacher. Or rather, that he was a 'transposed' teacher, one who had long ago left behind the traditional 'keys' of teaching and now strived to discover new territory. What was important to him was always what was still to be discovered, even in old, well-known areas. In that he was a great teacher – perhaps the only possible one.

Contradictions: this was his domain, but behind the irreconcilable juxtapositions he found a third way, an otherness, a merging. Ligeti's 'teaching' (which was, when it dealt with 'music', rather a philosophy of music) was first and foremost the unmasking of petrified structures, and not just those of the students. New areas of thought that could enrich music were then sought out. His main criterion was the 'magic' of good music whether it was 'simple' or 'complex', notated or not as in jazz. He liked to use the word 'complex' ('vertrackt'), which is not surprising given the nature of many of his works. Yet he did accept and sought out 'simple' musical trajectories: see the beginning of the Cello Concerto, the first movement of the Viola Sonata, or the beginning of the slow movement of the Violin Concerto – and there are many more examples.

And so I begin my rather fragmentary, unjust, and biased account of 'Ligeti as teacher'. I will interweave memories from 1974 up to 2003 when we finally lost touch. I did not visit him in Vienna where, due to illness, he had been forced to go back to the care of his wife Vera.

I joined Ligeti's class in 1974 as a postgraduate student and came regularly until his retirement in 1989. After that I would visit him often at home in his Mövenstraße flat, once together with his American student Sidney Corbett. He came twice with the whole class to visit my wife and I at home. The first time he came, he gave his Canadian student Denys Bouliane an extended interview in my studio. On a later occasion we listened to a wonderful *pianissimo* work for orchestra by Benedict Mason, full of a long-lost, far-away beauty. In such a situation Ligeti could be completely spellbound.

I also conducted two interviews with him, in 1993 and 2001. We had become used to each other rather than being friends. However, there was an indescribable mutual understanding between us for which I would venture to name a precise beginning in time: it was since Hubertus Dreyer had first premièred my *Partota* for solo piano in the Hochschule in 1986. I was a 'former student' with a special interest in tuning systems and Ligeti liked positions that were somehow out of the ordinary.

Of course, one of the consequences of this long acquaintance with him had nothing to do with music or artistic considerations in general: we, the students, had become a kind of organism in a way that is hard to describe, with everyone playing his or her role. We often utterly rejected each other, but the opposite could also happen. Some of us avoided the big meetings and preferred to see him as 'soloists', or they visited Ligeti on their own after the end of their studies rather than with the class. I never saw Silvia Fómina with the group, and Unsuk Chin came only at the beginning of her studies. But mind you, I myself attended only very infrequently and visited regularly only from the mid-1980s on, when a tightly knit group had built around Ligeti. Some of the 'regulars' were the young Hubertus Dreyer, Hans Peter Reutter, Mike Rutledge and Sidney Corbett who came later. Then there were Mari Takano, Kiyoshi Furukawa and Tamae Okatsu from Japan, with other guests either occasionally flying in from far away or becoming regular students: Benedict Mason and Malcolm Singer from England, Denys Bouliane and Sid McLauchlan from Canada, and Xiaoyong Chen, whom Ligeti helped when he came to Hamburg from China. Ligeti encouraged us to form a 'microtonal conspiracy' and this led to the formation of a group of composers and musicians named 'Chaosma'. For our first concerts Ligeti was able to secure the support of the Hamburg music agent Rolf Sudbrack and Jürgen Drews from the Goethe Institut in Munich. Yamaha Europe also became our first sponsor by donating several Yamaha DX7 IIs, the first digital synthesizer which allowed microtonal reprogramming. The Goethe Institut subsidized many a concert tour all over the world and I for one lectured and gave composition classes everywhere from New Zealand to South Africa.

As we all gathered to have a bite to eat (salami, cheese and pickles) around the little table we had painstakingly cleared for this purpose, one could feel the electricity in the air: some blossomed and many felt freed of an often uncomfortable tension. I do not think it was the feeling we were in the presence of a 'star'. Ligeti himself was totally unpretentious at home – unlike in the public space of the concert hall where he could become a hyper-nervous prima donna, a bit out of timidity, I believe, but more because he feared his music would fail. The tension we felt at these class meetings in Ligeti's home was a result of his profound self-questioning, his constant scepticism and his boundless intellectual searching. My wife always noticed that whenever I was speaking to him on the phone I spoke twice as fast. It was my typical reaction to his accelerated tempo but he would pull us all down into the spin of his maelstrom. It is thus not surprising that we felt relieved when we could listen to a piece of jazz or another type of music, which he would play either on the record player, from now extinct music cassettes or simply on the piano. I still have many of the ethnic music cassettes he gave me, which he always generously copied from his records for his students.

Nobody listened more eagerly nor enjoyed these meetings better than Ligeti himself. Yet none of us failed to notice the expression of deep boredom that would now and again appear on his face. At times there simply was not enough fresh blood in the class. I once told him that he was like a vampire who bled us dry of all of our ideas. A slight giggle to himself was his only reaction. As a teacher he was a taker rather than a giver, and whenever he discovered something good, a tiny little idea perhaps, which would drown out the humdrum chitchat about music, he would go to his record shelf, his musical treasure trove and the tiny little idea had to hold its own against the weight of the masters. He was not at all interested in self-promotion and would stop us if we were prone to that. He truly despised the boasting, self-important know-it-alls who occasionally joined us in the class.

I cannot recall a single instance of him 'lecturing'. Even his public seminars at the Hamburg University or in room 'Blau 200' at the Musikhochschule were rather either discussions with himself, or with Schubert or Mahler. 'Blau 200' was Ligeti's teaching room in the acoustically as well as aesthetically extremely poorly constructed new building of the Hochschule. A supporting round pillar stood nearly in the middle of the room while neither the windows nor the concrete walls let any fresh air in. In the end the neighbouring organists naturally had the better of Ligeti who quickly fled the tonal cadences and from then on taught at home.

He did not care whether the audience was able to follow his lectures or not. His talks were delivered in his famous stammering and rambling mode. As soon as an idea became obvious to him, and this could be after only three words of an incomplete sentence, he would break it off and start on the next fragment. Ligeti spoke in the form of a direct narration of his thoughts – the actual words always lagging slightly behind. But he much preferred to 'discover': if someone came up with an interesting idea, he would look up, wide-eyed, and come out with his soft short staccato 'yes'.

I had heard Fortner's Beethoven lectures in Freiburg, which had a quite similar approach: he would explain the specific architecture of musical forms by starting with the smallest of forms. I do not really remember that 'tonality' was a subject in Fortner's class or maybe, in this case, Ligeti has drowned out my recollections. His mind in upmost tension, Fortner would intimate through his typical falsetto-speech how ambiguous the process of finding a solution could be. In a similar fashion, Ligeti would simply emit 'hypotheses' on how Schubert's harmony was completely different from Beethoven's, stirring the listener to modify, amend or even reject them, at least in their presented form. His stammering, unfinished way of speaking gave his remarks the appearance of temporary snapshots of a much bigger, yet utterly indescribable super-idea, which, even if it could have been uttered, would have emerged as something alien to the art form under analysis. My somewhat erratic discourse on Ligeti's seminars may give you a glimpse of how 'sacred' the tonal structure of Schubert's late B♭ major sonata was for him ...

There were unforgettable moments in the class, for instance when Roberto Sierra, then a student from Puerto Rico, introduced us, early in the 1980s, to Simha Arom's recordings of the African Banda Linda horn ensembles. Another memorable event was when Hubertus Dreyer (now a musicologist in Tokyo) either played some new jazz recordings or improvised his own 'jazz' at the piano. I experienced Ligeti's love of anything new after my return from the US when I played recordings of Nancarrow's music that he did not have in his collection – he had discovered Nancarrow for himself during my absence in 1979 in Paris. We also listened to recordings of the *ars subtilior* of the late 14th century, among these the incredible *Le ray au soleyl*, an *opus dubium* by Johannes Ciconia which Annette Kreutziger-Herr (now a professor in Cologne) had brought to the class. Another highlight was the visit of Heinz-Otto Peitgen and Peter Richter, the two Bremen scientists who had developed the first high definition fractal images. All these exceptional encounters finally came together for the 'Ligeti Congress' which took place, in 1988, at the Hamburg Hochschule. Its president, Hermann Rauhe, had secured funding from the Deutsche Forschungsgemeinschaft and organized the event together with Ligeti's students and friends as a celebration of his 65th birthday. They all came – everybody Ligeti had talked so much about, always insisting that only pure research (without any other interest) could lead to new insights. There was the Nobel-Prize-winning biophysicist Manfred Eigen, the computer music specialists John Chowning and Jean-Claude Risset, the ethnomusicologists Simha Arom and Gerhard Kubik, the physicist Peter Richter and the musicologist Ursula Günther (who died in November 2006) who had coined the term *ars subtilior* to describe the style of the late 14th-century music. Many other outstanding musicologists also took part, some from Hamburg such as Peter Petersen or Constantin Floros who later wrote a monograph on Ligeti.

Even now, there is always a whiff of Ligeti whenever old members of the class, particularly those from the 1980s, email, phone or meet. I would not be surprised if, for many of us, he is present in every note we write: does what I am writing have to do only with the music or am I trying to impress someone? For Ligeti, music was also something that appealed to the senses, reaching out to the complete range of the listener's sensual potential. 'Aber Vorsicht!' – 'Be careful!' – he would then often say. Processes, which were 'conceivable' as musical structures, were dismissed if the sounding image, that is what one in fact heard, was meaningless. In his uncompromising judgement, Boulez's strict serialism and Xenakis's stochastic processes were doomed to fail.

One more word on the 'sensual nature' of his approach: he often mentioned hearing the extremely rapid Romanian folk music as a young boy. And so, at the bottom of Ligeti's musical ocean we find pulsation, even when it has seemingly been completely dissolved as in *Atmosphères*. Pulsation had no negative connotation for one who had grown up without the march music and *Volksmusik* which had scarred the West Germans of the 1950s. Nor did Ligeti have any reason to reject melody and melodic lines, another avant-garde taboo. In the class, we did not use pulse and melody mainly as a way to 'protest' against the avant-garde's decrees, for us it was also a means of redefining ourselves. Still, where would one find the 'new' in the old? How could we 'know' it as listeners? Our quest was misunderstood and inevitably we came under attack. We, along with our 'teacher', were labelled 'retro'.

We misunderstand Ligeti if we regard him only as a 'composer' or only as a 'composition teacher'. (In my view he accepted the Hamburg professorship in the early 1970s mainly for financial reasons.) What he really wanted was pure musical research, detached from the business side of music. Writing music and thinking about music were just his own personal means of expression. This was maybe one reason why he deeply hated – or better, had contempt for – the 'music business' that had created insidious ways of maintaining itself and its ideology. Again and again Ligeti made us aware of this farce. What was alarming to us was that we, as young composers, had to gain a foothold in that world and try to make a living there. As he grew older, Ligeti became more and more bitter. He felt that commercial interests reigned and that political stubbornness was pervasive in Germany. A basic assumption of composition is that a composer should always put himself in question and never become set in his ways. Ligeti demanded this of his students and was enraged to see that the music industry selfishly exploited, commercially and ideologically, not only new music but all types of music, fearlessly shifting from the realm of composition to that of interpretation in the most amateurish manner. Good connections were often more important than the best quality. He was shocked when, even in Hamburg, dilettantes conducted contemporary music concerts, particularly as this was the city Ligeti had chosen as his refuge to compose. (No one paid any attention to him here, he could cycle undisturbed around the Alster, a small lake near his flat.) Yet he said nothing in public – what could he do against this Hamburg 'amicitia'. For this reason he found Hamburg totally provincial and so continued to remind us of the importance of professionalism in writing and interpreting music, and always pointed out examples taken sometimes from the music of the old Flemish composers (Ockeghem) or from that of his friend György Kurtág.

Because of its insistent repetition of principles, much of the so-called 'new music' had become obsolete to him. This he always demonstrated to his students not only by referring to our own compositional attempts, but also by regularly playing recordings: these Ligetian analyses were often detrimental to many a still famous name because they unveiled the real source of certain ideas or their much revered models. Yet how enthusiastic he could be about really inspiring new compositions such as some late works by Gérard Grisey (for example *Vortex temporum*) or Claude Vivier's *Lonely Child*! Rather strange people like Harry Partch and, of course, Conlon Nancarrow also caused much excitement – Nancarrow had written another study for player piano for Ligeti, *For Ligeti,* and came to Hamburg in the early 1980s. Like Ligeti, we were all on a quest, and this multitude of alternative musical approaches quickly demonstrated to us the limitations of the saturated German avant-garde. Many of us went other ways than composing contemporary art music. Some became sound engineers and recording producers (Sid McLauchlan) or musicologists (Hubertus Dreyer), or even invented instruments (Benedict Mason). They and others still try to find new, untrodden musical paths, unexplored musical worlds like the ones based on pulsation or microtonal structures that the later Ligeti was committed to. The question was whether or not a composition still had to represent an 'example' of a theory, as was requested by the entire 'Heinz-Klaus Metzger world' (a term coined by Ligeti) and its followers.[2] When many of us sided with John Cage, Ligeti slyly accepted his approach, stating that it just could not be compared to the 'music' Haydn wrote. (He always dreamed of writing something matching the quality of Haydn's string quartets.) He also feared philosophical dilettantism or dealing with only half-understood philosophies. He was shocked by the dilettantism of the so-called 'complexism' that emerged from the Ferneyhough circle in Freiburg (although Ferneyhough himself always distanced himself from the complexism of his student Claus-Steffen Mahnkopf!). As much as Ligeti was interested in the other arts – particularly painting, architecture and poetry (which, in his opinion, included Derrida's 'philosophy', as an example of bad 'poetry' because as philosophy it did not really explain what it claimed to be about) – he did not like to plunder these areas before their influence had merged into a concept in his mind or a new, third way had been found.

Ligeti loved the indirectness of allusion (another one of his favourite terms). He created his own enchanted islands full of manifold echoes, but would only allow the work to come out of the studio when everything had fused together. He warned us not to compose 'music about music' and became more and more mistrustful of his students' 'neo-tonality' which emerged in the 1970s. It was perhaps for this reason that he became more and more critical of his opera *Le Grand Macabre*, a work he would describe as a collage in the sense of pop-art.

And how he would love to ramble and sometimes completely avoid talking about music. I remember something unconnected to his teaching: as he did not sleep very well he liked to ring people up late at night and talk for hours. Once, as we were discussing the birth of human culture, Ligeti speculated that we could not possibly know when it had begun. It could be much older than the cave-paintings at Lascaux, for instance, and since these were so perfect, there must have been previous attempts at image making on some perishable material which extinct cultures had undertaken tens of thousands of years ago. (In the meantime, examples of older depictions – figurines, images or geometrical forms– have indeed been found.) Ligeti also believed that musical culture could be as old as humanity. He was fascinated by what was remote and he loved to fantasize about these worlds.

And how blunt he could be, for instance when, after leafing through a student's score, he would mess up his hair with both hands and ask: 'Do you like this?' But when someone had a good idea, Ligeti, his head buried behind his hands and peeking through his fingers, would utter his staccato 'yes'. Often, because of some association, he would change the course of the discussion and branch out into some typical Ligeti direction, leaving the rest of us speechless. These bizarre and unexpected interconnections between all possible ways of thinking would stimulate both him and us as well. In my mind I see the smirk on his face when he remembered how the many churches were organized in and on the roof of the Church of the Holy Sepulchre in Jerusalem. Perhaps he was comparing it to the

---

[2] Heinz-Klaus Metzger (1932–2009) was the most important German 'new music' critic and theoretician after Adorno.

numerous new-music styles in Europe. He enjoyed making fun of such words as 'neophysites' or of the different forms Christian belief could take, all marvellous crazy nonsense that Ligeti recognized and loved. 'Crazy' ('verrückt') and 'bizarre' ('merkwürdig') were much-used words with which he would refer even to his favourites Partch, Nancarrow or Feldman. (Feldman was, for example, 'much more normal, but also crazy'.) I suppose that what he meant were extreme positions – his own included. Speaking about favourites: with Ligeti, everything was relative. Although he found Partch extremely interesting and even wanted, at some point, to have a 43-tone organ built in Partch's system, he could also say: 'He was not really a composer.' (This he certainly meant in the narrow European, 'Haydnesque' sense.)

Over and over again Ligeti would expose the great contemporary manipulators of clichés: take an infusion of Alban Berg and mix it with some meaningful crumbs that just happen to come along – and then, pushed by publishers, conductors and concert agents, you can pose as a 'great artist'. After that, Ligeti liked to play 'real' Berg or 'real' Schumann. It was extremely enlightening for the class to witness so many of its guiding lights fall forever into darkness. Yet it could also be embarrassing for us to see, so harshly demonstrated, where our own thinking came from and consequently the weakness of our own approach. Since the 1970s we liked to discuss the official new music scene, which was controlled then by Darmstadt, Stuttgart and Freiburg. (Cologne with Stockhausen had pulled out long before that.) The old avant-garde was our favourite adversary. We all wanted to free ourselves from it and find our own ways, even within 'tonality' in the broadest sense. Some of us went very far back and chose old tonal models but this also proved to be a false path as nothing new was likely to be discovered there ...

Ligeti often spoke of how pitch and metre in post-Schoenberg-Webern new music had fallen under a kind of haze. In one of my interviews he said:

> When I think of the avant-garde I have this image in my head: I am sitting in an airplane, the sky is blue and I see a landscape. And then the plane flies into a cloud: everything is grey-white. At first the grey seems interesting if you compare it to the earlier landscape, but it soon becomes monotonous. I then fly out of the cloud and again see the landscape, which has completely changed in the meantime.
>
> I believe that we have flown into such a cloud of high entropy and great disorder, particularly because of Schoenberg and the Viennese School but also due to the post-war generation in Darmstadt and Cologne – to which I more or less belonged. The instant I emerge out of the cloud I see, and this is being very critical, that the music we wrote was in fact rather ugly. With 'we' I mean my generation, myself included. This ugly music was a consequence of twelve-tone music, of total chromaticism.
>
> It is for this reason that I experiment with hybrid systems, as you also do, rather than with dogmatic or puristic ones.[3]

---

[3] 'György Ligeti und Manfred Stahnke: Gespräch am 29. Mai 1993', in *Musik – nicht ohne Worte: Beiträge zu aktuellen Fragen aus Komposition, Musiktheorie*

The word 'ugly' is not easy to construe. Ligeti cannot have meant it as the opposite of conventionally beautiful sound, as his late music is not really 'beautiful'. I can only find one reason why he rejected the impact of dodecaphony, an aspect which became clear in our many conversations. Many of the serial works of the 1950s and later did not focus on the power of pitch and interval, but rather on a somewhat blanket aural impression amid what seemed to be 'randomly' interacting structures. This often applied to the temporal framework as well, which, to Ligeti, frequently appeared arbitrary. I had analysed in detail 'Trope', the second movement, or 'formant' as Boulez calls it, of the Third Piano Sonata, and in the process had established an intense (if not tension-free) relationship to this piece. At the end of the 1950s Ligeti had written about this piece in *Die Reihe*[4] yet had not attempted a proper analysis as he had done with Boulez' *Structure Ia* (where he went so far as to uncover composition errors Boulez had made). Perhaps Ligeti meant that the anonymity of the material was 'ugly'. In fact, Boulez wanted to create a kind of 'anonymity' in his Third Sonata. Ligeti connected this, always with a twinkle in his eye, to Boulez' personality.

Ligeti's relationship to the older composers of the 20th century was fascinating. Messiaen and Stravinsky were masters and although Ligeti mimicked Boulez's disparaging gesture towards Shostakovich who was *persona non grata* in the eyes of many Western avant-gardists, he also drew increasingly nearer to him. Ligeti did not conceal the fact that he had refused to shake the composer's hand in Stockholm in the 1960s: at the time he believed Shostakovich to be a member of the Moscow *nomenklatura* and it was only after reading his memoirs that Ligeti realized how precarious Shostakovich's situation had been then.[5] In Germany there were 'officious' disparaging remarks about Gérard Grisey, Wilhelm Killmayer or Peter Kiesewetter – I remember only too well the mood in the Darmstadt of the 1970s and 80s, a tone which was dictated by many leading figures of the time. Ligeti was horrified to see with what stupidity, for example, Grisey's harmonic inventions were labelled as 'pretentiously arty' or dismissed as 'wallpaper-music'. He also made clear to us what ideology could bring about, in politics but also in art: a primitive unenlightened black-and-white view without any chance of discussion. Yet discussion was what the Ligeti class was all about although he would have never accepted to debate art principles or political views with 'fanatic believers'. Along with Ligeti, we always craved to find opportunities for 'falsification' (to use Karl Popper's terminology, which was central to Ligeti's thinking).[6] In other words, we were always trying to prove the impossibility of a given musical position, even in the works of colleagues. How we all suffered, yet how passionately we tried to defend ourselves. I mentioned earlier that I had studied with

und Musikwissenschaft, ed. Manfred Stahnke, Musik und 2 (Hamburg, 2000), pp. 121–60, at pp. 143f.

[4] *Die Reihe* was an influential German-language music journal, edited by Herbert Eimert and Karlheinz Stockhausen, and published by Universal Edition between 1955 and 1962.

[5] *Testimony: The Memoirs of Dmitri Shostakovich*, ed. Solomon Volkov (New York, 1979).

[6] Karl Popper, *The Logic of Scientific Discovery* (London, 1959); originally published as *Logik der Forschung* (1934).

Klaus Huber and Brian Ferneyhough, so naturally some of us, not just myself, but also the visiting Huber student Uros Rojko, tried to defend our position. And as a result, I think that Ferneyhough's *Cassandra's Dreamsong* was finally accepted in Ligeti's class.

Ligeti was fascinated by the sudden 'radiance' of a good composition. If it was coherent within itself (or, as Ligeti liked to put it, if it 'worked'), scientific falsification no longer applied. Of course, art was light-years away from science, but even so it should be as clear, disinterested and uncorrupted by politics, ideology or religion.

What does 'falsification' mean? It is based on a lack of faith: if I believe in a god, it is not possible for me to prove his non-existence. If I believe that music only has a social and political mission, I cannot accept the opposite standpoint. It is therefore not possible to 'falsify' faith. Let us look at the visual arts: maybe Ligeti hated schools of thought such as the one around Joseph Beuys precisely because they excluded discussion and surrounded the 'work' with a quasi-religious aura. According to Ernst Gombrich, the art historian who was extremely important for Ligeti, these objects were therefore no longer accessible in the old meaning of a work of art. I had to believe in Beuys or let it be. Ligeti taught us to be non-believers, but he also knew that some 'naïveté' had to be kept and enjoyed speculating about this. For him Messiaen was the great 'naïf' and because of this maybe a great composer. Stravinsky was the 'non-naïf' and for Ligeti he was peerless among the composers of the 20th century (surprisingly, Bartók came far behind). In the same way, to include John Cage in a traditional musical discourse was out of the question: 'art' or 'music' could be anything to him, and so these terms lost all meaning.

Many of us wondered whether Ligeti had detached himself from a 'broader' conception of art and adopted a retrogressive view. Or was his exploration of polymetrics and microtonality really a move forward into a new, unknown sphere? In the 1980s I overheard followers of Lachenmann say that whatever Ligeti was doing, Chopin had already done much better before him. Ligeti was regarded as an absolute reactionary. While such a statement is certainly derogatory (and Ligeti himself reported hearing this said during a visit with Klaus Huber's and Brian Ferneyhough's Freiburg group) it may be worthwhile to discuss how deeply Ligeti's thinking really was 'backward-oriented' in an artistic sense or whether his 'backwards' basically realigned him and his students in the direction of a 'forwards' or somewhere else. Let us try to explain it in the following way: perhaps what made Ligeti 'classical' was his evolutive outlook, which we encountered every time the class met. His knowledge of the musical past, which reached back to the 14th century, provided him with a kind of playground, to which he would always add new ideas and unusual scenarios. Unlike Cage he never left this playground, not even in his view of African or South-East Asian music. He would combine different musical approaches in a way typical to him, sometimes quite boldly (for example, in his harpsichord pieces *Passacaglia ungherese* and *Hungarian Rock* that he dismissed as unimportant 'pastiches'), or sometimes by indiscernibly melding everything together. His term 'allusion' (appropriate here rather than the less relevant 'quotation') applies to his Piano Études, positioned as they are between Bartók, Africa, Nancarrow (jazz or boogie mixed with

Bach), Chopin and maybe also Steve Reich. Ligeti's 'maximalism' thus even included minimalism. To us students he came across as an encyclopedia of confusing patterns. In class we could always feel how hard it was to grasp this man. In company he could be very pleasant, at times even soft and sensual, and with women he was awe-inspiring. Never have I seen someone seemingly melt away with such tenderness yet become bitterly hard and consequent when defending a point of view, always unhappy with himself and others, always already beyond the ideas we had just painstakingly gathered.

It became clear to us that Ligeti would consciously disregard certain points of view when he circumvented famous names such as Xenakis or Nono, and all those who had a naïve communist mindset. He had lived through the Hungarian variety of communism himself, he knew what thought control was, and he saw it in the West-German new music scene. Yet ultimately he did judge composers and their works according to purely musical criteria. For instance, his argument with Xenakis was: 'I fault Xenakis for applying often unproven and somewhat naïve mathematical manipulations to music without further consideration. He believed that what makes sense as an algorithm will also be meaningful as music.'[7]

Nono's completely naïve faith in the communist idea exasperated Ligeti. I well remember his account (around 2001) of a meeting with Nono in a communist café. There was a poster on the wall commemorating the 1956 communist victory in Hungary and Nono said to Ligeti, the refugee, something like 'And Hungary is also liberated now.' Ligeti could have explained to him the complexity of the Hungarian revolution from his point of view – a revolution in which the Hungarian fascists were also involved even if they did not play a major role. It is my impression that Ligeti rejected Nono's entire œuvre because, in the earlier works at least, he perceived a political idea in the background. Nono was never heard nor discussed in the class.

In a further attempt to draw yet another circle around Ligeti, let me repeat myself with variations: Ligeti was always seeking, across time and space, for new and exciting ideas and musical solutions. He was interested in the exploration of listening. To him it did not matter if it was 'high' or 'low' art – or not art at all as was often the case when he dealt with the daily acoustic life of Africa. This treasure hunter was always more curious than his students who were still trying to define themselves. Maybe he was lucky that he came from a time when 'art' had still been embedded in a complex discourse – one which we had already lost, not out of ignorance but because our current time painstakingly seeks out a new definition for itself. We who tend to play with old 'yellowed' material can hardly guess what 'art' once was. We also have a different notion of what 'serious' is. Ligeti was 'lost' in a different way than we are now. And he very much liked to discover true 'research' in a new area, be it pulsation or microtonality.

In the above-mentioned interview from 1993 I said to him: 'I would like to think that the most important thing to you is to 'listen': to open up new paths so that one can perceive what music once was in a

---

[7] 'György Ligeti und Manfred Stahnke: Gespräch am 29. Mai 1993', p. 123.

completely different way.' To this Ligeti replied: 'I would say, finding new concepts of listening was the most important thing.' And later after some meandering:

> I constantly strive to revise my own point of view. For example, when I had serious misgivings about the Darmstadt, Cologne or Paris avant-garde, I started something one could call postmodern. These were the two pastiche harpsichord pieces *Passacaglia ungherese* and *Hungarian Rock*, but also the final passacaglia of *Le Grand Macabre*. This piece was the result of a fundamental stylistic discussion I had with Hans-Christian von Dadelsen [one of his students in the 1970s]. Later in the Horn Trio I clearly alluded to traditional form models, even though the content is not traditional at all.

In the Horn Trio I suspected a link to certain views of two other students: 'May this be a reaction to Wolfgang von Schweinitz und Detlev Müller-Siemens?' Ligeti replied:

> Exactly, this was my composition class then. After that I veered away from the Horn Trio model and composed two choral cycles, the *Hölderlin Phantasies* and the *Hungarian Études*, and then the Piano Études, which go in a totally different direction altogether.

I threw in: 'Yet there are elements of the Horn Trio which return later again and again, for instance in the slow movements of the Piano Concerto or the Violin Concerto, the drawn-out, poignant almost Viennese-sounding melodies of the high strings in the Piano Concerto – an all but Mahlerian tone that is already anticipated in *Lontano* ...' Ligeti responded:

> Very well, some elements always return, others disappear. All this is not conscious on my part. It doesn't happen in the context of a theory of art. I have no such theory and that is why many people are disappointed. I have no message. One cannot pin me down to a unified compositional theory that could be verbalized. Instead, I always aim to try out new things. For this reason I once tried to describe it like this: I am like a blind man in a labyrinth, feeling his way around and constantly finding new doorways and entering rooms that he did not even know existed. And then he does something and never knows what the next step will be. And this continues in one direction, but it could also go on in a completely different one.[8]

Let us try to take a closer look at some of Ligeti's terms in a musical context by analysing one of his late Piano Études: what did Ligeti mean when he used the terms 'allusion', 'tonality', 'pulsation', 'meta-level', 'gestalt', 'super-signal', 'polyvalency', etc.?

If we look at the whole of Ligeti's Piano Études we can see that they have something in common, a similar approach, a model in a way, which repeats itself in different forms. Over and over again we come across canons, shifting pulsation patterns and pitch configurations which are more or less close to 'tonality' but far removed from Schoenberg's technique and its aftermath. These works are related to a high degree to some older étude

[8] Ibid., pp. 126f.

cycles – namely to those by Chopin. In each piece Ligeti proposes a basic idea, which continuously transforms, expands or even abolishes itself and reverts to its antipode – a model, which contains its own antithesis on a higher structural level. What interests us is this deviation, this 'difference' from what was first proposed. Perhaps we can find constants in the way Ligeti handles his material and this can help us to better understand his thinking. Let us take as an example the Étude no. 9, *Vertige*, and test the basic theorem of 'model and difference'. *Vertige* shows very clearly the original 'models' of the formal, pitch and rhythmic organization from which the deviations will be identified. The word 'difference' is appropriate because, firstly, it evokes the morphological process of 'differentiation' (the process of specialization of cells and tissues); secondly, it implies 'deviation'; and thirdly, there is even a distant link to Derrida's philosophy, namely in the notion of 'sublation'.[9] Ligeti liked to call this philosophy 'empty' or 'just a bit of fluff' – or perhaps he was just striking out at Derrida's self-irony in this way?

In fact, Ligeti's Études are more than just a collection of clever musically immanent manipulations. If we say that this body of work deals with our perception of *Gestalt*, we certainly come nearer to a first level of understanding: music providing a view on man in its purely acoustic form. Yet if we take account of Ligeti's titles (starting with *Désordre*), we notice a genuine 'deferral' (Derrida!)[10] which moves us away from the purely musical product. These titles are fraught with profound many-layered meanings; in the case of the first Étude, *Désordre* (which is dedicated to Boulez), both Boulez' serialism and Cage's world are meant here. Ligeti would always say that total serial organization and a throw of the dice led to similar results. Also hidden in the title (in the Latin word 'ordo') is a vast complex of thinking and ideas which used, as early as the Middle Ages, the 'canon' as a musical metaphor. Boulez also refers explicitly to this fundamental medieval terminology, as I tried to show in my analysis of the movement ('Formant') 'Trope' of his Third Piano Sonata (*tropus*: originally the 'grafting' of a grapevine).

On the Piano Étude no. 9, *Vertige*

With the Piano Étude *Vertige* (Vertigo), a case of *trompe-l'oreille*, Ligeti clearly sought to compose a musical counterpart to the *trompe-l'œil* found in the works of the Dutch graphic artist M. C. Escher, whose lithography *Ascending and Descending* (1960), for instance, shows monks in an endless illusory ascent and descent on the roof of a monastery.

---

[9] This is an English translation of the Hegelian word *Aufhebung*, which means a term which is both preserved and changed through its dialectical interplay with another term or concept.

[10] Derrida coined the word *différance*, replacing the 'e' with an 'a' to mean basically two different gestures. The first, relating to 'deferral', is the notion that words and signs can never fully summon forth what they mean, but can openly be defined through appeal to additional words, from which they differ. Thus, meaning is forever 'deferred' or postponed through an endless chain of signifiers. The second, relating to 'difference', concerns the force which differentiates elements from one another and, in so doing, engenders binary oppositions and hierarchies which underpin meaning itself.

In *Vertige* the model is an endlessly descending chromatic line, an idea no doubt inspired by Roger Shepard's continuously ascending or descending line.[11] This idea also appears in Jean-Claude Risset's *Computer Suite from Music for Little Boy* (1968) for computer-synthesized sounds, here in the modified form of an endless glissando. Both Shepard and Risset create the illusion of hearing endlessly upward or downward moving pitches by fading in and out partials, which are an octave apart from each other – the 'Shepard octaves'.

I remember a class trip we took in the mid-1970s to IRCAM in Paris, Boulez's then newly founded research institute. There we heard Shepard's and Risset's acoustical illusions, and also met John Chowning, the American computer-music specialist to whom both Wolfgang von Schweinitz (in 1976) and myself (in 1980) were 'sent' (as Ligeti liked to say) to study the new techniques of computer music. While in the United States, I also carried on research on microtonality with Harry Partch's collaborator and supporter Ben Johnston in 1979–80. (Partch had died in 1974.)

One of Ligeti's sources for *Vertige* was also certainly the often-mentioned descending melodies sung by Romanian professional mourners. In *Vertige* Ligeti does not use octaves but starts with canonic entries eight quavers apart, resulting in intervals of minor sixths (Example 41). By changing the spacing between the entries of the canon, different types of chords result. While the entries of the canon initially occur at a distance of eight semitones, i.e. a minor sixth, subsequent entries fluctuate between seven and five semitones, i.e. between a fifth or a fourth. The smallest distance is three semitones, or a minor third. It is obvious that Ligeti is trying to avoid the combination of fourth (or fifth) and tritone. Thus, the spacing of five or seven chromatic steps is never coupled with six, as the resulting chords would have been too close to the pitch system of the Second Viennese School (particularly Schoenberg and Webern) – something Ligeti strictly avoided in his Études.

Ligeti sometimes 'corrupts' (or rather 'renders more musical') his model by leaving out a chromatic step, for instance, in the five-part section of bar 31. The highest line (end of bar 30) G_2–Gb_2–F_2 leaps to Eb_2–D_2 and is cut off, the same happens to the line above it in bar 31, third quaver: F_2 jumps to Eb_2 but the chromatic line continues on the lower stave. Here Ligeti creates 'diatonic' interspersions by alternating semitones and whole tones.

Furthermore, he composes a 'formal process' and builds the 'super-signal' of a melody-like structure by pulling the whole pitch curve up or down. Thus he creates the illusion of an easily discernible 'form', into which all the subsignals merge. Or, he 'freezes' individual notes into long drawn-out super-lines, which we then perceive as 'melodies' (Example 42).

Let us look more closely at the beginning of the Étude and especially at its 'harmonies' or, put in a more neutral way, at its vertical component which seems to derive from the chromatic linear model. In doing so we must take into account that Ligeti always uses a pragmatic enharmonic notation

[11] See Albrecht Schneider, 'Was haben Ligetis Études pour Piano mit Shepard-Skalen zu tun? Über "auditorische Illusionen", *Vertige* und *Columna infinită*', in *Mikrotöne und mehr – Auf György Ligetis Hamburger Pfaden*, ed. Manfred Stahnke (Hamburg, 2005), pp 81–104.

Example 41 *Vertige*, bars 1–15

239

Example 42 *Vertige*, bars 16–27

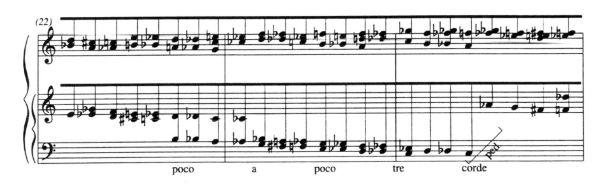

poco   a   poco   tre   corde

(ppp)   *cresc. poco a poco* - - - - - - -

mp
poco ped.
cresc. poco a poco - - - - - - -

emphasize the melody / *die Melodie hervorheben*

in order to make it easier for the performer to read. Ligeti introduces a rhythmical pattern (which quickly becomes asymmetrical) of incoming lines, at first sixths, and after a lone E major chord in first inversion (bar 2), fifths and superimposed fifths or fourths and superimposed fourths and fifths, and then, from bar 6 onwards also superimpositions of fourths. Major thirds, coupled with octaves, start to play a role in bar 8 and in bar 9 minor sixth chords are added. Ligeti builds always new constellations of thirds, fourths and fifths (including the 'omissions'), resulting in sixths, octaves and bigger intervals. In this way he 'naturally' creates allusions to 'tonal' chords and, from bar 24 onwards, he also uses major seconds, at first similarly to 'sixte ajoutée' chords (bar 30).

We could be tempted to go back and find parallels in music history or maybe suppose a development from 'jazz chords': beginning initially with two parts, Ligeti expands to three-, four- and five-part chords, which – given the tempo – are more and more difficult to play. The jazz terminology for bar 10 would be 'maj6/9' ($A-C\sharp_1-F\sharp_1-B_1$), or in bar 12 'sus4/7/9' ($A-D_1-G_1-B_1$). Among the first five-part chords that are not just simple triads with doubled octaves is a 'C major' chord with raised fourth und ninth ($E_1-C_2-D_2-E_2-F\sharp_2$) in bar 25.

The basic principle of the descending lines is even thwarted in the lower stave of bar 29 by a line proceeding in upward contrary motion ($B\flat-B-C-C\sharp-D$), whereby a sustained minor six-four chord appears on the note D. Similarly, we find in bars 33–4 the melodic line $B\flat_2-B_2-C_3-C\sharp_3-D_3-E\flat_3$, while this last $E\flat_3$ marks the beginning of another 'super-melody' built on sustained 'frozen' notes. Bass lines are often built out of 'frozen' chromatically related notes, which have been picked out of different chromatic lines. An example of this is the melody $E_1-B-B\flat-A-G\sharp-G-F\sharp-F$ from bar 34.

Did Ligeti create the chromatic lines first and then later fit in the vertical structure, that is, the chords? Or were the chords there first, leaving the chromatic sequences to adapt to them? I think both views are true. Sometimes Ligeti just simply lets the chromatic line go, and sees where it leads. Let us remember Ligeti's words: 'I am like a blind man in a labyrinth, feeling his way around, constantly finding new doorways and entering rooms that he did not even know existed.'[12]

On the other hand, he sometimes includes certain chords and moulds the chromatic lines around them. These tonal or 'jazz' chords are then apparently the trigger for the surrounding chromatic lines that in turn provide the chord's individual notes. Yet in this many-sided scheme this is only one of the poles that determine the structure. The other, as we mentioned, is the 'letting go of the lines', the play with 'chance' which is built into this process. Once the chromatic lines have begun they seem to produce these specific chords, out of the simultaneity of parallel lines, so to speak as a 'by-product'. Always crucial is the higher 'pitch curve' (or 'envelope') of the whole structure, which builds a kind of 'melodic line'. This envelope idea originated around 1956 when Ligeti was working with Gottfried Michael Koenig at the Electronic Studio in Cologne.

---

[12] See 'György Ligeti und Manfred Stahnke: Gespräch am 29. Mai 1993', pp. 126f.

Figure 17 *Vertige*: envelope in the first section

Bar	I	15	17	19	21	21	23	24	25
Highest pitch	B_1	C_2	Db_2	D_2	Eb_2	E_2	F_2	$F\sharp_2$	G_2

This essential structural element is present from the very beginning of *Vertige* till we reach D_3 in bar 29. This peak then marks the end of a first section of development, which is further stressed by the dramatic low B minor chord.

Again we are tempted to relate B_1, the first pitch of the implied chromatic line, to the closing B minor chord and so to assume that some kind of tonal structure supports this Étude. In bar 25ff. the bass line, B–Bb–G–E–C–F, leads straight to the B minor chord, and confirms the 'old' idea of the 'clausulas' which seems to lie under the surface (Example 43).

Example 43 *Vertige*, bars 25–9

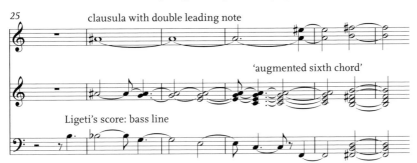

The bass line Bb–G–E–C forms a *penultima* which precedes the *ultima* F♯–B–D. We also observe the 'double leading-note clausula' in the use of Bb which leads in the octave to B, while F leads to F♯. Proof that this is no coincidence is provided by a similar passage in bar 38, which leads to A minor (Example 44). The *penultima* situation originates out of the context of the line Eb_3–D_3–B_2–Ab_2–F_2–Bb_1. This time the double Phrygian leading notes Bb_1 and F_2 also precede the double leading-note clausula before the A minor chord. Thus Ligeti surrounds his target chord minor with a Bb major chord (a semitone higher than A minor) and a G♯ minor (a semitone lower than A minor) chord which he then folds out in a melodic line.

Vertige is an example of a multi-layered codification. This is reflected in the interaction between the abstract pure chromaticism and the pre-existing language structure of tonality, and in the inextricable interweaving of linearity and verticality. Ligeti loved to play with forms, which out of the depths of time and space found their way in his head. This appears in always new constellations in all the Études. The Étude *Galamb borong* juxtaposes Debussy's whole-tone scale with the *sléndro* of the Indonesian gamelan. *Automne à Varsovie* plays with Chopin, mixing in Nancarrow or African metres. Our Étude *Vertige* also contains much Chopin, for instance allusions to op. 10, no. 3 (Example 45).

Bartók too is watching from afar, and Steve Reich is also nearby ... With Ligeti, allusions never end ... and they are like distant windows, suddenly opening onto an unlimited space, revealing a well-known godhead. (I always imagine the Greek gods to be personifications of potential human thoughts, which usually, as in the case of Apollo, for example, consist of multiple intertwined thoughts ...)

Translated by Louise Duchesneau

Example 44 *Vertige,* bars 34–9

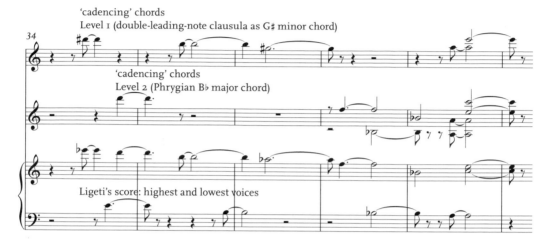

Example 45 Chopin, Étude in E major, op. 10 no. 3, bars 37–42

Ligeti during an interview at the NDR Festival celebrating his 70th Birthday in Hamburg (1993)

12 The Bigger Picture: Ligeti's Music and the Films of Stanley Kubrick

CIARÁN CRILLY

Stanley Kubrick performed a rare trick in his science-fiction masterpiece *2001: A Space Odyssey* (1968) by employing a substantial amount of concert music by an avant-garde composer without the composer's permission. Common practice dictates that music be part of the post-production process in filmmaking and involves the engagement of a specialist film scorer, working in response to the wishes of the director. Such instruction is commonly relayed via a music supervisor or editor. Contrary to this tradition, no creative contact between the director and the composer György Ligeti had taken place in *2001*.[1] This allowed Ligeti's scores to be subsumed by Kubrick's singular cinematic vision, unhindered by creative interference. The American director aimed to reject the post-silent convention of relating a story through words, instead creating a form of pure audio-visual expression. Ligeti's music is conspicuous in two of Kubrick's films: *2001* and *Eyes Wide Shut* (1999), his posthumously released final work.[2] In these films, music, and Ligeti's in particular, was central to Kubrick's strategy of subverting the traditional role of sound in narrative cinema as part of his own personal odyssey: the search for pure cinema.

When Ligeti died in 2006, many obituaries were prompt in highlighting the presence of his music in Stanley Kubrick's *2001: A Space Odyssey*.[3] It was almost as though it formed a central part of his compositional legacy. Following the film's release in 1968, a friend of the composer alerted Ligeti, who was hitherto unaware, to the presence of his music in this mainstream science-fiction masterpiece. And, of course, he was not the only composer whose output was commandeered to satisfy Kubrick's requirements in this instance; there are more famous and imitated sequences incorporating music in the film. The opening credits are accompanied by the 'Prelude'

---

[1] Of course, such contact had been originally intended, albeit with another composer, as Alex North had been engaged to supply an original score for *2001*.

[2] The music of Ligeti also makes an appearance in *The Shining* (1980), Kubrick's foray into the horror genre based on a novel by Stephen King. Although dominated by the music of Polish composer Krzysztof Penderecki, six of whose works appear, *The Shining* also features Ligeti's 1967 orchestral masterpiece *Lontano*, employed at three different points in the film. It is heard when Danny first sees the twin girls and as Wendy realizes the hotel's phone lines are no longer functioning. Its most striking occurrence is during an early scene in which Halloran shows Wendy the storeroom and 'shines' with Danny, telepathically asking him: 'How'd you like some ice-cream, Doc?' Also predominant in the film are the third movement of Bartók's *Music for Strings, Percussion and Celesta*, and several popular 1920s and 1930s ballads that evoke the Overlook Hotel's hidden past.

[3] See, for example, *The Daily Telegraph*'s obituary from 13 June 2006, whose second paragraph concluded: 'The effectiveness of the ethereal "Ligeti sound" and its ability to suggest mysterious webs of harmony was brought to a wide public by the film director Stanley Kubrick in 1968 when, on the soundtrack of *2001: A Space Odyssey*, he used Ligeti's *Atmosphères*, the *Requiem* of 1965 and *Lux aeterna* for unaccompanied choir.' See http://www.telegraph.co.uk/news/obituaries/1521105/Gyorgy-Ligeti.html, accessed 12 January 2009.

from Richard Strauss's *Also sprach Zarathustra*, perhaps linking the film's metaphysical musings on the future of humanity to the Nietzschean Superman. There are two lengthy space station sequences between which we hear all of Johann Strauss's waltz *On the Beautiful Blue Danube*. The employment of these two works is familiar to the point of frequent parody. Other than Ligeti's score, the one remaining musical work to feature was 'Gayane's Adagio' from Khachaturian's ballet *Gayane*, whose elegant breadth matches the infinite stillness of space.

Ligeti's *Lux aeterna* (1966), *Requiem* (1963–5) and *Atmosphères* (1961) are the credited works also featured, the latter being heard almost in its entirety during the celebrated Star Gate sequence. Since Ligeti had not been approached by Kubrick or the studio, there was the matter of copyright, and the fallout from the unauthorized use of his music is legendary.[4] There was the matter of the uncredited presence of an electronically manipulated version of *Aventures* (1962–3), heard in the final scenes before the appearance of the so-called Star Child. *Aventures* was not included in the closing credits, while the other three works were, but it was the fact that the musicians had been paid by the studio while the composer was not that hastened the possibility of legal action. MGM, the producers of *2001*, felt that Ligeti should be content with the eventual outcome, as 'he's now famous in America'.[5] Eventually, a rather modest financial settlement was agreed, leading Kubrick to recompense by ensuring that Ligeti's music would be used again in two of his later films with generous remuneration.[6] It is the use of his music in *2001* and *Eyes Wide Shut* that is of interest here, and how this music was wedded to the director's vision of a comprehensive audio-visual experience.

The function of music in film

The heightened role of music in *2001* breaks with tradition in a number of ways. In the post-silent era, music has generally been supplied by specialist film composers during post-production. There have been instances of composers with established reputations in the concert hall who have enjoyed success in the movie theatre as well, however these tend

---

[4] Apocryphal accounts often claim that Ligeti himself saw the film first, without prior knowledge of his music being used. Richard Steinitz recounts: 'On 22 October 1967 *Lontano* was premièred at the Donaueschingen Festival – and a few months later, Ligeti had a considerable shock. One day he received a letter from a friend in New York congratulating him on his contribution to the soundtrack of Stanley Kubrick's new film *2001 – A Space Odyssey*. Astonished, he attended its Vienna première and discovered that Kubrick had helped himself to large sections of three of Ligeti's recently recorded compositions.' Richard Steinitz, *György Ligeti: Music of the Imagination* (London, 2003), p. 161. See pp. 161–4 for details on the aftermath of this event.

[5] 'In the 1970s I saw a book on the making of *2001* and read that Ligeti had successfully sued MGM for taking his music. But it's not so. I never sued them. MGM wrote me such nice letters. They said Ligeti should be happy; he's now famous in America.' Ligeti interviewed by Michael John White, *Independent*, 18 October 1989. Quoted in Steinitz, *György Ligeti: Music of the Imagination*, p. 163.

[6] Steinitz, *György Ligeti: Music of the Imagination*, p. 163, reports that MGM would eventually pay Ligeti $3,500 in 1973, with $1,000 of that going to his lawyer, though his publishers 'graciously waived their shares'.

to be scarce. Notable instances include Sergei Prokofiev's scores for director Sergei Eisenstein and William Walton's Shakespearean collaborations with Laurence Olivier. Other 20th-century composers, such as Vaughan Williams and Copland, dabbled in the new art of film music, while Erich Korngold made a career-defining move from the European concert hall to the Hollywood studios. Even in the silent era, when music was the dominant element in film sound, the involvement of a 'concert hall' composer was a rarity.[7] Traditionally, the (almost) completed film is given over to the composer, who scores a series of musical cues communicated by the director or music editor, which has been standard practice in the Hollywood system since the mid-1930s. The director and music editor will have already decided roughly what kind of music is needed and when it is required, though the composer may have some room for negotiation.[8]

One of the most important functions of film music is suturing: creating seamlessness between the cuts, but, more importantly, between the reality of the moviemaking process and the fantasy of the audience's experience. Claudia Gorbman writes of music's ability to erase

> the spectator's potential recognition of the technological basis of filmic articulation. Gaps, cuts, the frame itself, silences in the soundtrack – any reminders of cinema's materiality which jeopardise the formation of subjectivity – the process whereby the viewer identifies as subject of filmic discourse – are smoothed over, or 'spirited away' ... by the carefully regulated operations of film music.[9]

Due to this and other functions, music's post-production status is not diminished in the eyes of the director or composer. Bernard Herrmann, the man behind the music for *Vertigo* (1958) and *North by Northwest* (1959), famously claimed: '[Hitchcock] only finishes a picture 60%. I have to finish it for him.'[10] In the more celebrated case of *Psycho* (1960), Hitchcock himself was known to have remarked that '33% of the effect ... was due to the music.'[11] Though some may dispute the percentage, no one could deny the indispensable nature of Herrmann's music to the final

---

[7] Among the most significant examples are Satie's score for René Clair's *Entr'acte* (1924), after a synopsis by the artist Francis Picabia, George Antheil's *Ballet Mécanique* (1925), originally composed for Fernand Léger's cubist-surrealist film of the same name, and Honegger's music for the Abel Gance epic *Napoléon* (1927). Dmitri Shostakovich was involved in composition for silent and sound film throughout his career for purely commercial reasons, yet these scores are not considered among his finest works.

[8] A celebrated example is the shower scene in Alfred Hitchcock's *Psycho* (1960), which he had originally wished to be without music, with only the sounds of stabbing, shrieking and splashing. Bernard Herrmann, Hitchcock's favourite film scorer, had other ideas and persuaded the director to hear music he had composed for the sequence. Hitchcock eventually admitted that 'the score significantly improved the scene'. Donald Spoto, *The Life of Alfred Hitchcock: The Dark Side of Genius* (London, 1983), p. 420.

[9] Claudia Gorbman, *Unheard Melodies: Narrative Film Music* (Bloomington, 1987), p. 58.

[10] Quoted in Steven C. Smith, *A Heart at Fire's Centre: The Life and Music of Bernard Herrmann* (Berkeley, 1991), p. 192.

[11] Quoted in ibid., p. 241.

product. Additionally, it was a dispute over severe editing of his score for *The Magnificent Ambersons* (1942) that resulted in a split with Orson Welles, for whom he had also scored *Citizen Kane* (1941).

A further convention of relevance to the Kubrick–Ligeti case is the traditional employment of a temp track in the early stages of editing. Some directors have been known to play music on set during filming for the purposes of mood and rhythmic pacing, but the use of temp tracks is almost universal.[12] The temp track is 'a dynamic mock-up of the soundtrack' or a 'veritable blueprint of a film's soundtrack' that is assembled for previews in which the action of an audience or production team is gauged.[13] It tends to be an assembly of pre-existing music, either classical tracks or cues from other movies. All too often 'directors and producers become so convinced, accustomed, and perhaps 'married' to the 'temp', that composers are often requested to emulate it'.[14] If one considers Ridley Scott's *Gladiator* (2000), for example, there is a strong impression that the film scorers were asked to get as close as possible to 'Mars' from Holst's *The Planets* without infringing copyright; such clear attempts at replication are common.[15]

Initially, Kubrick was to commission a score from the significant Hollywood composer Alex North, who had worked on *Spartacus* (1960) and was especially noted for his pioneering jazz-inflected score for Elia Kazan's *A Streetcar Named Desire* (1951). North's music was to be rejected in favour of the eventual composite score that consisted of music by composers known outside the realm of the cinema. Furthermore, much of this was music by a leader of the musical avant-garde, not simply established classics. Kubrick would later explain in an interview:

> However good our best film composers may be, they are not a Beethoven, a Mozart or a Brahms. Why use music which is less good when there is such a multitude of great orchestral music available from the past and from our own time?[16]

In the course of filming and editing, Kubrick began to employ the great music already available to him in a temp track as a guide, and he did so

---

[12] An example of playing music for psychological effect is supplied by Ken Russell, writing about work on his film *The Devils* (1971): 'The film to me is all about brainwashing, so I decided to play a symphony by Prokofiev on the set, hoping the actors would lose themselves – it is such possessing, freak-out music.' Quoted in Carl Wilkinson, *The Observer Book of Film* (London, 2007), p. 26.

[13] Ronald H. Sadoff, 'The Role of the Music Editor and the "Temp Track" as Blueprint for the Score, Source Music, and Scource Music of Films', *Popular Music* 25/2 (2006), pp. 165–83, at p. 166.

[14] Ibid.

[15] 'So frequent, consistent and confounding are the conventions that, upon watching a newly released film, music editors often comment 'I know what *that* was temped with!'' Ibid., p. 174.

[16] Stanley Kubrick in an interview with Michel Ciment (on *Barry Lyndon*), *The Kubrick Site*, http://www.visual-memory.co.uk/amk/doc/interview.bl.html, accessed 23 April 2008. It ought to be noted that North was paid, as were the performers on the recordings used, while Ligeti was not. See Steinitz, *György Ligeti: Music of the Imagination*, p. 162.

without the use of a music editor.[17] This track remained when he was asked to present a show reel to MGM producers and North began to feel that 'whatever I wrote to supplant Strauss's *Zarathustra* would not satisfy Kubrick, even though I used the same structure but brought it up to date in idiom and dramatic punch'.[18] When North attended a screening in New York, he realized that his music had been replaced by the guide music, and endured a shock parallel to that felt by the composer whose music actually *was* used.

Total film/pure cinema

When Erik Satie composed *Socrate* in 1918, he referred to Plato, upon whose Socratic dialogues the symphonic drama was based, as 'a perfect collaborator', someone with whom he clearly had no creative contact.[19] Furthermore, Plato was 'very gentle and never importunate', unlike, for example, the exacting Jean Cocteau, with whom Satie had recently worked on the ballet *Parade* (1917).[20] The idea of close collaboration was similarly uncomfortable for other 20th-century composers, among them Arnold Schoenberg. He once found his ideal collaborator in film to be an imaginary director in an imaginary film, in reality himself, in the *Musical Accompaniment for an Imaginary Film Scene* (1929–30), while he found the reality of film composition in Hollywood to be marked by rejection.[21] For Kubrick, while there were collaborations with composers such as Wendy Carlos, who provided electronic music for *A Clockwork Orange* (1971) and *The Shining*, he was happier in the company of composers whose reputation was made on the concert stage and not in the cinema. Ligeti would prove to be his 'perfect collaborator' as the director remained in control of the music editing process, and avant-garde music offered him a new sensory level.

Kubrick was to strive for creative totality after the Wagnerian model, the *Gesamtkunstwerk*, an ideal of auteurship summarized in this statement: 'One man writes a novel. One man writes a symphony. It is essential for one man to make a film'.[22] He also searched for something between total

---

[17] The only music credits at the end of *2001* are for the composers and performers.

[18] Quoted in Jerome Agel, ed., *The Making of Kubrick's '2001'* (New York, 1970), p. 199.

[19] Quoted in Nigel Wilkins, 'Erik Satie's Letters to Milhaud and Others', *Musical Quarterly* 66/3 (1980), pp. 404–28, at p. 418.

[20] Ibid.

[21] For an account of Schoenberg's relationship with the Hollywood establishment and its failure to acquiesce to his high demands, see Sabine M. Feisst, 'Arnold Schoenberg and the Cinematic Art', *Musical Quarterly* 83/1 (1999), pp. 93–113. Igor Stravinsky, like Schoenberg a resident of the Hollywood Hills, also experienced rejection from the local movie industry. He composed music with a film adaptation of Franz Werfel's *The Song of Bernadette* in mind, but was spurned in favour of Hollywood stalwart Alfred Newman. This music then found its way into the middle movement of Stravinsky's *Symphony in Three Movements*.

[22] Quoted in Garan Holcombe, 'Stanley Kubrick: The Legacy of a Cinematic Legend', *California Literary Review*, http://www.calitreview.com/Essays/stanley_kubrick_5008.htm, accessed 2 May 2008.

film and pure cinema. This he was able to achieve by reassessing cinema's narrative tools. Cinema is a visual medium, but an aural one too. The hierarchical norm of sound in film is voice, sound effect and music, usually in that order.[23] Yet, this is subverted by Kubrick. Michel Chion emphasizes how traditional narrative cinema is vococentric, favouring voice as the prime sonic element.[24] In fact, as Chion claims, it is verbocentric, conveyed by word. Kubrick was suspicious of an over-reliance on word as a primary narrative tool, famously declaring that the 'screenplay is the most uncommunicative form of writing ever devised'.[25] In *2001* and *Eyes Wide Shut*, Kubrick subverts this hierarchy, rejects voice as the main means of providing information and grants music a privileged position in the aural hierarchy. His sound world is robbed of semantic meaning, to invoke another Chion concept, and begins to approach something more absolute or abstract: a pure cinema.[26]

Analysis I: Music in *2001*

In *2001: A Space Odyssey*, the otherworldly nature of Ligeti's modernism, especially in the haunting vocal sonorities of the *Requiem* and *Lux aeterna*, contrasts with the classic role of modernist music in film, namely horror. Kubrick's own genre piece *The Shining* is a fine case in point, with a score consisting almost entirely of music by Bartók (*Music for Strings, Percussion and Celesta*), Penderecki (several works including *De natura sonoris*) and Ligeti again (*Lontano*). The tonal music in *2001* is, by contrast, assuring and affirmative: each of the tonal works in the film begins with a rising arpeggiated figure, one major (*Blue Danube*), one minor (*Gayane*) and one combining the two (*Also sprach Zarathustra*). Through these works, Kubrick describes a positive outcome for the future, loading each with hermeneutic intent. While Ligeti's music is otherworldly, Johann Strauss's conveys the grace and wonder of human technology, Richard Strauss's a higher force or being, and Khachaturian's represents humanity itself. These four sound worlds can be seen to represent, in turn, the Universe, Earth, God (as signification for a higher being) and Man. The cello monody in 'Gayane's Adagio' by Khachaturian invokes the solipsistic isolation of humanity, presaging the eventual isolation of the one astronaut to be left alive, Dave Bowman (Keir Dullea). Bowman then proceeds to eradicate the other remaining life force in one of the most poignant scenes in movie history: the computer HAL sings the *downward* arpeggio of 'Daisy, Daisy' (from the song *Bicycle Built For Two*) as he dies, becoming increasingly sluggish and deeper in register.

The celebrated Star Gate sequence, perhaps a psychedelic trip in the spirit of the age in which the film was made, is dominated by Ligeti's music. In fact, the Kyrie of the *Requiem* and *Atmosphères* are accorded the privilege of being heard in their entirety in the scene (save the virtually inaudible

---

[23] See Michel Chion, *Audio-Vision: Sound on Screen*, ed. and trans. Claudia Gorbman (New York, 1994), pp. 5–6.

[24] See ibid.

[25] Quoted in Agel, *The Making of Kubrick's '2001'*, p. 109.

[26] Semantic meaning is defined as 'that which refers to a code or a language to interpret a message'. Chion, *Audio-Vision*, pp. 5–6.

final seconds of *Atmosphères*): almost 17 minutes of music, accompanied only by the experimental visuals and the rumbling sound effect that communicates the movement of the pod in which Bowman is travelling. Ligeti's extra-musical analogy for micropolyphony, the technique at the heart of *Atmosphères*, was the appearance of crystals growing in a solution: the purpose of the technique is 'to arrest the process, to fix the supersaturated solution just at the moment before crystallisation'.[27] This finds a visual counterpart in Kubrick's strategy of capturing chemical reactions on glass slides via slit scan photography, which was to generate much of the Star Gate sequence imagery. The concept of sound moving out of the upper register and back in through the lowest, as expressed in *Atmosphères* with four high piccolos succeeded by double basses (bars 39–40), lends itself to the spatial and temporal limitless Kubrick was suggesting in this section, entitled 'Jupiter and Beyond the Infinite'. Perhaps more crucially, he wished for a musical avant-garde to match his avant-garde cinema.

Analysis II: Music in *Eyes Wide Shut*

In *Eyes Wide Shut*, the 'Waltz no. 2' from Shostakovich's Suite for Variety Stage Orchestra is heard in the opening and closing credits, and even enters the diegesis as Bill (Tom Cruise) is seen to switch it off on the radio before he and his wife Alice (Nicole Kidman) go out for the evening.[28] Chion cites the waltz as representing Life, while Ligeti's piano piece represents the Law in the film.[29] *Musica ricercata*, though an early work produced long before the distinctive Ligeti-sound had developed, is not a mere apprentice piece, and it has a novel structural premise. The first piece contains just two pitches (plus octave transpositions), the second three, and so on, until the final piece employs all 12 tones. The second of them is heard in *Eyes Wide Shut* and consists of three pitches that constitute a whole tone (E♯–F♯–G♮). It is played five times, each instance being a moment of drama or high tension. In its final presentation, the repeated hammering of G♮ seems to indicate a pounding heart as Bill is unnerved by his wife's discovery of a mask. Ligeti would reveal that these biting repetitions symbolized for him 'a knife through Stalin's heart' at the time the work was composed.[30]

Further to Chion's interpretation, I propose that Kubrick employs pitch references to portray Bill's gradual entrapment, which in turn is threefold: it consists of motives representing temptation, sin and retribution. The interval of the first motive contracts until it arrives at the interval of the last. The temptation motive, associated with an early love scene between the married couple and Bill's entrance at the house where the orgy is taking place, is a rising minor third (E–G). It is heard in the vocal line

[27] Quoted in Jonathan W. Bernard, 'Inaudible Structures, Audible Music: Ligeti's Problem, and his Solution', *Musical Analysis* 6/3 (1987), pp. 207–36, at p. 211.

[28] This is an example of what Sadoff identifies as 'scource' music; that is, something between score and source music, in this instance source music acting as score. See Sadoff, 'The Role of the Music Editor', p. 170. This Shostakovich suite is commonly (though erroneously) cited as the *Suite for Jazz Orchestra, No. 2*.

[29] Michel Chion, *Eyes Wide Shut*, trans. Trista Selous (London, 2002), p. 33.

[30] Quoted in Steinitz, *György Ligeti: Music of the Imagination*, p. 57.

of Chris Isaak's *Baby Did a Bad, Bad Thing* and the keyboard in the cue *Masked Ball*, composed by Jocelyn Pook, who supplied all the additional music cues in the film. This closes by a semitone to alternating F–G in the song *Strangers in the Night*, the sin motive associated with the orgy scenes now being witnessed by Bill. This closes in a further semitone to become F♮–F♯ (written E♯–F♯), the opening pitches of Ligeti's *Musica ricercata* no. 2 (*Mesto, rigido e ceremoniale*), accompanying the retribution of Bill's *ad hoc* trial. The notes alternate in a manner echoing the opening tones of *Strangers in the Night*, which has just been heard in a lush orchestral arrangement (the song title surely being a conscious joke in the context of the preserved anonymity of a masked orgy).[31] We are hearing, as well as seeing, the consequences of Bill's actions close in on him.

In the scene where Bill is led from the orgy to be confronted by a mock court (film timing from 01:19:28 onwards) two components must be taken into account. First, the pitch contraction from song to piano piece is manipulated by dynamic register and a move from diegetic to non-diegetic music: Ligeti's solo piano is suddenly louder and extrinsic. Second, there is a marked sense of the dialogue being structured around the music, which in turn lends rhythm to Kubrick's cutting. The contracting minor third is a miniature registral collapse that may be considered to have a precedent in a passage from the finale of Bartók's *Music for Strings, Percussion and Celesta* (up to bar 231); this is a work Kubrick must have been acquainted with as its third movement featured prominently in *The Shining*. A similar procedure occurs in *Atmosphères*, the centrepiece of Kubrick's Star Gate sequence, as the music is 'gradually compressed' into 'a dense knot, tied together by a minor third'.[32] Ligeti's ending, therefore, is Kubrick's beginning.

Kubrick declared *Eyes Wide Shut* to be his best film, and Michel Chion counts it, along with *2001* and *Barry Lyndon* (1975), to be among his three greatest movies.[33] This may seem surprising on account of the critical reception it received upon release, but this in turn makes more sense in light of Martin Scorsese's commentary from 2003:

> When *Eyes Wide Shut* came out a few months after Stanley Kubrick's death in 1999, it was severely misunderstood, which came as no surprise. If you go back and look at the contemporary reactions to any Kubrick picture (except the earliest ones), you'll see that all his films were initially misunderstood. Then, after five or ten years came the realization that *2001* or *Barry Lyndon* or *The Shining* was like nothing else before or since.[34]

We are left in no doubt that Scorsese counts this film of 'terrifying self-exposure' among Kubrick's finest.[35] I believe this evaluation, as well as those of Chion and the director himself, has much to do with greater

---

[31] Chion (*Eyes Wide Shut*, p. 34) suggests a link between the figures of adjacent notes, but the symbolism is taken a step further here to include earlier cues.

[32] Steinitz, *György Ligeti: Music of the Imagination*, p. 108.

[33] Chion, *Eyes Wide Shut*, p. 9.

[34] Martin Scorsese, 'Introduction', in *Kubrick: The Definitive Edition*, ed. Michael Ciment (London, 2003), p. vii.

[35] Ibid.

technical accomplishment in how *Eyes Wide Shut* exploits its music's narrative capabilities by treating the individual musical works as part of a single, comprehensive score. Where the marriage of sound and vision in *2001* is experimental, and undoubtedly influential, in *Eyes Wide Shut* it is refined and polished.

Conclusion

Kubrick said: 'I don't like to talk about *2001* much because it is essentially a non-verbal experience ... It attempts to communicate more to the subconscious and to the feelings than it does to the intellect.'[36] His control over the music editing process fed into the unifying goal of the total work of art in cinema. This he further achieved by subverting the normal vococentric, and thus verbocentric, status of narrative film, no longer dependent on *word* as its man source of narrative impetus. His greatest films expose and harness the expressive power of music, to create, not just visual poetry, but cinematic poetry. In such a context, maybe Bernard Herrmann's claim of the unscored Hitchcock film being only 60 per cent complete does not seem so excessive. *2001* was the ultimate embodiment of cinema as an audio-visual medium, not merely a visual one. A recent commentator Mario Falsetto asserts that:

> Kubrick's ambition in *2001* is, in some ways, to return to cinema the notion of film as experience, a notion that has often taken second place to the medium's narrative aspirations. Of course, the film is concerned with presenting and experimenting with narrative. At the same time, it seems equally concerned with creating a visual and aural experience so unique that audiences will feel that they are experiencing film for the first time.[37]

This is a seam running through Kubrick's entire œuvre. An emphasis on the purely visual is undoubtedly linked to his creative origins in photography and documentary making.[38] While music, and his own choice of music in particular, is accorded an increasingly significant role in all his films from *2001* onwards. Save a few exceptions, music had not been in the cinematic foreground to such an extent since the 1920s:

> It is true, music was an integral part of the film experience in the 'silent' era, films like René Clair's *Entr'acte* (1924) and Fernand Léger's *Ballet Mécanique* (1924–25) ... By the 1930s Sergei Eisenstein, for his film *Alexander Nevsky*, constructed an elaborate scheme to correlate the visual images with the score by Prokofiev. In this film as in a number of others, such as *2001: A Space Odyssey*, music often determines images.[39]

[36] Stanley Kubrick in an interview with Joseph Gelmis, quoted in Agel, *The Making of Kubrick's '2001'*, p. 7.

[37] Mario Falsetto, *Stanley Kubrick: Narrative and Stylistic Analysis* (Westport, 1994), pp. 44–5.

[38] Indeed, Kubrick termed *2001* a 'mythological documentary'. Quoted in James Gilbert, 'Auteur with a Capital A', in *Stanley Kubrick's 2001: A Space Odyssey: New Essays*, ed. Robert Phillip Kolker (New York, 2006), p. 33.

[39] James Monaco, *How to Read a Film* (New York, 1977), p. 39.

Kubrick's films belong to an elite lineage that links them to the audio-visual ideals of the silent cinema, which, as Samuel Beckett once noted, 'had barely emerged from its rudiments when it was swamped'.[40] Kubrick rejected the post-silent tradition of relating a story through words, creating a form of pure audio-visual expression that maybe the early cinema did not have the opportunity to attain fully. In his two great works of pure cinema, *2001: A Space Odyssey* and *Eyes Wide Shut*, music, and the music of Ligeti in particular, was free to convey the unhindered will of one of cinema's great artists.

[40] From a letter to Thomas McGreevey, 6 February 1936. Quoted in James Knowlson, *Damned to Fame: The Life of Samuel Beckett* (London, 1996), p. 226.

Ligeti at a rehearsal of Apparitions
(London, October 1989)

13 Invented Homelands: Ligeti's Orchestras

PAUL GRIFFITHS

Ligeti in interview[1] liked to present his creative life as a sequence of escapes: from the folk-art approved in Hungary between 1951 and 1956, from the serial mechanisms that were *de rigueur* in Western Europe around the time of his emigration, from the electronic sound synthesis to which he was immediately attracted once out of Hungary, from the cluster style with which he made his name, and then, when he was in his 50s, from an 'avant-garde' that had become the new mainstream and, simultaneously, from a revived Romanticism that was being put forward as the most promising alternative. Yet there were constancies, including the regular attention he gave the orchestra. As Table 1 shows, orchestral works appear throughout his composing life, with only three notable interruptions, all of which are merely apparent, since at these times, too, he had large-scale projects on the go. During his last few years in Hungary he was working towards *Apparitions* and the *Requiem*; in the late 1970s and early 1980s he was already struggling to write a piano concerto; and in the mid-1990s he was planning his second opera. By contrast, there were long gaps in his outputs in other genres: chamber music (nothing during the two decades after the Horn Trio), piano music (nothing during the two decades before *Monument–Selbstportrait–Bewegung*) and choral music, to mention three to which he contributed notably.

However, before considering orchestral music as having had the composer's most constant favour, one might want to consider how coherent this genre is – whether the orchestra is one land or many. Table 1 may already have provided a warning. Is there such a thing, in the music of the late 20th century and early 21st, as 'the orchestra'? Or should we think rather of 'an orchestra', assembled anew for each particular piece? Such questions – along with so many others – Ligeti's generation inherited from the most progressive composers of the first half of the 20th century, and not least from Stravinsky, whose work exemplifies two powerful currents. One was, indeed, the rejection, or at least inquisitive suspicion, of 'the orchestra' as a standard ensemble, for though Stravinsky sometimes laid out his music for a grouping that would not have surprised Beethoven (Symphony in C, *Ode*), he was equally capable of startling transmutations – an orchestra without violins, violas or clarinets (Symphony of Psalms), or one with no strings at all (Symphonies of Wind Instruments) – so that even those Beethovenian scores might appear particular confections. Alongside the more or less radical adjustments he made to orchestral normality, Stravinsky also devised or accepted a variety of reductions and refractions: the '18th-century' orchestra (*Pulcinella*, *Danses concertantes*, *The Rake's Progress*), the modern mixed dozen or so (*Rag-time*, *Concertino*), the jazz band (*Scherzo à la russe*, *Ebony Concerto*), the multicoloured monochrome grouping of pianos and percussion

[1] See, for example, *György Ligeti in Conversation with Péter Várnai, Josef Häusler, Claude Samuel and Himself* (London, 1983); Pierre Michel, *György Ligeti: compositeur d'aujourd'hui* (Paris, 1985) and *'Träumen Sie in Farbe?': György Ligeti im Gespräch mit Eckhard Roelcke* (Vienna, 2003).

Table 1 Scorings of Ligeti's orchestral works

Concert Românesc (1951)
2*.2§. 2. 2 – 3. 2.0.0 – 2 perc – str

Apparitions (1958–9)
3.0.3.3 – 6.3.3.1 – 4 perc, hp, hpd, pf, cel – 12.12.8.8.6

Atmosphères (1961)
4****.4.4*.3† – 6.4.4.1 – pf – 14.14.10.10.8

Fragment (1961)
0.0.0†. – 0.0.1.1 – hp, hpd, cel – 0.0.0.0.3

Aventures and *Nouvelles Aventures* (1962–5)
coloratura soprano, contralto, baritone
1*.0.0.0 – 1.0.0.0 – perc, hpd, pf + cel – 0.0.0.1.1

Requiem (1963–5)
soprano, mezzo-soprano, chorus
3**.3‡.3*‡§.3† – 4.4.3.1 – 3 perc, hp, hpd, cel – 12.12.10.8.6

Cello Concerto (1966)
vc
1.1.2.1 – 1.1.1.0 – hp – 8.7.6.5.4 (or 1.1.1.1.1)

Lontano (1967)
4**†. 4§. 4‡§. 3† – 4.3.3.1 – str

Ramifications (1968–9)
str: 7.0.2.2.1 (or multiples)

Chamber Concerto (1969–70)
1*. 1†.2‡. 0 – 1.0.1.0 – hpd + hmnm, pf + cel – 1.1.1.1.1

Melodien (1971)
1*. 1†§. 1. 1 – 2.1.1.1 – 1 perc, pf + cel – 8.6.6.4.3 (or 1.1.1.1.1)

Double Concerto (1972)
fl, ob
3***. 3†§. 2*‡. 2† – 2.1.1.0 – glock + vib + xyl – 0.0.4.6.4

Clocks and Clouds (1972–3)
5***†. 3. 5‡. 4† – 0.2.0.0 – glock, vib, 2 hp, cel – 0.0.4.6.4

San Francisco Polyphony (1973–4)
3**†.3†§. 3*‡.2† – 2.2.3.1 – 2 perc, hp, pf + cel – 12.12.10.8.6

Le Grand Macabre (1974–7)
solo voices, chorus
3.3.3.3 – 4.4†.3.1 – 4 perc, 3 kbd – 3.0.2.6.4

Piano Concerto (1985–8)
pf
1*. 1. 1ᵒᶜ. 1 – 1.1.1.0 – 1/2 perc – 8.7.6.5.4 (or 1.1.1.1.1)

Violin Concerto (1989–93)
vn
2*†ʳᵉᶜ. 1ᵒᶜ. 2*‡ᵒᶜᵒᶜ. 1ᵒᶜ – 2.1.1.0 – 2 perc – 5.0.3.2.1

Hamburg Concerto (1998–2003)
hn
2*. 1.††ᵒ*. 1 – 4.1.1.0 – 2 perc – 5.4.3.2.1 (or 1.1.1.1.1)

Key

* = piccolo/E♭ clarinet

† = alto flute/oboe
d'amore/basset horn/
contrabassoon/bass
trumpet

‡ = oboe da caccia/bass
clarinet

§ = cor anglais/contrabass
clarinet

ᵒᶜ = ocarina

ʳᵉᶜ = recorder

Superscript symbols show
doublings, a superscript ᵒ the
standard instrument (basset
horn also playing clarinet).

(*Les Noces*). A third possibility typical of the 1900–50 period was to increase the scope of the percussion within an otherwise normal ensemble, a broad development associated less with Stravinsky than with Varèse (*Arcana*) and Messiaen (*Turangalîla*), and earlier with Mahler, Berg and Webern.

Ligeti and his contemporaries thus had a variety of models before them of skewed, condensed or expanded orchestras, and they responded to those models vigorously. The most extraordinary orchestral reinvention of the 1950s was surely Stockhausen's in *Gruppen*, a work Ligeti heard at its first performance (in Cologne, where he was then living, on 24 March 1958). Quite apart from disposing the forces in three separate groups, this score brought the percussion up to parity with the other departments in an orchestra built on the scale of half a century before, the scale of Mahler, Strauss and *The Rite of Spring*, a complement of 12 percussionists being suggested, along with three keyboard players. During his two and a half years in Cologne, from February 1957 to the summer of 1959, Ligeti must have acquainted himself also with his colleagues' variations on the small-scale orchestra – with Stockhausen's *Kontra-Punkte* for ten players (1952–3), for example, or Nono's *Canti per 13* (1955).

Yet, characteristically, he went down neither of these paths. As Table 1 indicates, his use of percussion in the Cologne-period *Apparitions* was moderate for the time, and after the *Requiem* he scaled back. *Atmosphères* and *Lontano* have no percussion at all, except for a piano whose strings are gently brushed in the former, and untuned instruments are comprehensively excluded between the Cello Concerto and *Clocks and Clouds*. As for the *ad hoc* ensemble, Ligeti produced his only contributions during his most anarchic period: the septet of *Aventures* and *Nouvelles Aventures* (perhaps too small to count as any kind of orchestra) and the deliberately absurd ten-piece group of *Fragment*, a work he disowned, to the extent of excluding it from the compendium of recordings he supervised in his 70s. The case of the Chamber Concerto is different. By then the contemporary ensemble of 15 or so players was becoming a permanent fixture – though as yet without the stimulus this very work was to provide – and so here Ligeti was writing for a regular formation, almost as much as he had been just before in composing for string quartet and wind quintet. Only in the 1970s do we find a succession of works whose orchestration is exceptional: the Double Concerto, *Clocks and Clouds* (for a larger but not dissimilar outfit) and *Le Grand Macabre*, all curtailing the violins (represented by just three in the opera) and placing the winds on a roughly equal footing with the remaining strings. After that Ligeti preferred the kind of medium scale on which he had worked in his Cello Concerto, Chamber Concerto and *Melodien*.

Alongside this increasing focus on the moderate-sized ensemble may be traced another pattern, one of growing fascination with unusual wind instruments and unusual tunings. The introduction in the *Requiem* of the oboe da caccia, an instrument virtually unknown outside the St Matthew Passion, is the first intimation of a taste for orchestral strangers. Another Baroque visitor, the oboe d'amore, appears in almost every score from the Chamber Concerto to *San Francisco Polyphony*, followed by the ocarina and recorder in the piano and violin concertos (the treble recorder returning after more than four decades from the withdrawn *Ballad and Dance* of 1949–50 for school orchestra), after which the Horn Concerto welcomed further 18th-century guests: basset horns and natural French horns. Here (the ocarinas always excepted) Ligeti shows himself an observer of the period-instrument movement that coincided with his creative life. Further evidence of this comes in his frequent use of the harpsichord in scores from *Apparitions* to the Chamber Concerto but not thereafter, discreetly withdrawing it in course with the modern instrument's fall from grace among musicians performing 18th-century music. Yet of course there is no historicism in how these instruments are used. The harpsichord always belonged with other keyboard and tuned percussive instruments in a jangling group; the lowered oboes added subtle colour and perhaps were there to mute the 'concreteness' that had caused the composer to omit oboes from the first orchestral score he wrote as an émigré and limit them in the second;[2] and the ocarina, recorder and natural horn offered tunings that were appealingly wayward or simply different, going on serving a partiality for disintonation first revealed in *Ramifications*, with its string groups a quarter-tone apart. Most fundamentally, Ligeti handled unusual instruments – or usual ones – with the kind of sensitivity to effect he admired in Stravinsky, how a line for clarinet would necessarily be different from one for flute. 'That is also my idea, to take into account the specific properties of every instrument.'[3]

Rather strikingly, all Ligeti's works with large orchestral forces come from the decade between 1958 and 1967 (four scores) except for *San Francisco Polyphony* (1973–4), for which the circumstances were special: enthusiasm for the city and a wish to make use of material drafted for the abandoned *Oedipus* opera (which also supplied *Clocks and Clouds*). Ligeti could assuredly have secured commissions for more big orchestral works had he wanted. He lived to see *Atmosphères* taken up by prominent orchestras around the world, presented not only by such persistent allies as Peter Eötvös, Jonathan Nott and Esa-Pekka Salonen but also by some of the most prominent conductors around: Claudio Abbado, Riccardo Chailly, Christoph von Dohnányi and James Levine. Table 2 suggests how deeply his scores had penetrated orchestral programming internationally by the time of his death, his music far outdistancing that of his contemporaries in this respect and coming close to works one might consider staples of the repertory. *Lontano*, for example, enjoyed more performances in 2007 than Bartók's *Music for Strings, Percussion and Celesta*, and not so many fewer than Strauss's Four Last Songs. (It is ironic that Ligeti came to feel this to be one of his weakest pieces.)[4] Yet in 1978, a few years after *San Francisco Polyphony*, when he might have seemed ready to write another big work, having completed *Le Grand Macabre* in the interim, he assured Péter Várnai that 'if someone asked me now to write a work for the orchestra I should refuse, since I am at the moment interested in other things.'[5]

---

[2] See Ove Nordwall, *György Ligeti: eine Monographie* (Mainz, 1971), p. 36.

[3] *György Ligeti in Conversation*, p. 23.

[4] See Ligeti and Roelcke, *Träumen Sie in Farbe?*, p. 203.

[5] *György Ligeti in Conversation*, p. 23.

Table 2 Number of performances worldwide in 2007 of works by Ligeti and others

Concert Românesc	28	Adams: Violin Concerto	26
Apparitions	3	Berio: *Sinfonia*	13
Atmosphères	21	— *Rendering*	24
Fragment	0	Birtwistle: *Secret Theatre*	5
Requiem	6	Boulez: *Le marteau sans maître*	8
Cello Concerto	12	— *Notations I–IV*	10
Lontano	41	Feldman: *Neither*	4
Ramifications	28	Henze: Symphony no. 1	3
Chamber Concerto	44	Nono: *Il canto sospeso*	0
Melodien	23	Stockhausen: *Kontra-Punkte*	8
Double Concerto	1	— *Gruppen*	1
Clocks and Clouds	2	Takemitsu: *Rain Coming*	21
San Francisco Polyphony	8		
Piano Concerto	23	Bartók: *Music for Strings*	32
Violin Concerto	31	Mahler: Symphony no. 1	64
Hamburg Concerto	7	Strauss: *Four Last Songs*	55

Note: Figures for works published by Schott, Universal Edition and Boosey & Hawkes were obtained from their online data banks, those for Peters Edition works kindly supplied by Stefan Conradi.

'Other things' maintained their allure, for reasons we may partly guess. For instance, his developing and then continuing interest in non-standard tunings (an interest also referable to what was happening in the performance of Baroque music) may have helped turn him from the grand format to smaller ensembles, which could project microtonal deviations more surely and clearly. But equally, he cannot have failed to notice the growing importance of the contemporary ensemble, as *Die Reihe* – founded in 1958 and the destined home of his Chamber Concerto – was followed by the London Sinfonietta (1968), the Ensemble InterContemporain (1976), the Ensemble Modern (1980), Klangforum Wien (1985) and many more. Though he wrote nothing further expressly for such formations, he kept them in mind by making *Melodien* as well as his cello, piano and horn concertos available for performance with solo strings and so by an ensemble of 14–17 players. The Violin Concerto, requiring 23, may also be counted into this repertory, that of the chamber orchestra with bells and whistles – the tuned percussion that had nearly always played a part in Ligeti's scoring plus the new wind irregulars. This kind of ensemble seems always to have been waiting for Ligeti as he went through his successive self-transformations.

Three nowheres and a return

Thus standing apart, the four works for big orchestra – *Apparitions,*
Atmosphères, Lontano and *San Francisco Polyphony* – also stand together
in several respects. For one, each of the last three plays continuously,
whereas Ligeti's compositions for smaller forces are in several movements,
with the single exception of *Melodien*. It is as if, for Ligeti, the large mass
implied continuity – even, in the cases of *Atmosphères* and *Lontano*, infinite
continuity, going on after the notional (and notational) conclusion. Both
these works end with a slow fade, during which we may feel the music is
departing from us, like a planet that has drawn near and is retreating into
darkness. The first movement of *Apparitions* also closes as if moving on
elsewhere, passing the limits of the audible not only in its low dynamic
level but also in the extremely high register of the cluster here for three
violins. Indeed, the 'elsewhere' is realized in an absolutely direct fashion,
in that the violins are heard from offstage. No one we can see is making a
sound, and yet the music continues.

However, *Apparitions* is very different from its two symphonic-scale
successors in its chopped-up progress, the first movement, *Lento*, being
a concatenation of sounds, most of them clusters or noises, and the fast
second a quiver of ostinatos overtaken by a loud, tangled polyphony for 46
strings, which itself gives way to a quick exchange of rumbles, fanfares
and brute shocks ending in exhaustion. Ligeti gave this curious music
two different kinds of explanation. One had to do with a childhood dream
of finding his bedroom filled with a webwork spun by fantastic insects;[6]
the other with a critique of 'serial' music as he found it in Cologne and
Darmstadt soon after his 1956 emigration. According to his own account,
he had been trying since 1950 to realize his dream as sound, and had
completed a first attempt, *Víziók* (Visions), shortly before leaving Hungary,
a score he brought with him but lost. *Apparitions* was a second try, as he
made explicit in first publishing an account of his dream in his programme
note for the work, though he became ambivalent about the relevance.[7]

He did not rescind, however, what he had to say about the importance
to *Apparitions* of the musical situation he found in western Europe in the
late 1950s. There were two aspects to this, concerning, on the one hand,
the circle he joined by going to Cologne (the circle that 'Darmstadt' may
serve to label) and, on the other, composers who, though working in idioms
generally perceived as avant-garde, were regarded from the 'Darmstadt'
position as beyond the pale. Of course, boundaries were constantly shifting.
Luigi Nono, a founder member of the 'Darmstadt' group, got sidelined, or
sidelined himself, as the 1950s went on. And though Ligeti was regularly at
Boulez's side on the Darmstadt faculty between 1959 and 1966, his music
was not admitted to Boulez's performing repertory until 1971.

Ligeti always acknowledged what he owed to his contemporaries,
especially Boulez and Stockhausen, but he was always concerned also to
present himself as an outsider, being a little older, having had very different
experiences in his 20s (unlike his colleagues he had a whole mature

[6] Ibid., p. 25.
[7] Ibid.

output of tonal compositions behind him), and coming as an immigrant. *Apparitions* belongs with recent works by Boulez and Stockhausen in drawing on fixed repertories in various parameters (notably duration), but it may be understood, too, as a demonstration piece for views Ligeti expressed in his contemporary article 'Metamorphoses of Musical Form'.[8] Composition and essay alike, both appearing in 1960, caused consternation within new-music circles in Germany for their challenge perhaps not so much to serialism *per se* as to a doctrine of abstractness – abstractness defined in contrast not only with the *espressivo* past but also with the *espressivo* present, that of the Soviet bloc. Here was a composer arriving from within that region (the most notable one to do so during the entire Cold War period), one who rejected the old tonal language as decisively as any of his Western contemporaries – perhaps more decisively, because in doing so he was rejecting music he himself had composed, music he kept under wraps until the late 1960s – and yet who was willing to speak of sound as having plastic qualities: 'hacked, pulverized, melted, highly condensed'.[9]

To recognize those qualities was to open the possibility of an onomatopeia of sound, a music expressing itself by virtue not of syntactical relationship but of inherent metaphor. Ligeti's note on his electronic piece *Artikulation*, composed shortly before *Apparitions*, indicates how far he was prepared to go:

> Sounding planes and masses, which may succeed, penetrate or mingle with one another – floating networks that get torn up or entangled – wet, sticky, gelatinous, fibrous, dry, brittle, granular and compact materials, shreds, curlicues, splinters and traces of every sort – imaginary buildings, labyrinths, inscriptions, texts, dialogues, insects – states, events, processes, blendings, transformations, catastrophes, disintegrations, disappearances – all these are elements of this non-purist music.[10]

However, it is perhaps the notion of music as speech, tactfully buried here in a catalogue of connotations, that is conveyed most forcibly by *Apparitions* as much as *Artikulation*. The individual sounds of the orchestral work's first movement may be static samples of material, but in succession they create arching dynamics of expectancy that lead toward climaxes, these either silencing the music or turning it in another direction. And though events are certainly less static in the second movement, there is a similar dynamism arising from the shuffle of events toward climax and change.

In 'Metamorphoses of Musical Form' Ligeti several times speaks of new music as having experienced loss: the 'disintegration' the 12-note row underwent through the application of the new procedures devised by Boulez, Stockhausen and others, a 'decreasing sensitivity to intervals' caused by the density of such works as *Gruppen*. *Apparitions* accepts that condition of loss: it has no row and, for the most part, no intervals, only impalpable clusters, noises and ostinatos. Yet it speaks. Like someone

---

[8] *Die Reihe*, no. 7 (English edition 1965), pp. 5–19.
[9] Ibid., p. 14.
[10] Nordwall, *György Ligeti: eine Monographie*, p. 41.

ignorant of the language of those to be addressed, it uses signs and gestures to express itself vehemently.

Ligeti's references to living composers in 'Metamorphoses' are all to people whose 'Darmstadt' credentials were not in dispute: Boulez, Stockhausen (early), Nono, Pousseur, Gottfried Michael Koenig, Cage, Messiaen and Karel Goeyvaerts. Even the order of appearance affirms the author's rectitude, and moderates the criticism, situating it within the body of the elect. This is the group to which Ligeti wanted to belong – but not quite, preferring a place on the margins. He made the point over and over again in his conversations, declaring to Várnai, for example: 'I dislike the idea of being a member of a clique.'[11]

One name missing from the roll call of 'Metamorphoses' is that of Iannis Xenakis, representing another camp. Again Boulez's performing history affords an illustration. In 1963, under pressure, he commissioned Xenakis to write a piece for his Domaine Musical series, but other than that he conducted just one Xenakis piece in the 1970s and then left the composer alone again until 1990. Ligeti, too, distanced himself from Xenakis, particularly in defence of his originality in matters of texture music and multitudinous string polyphony. He conceded that Xenakis had been the first to write individual parts for all an orchestra's string players, in *Metastasis* (1953–4), but added that he did not know this work until after he had written *Apparitions* and *Atmosphères*,[12] while, by consistently giving 1950 as the date when he first imagined a dense, stationary music,[13] he established his own priority in any case. And one is encouraged to accept Ligeti's word because he was ready to acknowledge knowing other examples of texture-block music – Kagel's *Anagrama* and Stockhausen's *Carré* from within the Cologne circle, but also Penderecki's *Anaklasis* from right outside – before finishing *Atmosphères*.[14] The Kagel had been performed at the ISCM festival in Cologne in June 1960 that also saw the première of *Apparitions*, and the Stockhausen and Penderecki scores were both given for the first time at German festivals in October 1960.

All this history, relating to the style wars of half a century ago, still hangs around *Apparitions*, partly because of the composer's often-repeated testimony but perhaps more substantially because this contrarian work sets itself apart not only from Stockhausen and Xenakis but also from the norms of orchestral behaviour. Ligeti knew those norms well. By this time he had, as middle-class child, conservatory student and professor, been attending opera and orchestral performances for a quarter of a century; he also knew the orchestra back-to-front, as it were, from his teenage years as a timpanist,[15] and orchestral composition had been on his agenda since that time, when he started a symphony. *Apparitions* – a chain of discrete events for diverse ensembles and solo instruments – emphatically contradicts all that experience. Ligeti was placing himself creatively, as well

---

[11] *György Ligeti in Conversation*, p. 29.

[12] Ibid., p. 37; see also Michel, *György Ligeti: compositeur d'aujourd'hui*, pp. 156–7.

[13] See, for example, *György Ligeti in Conversation*, pp. 33 and 88, and Michel, *György Ligeti: compositeur d'aujourd'hui*, p. 133.

[14] *György Ligeti in Conversation*, p. 37.

[15] See Ligeti and Roelcke, *Träumen Sie in Farbe?*, p. 35.

as physically, in exile from everything he had known. Yet in doing so he was joining ranks with contemporaries who by no means shared his life story, for the orchestral works written around this time by Stockhausen, Boulez, Xenakis and others are every bit as different, as unaccommodating to orchestral routine. Orchestral writing, for younger composers at this period, was all about innovation, and *Apparitions* innovates with the best of them, in formal strategy and in introducing non-standard effects, such as the toneless gasps from brass players at the end. It is strange. (Ligeti's articulation of his boyhood dream was surely an attempt, by a musician versed in orthodoxy, to justify the unorthodox.) It is even disturbing, as the hapless orchestra fumbles and gesticulates to make itself understood. And in just the same measure – now far apart indeed from anything by any of Ligeti's contemporaries – it is comic, the at once marred and exaggerated expression looking forward to the black humour of the *Requiem*.

Atmosphères is not so obviously funny – though certainly it is still strange. Ligeti said that one piece grew out of the other, in that hearing the dense canon in the middle of the second movement of *Apparitions*, at the work's first performance (Cologne, 19 June 1960), gave him a starting point for *Atmosphères*,[16] which was commissioned for the 1961 Donaueschingen Festival. However, the separated sounds with which *Apparitions* creates its wordless sentences are no longer available. The movement from one sound to another is not abrupt but gradual; distinction is created only when one cluster comes to glow through another, and the one discontinuity does not register as such, the music seeming to disappear off the top of the pitch spectrum to reappear at the bottom, creating a sensation of vacant space that was to recur in most of Ligeti's larger scores. Time is almost unmarked, and, in this absence of rhythm, the music comes near being pure sound. Ligeti's admiration for Cage – which perhaps shows in his unconventional use of the piano, two players brushing strings in what is otherwise necessarily a score for sustaining instruments: winds and strings – may be implicated also in music where sounds are themselves, or, rather, where sound is itself, a single substance in more or less continuous, usually smooth change from the beginning of the piece to the end (and implicitly beyond).

To hear *Atmosphères* in a Cageian context is to lessen the gap between this work, completed in July 1961, and the dadaist pieces that came immediately after: the lecture on the future of music and the *Trois Bagatelles* for pianist, both projects conceived the following month, and *Fragment*, written in October. It is to lessen the widely understood gap, too, between what is precise, defined and mechanical in Ligeti's music – often comic, too – and what is intangible, the gap between his clocks and his clouds. Where *Atmosphères* and its aftermath of skits are concerned, there is a difference in levels of craft and aim, to be sure, but the orchestral piece can also be taken as a jape, if a serious one: music playing dumb. The person trying to communicate in an unknown language is now gagged and has hands and feet tied. We stare and strive to understand as we contemplate the vast spaces of this work, beautiful and empty, and beautiful in being

---

[16] See Michel, *György Ligeti: compositeur d'aujourd'hui*, p. 150.

empty. *Atmosphères* completes the losses begun in *Apparitions*, and Ligeti fittingly dedicated the score as a memorial, to Mátyás Seiber.

Atmosphères is a limit case, from a period of limit cases that included Cage's *4' 33"* and Boulez's *Structures Ia* (subject of Ligeti's famous analysis). Music cannot be more blurred than this, with scarcely a gesture to be discerned in the multicoloured mist. *Lontano*, which Ligeti completed six years later, again for Donaueschingen, and again for an orchestra without hard edges (not even a strummed piano this time), revisits the same space, created by sounds of great length, but even if there are still few objects in that space – no gestures that operate on the human timescale of bodily movement or vocal articulation until stately progressions arrive toward the end – there are forces to be felt and veils to be made out, with further veils behind them. The reason for this is straightforward: *Lontano* is made not of clusters but of single notes, tight chords and intervals spread across the pitch space, all these with almost constant, imperceptible changes of tone colour as instruments enter and leave the protracted unisons. Such a conception is more demanding of finesse in orchestration, and possibly *Lontano* owes its gleam to what Ligeti had discovered in the interim in writing (and hearing performed) his *Requiem* and Cello Concerto. The work – which owes its title to the musical marking 'da lontano' (from the distance), and which speaks of distance in so many respects – maintains its distance from the roughness that *Apparitions* and even *Atmosphères* had accepted as part of their nature as works of the avant-garde.

Atmosphères had been an absence of music, as traditionally understood. *Lontano* is an absence of a particular kind of music: the sumptuous symphonic music of the late 19th century – the kind of music that in 1967 formed the heartland of the orchestral repertory, and still does. This is music that is everywhere present, in concert halls and probably also in our homes, by way of radio or recording, but at the same time mysteriously vanished. We know a lot about this music. We can study different recorded performances, examine sketches, analyse scores, elucidate internal and external references. But we cannot make more of it, not without falling into absurdity and pastiche. Distance separates us from this music, and *Lontano* surveys that distance. The single note of the opening, extended far beyond what would be normal, is a living echo, indefinable in its mixture of flute tone (rather low in the instrument's register) with cello (rather high), to which other colours are added, and the piece goes on with these long rays of subtly mixed sound, as if the concert hall were breathing back what has soaked into its walls. Occasionally a combination of rays will suggest a melodic shape or harmonic progression or timbre more distinctly redolent of something in the standard repertory, especially the late Romantic repertory – Bruckner, Mahler or Wagner, as Ligeti himself suggested.[17]

Patterns from the past arrive also in *San Francisco Polyphony*, which might be regarded as a further reconnoitre of the same territory, undertaken not with clusters as in *Atmosphères*, not with single notes as in *Lontano*, but with melodies and ostinatos, or rather with melodies that degrade into ostinatos and ostinatos that develop into melodies. Sometimes, as in *Lontano*, the circumstances will, almost as if by chance, strike a quite

[17] *György Ligeti in Conversation*, p. 93.

particular chord; there is, for instance, a powerfully Bergian moment. But we may sense, too, that Ligeti is readmitting his own past. Since *Lontano* two things had happened, perhaps connected. In 1970 Ligeti had returned to Hungary for the first time since his emigration; and he had embarked on a cautious disclosure of his pre-emigration music, starting with a choral ballad of 1953, *Pápainé*, which was performed in Stockholm in the month *Lontano* was completed (May 1967). The bubbling-up of possibility in *San Francisco Polyphony*, so many of the ostinatos rotating upward-moving figures, hints too at a release of tension, a new enrichment, and yet it suggests, too, the composer's acknowledgement of his own more various past – a past not lost and gone forever, like that descried in *Lontano*, not abruptly cut off by his emigration into a radically different musical world, but silently present all the time and fizzing with vitality. And certainly there is this positive, optimistic side to *San Francisco Polyphony*, the only work of any kind Ligeti wrote for a United States institution, and one that ends – in a superb display of showmanship utterly against the spirit of *Lontano* and *Atmosphères* – with a bang.

Yet the piece has much in common with its predecessors. The vacant-space effect – of emptiness below a ceiling high in the audible frequency range, often emphasized by a floor in the extreme bass either simultaneous or supervening – reappears, and there are direct references back to *Lontano* in the arrival of a gauze of tritones in many registers and of another of Cs in several octaves. *San Francisco Polyphony* also continues to follow two historical paths at the same time: that of the composer's existence and that of composition in general, certainly as it was understood by the post-war avant-garde Ligeti had joined. Both paths identified a moment of rupture (emigration, fascism/war) after which a new start had to be made; both were leading through a gradual retrieval of the previously obliterated past, Ligeti's increasing recognition of his pre-1956 works from 1967 onwards being paralleled by, for instance, Berio's celestial railroad of quotations in his *Sinfonia* (1968–9) or Stockhausen's reintroduction of melody as guiding principle in *Mantra* (1969–70). Ligeti's abstention from the large orchestra after *San Francisco Polyphony* may also have something to do with his emigration – his mental emigration from a symphonic, tonal tradition that had been hijacked by Soviet-approved culture. The big orchestra had given him the means to say 'no', to defy that tradition in its own arena, achieving, no doubt, a more complete and complex defiance than had been possible with the blatantly anti-symphonic, anti-tonal material he had used before, that of electronic music. Once he no longer wanted to say 'no' but was beginning to say 'yes', both to his own past work and to the ideas it represented, the symphony orchestra was no longer relevant.

There was, however, a new battle to be fought. As Ligeti worked on *San Francisco Polyphony* he was also teaching at the conservatory in Hamburg and discovering a coming generation of composers, then in their early 20s, who were pushing to go much further in recuperating the past; Manfred Trojahn, Wolfgang von Schweinitz and Hans-Christian von Dadelsen, three pioneers of the 'New Romanticism', were all pupils of his at this time. By his own account he was surprised by the New Romantic corners and shadows he heard when his new work was played for the first time: 'While I was working on *San Francisco Polyphony* I thought that the city's atmosphere had a decisive influence on the music, but when I heard it performed I realized it is more Viennese: there are a number of expressive melodies in it reminiscent of Alban Berg or Mahler.'[18] He was right both times. The piece does convey something of the exhilarating freshness Ligeti would have found around him on his first visit to San Francisco, in 1972, and yet it does indeed have its revenants. Further along this path Ligeti was not prepared to go. The slam at the end sounds like a door closing, an action the sorcerer conjures not only for his apprentices but also for himself.

The one and the many

If the four works for big orchestra tell a story of refusal (of the past, even of musical incident) followed by incremental accommodation up to a point of new refusal, the larger and more diffuse array of works for smaller groupings describe rather a circle, around which certain features are held in common. As already noted, most of these works are in several movements, whether two (Cello Concerto, Double Concerto), four (*Romanian Concerto*, Chamber Concerto), five (Piano Concerto, Violin Concerto) or seven (*Hamburg Concerto*). That these scores also share a term in their titles is not insignificant. Five of them sport soloists, and all exhibit a spirit of play that Ligeti inherited from the Baroque by way of 20th-century neoclassicism. Given this was a composer both antiquarian and adventuresome (as shown in some of his instrumental choices), the title he chose for his last concerto was surely in reference to Bach's famous set, which he may humorously have felt he had outdone by chalking up seven.

To those seven one might add an eighth, in *Melodien*, which, if played with solo strings, is a concerto for everybody quite as much as the Chamber Concerto – perhaps more so, since, as the title suggests, this is music of melodies, and those melodies are played most often by soloists. The piece is, indeed, an anterior, and in many ways superior, *San Francisco Polyphony*, again displaying some of the frequent features of Ligeti's writing for large ensemble: the sense of space between the topmost and bottommost registers, the octave Cs (occurring here at the midpoint), the slowly changing clouds that are often clouds of precise mechanisms. Ligeti disclosed that he began the composition by sketching a 'harmonic skeleton',[19] and very possibly this manner of composition was something else *Melodien* shared with other works, especially *Lontano* and *San Francisco Polyphony*. Its opening provides a signal instance of another common atmosphere in Ligeti's music, that of music swept up into the uppermost treble, where the composer may have been recalling his experiences trying to listen to western musical broadcasts in Soviet-dominated Hungary: 'I could hear the piccolo and the xylophone but none of the lower instruments on account of the jamming.'[20] Bars 14ff. of *Melodien*, scored for the two

---

[18] Ibid., pp. 66–7.

[19] See Marc Chemillier, 'Analysis and Computer Reconstruction of a Musical Fragment of György Ligeti's *Melodien*', *Muzica* 6/2 (1994), pp. 34–48, http://mediatheque.ircam.fr/articles/textes/Chemillier94a/#fn0, accessed 15 August 2010.

[20] Ligeti and Roelcke, *Träumen Sie in Farbe?*, p. 75.

instruments Ligeti names plus celesta, clarinet and string harmonics in the same register, might have been designed to pierce through any such attempt to block.

Each of the two halves of *Melodien* moves from one pitch class – a single superhigh A in the first half, the octave Cs in the second – through a process of increasing differentiation. Examples 46–8 shows some stages in this process near the beginning of the second half, where the melodies are generally in even note values, with some notes of half value.

The first idea describable as a melody, not a sustained note, tremolo or ostinato, enters on oboe and clarinet in octaves at bar 75, and has the elementary character of plainsong, whose neumatic notation would even serve to express it (Example 46).

Example 46 *Melodien*, bars 72–5

The marking 'as though sounding from the distance' (*da Lontano*, one might say) might imply a distance of time as much as space. Next come two successive melodies from the flute (Example 47), the first starting in the same modal region (C Dorian), the second a variation in something like an inversion of the same five-note mode, but with a sixth note.

Example 47 *Melodien*, bars 79–81

A few bars later (Example 48) the music has grown into scales of up to 12 notes, but with diatonic features remaining, such as the recurrence of B♭ as initial or final note, the triads that the melodies often outline, and the tritones that will swivel a melody from one mode into another, rather as chords of tritones act as turning points in *Lontano* and *San Francisco Polyphony*. The passage underscores what Ligeti meant in describing his music as neither tonal nor atonal. The tonal elements are unstable, flickering, just as the music flickers rhythmically, with its several pulse rates out of alignment, and just as it flickers in its references, whether generic (plainsong in Example 46) or specific (Janáček in the rising figure in F♯ of Example 47). A whole thousand-year history of music, from chant to row, unfolds here in the space of eight bars, or about 30 seconds, given the prescribed tempo of crotchet = 68. Indeed, there is more than that, for some of these melodies imply modalities not yet encountered, at least in Western music. Starting out, one may imagine, with a completely abstract concept, that of unison moving into total chromaticism, Ligeti discovers aspects of different pasts, real and imaginary, entering his music as if by accident. The micropolyphony of *Atmosphères* and the *Requiem*, made of many essentially similar lines, was to remain a possibility, important in the Double Concerto and *Clocks and Clouds*, for instance, and still in the last concertos, but in *Melodien* Ligeti had discovered how a basically homogeneous kind of music, defined by certain harmonic rules, could

Example 48 *Melodien*, bars 79–84

(*) Siehe Fußnote Seite 21 (**) Individuelle Bogen Wid-Einteilung, ad lib.
See footnote, page 21   Individual bowing, ad lib.

be constituted from a variety of idiolects in different instrumental parts. Folk-music modalities, which had been a source when he was in Hungary, were now a product. And the orchestra had become an assembly of almost independent but confluent individuals – individuals moving, one may note, within the same space, for *Melodien* smartly disposes of traditional registral hierarchies. One descending flourish in the cello apart, the melodizing instruments of Example 48, from cello to double bass, are all operating within a comfortable soprano register. The orchestra has become a polyphony of treble voices.

Not only *San Francisco Polyphony* benefited from this; there are moments in *Clocks and Clouds* that babble in highly restricted modes, and the 'Collage' in the third scene of *Le Grand Macabre* presents a simultaneity of diverse languages for four soloists appearing as devils: 'One is a violinist who plays a Scott Joplin-type ragtime on his violin, which is deliberately mistuned. The bassoon player intones a distorted Greek Orthodox hymn ... . The third devil plays a mixture of a Brazilian and Spanish, half-samba, half-flamenco tune on his E-flat clarinet. The fourth plays on his piccolo a march that is half-Scottish, half-Hungarian – more exactly, a Hungarian pentatonic tune that is made to sound like bagpipe music. And the overall harmonic structure is twelve-note.'[21] However, the works Ligeti wrote after his opera take the idea of fake folk (and art) music, of retrieval by synthesis, much further.

Before this period – before the late 1970s, that is – Ligeti said little in the West about folk music, which he probably felt belonged to the world he had abandoned in leaving Hungary. *Melodien* may have taught him that this was not so; certainly his interest in folk music, of many different kinds, picked up immensely a few years later. In 1978 he wrote to a contact in Romania asking for folk materials;[22] soon afterwards came discoveries that left their mark on his music and on his memory, so that two decades afterwards he was able to date them with precision: Caribbean music, encountered in 1979–80 thanks to another Hamburg student, Roberto Sierra, who came from Puerto Rico, and then in 1982 African music, starting with that of the Banda Linda of the Central African Republic, recorded by Simha Arom.[23] Later came Thai music, Burmese,[24] and that of Melanesia.

We may imagine that Ligeti was opened to these new enthusiasms – rapidly to become new influences – by the invented modalities he had found arising under his fingers as he composed *Melodien*, but there was also the impetus of an impasse. Sierra was, as it were, the counterpoise to Trojahn, Schweinitz and Dadelsen, a student who proposed fresh paths, not old ones. Moreover, folk music was no longer to be disowned with the Hungarian past, for Ligeti was going on releasing or rereleasing his pre-1956 compositions (an almost three-decade process not completed until the mid-1990s) and he was returning to Hungary occasionally (notably in 1983, for his 60th birthday celebrations), finding that the clamps he

---

[21] *György Ligeti in Conversation*, p. 59.

[22] See Rachel Beckles Willson, *Ligeti, Kurtág, and Hungarian Music During the Cold War* (Cambridge, 2007), p. 187.

[23] See Ligeti and Roelcke, *Träumen Sie in Farbe?*, p. 133.

[24] Ibid., p. 138.

had known on creativity were now removed. Folk music did not mean restriction and the past; it could be innovation and the future. He could be another Bartók.

It need be no surprise, then, that Bartók's shadow can be made out behind the exuberant polymodal, polyrhythmic, multicoloured surfaces of the first large-format piece he completed after his opera: the Piano Concerto, which he finished in 1988 after nearly a decade of work. Ligeti may have created the work out of a struggle not to recapitulate Bartók,[25] but that is indeed what he did, if not in his five-movement form, which lacks Bartókian symmetry, then in his references to the theme of the first movement of the *Music for Strings, Percussion and Celesta*, which come repeatedly, especially in the second, third and fifth movements. We know this was a work he admired, for he remarked how: 'Bartók's sonority, especially in the fugal first movement of the *Music for Strings, Percussion and Celesta*, has always been a model for me.'[26] Not the sonority, now, but the melody of that movement – albeit mediated by his thematic use of descending chromatic scale fragments in his immediately preceding Études for solo piano – forms one strand, perhaps the most pervasive, threading through the glorious tangle of the Piano Concerto, a work Ligeti ended with a bang recalling that of *San Francisco Polyphony*, only now with a sense not of slamming a door but of popping a champagne cork.

Ligeti scored his Piano Concerto, as earlier his Cello Concerto, for a fairly standard chamber orchestra, though, as already noted, both works may be played with solo strings. Finishing the piece, so long in the making, seems to have been a release, and he moved swiftly on to a new book of piano études, a commission for the King's Singers (*Nonsense Madrigals*) and another concerto, for violin. For this he again chose a modest-sized ensemble, but now a hand-picked one, evenly balanced between strings and winds, incorporating an entire sub-ensemble of hazily tuned and undervalued wind instruments (including not only the ocarinas and recorder but also two swanee whistles played by percussionists), and complicating the harmony also with untempered harmonics. The instrumentation would appear to have been chosen with these non-standard tunings in view (or earshot). One of the five orchestral violins plays roughly a quarter-tone sharp, one of the three violas slightly more than a semitone flat, these two instruments having been respectively tuned to seventh and fifth harmonics produced by the double bass, while the horns and trombones sometimes project natural harmonics directly and microtonal deviations are also required occasionally from the woodwind. The most conspicuous homogenizing feature of the western orchestra, demonstrated at each concert as everyone tunes to the oboe's A, is here set aside. There is no agreement about tuning, and so there can be no harmonic agreement – or rather, it is in manifest disagreement, in confusion teetering on the borders of chaos, that this remarkable concerto finds its being.

It opens with magical iridescence as the soloist leads all the violins and violas in cascades of natural harmonics on open strings, the mistuned (but

---

[25] See Beckles Willson, *Ligeti, Kurtág, and Hungarian Music During the Cold War*, p. 183.

[26] Michel, *György Ligeti: compositeur d'aujourd'hui*, p. 168.

for this music rightly tuned) members included. When abrupt scales start to emerge from the glistening texture, played by the soloist with marimba reinforcement, it is their equally tempered intervals that sound out of tune in this environment. Rather as in the Berg concerto (perhaps the predecessor most closely on Ligeti's mind), from the primeval sound of the violin's native fifths comes a whole musical world, developing in this case from harmonics and misaligned tunings. Richard Steinitz[27] very plausibly suggests that, as before with *San Francisco Polyphony* and *Clocks and Clouds*, this work became the repository for ideas Ligeti had been forming towards an opera, in this case *The Tempest*, the rainbows of harmonics and the earthy scales sounding for the Ariel and Caliban aspects of Prospero's island.

If in the Piano Concerto Ligeti had engaged with Bartók more directly than since his years in Budapest, here he draws even nearer home by creating for his second movement a solo violin melody, heard first almost unaccompanied, that looks back more than 40 years to the solo cello melody of his Cello Sonata's adagio – but with the crucial difference that the new line, though plainly diatonic and contained within the span of an octave, is ambiguous in its tonality (as also in its metre). D, G and A are explored as potential resting points, but this is a melody with no certain ground, a folksong for the homeless. It is repeated at different pitch levels in a sequence of variations, of which the third places a dazzling hocket for solo violin and piccolo over the melody on trumpet with trombone support and the next has the soloist playing in 4/4 against the 3/4 of the melody on horns producing natural harmonics. The composer's draft[28] is explicit about his sources for these inventions: Machaut and a more recent enthusiasm, Pygmy music. No less bizarre are the passages that come before and after these, in which the orchestra is joined by the quartet of ocarinas, performing the melody in offbeat harmonizations, with an effect simultaneously of mockery and wonder.

The third movement also has a central melody, but one that runs right through the solo part, constantly shape-shifting. Example 48 shows its

Example 48 Violin Concerto, third movement, *Intermezzo*, 33–7

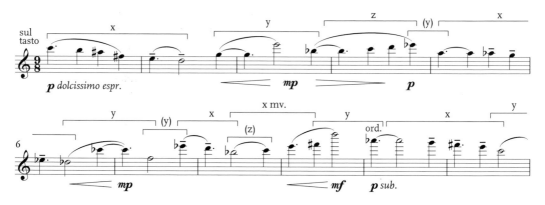

[27] See Richard Steinitz, *György Ligeti: Music of the Imagination* (London, 2003), p. 334.
[28] Reproduced in ibid., p. 335.

beginning, marking elements that keep returning: a descent in chromatic, major-third and whole-tone steps (*x*), a lift through a sixth or diminished seventh followed by a tritone fall (*y*) and a scalar rise (*z*). The entire 76-bar melody is made of these, but in perpetual variation of detail and mode, and in restless tension, too, with the notated 'Bulgarian' metre. It is a fractal line, like the track of a memory trying to remember something forgotten, piece it together from fragments retained in the revolving mind, sometimes making semi-fresh starts that are prompted by, or that prompt, shifts in the prevailing harmony. At first there is only the melody and its background of microtonal harmony and raining chromatic scales, but a third of the way through a horn starts sporting in the harmonic series, and then woodwinds add counterpoints, placing the soloist's elements together in ways that are modally and metrically more rudimentary; Ligeti's marking is 'cheeky'. Example 49 (see pp. 276–7) comes from early in this process. The solo violin's search for its lost melody goes on, with an intensity both in the elements themselves and in the repeated retries, while reed instruments propose spurious simplicities. One may note, too, how the orchestra has become an array of high voices, as in *Melodien*, but now with melodies that are far more sharply characterized.

Ligeti, in this scintillant concerto, was able to review the place where he began, as represented by melody typical of central European folksong, now from within a world stretching as far as Machaut and equatorial Africa. And, while acknowledging the pathos of being separated from a locus of origin, he was able to rejoice in itinerancy, to measure his closeness to places of diverse kinds. The Violin Concerto is the richest of his invented homelands, and may persuade us that feelings of belonging are complex, ambiguous, mutable and probably illusory.

276

Example 49 Violin Concerto, third movement, *Intermezzo*, bars 33–7

*) Clarinets soli: the players subdivide the conductor's beat according to their own time-signature. They play synchronized exactly.
Klarinetten soli: die Spieler unterteilen die Schläge des Dirigenten gemäß ihres eigenen asymmetrischen Metrums. Sie spielen streng synchron.

Ligeti and Ines Gellrich at the NDR Festival for Ligeti's 75th birthday in Hamburg (June 1998)

Bibliography

Agel, Jerome, ed., *The Making of Kubrick's 2001* (New York, 1970)

Arom, Simha, 'The Use of Play-Back Techniques in the Study of Oral Polyphonies', *Ethnomusicology* 20/3 (1976), pp. 483–519

——*African Polyphony and Polyrhythm: Musical Structure and Methodology* (Cambridge, 1991)

——'Une parenté inattendue: polyphonies médiévales et polyphonies africaines', in *Polyphonies de tradition orale: histoire et traditions vivantes, Actes du Colloque de Royaumont 1990*, ed. Michel Huglo and Marcel Pérès (Paris, 1994)

——'Musiques traditionnelles et création contemporaine', in *Catalogue de l'exposition André Jolivet – 'Les objets de Mana'* (Paris, 2003), pp. 27–32

——'L'aksak: principes et typologie', *Cahiers de musiques traditionnelles* 17, 'Formes Musicales' (2004), pp. 11–48

Bauer, Hans-Günther, *Requiem-Kompositionen in Neuer Musik: Vergleichende Untersuchungen zum Verhältnis von Sprache der Liturgie und der Musik* (Tübingen, 1984)

Beckles Willson, Rachel, *Ligeti, Kurtág, and Hungarian Music During the Cold War* (Cambridge, 2007)

——'Veress and the Steam Locomotive in 1948', in *Sándor Veress: Komponist – Lehrer – Forscher*, ed. Doris Lanz and Anselm Gerhard (Kassel, 2008), pp. 20–5

Beethoven, Ludwig van, *Symphony No. 3 op. 55 in E flat Major* Eroica (London, n.d.)

Benjamin, Walter, 'On Some Motifs in Baudelaire', in *Illuminations*, trans Harry Zohn, ed. Hannah Arendt (New York, 1968), pp. 155–200

Bernard, Jonathan W., 'Inaudible Structures, Audible Music: Ligeti's Problem, and his Solution', *Musical Analysis* 6/iii (1987), pp. 207–36

——'Voice Leading as a Spatial Function in the Music of Ligeti', *Music Analysis* 13 (1994), pp. 227–53

——'Ligeti's Restoration of Interval and Its Significance for His Later Works', *Music Theory Spectrum* 21 (1999), pp. 1–31

——'A Key to Structure in the Kyrie of György Ligeti's Requiem', *Mitteilungen der Paul Sacher Stiftung* 16 (2003), pp. 42–7

Bónis, Ferenc, 'Musical Life: Three days with Sándor Veress the composer, Part II', *New Hungarian Quarterly* 29/109 (Spring 1988), pp. 217–25

——'Musical Life: Three days with Sándor Veress the composer, Part III', *New Hungarian Quarterly* 29/111 (Autumn 1988), pp. 208–14

Bori, Imre, 'A szintézisteremtő', in *Magyar Orpheus* (Budapest, 1999), pp. 351–69

Bossin, Jeffery, 'Report from Berlin', *Current Musicology* 37/38 (1984), pp. 237–78

Boulez, Pierre, *Orientations: Collected Writings*, ed. Jean-Jacques Nattiez (London, 1986)

Bouliane, Denys, 'György Ligeti im Gespräch mit Denys Bouliane', in *Neuland – Ansätze zur Musik der Gegenwart* 5 (Cologne, 1984/5), pp. 72–90

—— 'Geronnene Zeit und Narration – György Ligeti im Gespräch', *Neue Zeitschrift für Musik* 149/5 (1988), pp. 19–25

—— 'Stilisierte Emotion – György Ligeti im Gespräch mit Denys Bouliane', *MusikTexte– Zeitschrift für neue Musik* 28–9 (March 1989), pp. 52–62

Braunfels, Michael, *Die Krankheit der verwalteten Musik* (Zurich, 1975)

Brecht, Bertolt, *Brecht on Theatre: The Development of an Aesthetic*, ed. and trans. John Willett (London, 1964)

Chemillier, Marc, 'Analysis and Computer Reconstruction of a Musical Fragment of György Ligeti's *Melodien*', *Muzica* 6/2 (1994), pp. 34–48; http://mediatheque.ircam.fr/articles/textes/Chemillier94a/#fno, accessed on 14/08/10

Chion, Michel, *Audio-Vision: Sound on Screen*, ed. and trans. Claudia Gorbman (New York, 1994)

—— *Eyes Wide Shut*, trans. Trista Selous (London, 2002)

Clendinning, Jane Piper, 'The Pattern-Meccanico Compositions of György Ligeti', *Perspectives of New Music* 31/1 (Winter, 1993), pp. 192–234

—— 'Structural Factors in the Microcanonic Compositions of György Ligeti', in *Concert Music, Rock, and Jazz since 1945*, ed. Elizabeth W. Marvin and Richard Hermann (Rochester, NY, 1995), pp. 229–56

Czigány, György, 'Vers, zene, Weöres Sándor', in *Magyar Orpheus* (Budapest, 1999), pp. 564–70

Czigány, Lóránt, *The Oxford History of Hungarian Language* (Oxford, 1984), pp. 453–4

Deming, Alison Hawthorne, 'Science and Poetry: A View from the Divide', in *The Measured Word, On Poetry and Science*, ed. Kurt Brown (Athens, 2001), pp. 181–97

Dibelius, Ulrich, 'Ligetis Horntrio', *Melos* 46/1 (1984), pp. 44–61

—— *Ligeti: Eine Monographie in Essays* (Mainz, 1994)

—— 'Gespräch über Ästhetik', in *Ligeti: Eine Monographie in Essays*, pp. 253–73

Drott, Eric, 'Ligeti in Fluxus', *Journal of Musicology* 21 (2004), pp. 201–40

Duchesneau, Louise, 'György Ligeti on his Violin Concerto', *Ligeti Letter* 2 (Hamburg, 1993), pp. 1–7

Dwyer, Benjamin, 'Laughing at the Chaos – György Ligeti (1923–2006)', *Journal of Music in Ireland* (Sept./Oct. 2007), p. 16

Fahlström, Susanna, *Form and Philosophy in Sándor Weöres' Poetry*, Studia Uralica Upsaliensia 32 (Uppsala, 1999)

Falsetto, Mario, *Stanley Kubrick: Narrative and Stylistic Analysis* (Westport, 1994)

Feisst, Sabine M., 'Arnold Schoenberg and the Cinematic Art', *Musical Quarterly* 83/1 (1999), pp. 93–113

Floros, Constantin, *et al.*, eds., *Für György Ligeti: Die Referate des Ligeti-Kongresses Hamburg 1988*, Hamburger Jahrbuch für Musikwissenschaft 2 (Laaber, 1991)

Gann, Kyle, *The Music of Conlon Nancarrow* (Cambridge, 1995)

Gervasoni, Pierre, 'Interview with György Ligeti', *World*, 27 September 1997; reprinted online at http://members.lycos.fr./yrol/MUSIC/ LIGETI/ligeti2.htm, trans. Josh Ronsen, October 2003, accessed 10 August 2010

Gilbert, James, 'Auteur with a Capital A', in *Stanley Kubrick's 2001: A Space Odyssey: New Essays*, ed. Robert Phillip Kolker (New York, 2006)

Goehr, Lydia, *The Quest for Voice: On Music, Politics and the Limits of Philosophy* (Oxford, 1998)

Gojowy, Detlef, 'György Ligeti über eigene Werke – Ein Gespräch mit Detlef Gojowy aus dem Jahre 1988', in *Für György Ligeti: Die Referate des Ligeti-Kongresses Hamburg 1988*, ed. Constantin Floros *et al.*, Hamburger Jahrbuch für Musikwissenschaft 2 (Laaber, 1991), pp. 349–63

Gorbman, Claudia, *Unheard Melodies: Narrative Film Music* (Bloomington, 1987)

Griffiths, Paul, *György Ligeti* (London, 1983; rev. edn 1997)

——'Music's Magic Show', *Hungarian Quarterly* 42/162 (Summer 2001), pp. 146–9

——*A Concise History of Western Music* (Cambridge, 2006)

Hamvas, Béla, 'A Medúza', in *Magyar Orpheus* (Budapest, 1999), pp. 213–17

Harvey, Jonathan, *The Music of Stockhausen* (London, 1975)

Häusler, Josef, 'György Ligeti talking to Josef Häusler (1968/69)', Sarah E. Soulsby, in *György Ligeti in Conversation with Péter Várnai, Josef Häusler, Claude Samuel and Himself* (London, 1983), pp. 83–110

Hicks, Michael, 'Interval and Form in Ligeti's *Continuum* and *Coulée*', *Perspectives of New Music* 31/1 (Winter, 1993), pp. 172–90

Hofstadter, Douglas R., *Gödel, Escher, Bach: An Eternal Golden Braid* (Hassocks, 1979)

Hohmaier, Simone, '"Veress war ein Vorbild, aber kein guter Lehrer": Zur Frage einer kompositorischen Veress-Rezeption bei Kurtág und Ligeti', in *Sándor Veress: Komponist – Lehrer – Forscher*, ed. Doris Lanz and Anselm Gerhard (Kassel, 2008), pp. 142–58

Holcombe, Garan, 'Stanley Kubrick: The Legacy of a Cinematic Legend', *California Literary Review*, http://www.calitreview.com/Essays/stanley_ kubrick_5008.htm, accessed 10 August May 2010

Isgitt, David, 'An Analysis of Periodic Rhythmic Structures in the Music of Steve Reich and György Ligeti' (Master of Music thesis, University of North Texas, 2002)

Jack, Adrian, 'Ligeti Talks to Adrian Jack', *Music and Musicians* 22/11 (1974), pp. 24–30

Jeppesen, Knud, *Der Palestrinastil und die Dissonanz* (Leipzig, 1925)

Kaufmann, Harald, 'Strukturen im Strukturlosen: Über György Ligetis "Atmosphères"', in *Spurlinien: Analytische Aufsätze über Sprache und Musik* (Vienna, 1969), pp. 107–17

Kertész, Imre, 'Wem gehört Auschwitz?', in *Eine Gedankenlänge Stille, während das Erschießungskommande neu lädt* (Reinbek, 2002), pp. 145–54

——— 'Hommage à Fejtő', in *Európa nyomasztó öröksége* (Budapest, 2008), pp. 203–16

Knowlson, James, *Damned to Fame: The Life of Samuel Beckett* (London, 1996)

Kolleritsch, Otto, ed., *György Ligeti: Personalstil – Avantgardismus – Popularität*, Studien zur Wertungsforschung 19 (Vienna, Graz, 1987)

Kroó, György, *Szabolcsi Bence*, vol. 2 (Budapest, 1994)

Kubik, Gerhard, 'Die Amadinda-Musik von Buganda', in *Musik in Afrika*, ed. Artur Simon, Veröffentlichung des Museum für Völkerkunde Berlin, Folge 40, Abteilung Musikethnologie IV (Berlin, 1983), pp. 139–65

——— *Zum Verstehen afrikanischer Musik, ausgewählte Aufsätze* (Leipzig, 1988)

Kubrick, Stanley, 'Interview with Michel Ciment', *The Kubrick Site*, http://www.visual-memory.co.uk/amk/doc/interview.bl.html, accessed 23 April 2008

Lachenmann, Helmut, 'Die gefährdete Kommunikation', in *Musik als existentielle Erfahrung: Schriften 1966–1995*, ed. Josef Häusler (Wiesbaden, 1996), pp. 99–103

Lavoie, Marie-Noëlle, 'Identité, emprunts et régionalisme: judaïcité dans les œuvres de Milhaud durant l'entre-deux-guerres', *Musique, arts et religion dans l'entre-deux-guerres*, ed. Sylvain Caron and Michel Duchesneau (Lyons, 2009), pp. 57–70

Lethen, Helmut, *Cool Conduct: The Culture of Distance in Weimar Germany* (Berkeley, 2001)

Lichtenfeld, Monika, 'Gespräch mit György Ligeti', *Neue Zeitschrift für Musik* 142 (1981), pp. 471–3

——— ed., *György Ligeti: Gesammelte Schriften*, 2 vols. (Mainz, 2007)

Ligeti, György, 'Kótaismertetések', *Zene-pedagógia* 2/3 (March 1948), p. 43

——— 'Neues aus Budapest: von Bartók bis Veress', *Melos* 16/2 (February 1949), pp. 60–1

——— 'Wandlungen der musikalischen Form', *Die Reihe* 7 ('Form – Raum') (1960), pp. 5–17

——— 'Metamorphoses of Musical Form', *Die Reihe* 7 ('Form–Space'), trans. Cornelius Cardew (Pennsylvania, 1965), pp. 5–19

——— 'Auf dem Weg zu *Lux aeterna*', *Österreichische Musikzeitschrift* 24 (1969), pp. 80–8

——— *Continuum*, score (Mainz, 1970)

—— *Éjszaka/Night/Nacht – Reggel/Morning/Morgen*, Two Unaccompanied Choruses (1955), score (Mainz, 1973)

—— *Poème Symphonique for 100 Metronomes*, score (Mainz, 1982)

—— *György Ligeti in Conversation with Péter Várnai, Josef Häusler, Claude Samuel and Himself* (London, 1983)

—— 'Fragen und Antworten von mir selbst', trans. Geoffrey Skelton, in *György Ligeti in Conversation*, pp. 124–37

—— 'Aspekte der Webernschen Kompositionstechnik', in *Musik-Konzepte, Sonderband: Anton Webern II*, ed. Heinz-Klaus Metzger, Rainer Riehn (Munich, 1984), pp. 51–104

—— 'Begegnung mit Kurtág im Nachkriegs-Budapest', in *György Kurtág, Musik der Zeit 5* (Bonn, 1989), pp. 14–16

—— 'Foreword', in Simha Arom, *African polyphony and polyrhythm, Musical structure and methodology* (Cambridge, 1991), pp. xvii–xviii

—— 'Rhapsodische, unausgewogene Gedanken über Musik, besonders über meine eigenen Kompositionen', *Neue Zeitschrift für Musik* 1 (1993), pp. 20–9

—— 'Meine Kölner Zeit', in *Neue Musik in Köln, 1945–1971* (Cologne, 1994), pp. 16–19

—— 'Preface', trans. Lindsay Gerbracht, *Sonata for Solo Viola* (Mainz, 2001)

—— 'Between Science, Music and Politics', in *Kyoto Prizes & Inamori Grants 2001* (Kyoto, 2002), pp. 231–65

—— *Le Grand Macabre*, revised version 1996, study score (Mainz, 2003)

—— *Gesammelte Schriften*, ed. Monika Lichtenfeld, 2 vols. (Mainz, 2007)

—— 'Fritz Cerha, herzlichst, zum siebzigsten Geburtstag', in *Gesammelte Schriften*, vol. 1, pp. 473–8

—— 'Neue Musik in Ungarn', in *Gesammelte Schriften*, vol. 1, pp. 51–5

—— 'Neues aus Budapest: Zwölftonmusik oder "Neue Tonalität"?', in *Gesammelte Schriften*, vol. 1, pp. 56–60

—— 'Konvention und Abweichung – Die "Dissonanz" in Mozarts Streichquartett C-Dur KV 465 (1990)', in *Gesammelte Schriften*, vol. 1, pp. 271–8

—— 'Tendenzen der Neuen Musik in den USA: Steve Reich – Terry Riley – Harry Partch (1972)', in *Gesammelte Schriften*, vol. 1, pp. 456–68

—— 'Begegnung mit Steve Reich (2002)', in *Gesammelte Schriften*, vol. 1, pp. 520–1

—— 'Musikalische Erinnerungen aus Kindheit und Jugend (1972)', in *Gesammelte Schriften*, vol. 2, pp. 11–12

—— 'Mein Kölner Jahr 1957 (1993)', in *Gesammelte Schriften*, vol. 2, pp. 29–32

—— 'Zwischenbilanz in Toronto (1973)', in *Gesammelte Schriften*, vol. 2, pp. 108–12

—— 'Paradigmenwechsel der achtziger Jahre', in *Gesammelte Schriften*, vol. 2, pp. 116–18

—— 'Rhapsodische Gedanken über Musik, besonders über meine eigenen Kompositionen (1991)', in *Gesammelte Schriften*, vol. 2, pp. 123–35

—— '*Monument-Selbstportrait-Bewegung* Drei Stücke für zwei Klaviere (1976)', in *Gesammelte Schriften*, vol. 2, pp. 277–80

—— 'Zu meinem Klavierkonzert (1988)', in *Gesammelte Schriften*, vol. 2, pp. 296–300

Lobanova, Marina, *György Ligeti: Style, Ideal, Poetics* (Berlin, 2002)

Metzger, Heinz-Klaus, and Rainer Riehn, eds., *Helmut Lachenmann, Musik-Konzepte 61–2* (Munich, 1988)

Michel, Pierre, *György Ligeti: compositeur d'aujourd'hui* (Paris, 1985)

Monaco, James, *How to Read a Film* (New York, 1977)

Nettl, Bruno, 'Displaced Musics and Immigrant Musicologists: Ethnographical and Biographical Perspectives', in *Driven into Paradise: The Musical Migration from Nazi Germany to the United States*, ed. Reinhold Brinkmann and Christoph Wolff (Berkeley, 1999), pp. 54–65

Nordwall, Ove, *György Ligeti: eine Monographie* (Mainz, 1971)

Oehlschlägel, Reinhard, '"Ja, ich war ein utopischer Sozialist" – György Ligeti im Gespräch mit Reinhard Oehlschlägel (1978 and 1988)', *MusikTexte – Zeitschrift für neue Musik* 28–9 (March 1989), pp. 85–102

Peitgen, Heinz-Otto, Hartmut Jürgens and Dietmar Saupe, *Chaos and Fractals* (New York, 1992)

Pethő, Ildikó, 'Weöres Sándor korai zenei kísérletei, a zenei sorozat', in *Modern – magyar – irodalom – történet*, ed. Orsolya Kolozsi and Tímea Urbanik (Szeged, 2006), p. 59

Popper, Karl, *The Logic of Scientific Discovery* (London, 1959)

Rahn, Jay, 'Text-Tune Relationships in the *Hora Lunga* Versions Collected by Bartók', *Yearbook of the International Folk Music Council* 8 (1976), pp. 89–96

Roelcke, Eckhard, '*Träumen Sie in Farbe?*': *György Ligeti im Gespräch mit Eckhard Roelcke* (Vienna, 2003)

Roig-Francolí, Miguel, 'Harmonic and Formal Processes in Ligeti's Net-Structure Compositions', *Music Theory Spectrum* 17 (1995), pp. 242–67

Romsics, Ignác, *Hungary in the Twentieth Century*, trans. Tim Wilkinson (Budapest, 1999)

Ross, Alex, 'Ligeti Split', *The New Yorker*, 28 May 2001, http://www.therestisnoise.com/2004/05/ligeti_2001.html, accessed 15 August 2010

Sadoff, Ronald H., 'The Role of the Music Editor and the "Temp Track" as Blueprint for the Score, Source Music, and Scource Music of Films', *Popular Music* 25/2 (2006), pp. 165–83

Sallis, Friedemann, 'Formal Problems in *Threnos in memoriam Béla Bartók* (1945) by Sándor Veress', *Mitteilungen der Paul Sacher Stiftung* 8 (1995), pp. 37–8

—— *An Introduction to the Early Works of György Ligeti* (Cologne, 1996)

—— 'La transformation d'un héritage: *Bagatelle* op. 6 n° 2 de Béla Bartók et *Invenció* (1948) pour piano de György Ligeti', *Revue de musicologie* 83/2 (1997), pp. 281–93

—— 'Teaching as a Subversive Art: Sándor Veress's "Billegetőmuzsika (Fingerlarks)" and György Kurtág's "Játékok (Games)"', in *Sándor Veress: Komponist – Lehrer – Forscher*, ed. Doris Lanz and Anselm Gerhard (Kassel, 2008), pp. 159–71

Salmenhaara, Erkki, *Das musikalische Material und seine Behandlung in den Werken 'Apparitions', 'Atmosphères', 'Aventures' und 'Requiem' von György Ligeti* (Regensburg, 1969)

Schneider, Albrecht, 'Was haben Ligetis Études pour Piano mit Shepard-Skalen zu tun? Über "auditorische Illusionen", *Vertige* und *Columna infinită*, *Mikrotöne und mehr – Auf György Ligetis Hamburger Pfaden*, ed. Manfred Stahnke (Hamburg, 2005), pp. 81–104

Schultz, Wolfgang-Andreas, 'Avant-garde and Trauma – 20th-Century Music and the Experiences from the World Wars', http://www.wolfgangandreasschultz.de/schultz_avantgarde_en.pdf

Scorsese, Martin, 'Introduction', in *Kubrick: The Definitive Edition*, ed. Michael Ciment (London, 2003), p. vii

Searby, Michael D., *Ligeti's Stylistic Crisis: Transformation in his Musical Style, 1974–1985* (Lanham, Toronto, Plymouth, 2010)

Seherr-Toss, Peter von, *György Ligetis Oper Le Grand Macabre. Erste Fassung, Entstehung und Deutung. Von der Imagination bis zur Realisation einer musikdramatischen Idee* (Eisenach, 1998)

Simon, Artur, ed., *Musik in Afrika*, Veröffentlichung des Museum für Völkerkunde Berlin, Folge 40, Abteilung Musikethnologie IV (Berlin, 1983)

Smith, Steven C., *A Heart at Fire's Centre: The Life and Music of Bernard Herrmann* (Berkeley, 1991)

Spoto, Donald, *The Life of Alfred Hitchcock: The Dark Side of Genius* (London, 1983)

Stahnke, Manfred, ed., *Musik – nicht ohne Worte: Beiträge zu aktuellen Fragen aus Komposition, Musiktheorie und Musikwissenschaft*, Musik und 2 (Hamburg, 2000)

—— 'György Ligeti und Manfred Stahnke: Gespräch am 29. Mai 1993', in *Musik – nicht ohne Worte*, pp. 121–60

Steinitz, Richard, 'Music, Maths & Chaos', *Musical Times* 137/1837 (March 1996), pp. 14–20

—— *György Ligeti: Music of the Imagination* (London, 2003)

Szigeti, István, 'A Budapest Interview with György Ligeti', *New Hungarian Quarterly* 25 (Summer 1984), pp. 205–10

Szitha, Tünde, 'A Conversation with György Ligeti', *Hungarian Musical Quarterly* 3/1 (1992), pp. 13–17

Taruskin, Richard, 'A Sturdy Musical Bridge to the Twenty-first Century', in *The Danger of Music and Other Utopian Essays* (Berkeley, Los Angeles, London, 2009), pp. 98–103

Toop, Richard, *György Ligeti* (London, 1999)

Tüskés, Tibor, 'Weöres és a *Sorsunk*', in *Magyar Orpheus* (Budapest, 1999), pp. 177–91

—— *A határtalan énekese, Fotográfiák, levelek, dokumentumok, Irások Weöres Sándorról* (Budapest, 2003)

Vajda, Miklós: '"If Any Harm Comes of This, I'll Kill You!": The True Story of Six Hungarian Poets' Grand Tour of Britain in 1980', *Hungarian Quarterly* 171 (Autumn 2003), pp. 85–96

Várnai, Péter, 'György Ligeti talking to Péter Várnai (1978)', trans. Gabor J. Schabert, in *György Ligeti in Conversation with Péter Várnai, Josef Häusler, Claude Samuel and Himself* (London, 1983), pp. 13–82

Veress, Sándor, 'Introductory Words', *Billegetőmuzsika* (Budapest, 1947)

—— 'Folk Music in Musical and General Education', *Journal of the International Folk Music Council* 1 (1949), pp. 42–3

Volkov, Solomon, ed., *Testimony: The Memoirs of Dmitri Shostakovich* (New York, 1979)

Weissmann, John, 'Guide to Contemporary Hungarian Composers: (1) The Early Decades of the Twentieth Century', *Tempo* 44 (Summer 1957), pp. 24–30

Weöres, Sándor, *Tűzkút* (Paris, 1964)

—— *Der von Ungern: Gedichte und fünf Zeichnungen*, trans. Barbara Frischmuth and Robert Stauffer (Frankfurt am Main, 1969)

—— *Selected Poems of Sándor Weöres and Ferenc Juhász*, ed. and trans. Edwin Morgan (London, 1970)

—— *Hvisking I morket* (Oslo, 1977)

—— *Der von Ungern; Poesiealbum 135: Sándor Weöres*, trans. Annemarie Bostroem *et al.* (Berlin, 1978)

—— *Egybegyűjtött írások I–III*, 3 vols. (Budapest, 1981)

—— *Dix-neuf poèmes* (Paris, 1984)

—— *If All the World Were a Blackbird*, trans. Alexander Fenton (Aberdeen, 1985)

—— *Eternal Moment: Selected Poems*, trans. William Jay Smith *et al.* (London, 1988)

Wilkins, Nigel, 'Erik Satie's Letters to Milhaud and Others', *Musical Quarterly* 66/3 (1980), pp. 404–28

Wilkinson, Carl, *The Observer Book of Film* (London, 2007)

Zenck, Martin, '"Die ich rief, die Geister / Werd ich nun nicht los" – Zum Problem von György Ligetis Avantgarde-Konzeption', in *György Ligeti: Personalstil – Avantgardismus – Popularität*, ed. Otto Kolleritsch, Studien zur Wertungsforschung 19 (Vienna, Graz, 1987), pp. 153–78

Recordings

Banda Polyphony, Central African Republic, recorded by Simha Arom, Musics & Musicians of the World, Auvidis-Unesco, International Music Council, LP D8043 (1976)

Ligeti, György, *Ligeti*, Wergo WER60095 (1984)

Ligeti, György, *Ligeti: Études pour piano – 1er livre, Trio pour violon, cor et piano*, Érato, ECD 75555 (1990)

Ligeti, György, *Complete A Capella Choral Works*, György Ligeti Edition 2, Sony Classical 62305 (1997)

Ligeti, György, *Works for Piano*, György Ligeti Edition 3, Sony Classical 62308 (1997)

Ligeti, György, *Vocal Works*, György Ligeti Edition 4, Sony Classical 62311 (1996)

Ligeti, György, *Mechanical Music*, György Ligeti Edition 5, Sony Classical 62310 (1997)

Ligeti, György, *Chamber Music*, György Ligeti Edition 7, Sony Classical 62309 (1998)

Ligeti, György, *Le Grand Macabre*, György Ligeti Edition 8, Sony Classical, SK 62312

Ligeti, György, *Melodien, Chamber Concerto, Piano Concerto, Mysteries of the Macabre*, György Ligeti – The Ligeti Project I, Teldec Classics 5873-83953-2 (2001)

Ligeti, György, *Atmosphères, Chamber Concerto, Etc.*, György Ligeti – The Ligeti Project II, Teldec Classics 8573-88261-2 (2002)

Ligeti, György, *Aventures, Nouvelle Aventures, Etc.*, György Ligeti – The Ligeti Project V, Teldec Classics 8573-88262-2 (2004)

Nancarrow, Conlon, *Studies for Player Piano*, vols. I & II, Wergo WER 6168–2 (1999)

Stravinsky, Igor, 'Symphonies, Rehearsals and Talks', *Igor Stravinsky, 1882–1972*, vol. IV, CD I, Sony Classical 46294 (2007)

Index